Studio

ROUGE

Teacher's Guide

www.pearsonschools.co.uk

✓ Free online support
✓ Useful weblinks
✓ 24 hour online ordering

0845 630 33 33

Tracy Traynor

ALWAYS LEARNING

PEARSON

Published by Pearson Education Limited, Edinburgh Gate, Harlow, Essex, CM20 2JE.

www.pearsonschoolsandfecolleges.co.uk

Edited by Sara McKenna
Designed by Emily Hunter-Higgins
Typeset by Kamae Design, Oxford
Original illustrations © Pearson Education Limited 2013
Illustrated by Caron at KJA Artists
Cover design by Emily Hunter-Higgins
Cover photos © Main picture: Studio Natacha Nicaise/Natacha Nicaise; Mountain: Shutterstock/M.M.G.; Skateboarder: Getty Images/PhotoDisc; Parkour: Corbis/Cardinal; Eiffel Tower: Shutterstock/Ints Vikmanis; La Défense square arch: Shutterstock/Alexander Mul

First published 2013

17 16 15 14 13
10 9 8 7 6 5 4 3 2 1

British Library Cataloguing in Publication Data
A catalogue record for this book is available from the British Library

ISBN 978 1 447 96028 7

Printed in the UK by Henry Ling Ltd.

Acknowledgements
Every effort has been made to contact copyright holders of material reproduced in this book. Any omissions will be rectified in subsequent printings if notice is given to the publishers.

Contents

Introduction

Course description

Studio is a fully differentiated 11–14 French course in three stages – *Studio 1* for Year 7, *Studio 2* for Year 8 and *Studio 3* for Year 9. The Year 7 resources also include a separate short book, *Accès Studio*, which enables flexibility in teaching the language according to pupils' prior experience of learning French at Key Stage 2. In *Studio 3 Rouge* pupils can be assessed at National Curriculum levels 4 to 7.

The course has been written to reflect the world pupils live in, using contexts familiar to them in their everyday lives and teaching them the vocabulary that they need to communicate with young French people of their own age on topics that interest and stimulate them. They are introduced to young French people and given insight into the everyday life and culture of France and other French-speaking countries, encouraging intercultural understanding.

At the same time, *Studio* ensures that pupils are taught the language learning skills and strategies that they need to become independent language learners. The elements of the 2014 Programme of Study for Key Stage 3 Modern Languages (grammar and vocabulary, and linguistic competence) are fully integrated into the course. In addition, pupils have the chance to experience cross-curricular studies and are given regular opportunities to develop and practise the personal, learning and thinking skills required to operate as independent enquirers, creative thinkers, reflective learners, team workers, self-managers and effective participators.

Studio ActiveTeach (see details on pp. 5–6) provides easy-to-use and exciting technology designed to add dynamism and fun to whole-class teaching. For individual pupil use, *Studio ActiveLearn* provides a wealth of exciting differentiated material for pupils to access individually via computers or mobile devices, in class or for homework.

Differentiation

Studio 3 Rouge is written for those pupils focused on progressing as quickly as possible through the National Curriculum levels in Year 9 with the target of working at Level 7 by the end of the book. Clearly, pupils will work at different levels and at different paces, and every module caters for the given range of National Curriculum levels in the following ways:

- There are differentiated activities within the target range of NC Levels in listening, speaking, reading and writing throughout the Pupil Book.
- Ideas are given in the Teacher's Guide for simplifying and extending the Pupil Book activities.
- *En plus* units at the end of every module contain longer reading and listening passages to provide opportunities for extension work.
- The *À toi* section at the back of the Pupil Book provides extra reading and writing activities at reinforcement and extension levels.
- The *Studio 3 Rouge* workbook provides further reading and writing activities at reinforcement and extension levels.

Studio 3 Rouge

Pupil Book

- Full coverage of the 2014 Programmes of Study for Key Stage 3 MFL
- Assessment right from the start
- Exciting video introducing pupils to the lives of young people in France
- Fully integrated grammar explanations and practice ensuring logical and rigorous progression
- Opportunities for cross-curricular topics and emphasis on language learning skills
- Fully integrated opportunities for PLTS

The Pupil Book consists of five core subdivided as follows:

- Five double-page core units – these contain the core material that must be taught to ensure that all the key language and grammar is covered in Year 9.
- *Bilan* – this is a checklist of 'I can' statements, allowing pupils to check their progress as part of Assessment for Learning.
- *Révisions* – optional revision activities that can be used as a 'mock' test preceding the end of module *Contrôle* in the Assessment Pack.
- *En plus* – an optional unit in which no new core language is introduced. The unit can therefore be missed out if you are short of time. However, these units contain lots of useful activities and tips for developing language learning skills, including longer reading and listening passages and opportunities for oral presentations.
- *Je parle* and/or *J'écris* – an extra challenge to develop speaking or writing skills.
- *Studio Grammaire* – two pages (or four, in Module 4) where the key grammar points introduced in the module are explained fully and accompanied by practice activities.
- *Vocabulaire* – two pages of module word lists for vocabulary learning and revision, plus a *Stratégie* tip box to help pupils acquire the skills they need to learn vocabulary and structure and understand texts more effectively.

At the back of the Pupil Book there are four further sections:

- *À toi* – self-access differentiated reading and writing activities. *À toi A* contains reinforcement activities for lower-ability pupils, and *À toi B* contains extension activities for higher-ability pupils. These are ideal for use as homework.
- Verb tables.
- *Speaking and writing skills* – one page of tips on how to improve speaking and writing skills.
- *Mini-dictionnaire* – a comprehensive French-English glossary, organised alphabetically and containing all the vocabulary encountered in *Studio 3 Rouge*. There is also a list of the French rubrics used in the Pupil Book.

Teacher's Guide

The Teacher's Guide contains all the support required to help teachers use *Studio 3 Rouge* effectively in the classroom:

- Clear and concise teaching notes, including lesson starters, plenaries and PLTS references for every unit.
- Full cross-referencing to the 2014 National Curriculum Programme of Study
- Cross-referencing to the Foundation Certificate of Secondary Education in French (Revised specification with first testing in 2014).
- Overview grids for each module highlighting grammar content and skills coverage.
- Answers to all the activities.
- The complete audioscript for all the listening activities in the *Studio 3 Rouge* Pupil Book.
- Guidance on using the course with the full ability range.

With the Teacher's Guide there is an accompanying customisable scheme of work offering complete help with planning, and showing how the course covers the National Curriculum Programme of Study.

The Teacher's Guide is available as a printed, spiral-bound book (scheme of work supplied as downloadable Word files with instructions on how to access them inside the front cover). Alternatively both the complete Teacher's Guide content and scheme of work can be purchased and accessed as Word files online (via the *ActiveTeach* Library). From there they can be downloaded and printed off as necessary.

ActiveTeach

ActiveTeach is a powerful and motivating resource combining the 'book on screen' and a wealth of supporting materials – providing you with the perfect tool for whole-class teaching.

- Use the on-screen Pupil Book with all the listening activities included.
- Zoom in on areas of text and activities to facilitate whole-class teaching.
- Build your own lessons and add in your own resources to help personalise learning.
- Use fun and motivating electronic flashcards to teach new vocabulary.
- Consolidate language using the whole-class interactive games.
- Use the video clips to introduce your pupils to the lives of young French people.
- Teach and revise grammar using PowerPoint® presentations, followed by interactive grammar activities on key grammar points.
- Download and print off a variety of extra worksheets for starters, plenaries, consolidation of grammar, thinking skills, language-learning skills, development of the four skills (reading, writing, speaking and listening), self assessment and vocab lists. These are ideal for follow-up work, cover lessons and homework.
- You can also download and print off worksheets with a current topical and cultural focus. These are updated half-termly, and, once up online, will remain there to be accessed or downloaded at any time.

The wide variety of worksheets in *ActiveTeach* (mentioned above) can be used to consolidate and extend pupils' learning as follows:

Module 1

Listening skills	Transcription
Learning skills	Learning vocabulary
Thinking skills	Logic puzzle
Grammar skills	The near future tense
Grammar skills	The perfect tense
Learning skills	Using spider diagrams
Grammar skills	Using three tenses
Assignment	Mon blog (with NC assessment)

Module 2

Reading skills	Reading unfamiliar texts
Thinking skills	Odd one out!
Grammar skills	Using negatives
Grammar skills	The future tense
Thinking skills	Making connections
Grammar skills	Using three tenses together
Assignment	Le sport et le fitness (with NC assessment)

Module 3

Reading skills	Reading a poem
Learning skills	Looking up nouns in a dictionary
Thinking skills	Cracking the code
Grammar skills	Using modal verbs
Grammar skills	The imperfect tense

Learning skills	Using different tenses
Thinking skills	Logic puzzle
Assignment	Mon CV (with NC assessment)

Module 4

Grammar skills	Asking questions
Listening skills	Listening for gist and detail
Grammar skills	Using the conditional
Learning skills	Learning by heart
Thinking skills	Logic puzzle
Thinking skills	Drawing from text
Reading skills	Reading complicated texts
Assignment	Le centre de vacances (with NC assessment)

Module 5

Thinking skills	Unravelling texts
Learning skills	Improving writing
Grammar skills	Direct object pronouns
Thinking skills	Fact or opinion?
Learning skills	Recognising patterns
Grammar skills	Using complex structures
Assignment	Une poésie (with NC assessment)

Assignment (*Défi*)

The worksheets include a collaborative assignment or challenge (*Défi*) to be carried out in pairs or groups.

The assignments consist of two worksheets, one containing the instructions for the task, the other providing preparation tasks and language to help the pupils.

The focus of the assignments is to help the pupils develop further their extended speaking and writing skills in cross-curricular contexts while fostering PLTS.

Audio

The audio files for the course contain all the recorded material for the listening activities in the Pupil Book. These audio files are also contained on *ActiveTeach* so only teachers who do not purchase *ActiveTeach* will need to buy the Audio Files. The different types of activities can be used for presentation of new language, comprehension and pronunciation practice. The material includes dialogues, interviews and songs recorded by native speakers.

After purchasing the audio files for *Studio,* you can access and download them online from the *ActiveTeach* Library. From there they can be saved onto your computer or network for future use.

Please note: the audio files and *ActiveTeach* do not contain the listening material for the end of module tests and end of year test. This material can be found in the Assessment Pack (see below).

Workbooks

The *Studio 3 Rouge* workbook contains one or two pages of activities for each double-page unit in the Pupil Book. It fulfils a number of functions:

- It provides self-access reading and writing activities designed to offer the pupils enjoyable ways of consolidating and practising the language they have learned in each unit.
- It gives extra practice in grammar and thinking skills, with integrated activities throughout.
- Revision pages at the end of each module (*Révisions*) help pupils revise what they have learned during the module.
- Module word lists (*Vocabulaire*) with English translations are invaluable for language learning homework.
- The *J'avance* pages at the end of each module allow pupils to record their National Curriculum level in listening, speaking, reading and writing and set themselves improvement targets for the next module.
- Level descriptors in pupil-friendly language at the back of the workbook allow pupils to see what they must do to progress through the levels in all four skills.

The Workbooks are available as print books sold in packs of 8 or can be downloaded as PDFs from the *ActiveTeach* Library.

Assessment Pack

The Assessment Pack contains all the assessment material required to assess pupils in Year 8 in all four skills, as well as self-assessment sheets.

- End of module tests in all four skills – listening, speaking, reading and writing.
- End of year test in all four skills.
- Covers levels 4 to 7.
- Target setting sheets.

The assessment pages and the audio can be downloaded online from the *ActiveTeach* Library. There you will find Word files and PDF versions of the test sheets, alongside the sound files for the listening tests.

Grammar coverage

Grammar is fully integrated into the teaching sequence in *Studio* to ensure that pupils have the opportunity to learn thoroughly the underlying structures of the French language. All units have a grammar objective so that pupils can see clearly which grammar structures they are learning. The key grammar points are presented in the *Studio Grammaire* boxes on the Pupil Book pages and fuller explanations and practice are provided in the *Studio Grammaire* pages at the end of each module. In addition, there are grammar PowerPoint® presentations in *ActiveTeach* for presenting new grammar concepts to classes, followed by interactive practice activities that can be used with whole classes or for individual practice. Worksheets focusing on the key grammar topics taught in *Studio 3 Rouge* are also provided in *ActiveTeach* and can be printed off for individual pupil use.

Grammar points explained and practised in *Studio 3 Rouge*:

- present tense of regular *–er*, *–ir* and *–re* verbs
- *depuis* + present tense
- perfect tense of regular verbs
- perfect tense of irregular verbs
- perfect tense with *avoir*/*être*
- imperfect tense
- the near future (*aller* + infinitive)
- future tense (e.g. *je mangerai*)
- the conditional
- using a range of tenses (present, perfect, imperfect, near future, future, conditional)
- reflexive verbs
- modal verbs (*vouloir*, *pouvoir*, *devoir*)
- *il faut* + infinitive
- the imperative
- negatives (*ne … pas, ne … jamais* and *ne … plus*)
- adjective agreement
- *meilleur*
- *à* + definite article
- direct object pronouns (*me, te, nous, vous, le/la/l', les*)
- emphatic pronouns
- the pronoun *y*
- question forms (inversion, *est-ce que*)
- question words
- expressions with *avoir* (*avoir raison, avoir faim*, etc.)
- *ce qui, ce que*
- nouns for jobs
- two meanings of *il y a*

Coverage of the Programmes of Study in *Studio 3 Rouge*

In *Studio* the 2014 National Curriculum Programme of Study is covered comprehensively. The Programme of Study is as follows:

1 Grammar and vocabulary

Pupils should be taught to:

- identify and use tenses or other structures which convey the present, past, and future as appropriate to the language being studied
- use and manipulate a variety of key grammatical structures and patterns, including voices and moods, as appropriate
- develop and use a wide-ranging and deepening vocabulary that goes beyond their immediate needs and interests, allowing them to give and justify opinions and take part in discussion about wider issues
- use accurate grammar, spelling and punctuation.

2 Linguistic competence

Pupils should be taught to:

- listen to a variety of forms of spoken language to obtain information and respond appropriately
- transcribe words and short sentences that they hear with increasing accuracy
- initiate and develop conversations, coping with unfamiliar language and unexpected responses, making use of important social conventions such as formal modes of address
- express and develop ideas clearly and with increasing accuracy, both orally and in writing
- speak coherently and confidently, with increasingly accurate pronunciation and intonation
- read and show comprehension of original and adapted materials from a range of different sources, understanding the purpose, important ideas and details, and provide an accurate English translation of short, suitable material
- read literary texts in the language, such as stories, songs, poems and letters, to stimulate ideas, develop creative expression and expand understanding of the language and culture

- write prose using an increasingly wide range of grammar and vocabulary, write creatively to express their own ideas and opinions, and translate short written text accurately into the foreign language.

The table below outlines the points from the Programme of Study in short form, and shows where they are covered in *Studio 3 Rouge*. The content of the course is also matched to the Programme of Study unit by unit throughout this Teacher's Guide.

1 Grammar and vocabulary (GV)	
GV1 Tenses	M1 U1, M1 U3, M1 U4, M2 U5, M3 U3, M4 U4
GV2 Grammatical structures	M2 U2, M3 U2, M4 U2, M5 U3
GV3 Developing vocabulary Opinions and discussions	M2 U1, M3 U1, M4 U2, M5 U4 M1 U2, M2 U2, M5 U1, M5 U4
GV4 Accuracy	M1 *J'écris*, M2 *J'écris*, M3 U4, M3 *Gram*,
2 Linguistic competence (LC)	
LC1 Listening and responding	M1 U5, M2 *En plus*, M3 U2, M4 U4, M5 U2
LC2 Transcription	M4 U1, M4 U5
LC3 Conversation Conversation (dealing with the unexpected) Conversation (using modes of address)	M1 U1, M2 U2, M3 U4, M4 U2, M5 U4 M1 U2, M2 U2, M5 U1 *Studio* 1
LC4 Expressing ideas (speaking) Expressing ideas (writing)	M1 *Je parle*, M2 *En plus*, M3 *Je parle*, M5 *Je parle* M1 *J'écris*, M2 *J'écris*, M4 *J'écris*
LC5 Speaking coherently and confidently Accurate pronunciation and intonation	M1 *Je parle*, M2 *En plus*, M3 *Je parle*, M5 *Je parle* M2 *En plus*, M3 U3
LC6 Reading comprehension Translation into English	M1 *En plus*, M2 U1 (authentic), M4 U5 (authentic), M4 *En plus* (adapted from authentic), M5 *En plus* (adapted from authentic) M1 *Gram*, M2 *Gram*, M4 *Gram*, M5 *Gram*
LC7 Literary texts	Worksheet 3.1
LC8 Writing creatively Translation into French	M1 *J'écris*, M2 U3, M2 *J'écris*, M3 U3, M4 U5 M1 *En plus*, M3 *Gram*, M4 *Gram*, M5 *Gram*

National Curriculum Levels in *Studio*

The 2014 National Curriculum no longer includes Level Descriptors for Levels 1–8 and exceptional performance. In order to ensure sound progression, as well as to aid progress tracking and reporting, *Studio* keeps the levels in place, using the level descriptors as they were in the previous Curriculum. In the course they feature in the following ways:

- All activities in the course are levelled (in the teacher's notes) from Levels 1–7
- End of Module Assessments for *Studio* have been written using the National Curriculum Levels to indicate the level of challenge
- Workbooks contain self assessment and target setting pages based around the old National Curriculum Levels.

As the new National Programmes of Study become established in schools from 2014, their use in Studio, as well as the use of the older NC Level descriptors, will be reviewed to make sure that the course provides the most valid and up to date account of how achievement is measured and progress is tracked.

Coverage of Personal Learning and Thinking Skills in *Studio 3 Rouge*

Activities supporting PLTS development are included throughout the course. Key examples are highlighted in the Teacher's Guide using the PLTS icon PLTS: one PLTS is identified in each unit, with Modules 1–5 all featuring the full range of PLTS. A selection of these is listed below, with details of how they meet the curriculum requirements.

Personal Learning and Thinking Skills	
I Independent enquirers	Pupil Book activities throughout the course (e.g. M2 U3 ex. 4, M4 U5 ex. 1); ICT-/other research-based activities (e.g. M5 U3 extension suggestion after ex. 5)
C Creative thinkers	Regular activities developing skills strategies (how to improve listening/speaking, etc.) (e.g. M5 *En plus* ex. 2); activities requiring pupils to identify patterns and work out rules (e.g. M1 U4 Starter 2); activities requiring creative production of language (M2 U1 ex. 8 and all *Je parle/J'écris* sections)
R Reflective learners	Ongoing opportunities to assess work and identify areas for improvement (e.g. M2 U2 ex. 7, M5 U4 ex. 2), including all *Bilans* and Plenaries (e.g. M3 U5 Plenary) and all *Je parle/J'écris* sections
T Team workers	Regular pair- and teamwork activities (M4 U2 ex. 3), including many Starters; regular peer assessment (e.g. M3 U3 ex. 5 and all *Je parle/J'écris* section); links with partner schools (e.g. M1 U1 ex. 7 suggestion)
S Self-managers	Ongoing advice on managing learning (e.g. M2 *En plus* ex. 3, M4 U3 ex. 1 reinforcement suggestion), including strategies to improve learning (e.g. M5 U1 ex. 8)
E Effective participators	Opportunities throughout the course for pupils to contribute (e.g. M1 U2 ex. 7, M3 U4 ex. 7), including discussions based on module openers, presentations (e.g. M4 *En plus* Starter 1 and all *Je parle* sections) and all Plenaries (e.g. M5 U2 Plenary)

Pupils may find the following short forms useful as a reference in class:

I am a/an …	Today I …		
Independent enquirer	PLTS	**I**	worked on my own to find out something new
Creative thinker	PLTS	**C**	used what I know to work out or create something new
Reflective learner	PLTS	**R**	thought about what I've learned and how I can improve
Team worker	PLTS	**T**	worked well with other people
Self-manager	PLTS	**S**	took responsibility for improving my learning
Effective participator	PLTS	**E**	took part in the lesson in a positive way

Coverage of the Foundation Certificate of Secondary Education in French in *Studio 3 Rouge*

Studio can be used to teach the Key Stage 3 FCSE qualification from AQA. The following table shows where each of the FCSE units and sub-topics for the Revised Specification (2014) can be taught using *Studio 3 Rouge*. Many of the FCSE units and subtopics that do not appear in the *Studio 3 Rouge* or *Vert* grid are covered in *Studio 1* or *Studio 2 Rouge/Vert*. A separate leaflet is also available showing the FCSE Revised Specification coverage across all three stages of *Studio* (*Studio 1*, *Studio 2 Rouge/Vert*, *Studio 3 Rouge/Vert*).

Unit 1 – Relationships, family and friends

Sub-topics	Where in *Studio 3 Rouge*
Reading and listening	
Family and step family	
Personal details about family	
Mini biography of family	
Rank in family	
Personal details about friends	
Girlfriend, boyfriend	M1 U4
Relationships and reasons for good and bad relations within family and friends	M5 U1
Issues	M5 U1
Taking sides in an argument	M5 U1
Pets	
Clothes	
Family celebrations	
Prepositions	
Numbers	
Speaking and writing	
Personal information	
Family/friends	
Meeting up with friends/activities	M1 U3. M1 U4
Descriptions	M1 U2
Hobbies/free-time activities	M1 U3, M1 U4

Unit 2 – Education and future plans

Sub-topics	Where in *Studio 3 Rouge*
Reading and listening	
Education School: teachers problems transport timetable uniform facilities type of school location subjects rules school clubs sport progress report items in school bag	M4 *En plus*
Future plans	
Plans for after school	M3 U1
Plans for jobs and careers	M3 U1
Plans for future study	M3 U5
Advantages and disadvantages of jobs	M3 U1
Advantages and disadvantages of staying on at school	M3 U3
Time	
Prepositions of place	
Alphabet	
Numbers	
Sequence	
Speaking and writing	
Physical description of school	
School activities	
Opinions	
Uniform	
Future plans	M3 U1, M3 U5

Unit 3 – Holidays and travel

Sub-topics	**Where in *Studio 3 Rouge***
Reading and listening	
Holidays	M4 U1
Types of holiday	M4 U2
Camping	M4 U2
Activities	M4 U1, M4 U2, M4 U3
Travel	
Accommodation	M4 U1
Weather on holiday	
Problems on holiday	M4 U4
Holiday experiences	M4 U4
Speaking and writing	
Destination	M4 U1
Travel	
Accommodation	M4 U1
Activities	M4 U1, M4 U2, M4 U3

Unit 4 – Leisure

Sub-topics	**Where in *Studio 3 Rouge***
Reading and listening	
Hobbies	M1 U3, M1 U4
Free time/hobbies	M1 U3, M1 U4
Television	
Films	
Cinema	
Music	M1 U5, M1, *En plus*
Gardening	
Going out	M1 U3, M1 U4
Theatre visit	
Clubs	
Around town	
Leisure centre	
Speaking and writing	
Hobbies/activities	M1 U3, M1 U4
Preferences	M1 U3, M1 U4
Going out	M1 U3, M1 U4
Pocket money	

Unit 5 – Healthy lifestyle

Sub-topics	**Where in *Studio 3 Rouge***
Reading and listening	
Healthy living	M2 U4, M2, *En plus*
Food/drink	M2 U3
Healthy/unhealthy eating	M2 U3, M2 U4
Fast food	M2 U3, M2 U4
Exercise	M2 U2, M2 U4, M2 U5, M2 *En plus*
Life as a footballer	
Sports	M2 U1, M2 U4
Leisure centres	
Alcohol	
Smoking	
Illness	
Chemist's	
Stress	
Exam pressure	
Health farms	M2 U4
Speaking and writing	
State of health	M2 *En plus*
Activities	M2 U4, M2 U5, M2 *En plus*
Eating and drinking	M2 U3, M2 U4
Opinions	M2 U2

Unit 6 – Food and drink

Sub-topics	Where in *Studio 3 Rouge*
Reading and listening	
Food/drink vocabulary items	M2 U3
Eating out	
Opinions about food and drink	M2 U3
Shopping for food	
Unhealthy/healthy food choices	M2 U3 M2 U4
Speaking and writing	
Food and drink habits	M2 U3, M2 U4
Eating out	
Opinions about food and drink	M2 U3

Unit 7 – Local area and environment

Sub-topics	Where in *Studio 3 Rouge*
Reading and listening	
Facilities	
Locations	
Preferences	M5, U2, M5 U3
Environment	M5 U2
Recycling	M5 U2
Weather	
Speaking and writing	
Local area	
Activities	
Environment	M5 U2

Unit 8 – Celebrations

Sub-topics	Where in *Studio 3 Rouge*
Reading and listening	
Birthdays	
Various festivals	M1 *En plus*
Parties	
Celebrating	
Engagements and weddings	
Celebrating success	
Carnival	M1 *En plus*
End of exams	
Speaking and writing	
Parties	
Opinions	
Special celebrations	M1 *En plus*

Games and other teaching suggestions

Reading aloud

There are many reading activities in the Pupil Book which give scope for further activities.

1 You can use the texts to practise reading aloud. As an incentive, award five points to a pupil who can read a text without any errors. Points could also be given to teams, depending on seating arrangements – tables, rows, sides of the room.
2 Set a challenge – 'I bet no one can read this without a single mistake' or ask a volunteer pupil to predict how many mistakes he/she will make before having a go, then seeing if he/she can do better than predicted.
3 Texts could be read round the class with pupils simply reading up to a full stop and then passing it on to someone else in the room. They enjoy this activity if it is fast. Alternatively, pupils can read as much or as little as they want before passing it on.
4 You can also read a text, pause, and have the pupils say the next word.

Reading follow-up

Motivation and participation can be enhanced by dividing the class into two teams and awarding points. Once they know a text very well, pupils should be able to complete a sentence from memory, hearing just the beginning. Move from a word to a phrase to a sentence: i.e. you say a word, the pupils give the word in a short context and then in a longer context.

1 You read aloud and stop (or insert the word 'beep') for pupils to complete the word or sentence.
2 You read aloud and make a deliberate mistake (either pronunciation or saying the wrong word). Pupils put up their hand as soon as they spot a mistake.
3 *Hot potato*: Pupils read a bit and pass it on quickly to someone who may not be expecting it.
4 *Marathon*: A pupil reads aloud until he/she makes a mistake. Pupils have to put up their hand as soon as they hear a mistake. A second pupil then takes over, starting at the beginning again and trying to get further than the previous pupil.
5 *Random reading*: You read a phrase at random and the pupils have to say the next bit.
6 You can play music and get the pupils to pass an object round the class. When the music stops, the person with the object has a turn. Let a pupil control the music, facing away from the class.

Mime activities

Mimes are a motivating way to help pupils to learn words.

1 You say a word, for example a job, sport or hobby, or an adjective, and the pupils mime it. This can be done silently with the whole class responding. Alternatively, it can be done as a knock out game starting with six volunteers at the front who mime to the class as you say each word. Any pupil who does the wrong mime or who is slow to react is knocked out. Impose a two-minute time limit.
2 Pupils say a word or phrase and you mime it – but only if the pupils say it correctly. This really puts you on the spot and gets the pupils trying very hard. You could also insist that the pupils say it from memory.
3 You mime and pupils say the word or phrase.
4 Send five or six pupils out of the room. They each have to decide on an adjective which sums up their character. They return to the room individually or together, each one miming their character adjective. The remaining pupils then guess the adjective. Get them to use a sentence, e.g. *Daniel est intelligent*.
5 *Envoyé spécial*: One person goes out of the room. The rest of the class decides on a character adjective to mime. The volunteer comes back into the room and has to guess the adjective that the class is miming. Again, encourage the use of whole sentences.
6 *Class knock-down*: As *Envoyé spécial*, but this time everyone in the class can choose different qualities to mime. The volunteer returns to the room with everyone doing his/her own mime. The volunteer points to each pupil and names the character adjective. If the volunteer is correct, the pupil sits down. This works well as a timed or team activity. The aim is to sit your team down as quickly as possible.
7 A version of charades is a good activity at the end of the lesson. Organise two teams, A and B. Have all the adjectives written down on separate cards, masculine forms only. Put the cards in a pile at the front. A volunteer from Team A comes to the front, picks up the first card and mimes it. The rest of the team must not see the word on the card. Anyone from Team A can put up his/her hand and is then invited by the volunteer to say the word. If correct, the volunteer picks up the next card and mimes it. The aim is to get through the whole list as quickly as possible. Note down the time for Team A. Team B then tries to beat that time.

Translation follow-up

Motivation and participation can be enhanced by dividing the class into two teams and awarding points. Once they know the text very well, you should be able to say any word, phrase or sentence from the text at random for the pupils to translate into English without viewing the text.

1 You translate the text and stop (or insert the word 'beep') for pupils to complete the word or sentence.
2 You translate, making a deliberate mistake. Pupils put up their hand as soon as they spot a mistake.
3 *Hot potato*: A pupil translates a bit and passes it on quickly to someone who may not be expecting it.
4 *Marathon*: A pupil translates until he/she makes a mistake. Pupils have to put up their hand as soon as they hear a mistake. A second pupil then takes over, starting from the beginning again and trying to get further than the previous pupil.
5 *Random translation*: You read a phrase in French at random and the pupils have to translate it.
6 One half of the class has their books open, the other half has them closed. The half with their books open reads a sentence in French at random. The other side has to translate. Do about five then swap round.
7 You can play music and get the pupils to pass an object round. When the music stops, the person with the object has a turn. Let a pupil control the music, facing away from the class.

Writing follow-up (text dissection)

Whiteboards are a useful tool. They do not need to be issued to every pupil. Pupils can work in pairs or groups or they can pass the whiteboards on. You could also divide the class into teams, with one whiteboard per team.

After reading a text in some detail:

1 Display some anagrams of key words from the text and ask pupils to write them correctly. You will need to prepare these in advance and check carefully. Award points for correct answers on each board.
2 Display some jumbled phrases from the text, e.g. *foot au je dimanche joue le*. Pupils rewrite the phrase correctly in their exercise books or on the board. They could work in teams, producing one answer per team on paper.
3 Display an incorrect word or phrase in French and ask pupils to spot the mistake and correct it. This can also be done as 'spot the missing word' or 'spot the word that is in the wrong place'.
4 Ask pupils to spell certain words from memory. Differentiate by first reading out a few words in French and then giving a few in English for them also to write out in French.
5 *Mini-dictée*: Read four or five short sentences in French for pupils to write out. Again, this could be a group exercise.
6 Give pupils phrases in English to write out in French.

Comprehension follow-up

1 Ask questions in English about the text.
2 Ask questions in French about the text.
3 True or false?
4 Who … ?

Vocabulary treasure hunt

1 Find the word for …
2 Find (three) opinions.

Grammar treasure hunt

1 Find (three) adjectives.
2 Find (two) feminine adjectives.
3 Find a verb in the *nous* form.
4 Find a plural noun.
5 Find a negative.

A variation on pairwork

Musical pass the mobile phone: One pupil controls the music, facing away from the class. While the music is playing, a toy or old mobile phone is passed from pupil to pupil. As soon as the music stops, the music operator (who is ideally also equipped with a phone) says the first statement of a dialogue. The other pupil who has ended up with the phone replies. They can, if they like, disguise their voice. The music operator tries to guess who is speaking. The game then continues.

Symbols used in these teaching notes

extension material/suggestion for extending an activity

reinforcement material/suggestion for reinforcing language

example of an activity which supports personal learning and thinking skills development

thinking skills activity (workbooks only)

1 Module 1: Ma vie sociale d'ado

Unit & Learning objectives	Programme of Study references	Key language	Grammar and other language features
1 Planète Facebook (pp. 8–9) Talking about Facebook Using present tense verbs	**GV1** Tenses (present) **LC3** Conversation **LC6** Reading comprehension **LC4** Expressing ideas (writing)	*Je vais sur ma page perso.* *Je lis mes messages.* *Je poste des messages.* *On organise des sorties.* *On partage des photos.* etc. *de temps en temps, quelquefois*, etc.	**G** regular *–er* verbs – developing reading skills
2 Comment tu trouves …? (pp. 10–11) Giving your opinion about someone Using direct object pronouns	**GV2** Grammatical structures (direct object pronouns; adjectival agreement) **GV3** Opinions and discussions **LC3** Conversation (dealing with the unexpected) **LC5** Speaking coherently and confidently	*arrogant(e), beau/belle, charmant(e), drôle*, etc.	**G** direct object pronouns **G** adjective agreement – developing writing skills
3 Tu viens aussi? (pp. 12–13) Arranging to go out Using the near future tense	**GV1** Tenses (near future) **GV3** Developing vocabulary **LC3** Conversation **LC6** Reading comprehension	*Je vais/On va …* *aller au cinéma/en ville* *faire les magasins* *Tu viens avec moi/nous?* etc. *Oui, merci. Je veux bien.* *Génial! Bonne idée.* etc. *ce matin, demain matin, dimanche soir*, etc.	**G** the near future tense – developing reading skills
4 Ça s'est bien passé? (pp. 14–15) Describing a date Using the perfect tense	**GV1** Tenses (perfect) **LC2** Transcription **LC3** Conversation (dealing with the unexpected) **LC6** Reading comprehension	*Je suis sorti(e) avec …* *Je suis/On est allé(e)(s) …* *au cinéma/à une fête/en ville* *J'ai bavardé.* *On a bu du coca.* *Je suis resté(e) à la maison.* etc. *hier, samedi dernier, le weekend dernier* *C'était cool/génial/un désastre*, etc.	**G** the perfect tense with *avoir/être* – developing reading skills

Unit & Learning objectives	Programme of Study references	Key language	Grammar and other language features
5 Fou de musique! (pp. 16–17) Describing a music event Using three tenses	**GV1** Tenses (past, present and future) **GV4** Accuracy (grammar; spelling; punctuation) **LC1** Listening and responding **LC4** Expressing ideas (writing)	*un concert gratuit* *en plein air* *télécharger les nouveautés* *une chanson* *la mélodie* *les paroles (f)* *l'ambiance (f)* *son nouvel album* etc.	– developing reading skills
Bilan et Révisions (pp. 18–19) Pupils' checklist and practice exercises			
En plus: La Fête de la Musique (pp. 20–21) Finding out about music festivals around the world	**LC3** Conversation **LC6** Reading comprehension **LC8** Writing creatively **LC8** Translation into French	Review of language from the module	– developing reading skills
Je parle (pp. 22–23) Extended speaking practice	**GV1** Tenses (past, present and future) **LC4** Expressing ideas (speaking) **LC5** Speaking coherently and confidently	Review of language from the module	**G** two meanings of *il y a* – developing speaking skills – checking your work
J'écris (pp. 24–25) Extended writing practice	**GV3** Developing vocabulary **GV4** Accuracy (grammar; spelling; punctuation) **LC4** Expressing ideas (writing) **LC8** Writing creatively	Review of language from the module	– developing writing skills – checking your work
Studio Grammaire (pp. 26–27) Detailed grammar summary and practice exercises			**G** the present tense **G** direct object pronouns **G** the near future tense **G** the perfect tense
À toi (pp. 118–119) Self-access reading and writing at two levels			

1 Planète Facebook

Learning objectives
- Talking about Facebook
- Using present tense verbs

Programme of Study references
GV1 Tenses (present)
LC3 Conversation
LC6 Reading comprehension
LC4 Expressing ideas (writing)

Grammar
- regular *–er* verbs

Key language
Je vais sur ma page perso.
Je lis mes messages.
Je poste des messages.
Je modifie mes préférences.
J'invite mes copains.
Je fais des quiz.
Je joue à des jeux.
Je regarde des photos.
Je commente des photos.
Je passe des heures …
On organise des sorties.
On partage des photos.
On s'envoie …
des liens vers des vidéos
de temps en temps
quelquefois
souvent
tous les jours
tous les weekends
tout le temps
une fois/deux fois …
… par jour/semaine/mois

PLTS
T Team workers

Cross-curricular
ICT: making contact on social networks

Resources
Audio files:
01_Module1_Unit1_Ex1.mp3
02_Module1_Unit1_Ex4.mp3
Workbooks:
Cahier d'exercices Rouge, page 3
ActiveTeach:
Starter 1 resource
Starter 2 resource
p.008 Grammar
p.008 Grammar practice
p.009 Listening skills
ActiveLearn:
Listening, Reading
Grammar, Vocabulary

Starter 1
Aim
To review present tense verbs

Write up the following. Give pupils two minutes to find the French versions of the verbs in the texts in exercise 1.

I have	I spend
I make comments on	I look at
I go	we send (each other)
we organise	I love
I do	I play
I meet up with	we share
I change	I read

(**Answers:** *j'ai, je commente, je vais, on organise, je fais, je retrouve, je modifie, je passe, je regarde, on s'envoie, j'adore, je joue, on partage, je lis*)

1 Écoute et lis. (Listening L3–4)
Listening. Pupils listen to three people talking about what they do on Facebook, following the text at the same time. Some vocabulary is glossed for support.

Audioscript Track 1

– *J'adore Facebook! Je vais tous les jours sur ma page perso. Je lis mes messages et je poste des messages sur le mur de mes copains. De temps en temps, je modifie aussi mes préférences.*
– *Je passe des heures sur Facebook. Je regarde et je commente les photos de mes amis. C'est marrant de faire ça! Quelquefois, je fais aussi des quiz ou je joue à des jeux. J'ai plein d'amis sur Facebook.*
– *Je retrouve toutes mes copines sur Facebook. On partage des photos et on s'envoie des liens vers des vidéos. J'invite aussi mes copines chez moi ou on organise des sorties. Facebook, c'est indispensable à ma vie sociale!*

2 Relis le texte. Qui dit ça? (Reading L3–4)
Reading. Pupils read the text in exercise 1 again and identify the speaker for each of the English statements. Draw their attention to the tip box on reading skills.

Answers
1 Antoine **2** Antoine **3** Léa **4** Mina **5** Mina **6** Léa **7** Mina **8** Mina **9** Léa **10** Antoine

3 Écris les phrases de l'exercice 2 en français. (Writing L3)
Writing. Pupils translate the sentences in exercise 2 into French.

Answers

1 Je fais des quiz ou je joue à des jeux.
2 Je passe des heures sur Facebook.
3 On s'envoie des liens vers des vidéos.
4 Je lis mes messages.
5 Je vais sur ma page perso.
6 J'invite aussi mes copines chez moi.
7 Je modifie mes préférences.
8 Je poste des messages sur le mur de mes copains.
9 On partage des photos.
10 Je regarde et je commente les photos de mes amis.

Studio Grammaire: the present tense (regular *–er* verbs)

Use the *Studio Grammaire* box to review regular *–er* verbs and some common irregular verbs in the present tense. There is more information and further practice on Pupil Book p. 26.

Give pupils working in pairs one minute to choose and memorise an irregular verb (*avoir*, *être*, *faire* or *lire*). Choose pairs to say their verb paradigm aloud, each person taking it in turn to say a verb form (e.g. *j'ai – tu as*, etc.).

Starter 2

Aim

To review the language for Facebook activities

Write up the following. Give pupils two minutes to identify which of the activities you would do on Facebook.

1 *Je commente les photos de mes amis.*
2 *On fait des quiz.*
3 *Je vais à la crêperie.*
4 *Je vais sur ma page perso.*
5 *On s'envoie des liens vers des vidéos.*
6 *J'éteins mon portable.*
7 *On mange un kilo de bananes.*
8 *On partage des photos.*
9 *On fait du bowling.*
10 *J'invite mes copains chez moi.*
11 *J'achète des souvenirs.*
12 *Je participe à un défilé.*

(**Answers:** 1, 2, 4, 5, 8, 10)

Check answers, asking pupils to translate each sentence into English.

Alternative Starter 2:

Use ActiveTeach p.008 Grammar practice to practise regular and irregular present tense verbs.

4 Écoute. Note les activités et la fréquence. (1–4) (Listening L4)

Listening. Pupils read the key language supplied, and then listen to four people talking about what they do on Facebook. Pupils note the activities and how often they are done.

Audioscript Track 2

1
– Bonjour, Théo. T'es sur Facebook?
– Ah oui, bien sûr, je suis sur Facebook!
– Et qu'est-ce que tu fais sur Facebook?
– Alors … je lis mes messages, je poste des messages sur le mur de mes copains …
– Tu fais ça souvent?
– Ah oui, je fais ça tous les jours. Et puis, quelquefois, je partage aussi des photos.
– Tu partages des photos?
– Oui, quelquefois, je partage des photos avec mes copains.
– D'accord. Merci, Théo.

2
– Et toi, Julie. Qu'est-ce que tu fais sur Facebook?
– Je retrouve toutes mes copines sur Facebook! Tous les weekends, on organise des sorties, pour aller en ville ou au ciné … – D'accord. Et à part ça?
– À part ça, je modifi e mes préférences …
– Tu modifi es souvent tes préférences?
– Eh bien, une ou deux fois par mois.
– Bon, merci, Julie.

3
– Salut, Yusuf. Que fais-tu sur Facebook?
– Moi, j'aime surtout commenter les photos de mes copains.
– Tu commentes leurs photos?
– Oui, je laisse tout le temps des commentaires sur les photos de mes copains. Et puis, de temps en temps, je fais des quiz …
– Tu fais des quiz? Et est-ce que tu regardes des vidéos?
– Oui, on s'envoie souvent des liens vers des vidéos – sur YouTube, par exemple.
– Merci bien, Yusuf.

4
– Et toi, Manon. Que fais-tu sur Facebook?
– Je ne suis pas sur Facebook.
– Tu n'es pas sur Facebook? Ah bon. Pourquoi?
– Parce que mes parents n'aiment pas ça. Ils pensent que Facebook, c'est mauvais pour les jeunes.
– Mauvais pourquoi?
– Ben, parce qu'on passe trop de temps sur Facebook et on ne fait pas nos devoirs, par

exemple.
– Dommage. Bon, merci, Manon.

Answers

Théo: reads and posts messages – every day shares photos (with friends) – sometimes

Julie: arranges to go out (to town or cinema with friends) – every weekend updates her likes – once or twice a month

Yusuf: comments on (friends') photos – all the time does quizzes – from time to time sends video links – often

Manon: not on Facebook, parents don't like it/think it's bad for young people

5 En tandem. Fais un dialogue. Utilise les renseignements A ou B. (Speaking L4)

Speaking. In pairs: pupils make up a dialogue, using one of the two sets of prompts supplied. A sample opening is given.

6 Lis le texte. Note vrai (V) ou faux (F). (Reading L4)

Reading. Pupils read the exchange of views on Facebook and then the sentences about it, writing V (true) or F (false) for each one. Some verb forms are glossed for support.

Answers

1 F **2** V **3** V **4** F **5** F **6** V

Discuss in pairs or as a class whose advice pupils agree/disagree with, using *Je suis d'accord avec …/Je ne suis pas d'accord avec …* Remind pupils of the expressions *avoir raison* and *avoir tort*, and encourage them to include these, e.g. *À mon avis, Vincent a raison/tort.*

7 Écris un court exposé avec comme sujet «Facebook et moi». (Writing L4)

Writing. Pupils prepare a short presentation text on the subject *Facebook and me.* They can use the details supplied in activities 1 and 5, as well as ideas of their own. A list of language to include is supplied for support.

PLTS T

If you have connections with a partner school, pupils could make contact on a social network with their French peers.

Plenary

Review the endings for regular *–er* verbs in the present tense using *retrouver.* Write *retrouv* on the board six times. Elicit the forms for each subject pronoun, asking pupils to write up the ending each time. Repeat with *inviter.*

Workbook, page 3

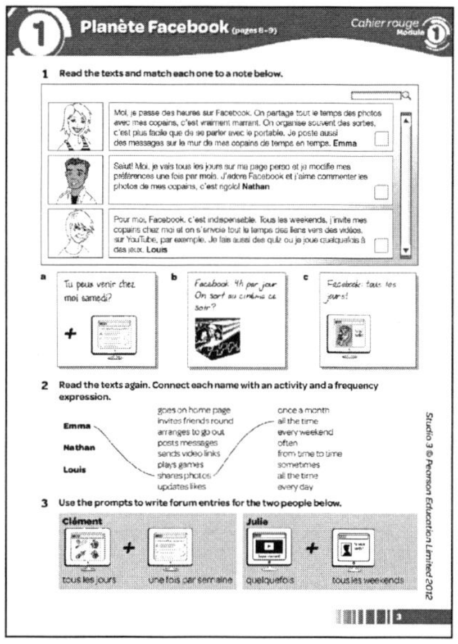

Answers

1 Emma – **b** Nathan – **c** Louis – **a**

2 Emma: shares photos all the time; arranges to go out often; posts messages from time to time.

Nathan: goes on home page every day; updates likes once a month.

Louis: invites friends round every weekend; sends video links all the time; plays games sometimes.

3 (Example answers:)

Clément: Salut! J'adore Facebook et tous les jours, j'aime commenter les photos de mes copains. C'est rigolo! Je fais aussi des quiz une fois par semaine.

Julie: Pour moi, Facebook, c'est indispensable. Moi et mes copains, on s'envoie quelquefois des liens vers des vidéos et tous les weekends, on organise des sorties.

Worksheet 1.1 Transcription

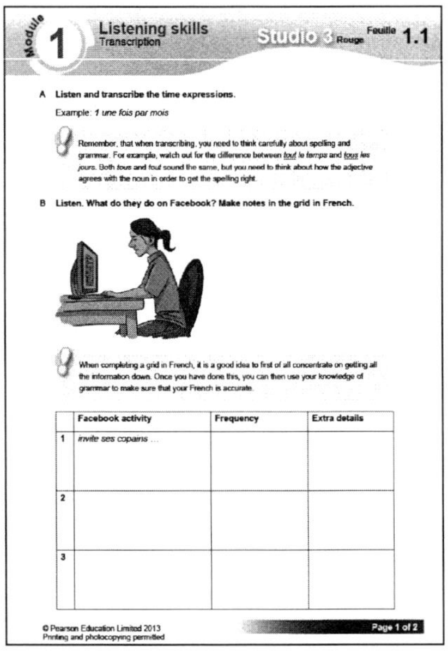

Module 1 Listening skills
Transcription
Studio 3 Rouge Feuille 1.1

A Listen and transcribe the time expressions.

Example: *1 une fois par mois*

Remember, that when transcribing, you need to think carefully about spelling and grammar. For example, watch out for the difference between *tout le temps* and *tous les jours*. Both *tous* and *tout* sound the same, but you need to think about how the adjective agrees with the noun in order to get the spelling right.

B Listen. What do they do on Facebook? Make notes in the grid in French.

When completing a grid in French, it is a good idea to first of all concentrate on getting all the information down. Once you have done this, you can then use your knowledge of grammar to make sure that your French is accurate.

	Facebook activity	Frequency	Extra details
1	*invite ses copains …*		
2			
3			

© Pearson Education Limited 2013
Printing and photocopying permitted
Page 1 of 2

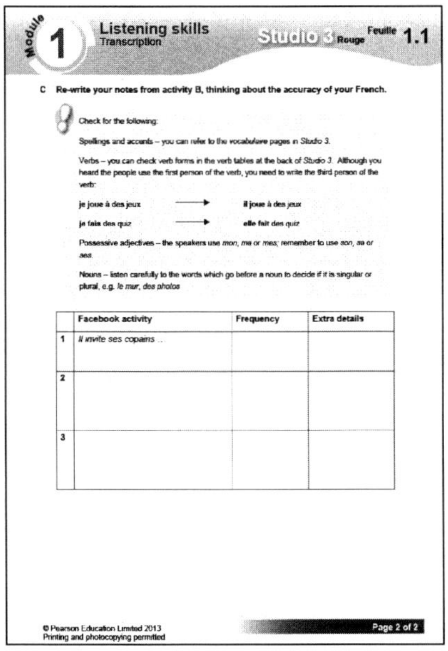

Module 1 Listening skills
Transcription
Studio 3 Rouge Feuille 1.1

C Re-write your notes from activity B, thinking about the accuracy of your French.

Check for the following:

Spellings and accents – you can refer to the *vocabulaire* pages in *Studio 3*.

Verbs – you can check verb forms in the verb tables at the back of *Studio 3*. Although you heard the people use the first person of the verb, you need to write the third person of the verb:

je joue à des jeux → **il joue à des jeux**

je fais des quiz → **elle fait des quiz**

Possessive adjectives – the speakers use *mon, ma* or *mes*; remember to use *son, sa* or *ses*.

Nouns – listen carefully to the words which go before a noun to decide if it is singular or plural, e.g. *le mur, des photos*

	Facebook activity	Frequency	Extra details
1	*Il invite ses copains …*		
2			
3			

© Pearson Education Limited 2013
Printing and photocopying permitted
Page 2 of 2

Answers

1 une fois par mois
2 trois fois par semaine
3 tous les soirs
4 tout le temps
5 tous les weekends

B & C

	Facebook activity	Frequency	Extra details
1	Il invite ses copains au cinéma. Il laisse des commentaires sur les photos de ses copains. Il fait aussi des quiz.	tous les weekends de temps en temps quelquefois	indispensable à sa vie sociale
2	Elle va sur sa page perso. Elle lit ses messages. Elle regarde les photos de ses amis.	une ou deux fois par semaine souvent quelquefois	Elle aime assez Facebook. / Elle préfère retrouver ses amis en ville.
3	Il joue à des jeux. Il poste des messages sur le mur de ses copains. Il partage des photos.	tout le temps tous les soirs souvent	Il passe des heures sur Facebook. / Il a plein d'amis sur Facebook.

1 2 Comment tu trouves ...?

Learning objectives

- Giving your opinion about someone
- Using direct object pronouns

Programme of Study references

GV2 Grammatical structures (direct object pronouns; adjectival agreement)

GV3 Opinions and discussions

LC3 Conversation (dealing with the unexpected)

LC5 Speaking coherently and confidently

FCSE links

Unit 1: Relationships, family and friends (Descriptions)

Grammar

- direct object pronouns
- adjective agreement

Key language

arrogant(e)
beau/belle
charmant(e)
drôle
égoïste
généreux/généreuse
gentil(le)
jaloux/jalouse
joli(e)
lunatique
pénible
timide

PLTS

E Effective participators

Cross-curricular

English: direct object pronouns

Resources

Audio files:
03_Module1_Unit2_Ex1.mp3
04_Module1_Unit2_Ex4.mp3

Workbooks:
Cahier d'exercices Rouge, page 4

ActiveTeach:
Starter 2 resource
p.010 Flashcards
p.010 Grammar
p.010 Grammar practice
p.010 Grammar
p.011 Learning skills

ActiveLearn:
Listening, Reading
Grammar, Vocabulary

Starter 1

Aim

To review adjective agreement

Give pupils two minutes to look at the adjectives labelled a–l in exercise 1 on page 10 of the Pupil Book and identify who each could refer to: a boy, a girl or both.

(**Answers:** boy – *arrogant, beau, charmant; girl – généreuse, gentille, jalouse, jolie; both – drôle, égoïste, lunatique, pénible, timide*).

Check answers. You could extend the activity by asking pupils to supply the feminine forms of *arrogant, beau, charmant* and the masculine forms of *généreuse, gentille, jalouse, jolie*.

Alternative Starter 1:

Use ActiveTeach p.010 Flashcards to introduce adjectives for character description and/or direct object pronouns.

1 Écoute et note les adjectifs dans le bon ordre. (1–12) (Listening L3)

Listening. Pupils listen to people discussing two people they know and note the adjectives used in the order they are mentioned.

Audioscript Track 3

Comment tu trouves Romain?

1 *Je le trouve timide.*
2 *Je le trouve beau!*
3 *Je le trouve arrogant.*
4 *Je le trouve charmant.*
5 *Je le trouve lunatique.*
6 *Je le trouve pénible!*

Comment tu trouves Ophélie?

7 *Je la trouve gentille.*
8 *Je la trouve jolie.*
9 *Je la trouve drôle.*
10 *Je la trouve jalouse.*
11 *Je la trouve égoïste.*
12 *Je la trouve généreuse.*

Answers

1 l **2** b **3** a **4** c **5** j **6** k **7** g **8** i **9** d **10** h **11** e **12** f

Studio Grammaire: direct object pronouns

Use the *Studio Grammaire* box to cover direct object pronouns. There is more information and further practice on Pupil Book p. 26.

Point out the tip box on how pupils can use direct object pronouns to raise their writing and speaking level.

Studio Grammaire: adjective agreement

Use the *Studio Grammaire* box to review adjective agreement.

2 Réécris les phrases suivantes, en utilisant *le, la* ou *les.* (Writing L2)

Writing. Pupils rewrite the sentences, replacing the objects of the sentences with direct object pronouns.

Answers

1 Je le trouve drôle.
2 Je la trouve jalouse.
3 Je les trouve beaux.
4 Je les trouve gentilles.
5 Je le trouve pénible.
6 Je les trouve généreux.

Pupils use a dictionary to research six more adjectives they could use to describe people.

3 En tandem. Comment tu trouves les célébrités? Utilise les photos ou tes propres idées. (Speaking L4)

Speaking. In pairs: pupils discuss their opinions of celebrities, using the people pictured as prompts or their own ideas. A structure is supplied.

Starter 2

Aim

To review direct object pronouns

Write up the following, replacing each underlined word (the answer) with a line. Give pupils two minutes to complete the sentences with the appropriate direct object pronoun.

1 *Anna? Je la trouve charmante.*
2 *Ben? Je le trouve drôle.*
3 *Charlotte? Je la trouve généreuse.*
4 *Daisy et Eddie? Je les trouve égoïstes.*
5 *Mes frères? Je les trouve pénibles.*
6 *George? Je le trouve lunatique.*

Alternative Starter 2:

Use ActiveTeach p.010 Grammar practice to practise direct object pronouns.

4 Écoute et lis l'histoire. (Listening L4)

Listening. Pupils listen to the story of an exchange visit romance, following the text in their books at the same time. Some vocabulary is glossed for support.

Audioscript Track 4

– *Lundi …*
– *Laura, regarde! Voilà les élèves de l'échange anglais qui arrivent!*
– *Alors, Charlotte, tu aimes les mecs anglais?*
– *Ah oui, je les trouve adorables! J'adore leur accent!*
– *Salut! Je suis Matthieu, ton partenaire d'échange.*
– *Oh, hello! I mean, bonjour. Je m'appelle Jack.*

– *Regarde le garçon avec le tee-shirt rouge. Comment tu le trouves?*
– *Il a l'air sympa, mais je préfère Matthieu. Je le trouve vraiment bien!*

– *Hé, Jack! Regarde les deux filles là-bas. Comment tu trouves la blonde?*
– *Pas mal. Mais je préfère sa copine. Je la trouve très jolie.*

– *Mercredi …*
– *Oh! Pardon.*
– *Il est un peu timide, mais carrément charmant et poli!*

– *Vendredi …*
– *Voici mon numéro de portable. Envoie-moi un SMS.*
– *Oh, là là! D'accord, il est assez beau, mais je le trouve trop arrogant et lunatique.*

5 Relis l'histoire et choisis la bonne réponse. (Reading L4)

Reading. Pupils read the story in exercise 4 again and then complete the sentences about it by choosing the correct option from the two given each time.

Answers

1 Les élèves qui arrivent en car sont anglais.
2 Charlotte aime les mecs anglais.
3 Laura trouve Matthieu beau.
4 Jack trouve Laura très jolie.
5 Laura pense que Jack est charmant et poli mais timide.
6 Jack donne son numéro de téléphone à Laura.
7 À la fin de l'histoire, Charlotte trouve Jack lunatique.

6 Quelle est ton opinion des quatre personnages? Écris ta réponse aux questions. (Writing L4)

Writing. Pupils give their opinions of the four people in the exercise 4 story by writing their own reply to the question about each of them. Draw their attention to the tip box on qualifiers and encourage them to use these in their descriptions.

7 À quatre. Écris un sketch. Utilise les renseignements suivants ou tes propres idées. Mémorise et joue le sketch! (Speaking L4)

PLTS E

Speaking. Pupils write a sketch, using the details supplied or their own ideas. They then memorise it and act it out in groups of four. The scenario and a sample opening are supplied.

Plenary

Review direct object pronouns and adjectives used to describe character. Ask about celebrities/pupils in the class, using *Comment tu trouves ... ?* Pupils reply using direct object pronouns, e.g. *Je la trouve drôle*.

Workbook, page 4

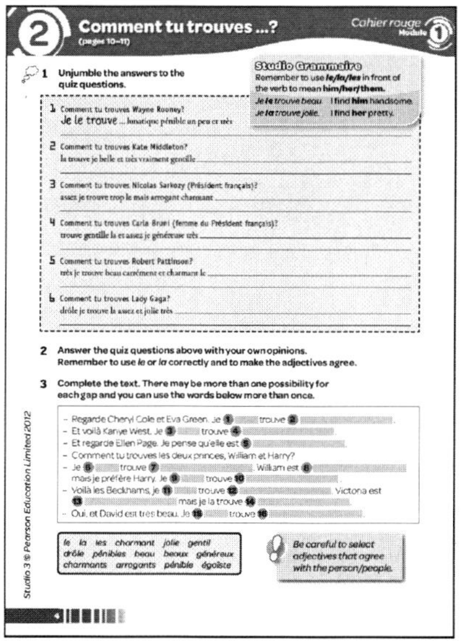
2 Comment tu trouves ...? (pages 10–11)
Cahier rouge Module 1

1 Unjumble the answers to the quiz questions.

Studio Grammaire

2 Answer the quiz questions above with your own opinions. Remember to use *le* or *la* correctly and to make the adjectives agree.

3 Complete the text. There may be more than one possibility for each gap and you can use the words below more than once.

le la les charmant jolie gentil drôle pénibles beau beaux généreux charmants arrogants pénible égoïste

Be careful to select adjectives that agree with the person/people.

Answers

1 **1** Je le trouve un peu pénible et très lunatique.
2 Je la trouve vraiment belle et très gentille.
3 Je le trouve trop arrogant mais assez charmant.
4 Je la trouve très gentille et assez généreuse.
5 Je le trouve carrément beau et très charmant.
6 Je la trouve assez jolie et très drôle.
2 (Answers will vary.)
3 (Example answers:)
1 les **2** pénibles **3** le **4** généreux **5** jolie
6 les **7** charmants **8** beau **9** le **10** drôle
11 les **12** beaux **13** jolie **14** égoïste **15** le
16 charmant

Worksheet 1.2 Learning vocabulary

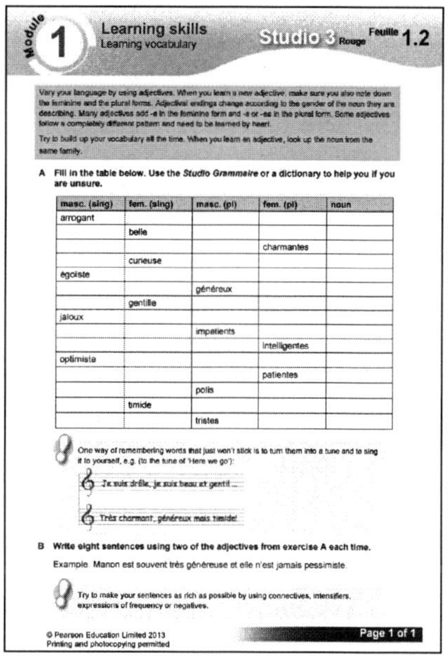
Module 1 Learning skills Learning vocabulary Studio 3 Rouge Feuille 1.2

A Fill in the table below. Use the *Studio Grammaire* or a dictionary to help you if you are unsure.

masc. (sing)	fem. (sing)	masc. (pl)	fem. (pl)	noun
arrogant				
	belle			
			charmantes	
	curieuse			
égoïste				
		généreux		
	gentille			
jaloux				
		impatients		
			intelligentes	
optimiste				
			patientes	
		polis		
	timide			
		tristes		

B Write eight sentences using two of the adjectives from exercise A each time.

Example: Manon est souvent très généreuse et elle n'est jamais pessimiste.

© Pearson Education Limited 2013 Printing and photocopying permitted

Page 1 of 1

Answers

A

masc. (sing.)	fem. (sing.)	masc. (pl)	fem. (pl)	noun
arrogant	arrogante	arrogants	arrogantes	l'arrogance
beau	*belle*	beaux	belles	la beauté
charmant	charmante	charmants	*charmantes*	le charme
curieux	*curieuse*	curieux	curieuses	la curiosité
égoïste	égoïste	égoïstes	égoïstes	l'égoïsme
généreux	généreuse	*généreux*	généreuses	la générosité
gentil	*gentille*	gentils	gentilles	la gentillesse
jaloux	jalouse	jaloux	jalouses	la jalousie
impatient	impatiente	*impatients*	impatientes	l'impatience
intelligent	intelligente	intelligents	*intelligentes*	l'intelligence
optimiste	optimiste	optimistes	optimistes	l'optimisme
patient	patiente	patients	*patientes*	la patience
poli	polie	*polis*	polies	la politesse
timide	*timide*	timides	timides	la timidité
triste	triste	*tristes*	tristes	la tristesse

B (Answers will vary.)

1 3 Tu viens aussi?

Learning objectives
- Arranging to go out
- Using the near future tense

Programme of Study references

GV1 Tenses (near future)
GV3 Developing vocabulary
LC3 Conversation
LC6 Reading comprehension

FCSE links

Unit 1: Relationships, family and friends (Meeting up, Free-time activities)

Unit 4: Leisure (Hobbies, Free time, Going out, Preferences)

Grammar
- the near future tense

Key language

Je vais/On va …
aller au cinéma/en ville
aller à la patinoire/à une fête
faire les magasins
faire un piquenique
Tu viens avec moi/nous?
Tu veux m'/nous accompagner?
Ça t'intéresse?
On se retrouve où/à quelle heure?
chez moi/toi
Il y a une séance à …
À plus.
À demain/samedi.
Oui, merci. Je veux bien.
D'accord, si tu veux.
Génial! Bonne idée!
Pourquoi pas?
Je n'ai pas trop envie.
Tu rigoles!
C'est vraiment nul!
J'ai horreur de ça!
ce matin/soir
cet après-midi
demain matin
samedi après-midi
dimanche soir
hier
samedi dernier
le weekend dernier
l'année dernière

PLTS

S Self-managers

Resources

Audio files:
05_Module1_Unit3_Ex2.mp3
06_Module1_Unit3_Ex5.mp3

Workbooks:
Cahier d'exercices Rouge, page 5

ActiveTeach:
Starter 1 resource
p.012 Grammar
p.012 Grammar practice
p.013 Video 1
p.013 Video worksheet 1
p.013 Class activity
p.013 Thinking skills
p.013 Grammar skills

ActiveLearn:
Listening, Reading
Grammar

Starter 1

Aim

To review adjective agreement

Write up the following. Give pupils two minutes working in pairs to translate the expressions into English. (You could supply the English versions in random order if they need support.)

ce matin
ce soir
demain matin
samedi soir
cet après-midi
dimanche
demain soir

Check answers. (Answers: this morning, this evening, tomorrow morning, Saturday night, this afternoon, Sunday, tomorrow evening)

1 Trouve le bon texte pour chaque photo. (1–6) (Reading L4–5)

Reading. Pupils read the texts and match each of them to the appropriate photo.

Answers

Pupils check their answers using the exercise 2 recording.

2 Écoute et vérifie. Note aussi si on accepte (✓) ou refuse (✗) l'invitation. (1–6) (Listening L4–5)

Listening. Pupils listen to six conversations and confirm their answers to exercise 1. They also note for each conversation whether the person accepts the invitation (writing a tick) or refuses it (writing a cross).

Audioscript Track 5

1 – *Salut, c'est moi. Je vais aller au cinéma samedi soir. Il y a une nouvelle comédie avec Ben Stiller. Ça t'intéresse?*
– *Ah oui, merci. C'est gentil. Je veux bien!*

2 – *Coucou, Antoine. Qu'est-ce que tu fais demain matin? Je vais aller à la patinoire. Tu viens avec moi?*
– *Ah non, merci. J'ai horreur de ça!*

3 – *Salut, Chloé. Qu'est-ce que tu fais demain soir? On va aller à un concert de rock et on a un billet de trop. Ça t'intéresse?*
– *Ben … Non merci. Je n'ai pas trop envie.*

4 – *Salut, Marc! Je vais aller à une fête d'anniversaire ce soir. C'est la fête de mon meilleur copain, Guillaume. Tu veux m'accompagner?*
– *Mouais. D'accord, si tu veux. Pourquoi pas?*

5 – *T'es libre cet après-midi? Ma soeur Marie et moi voulons aller en ville. On va faire les magasins. Tu viens avec nous?*
– *Tu rigoles! C'est vraiment nul!*

6 – *Ça va, Mohammed? T'es invité à sortir avec ma famille et moi dimanche. On va faire un piquenique dans le parc. Tu veux nous accompagner?*
– *Génial! Bonne idée! J'adore les piqueniques.*

Answers

1 C ✓ **2** B × **3** F × **4** A ✓ **5** D × **6** E ✓

Studio Grammaire: the near future tense

Use the *Studio Grammaire* box to review the near future tense. There is more information and further practice on Pupil Book p. 27.

R Pupils translate the following phrases into French, using the near future tense. Elicit the infinitives required first, if the class needs more support.

1 I'm going to meet **2** she's going to give
3 we're going to watch **4** they're going to sing

3 En tandem. Fais cinq mini-dialogues. Utilise les détails suivants. (Speaking L4–5)

Speaking. In pairs: pupils read the key language box, then put together and perform five mini-dialogues using the picture plus text prompts supplied. A sample exchange is given.

Starter 2

Aim

To review times

Read out the following times for the pupils to write down as digits.

1 *six heures cinq*
2 *onze heures et demie*
3 *dix heures et quart*
4 *trois heures moins le quart*
5 *sept heures vingt-cinq*
6 *cinq heures moins dix*

Check answers. (**Answers**: 6.05, 11.30, 10.15, 2.45, 7.25, 4.50)

Alternative Starter 2:

Use ActiveTeach p.013 Class activity to practise time expressions or ActiveTeach p.012 Grammar practice to practise the near future tense.

4 Lis les informations sur Internet et réponds à la question en anglais. (Reading L4)

Reading. Pupils read the cinema website information and answer the question about it in English. Draw their attention to the tip box on the false friend *séances*.

Answers

4 and 7

5 Écoute et note les renseignements en anglais. (1–4) (Listening L5)

Listening. Pupils read the key language box, then listen to four conversations and for each one note the details listed.

Audioscript Track 6

1 – *Allô, oui?*
– *Salut, c'est moi. Je vais aller au cinéma ce soir. Tu viens?*
– *Oui, je veux bien. On va voir quel fi lm?*
– *Arthur 3. C'est un dessin animé. Ça t'intéresse?*
– *Ça m'intéresse bien. Ça commence à quelle heure?*
– *Attends. Je vais regarder sur Internet. Il y a une séance à huit heures cinq.*
– *On se retrouve où et à quelle heure?*
– *Rendez-vous chez moi à sept heures et demie. D'accord?*
– *D'accord. À plus!*

2 – *Allô?*
– *Salut. Tu veux aller au cinéma samedi après-midi avec Rémi et moi?*
– *Ça dépend. Qu'est-ce que vous allez voir?*
– *On va voir un nouveau fi lm d'action qui s'appelle Les Diables Rouges. Tu viens?*
– *Pourquoi pas? Ça commence à quelle heure?*
– *Il y a une séance à deux heures et quart. Ça va?*
– *Oui, ça va. Alors, on se retrouve où et à quelle heure?*
– *On se retrouve chez toi à deux heures moins le quart?*
– *D'accord. À samedi, alors.*
– *À samedi. Au revoir!*

3 – *Allô, oui?*
– *Salut, ça va? Je vais aller au cinéma demain matin. Tu veux m'accompagner?*
– *Bonne idée. Qu'est-ce qu'on va voir?*
– *Planète Zéro. C'est un fi lm de science-fiction. Tu aimes ça?*
– *Ouais, j'aime bien ça … La séance est à quelle heure?*

– Je vais aller à la séance d'onze heures vingt-cinq. D'accord?
– D'accord. On se retrouve là-bas?
– OK. On se retrouve à onze heures et quart devant le cinéma
– OK. À demain!
– À demain! Ciao.

4 *– Allô?*
– Salut, c'est moi. T'es libre cet après-midi?
– Euh … oui. Pourquoi?
– Parce que Julie et moi, on va aller au cinéma. Tu viens avec nous?
– Ça dépend. Vous allez voir quel film?
– On va voir Ma Vie d'Enfer. C'est une nouvelle comédie. Ça t'intéresse?
– Oui, je veux bien, merci. Vous y allez à quelle heure?
– On va aller à la séance de trois heures moins dix.
– D'accord. On se retrouve où et à quelle heure?
– On se retrouve chez Julie, à deux heures et demie. Ça va?
– Oui, c'est super. À plus, alors.
– Oui, à plus!

Answers

1 When? this evening
Type of film: cartoon
Time: 8.05
Meeting place & time: my house, 7.30

2 When? Saturday afternoon
Type of film: action film
Time: 2.15
Meeting place & time: your house, 1.45

3 When? tomorrow morning
Type of film: science fiction
Time: 11.25
Meeting place & time: 11.15, in front of cinema

4 When? this afternoon
Type of film: comedy
Time: 2.50
Meeting place & time: Julie's house, 2.30

6 En tandem. Lis le dialogue à voix haute, puis change les mots soulignés. (Speaking L5)

Speaking. In pairs: pupils read the dialogue aloud. They then make up their own version, changing the underlined details.

7 Lis et écris le SMS en français ‹‹correct››. (Writing L4–5)

Writing. Pupils read the text message and rewrite it, converting text-speak to standard French. Draw their attention to the tip box on how to work out key features of text-speak.

Answers

Salut, Jack. Ça va?
Qu'est-ce que tu fais ce soir?
Je vais aller au ciné(ma). Tu viens?
Rendez-vous chez moi à sept heures. D'accord?

PLTS S

Read together through *Stratégie 1* on Pupil Book p. 29, covering the vocabulary-memorising technique of thinking about French words within English sentences. Set pupils the challenge of choosing and learning ten words using this approach, either in the classroom or at home.

Plenary

Ask the class to summarise how the near future tense is formed, giving you examples from the unit.

Make sentences using the near future tense and appropriate time expressions round the class, with each pupil adding a word (e.g. *Je – vais – aller – à – la – piscine – demain – après-midi.*). When a sentence is complete, start a new one. Pupils should try to avoid repeating verbs, places and time expressions.

Workbook, page 5

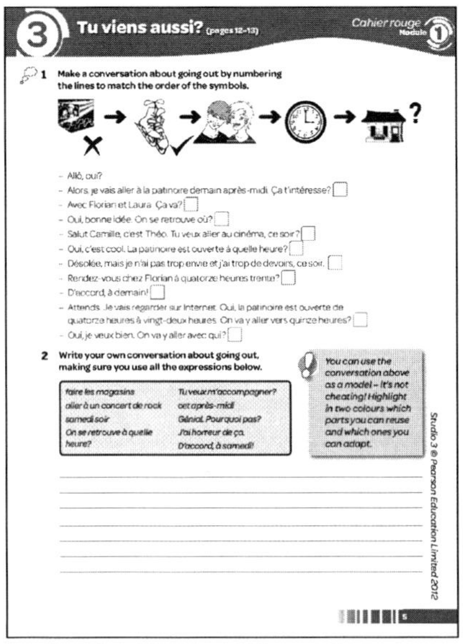
3 Tu viens aussi? (pages 12–13) Cahier rouge Module 1

1 Make a conversation about going out by numbering the lines to match the order of the symbols.

– Allô, oui?
– Alors, je vais aller à la patinoire demain après-midi. Ça t'intéresse? ☐
– Avec Florian et Laura. Ça va? ☐
– Oui, bonne idée. On se retrouve où? ☐
– Salut Camille, c'est Théo. Tu veux aller au cinéma, ce soir? ☐
– Oui, c'est cool. La patinoire est ouverte à quelle heure? ☐
– Désolée, mais je n'ai pas trop envie et j'ai trop de devoirs, ce soir. ☐
– Rendez-vous chez Florian à quatorze heures trente? ☐
– D'accord, à demain! ☐
– Attends. Je vais regarder sur Internet. Oui, la patinoire est ouverte de quatorze heures à vingt-deux heures. On va y aller vers quinze heures? ☐
– Oui, je veux bien. On va y aller avec qui? ☐

2 Write your own conversation about going out, making sure you use all the expressions below.

faire les magasins / *Tu veux m'accompagner?*
aller à un concert de rock / *cet après-midi*
samedi soir / *Génial. Pourquoi pas?*
On se retrouve à quelle heure? / *J'ai horreur de ça.*
D'accord, à samedi!

You can use the conversation above as a model – it's not cheating! Highlight in two colours which parts you can reuse and which ones you can adapt.

Studio 3 © Pearson Education Limited 2012

5

Answers

1 1, 4, 6, 9, 2, 7, 3, 10, 11, 8, 5

- – Allô, oui?
- – Salut Camille, c'est Théo. Tu veux aller au cinéma, ce soir?
- – Désolée, mais je n'ai pas trop envie et j'ai trop de devoirs, ce soir.
- – Alors, je vais aller à la patinoire demain après-midi. Ça t'intéresse?
- – Oui, je veux bien. On va y aller avec qui?
- – Avec Florian et Laura. Ça va?
- – Oui, c'est cool. La patinoire est ouverte à quelle heure?
- – Attends. Je vais regarder sur Internet. Oui, la patinoire est ouverte de quatorze heures à vingt-deux heures. On va y aller vers quinze heures.
- – Oui, bonne idée. On se retrouve où?
- – Rendez-vous chez Florian à quatorze heures trente?
- – D'accord, à demain!

2 (Example answer:)

- – Allô, oui?
- – Salut Sarah, c'est Émilie. Tu veux faire les magasins en ville cet après-midi?
- – Désolée, mais j'ai horreur de ça et j'ai trop de devoirs, ce soir.
- – Alors, je vais aller à un concert de rock samedi soir. Tu veux m'accompagner?
- – Génial, pourquoi pas? On se retrouve à quelle heure?
- – Rendez-vous chez moi à sept heures et demie?
- – D'accord, à samedi!

Worksheet 1.3 Logic puzzle

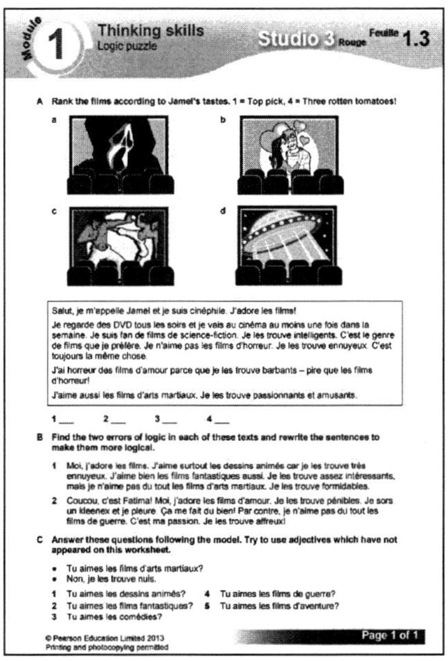

Module 1 Thinking skills
Logic puzzle
Studio 3 Rouge Feuille 1.3

A Rank the films according to Jamel's tastes. 1 = Top pick, 4 = Three rotten tomatoes!

a b c d

Salut, je m'appelle Jamel et je suis cinéphile. J'adore les films!

Je regarde des DVD tous les soirs et je vais au cinéma au moins une fois dans la semaine. Je suis fan de films de science-fiction. Je les trouve intelligents. C'est le genre de films que je préfère. Je n'aime pas les films d'horreur. Je les trouve ennuyeux. C'est toujours la même chose.

J'ai horreur des films d'amour parce que je les trouve barbants – pire que les films d'horreur!

J'aime aussi les films d'arts martiaux. Je les trouve passionnants et amusants.

1 ___ 2 ___ 3 ___ 4 ___

B Find the two errors of logic in each of these texts and rewrite the sentences to make them more logical.

1 Moi, j'adore les films. J'aime surtout les dessins animés car je les trouve très ennuyeux. J'aime bien les films fantastiques aussi. Je les trouve assez intéressants, mais je n'aime pas du tout les films d'arts martiaux. Je les trouve formidables.

2 Coucou, c'est Fatima! Moi, j'adore les films d'amour. Je les trouve pénibles. Je sors un kleenex et je pleure. Ça me fait du bien! Par contre, je n'aime pas du tout les films de guerre. C'est ma passion. Je les trouve affreux!

C Answer these questions following the model. Try to use adjectives which have not appeared on this worksheet.

- Tu aimes les films d'arts martiaux?
- Non, je les trouve nuls.

1 Tu aimes les dessins animés?
2 Tu aimes les films fantastiques?
3 Tu aimes les comédies?
4 Tu aimes les films de guerre?
5 Tu aimes les films d'aventure?

© Pearson Education Limited 2013
Printing and photocopying permitted
Page 1 of 1

Answers

A 1 d 2 c 3 a 4 b

B Other adjectives/phrases may be acceptable.

1 Moi, j'adore les films. J'aime surtout les dessins animés car je les trouve très amusants. J'aime bien aussi les films fantastiques. Je les trouve assez intéressants, mais je n'aime pas du tout les films d'arts martiaux. Je les trouve ennuyeux.

2 Coucou, c'est Fatima! Moi, j'adore les films d'amour. Je les trouve tristes. Je sors un kleenex et je pleure. Ça me fait du bien! Par contre, je n'aime pas du tout les films de guerre. Je déteste ça. Je les trouve affreux!

C (Answers will vary.)

Worksheet 1.4 The near future tense

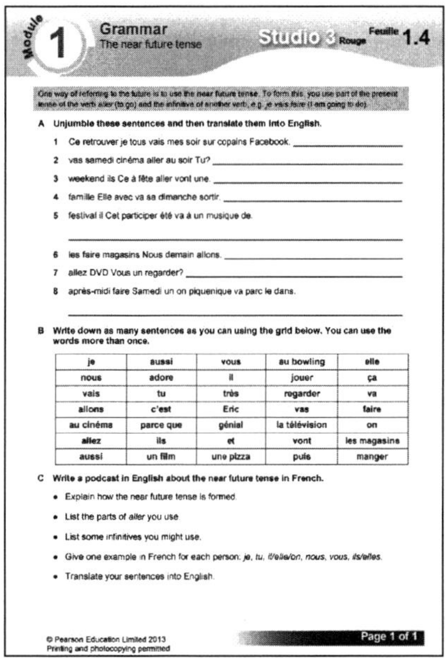

Module 1 Grammar
The near future tense
Studio 3 Rouge Feuille 1.4

One way of referring to the future is to use the near future tense. To form this, you use part of the present tense of the verb *aller* (to go) and the infinitive of another verb, e.g. *je vais faire* (I am going to do).

A Unjumble these sentences and then translate them into English.

1 Ce retrouver je tous vais mes soir sur copains Facebook. ___
2 vas samedi cinéma aller au soir Tu? ___
3 weekend ils Ce à fête aller vont une. ___
4 famille Elle avec va sa dimanche sortir. ___
5 festival il Cet participer été va à un musique de. ___
6 les faire magasins Nous demain allons. ___
7 allez DVD Vous un regarder? ___
8 après-midi faire Samedi un on piquenique va parc le dans. ___

B Write down as many sentences as you can using the grid below. You can use the words more than once.

je	aussi	vous	au bowling	elle
nous	adore	il	jouer	ça
vais	tu	très	regarder	va
allons	c'est	Eric	vas	faire
au cinéma	parce que	génial	la télévision	on
allez	ils	et	vont	les magasins
aussi	un film	une pizza	puis	manger

C Write a podcast in English about the near future tense in French.

- Explain how the near future tense is formed.
- List the parts of *aller* you use.
- List some infinitives you might use.
- Give one example in French for each person: *je, tu, il/elle/on, nous, vous, ils/elles*.
- Translate your sentences into English.

© Pearson Education Limited 2013
Printing and photocopying permitted
Page 1 of 1

Answers

A 1 Ce soir, je vais retrouver tous mes copains sur Facebook.
Tonight I am going to meet all my friends on Facebook.

2 Tu vas aller au cinéma samedi soir?
Are you going to go to the cinema on Saturday evening?

3 Ce weekend, ils vont aller à une fête.
This weekend they are going to go to a party.

4 Elle va sortir avec sa famille dimanche.
She is going to go out with her family on Sunday.

5 Cet été, il va participer à un festival de musique.
In the summer he is going to take part in a music festival.

6 Nous allons faire les magasins demain.
We are going to go shopping tomorrow.

7 Vous allez regarder un DVD?
Are you going to watch a DVD?

8 Samedi après-midi, on va faire un piquenique dans le parc.
On Saturday afternoon we are going to have a picnic in the park.

B (Answers will vary.)

C (Answers will vary.)

Video

The video component provides opportunities for speaking activities in a plausible and stimulating context. The StudioFR team, whom pupils met in Studio 1 and 2 – Marielle, Samira, Hugo, Alex and Mehdi – make video reports on a range of topics to send to StudioGB, their counterparts in the UK. Each video is around three minutes long.

Episode 1: Le speed dating

Marielle decides to take the team speed dating, where Samira and Hugo emerge as StudioFR's first couple. Video worksheet 1 can be used in conjunction with this episode.

Answers to video worksheet (ActiveTeach)

1 A – It has to be Marielle, as she's so sociable and full of romantic ideas.
– Questions like *Qu'est-ce que tu aimes faire?* are likely, to find out about shared interests.

B (Answers will vary.)

2 A She is looking at her *page perso* (home page).

B Each person fills out a piece of paper. They meet, and if they like each other, they'll go out together.

3 A It means 'What are you going to do this weekend?' (near future tense).

B She likes shopping and fashion.

C He is going to surf the internet.

D It's to show that they are talking to the camera, so they can say what they really think about each other.

E She thinks he's a pain (*pénible*). He thinks she is good-looking but selfish (*belle mais trop égoïste*). They aren't compatible because they have so little in common.

4 A Go for a picnic.

B Horror films.

C He thinks she's nice but she thinks he's shy.

D The boy.

5 A *Jolie* (pretty), *lunatique* (moody), *arrogant* (arrogant).

B Because she can't believe how arrogant he is to think (wrongly) that she would want to go out with him!

6 A Too shy, funny but arrogant.

B A pain, generous but jealous.

C Because they realise that they both like each other.

D She's going to post the results on the Studio home page.

E No! He gets brushed off with the words *Tu rigoles!* – 'You're joking!'

1 4 Ça s'est bien passé?

Learning objectives
- Describing a date
- Using the perfect tense

Programme of Study references
GV1 Tenses (perfect)
LC2 Transcription
LC3 Conversation (dealing with the unexpected)
LC6 Reading comprehension

FCSE links
Unit 1: Relationships, family and friends (Girlfriend, boyfriend, Meeting up, Free-time activities)
Unit 4: Leisure (Hobbies, Free time, Going out, Preferences)

Grammar
- the perfect tense with *avoir/être*

Key language
Je suis sorti(e) avec …
Je suis/On est allé(e)(s) …
au cinéma/à une fête/en ville
J'ai/On a …
bavardé
bu du coca
fait les magasins
fait une promenade
joué au bowling
mangé un hamburger
regardé un DVD
bien rigolé
On a dansé ensemble.
Je suis resté(e) à la maison.
C'était …
cool/génial
intéressant/marrant
romantique/sympa
affreux/bizarre
ennuyeux/horrible
nul/un désastre

PLTS
C Creative thinkers

Resources
Audio files:
07_Module1_Unit4_Ex2.mp3
08_Module1_Unit4_Ex4.mp3
Workbooks:
Cahier d'exercices Rouge, page 6
ActiveTeach:
Starter 1 resource
Starter 2 resource
p.014 Flashcards
p.014 Flashcards
p.014 Grammar
p.014 Grammar practice
p.015 Video 2
p.015 Video worksheet 2
p.015 Grammar skills
p.015 Learning skills
ActiveLearn:
Listening, Reading
Grammar, Vocabulary

Starter 1
Aim

To review the perfect tense

Write up the following, replacing each underlined word (the answer) with a line. Give pupils two minutes to complete the verbs, using the words supplied.

lu allé dansé pris fait allée vu bu

1 *j'ai bu (boire)*
2 *il a dansé (danser)*
3 *nous avons fait (faire)*
4 *elle est allée (aller)*
5 *vous avez pris (prendre)*
6 *tu as vu (voir)*
7 *j'ai lu (lire)*
8 *je suis allé (aller)*

Check answers. Ask pupils what tense is used in all the examples and get them to translate the verbs into English.

Alternative Starter 1:
Use both sets of ActiveTeach p.014 Flashcards to introduce language for describing a date in the past.

1 Fais correspondre les photos et les deux bonnes phrases. (1–6) (Reading L4–5)

Reading. Pupils read the key language box and then find the correct pair of sentences for each picture.

Answers

Pupils check their answers using the exercise 2 recording.

2 Écoute et vérifie. (1–6) (Listening L4–5)

Listening. Pupils listen to check their answers to exercise 1.

Audioscript Track 7

1 *Je suis allé à une fête avec Emma. On a dansé ensemble.*
2 *J'ai mangé un hamburger avec Baptiste. On a aussi bu du coca.*
3 *J'ai fait une promenade avec Chloé. On a bavardé tout le temps.*
4 *Je suis restée à la maison avec Max. On a regardé un DVD.*
5 *Je suis allé en ville avec Kali. On a fait les magasins.*
6 *J'ai joué au bowling avec Enzo. On a bien rigolé.*

Answers

1 a, i **2** f, g **3** b, h **4** e, l **5** c, j **6** d, k

Studio Grammaire: the perfect tense with *avoir/être*

Use the *Studio Grammaire* box to review the perfect tense with *avoir* and *être*. There is more information and further practice on Pupil Book p. 27.

R Ask pupils to identify the two verbs in the sentences in exercise 1 which form the perfect tense with *être* (*aller*, *rester*).

3 En tandem. Jeu de mémoire. Qui peut faire la phrase la plus longue?

(Speaking L4–5)

Speaking. In pairs: pupils play a memory game, working together to make the longest sentence they can. A sample exchange is given. Ask pairs to keep count of the number of items in their longest sentence to see which pair manages to include most items. Encourage them to be imaginative in adapting the sentences, e.g. *J'ai mangé une pizza avec Alex*.

Starter 2

PLTS C

Aim

To review the present and perfect tenses;
To identify and apply grammatical patterns

Write up the following. Give pupils three minutes to copy and complete the grid.

present	English	perfect	English
je danse			I danced
		j'ai lu	
	I see		
	I stay	*je suis resté(e)*	
je prends			
	I go		

Check answers. Ask pupils when the perfect tense is used.

Alternative Starter 2:
Use ActiveTeach p.014 Grammar practice to practise the perfect tense.
(Answers: present: *je danse, je lis, je vois, je reste, je prends, je vais*
English: I dance, I read, I see, I stay, I take, I go
perfect: *j'ai dansé, j'ai lu, j'ai vu, je suis resté(e), j'ai pris, je suis allé(e)*
English: I danced, I read, I saw, I stayed, I took, I went)

4 Écoute et complète le tableau. (1–4)

(Listening L5)

Listening. Pupils read the key language supplied and copy out the table. They listen to four conversations about what people did at the weekend and complete the table with the details. Some language is glossed for support.

Audioscript Track 8

1 *– Alors, tu es sortie hier?*
– Oui, je suis allée à une fête avec Guillaume.
– Ça s'est bien passé?
– … on a bavardé …
– Bavardé? C'est tout? Vous avez dansé ensemble?
– Oui, on a dansé ensemble.
– C'était comment?
– C'était romantique!

2 *– Qu'est-ce que tu as fait samedi soir?*
– Je suis allé au cinéma avec Lara.
– Qu'est-ce que vous avez vu comme film?
– Ben … On a vu un film de science-fiction.
– Et ensuite? Qu'est-ce que vous avez fait?
– Alors … ensuite, on a mangé une pizza …
– Ça s'est passé comment, alors?
– Bof, c'était ennuyeux.

3 *– Salut! Tu as passé un bon weekend?*
– Pas mal, et toi?
– Pas mal non plus. Samedi soir, je suis allée chez Thomas.
– Qu'est-ce que vous avez fait?
– On a regardé un peu la télé et après on a écouté de la musique!
– Ça s'est bien passé?
– Non! C'était un désastre!
– Un désastre? Pourquoi?
– Parce qu'il adore le rap et moi, j'ai horreur de ça! On a écouté du rap toute la soirée! Beurk!

4 *– Dis-moi, tu es sorti samedi après-midi?*
– Oui, je suis allé en ville avec Chloé.
– Qu'est-ce que vous avez fait en ville?
– On a fait les magasins. Elle a acheté un tee-shirt et moi, j'ai acheté un jean.
– Ça s'est passé comment?
– C'était sympa.
– Tu la trouves bien, alors, Chloé?
– Oui, je la trouve très jolie!

Answers

	où?	activité(s)	opinion
1	fête	bavardé, dansé	☺
2	cinéma	vu film science-fiction, mangé pizza	☹
3	chez Thomas	regardé télé, écouté musique	☹
4	en ville	fait magasins, acheté tee-shirt et jean	☺

5 En tandem. Complète le dialogue en utilisant tes propres idées. (Speaking L5)

Speaking. In pairs: pupils complete the dialogue framework supplied using their own ideas and then perform the dialogue.

6 Lis les textes et réponds aux questions en anglais. (Reading L5)

Reading. Pupils read the three texts in which people talk about what they did at the weekend. They then answer the questions in English. Draw their attention to the tip box on reading skills.

Answers

1 Nathan **2** Medhi **3** Rémi **4** Medhi **5** Nathan **6** Rémi **7** Nathan

7 En tandem. Jeu de conséquences. Complète une phrase à tour de rôle et en secret. Puis plie le papier. (Writing L5)

Writing. In pairs: pupils play 'Consequences' in French, taking it in turn to write a sentence, then fold the paper and pass it to their partner to write the next sentence. A framework is supplied.

8 Lis ton jeu de conséquences à voix haute. C'est rigolo? (Speaking L5)

Speaking. Pupils read aloud to the class what they wrote in exercise 7. Ask the class to vote on the funniest one.

Plenary

Ask the class when the perfect tense is used and how it is formed, giving you examples from the unit.

Give phrases from the unit using the infinitive, e.g. *faire une promenade*. Pupils make up a sentence using the perfect tense, e.g. *J'ai fait une promenade*. Encourage them to use different subject pronouns.

Workbook, page 6

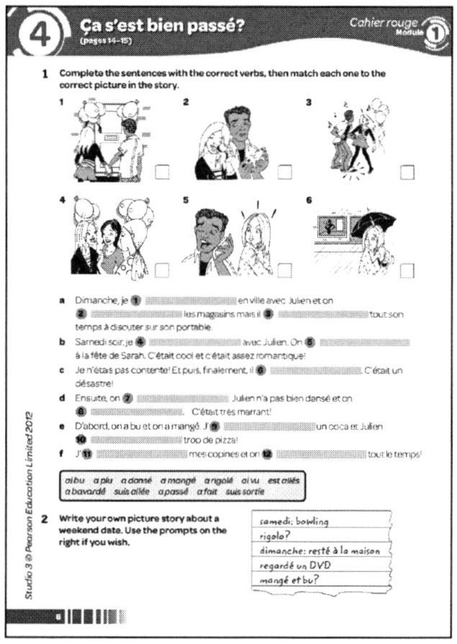
4 Ça s'est bien passé? (pages 14–15) Cahier rouge Module 1

1 Complete the sentences with the correct verbs, then match each one to the correct picture in the story.

a Dimanche, je (1) ______ en ville avec Julien et on (2) ______ les magasins mais il (3) ______ tout son temps à discuter sur son portable.
b Samedi soir, je (4) ______ avec Julien. On (5) ______ à la fête de Sarah. C'était cool et c'était assez romantique!
c Je n'étais pas contente! Et puis, finalement, il (6) ______. C'était un désastre!
d Ensuite, on (7) ______. Julien n'a pas bien dansé et on (8) ______. C'était très marrant!
e D'abord, on a bu et on a mangé. J'(9) ______ un coca et Julien (10) ______ trop de pizza!
f J'(11) ______ mes copines et on (12) ______ tout le temps!

ai bu a plu a dansé a mangé a rigolé ai vu est allés a bavardé suis allée a passé a fait suis sortie

2 Write your own picture story about a weekend date. Use the prompts on the right if you wish.

samedi: bowling
rigolo?
dimanche: resté à la maison
regardé un DVD
mangé et bu?

Studio 3 © Pearson Education Limited 2012

6

Answers

1 **a 1** suis allée **2** a fait **3** a passé
b 4 suis sortie **5** est allés
c 6 a plu
d 7 a dansé **8** a rigolé
e 9 ai bu **10** a mangé
f 11 ai vu **12** a bavardé
1 b **2** e **3** d **4** f **5** a **6** c

2 (Example answer:)

Samedi soir, je suis sortie avec Thomas. On est allés au bowling. C'était rigolo!

D'abord, on a bu et on a mangé. J'ai bu un Orangina et Thomas a mangé trop de frites!

Ensuite, on a fait du bowling, c'était très marrant! J'ai gagné!

Dimanche, je suis restée à la maison avec Claire et on a regardé un DVD. C'était super!

Worksheet 1.5 The perfect tense

Module 1 Grammar
The perfect tense
Studio 3 Rouge Feuille 1.5

Most verbs form the perfect tense with the correct part of *avoir* followed by the past participle.
To form the past participle, change the infinitive as follows:
-er → é -ir → i -re → u
Don't forget the irregular verbs – you will need to learn these by heart!
Examples: faire → fait prendre → pris voir → vu
A few important verbs take *être* instead of *avoir*. Verbs that take *être* need agreement on the past participle:
-e with a feminine subject (e.g. *elle est allée*)
-s with a plural subject (e.g. *vous êtes allés*)
Watch out for verbs that are feminine and plural (e.g. *elles sont allées*).

A Complete the table to describe what Odyssée did yesterday and what she is doing today.

hier (dimanche)	aujourd'hui (lundi)
1 J'ai fait une promenade avec Simon.	1 ______ mon travail.
2 ______ en ville.	2 Je vais à l'école.
3 J'ai mangé au fastfood.	3 ______ à la cantine.
4 ______ les magasins.	4 Je fais mes devoirs.
5 J'ai joué au bowling.	5 ______ aux jeux vidéo.

B Complete these sentences with the correct form of the perfect tense using the verbs in brackets.

1 Samedi, Tariq (jouer) ______ au foot.
2 Hier soir, on (rigoler) ______.
3 Dimanche, je (sortir) ______. J' (voir) ______ un film.
4 Hier soir, tu (manger) ______ un hamburger et tu (boire) ______ un coca.
5 Vous (prendre) ______ un taxi et vous (aller) ______ en ville.
6 Mes deux sœurs (aller) ______ en ville.
Elles (regarder) ______ un film d'horreur.

C Rewrite the following text in the past tense.

Eva fait les magasins avec ses copines. Elle regarde les vêtements et elle bavarde avec ses amies. Ensuite, elles vont au café où elles jouent au babyfoot, elles mangent des frites et elles boivent du coca.

Hier, Eva ______

Page 1 of 1

Answers

A 1 **Je fais** mon travail.
2 **Je suis allé(e)** en ville.
3 **Je mange** à la cantine.
4 **J'ai fait** les magasins.
5 **Je joue** aux jeux vidéo.

B 1 Samedi, Tariq **a joué** au foot.
2 Hier soir, on **a rigolé**.
3 Dimanche, je **suis sorti(e)**. J'ai vu un film.
4 Hier soir, tu **as mangé** un hamburger et tu as bu un coca.
5 Vous **avez pris** un taxi et vous **êtes allé(e)(s)** en ville.
6 Mes deux sœurs **sont allées** en ville. Elles **ont regardé** un film d'horreur.

C *Hier, Éva* a fait les magasins avec ses copines. Elle a regardé les vêtements et elle a bavardé avec ses amies. Ensuite, elles sont allées au café où elles ont joué au babyfoot, elles ont mangé des frites et ells ont bu du coca.

Worksheet 1.6 Using spider diagrams

Module 1 Learning skills
Using spider diagrams
Studio 3 Rouge Feuille 1.6

Spider diagrams allow you to structure your thoughts and ideas. They can be useful if you are giving a spoken presentation or doing a piece of extended writing. There is no right or wrong way to create spider diagrams. Choose the style that suits you best or create your own style.

Tips on creating spider diagrams in French:

- Write your topic in the middle of the page.
- Use colour.
- Use thick and thin lines.
- Write in key words.
- Always include at least one complex French phrase for each branch of your spider diagram.

Here are a few ways in which to create complex phrases:

- Use *où* (where) and *qui* (who).
- Use sequencers such as *puis*, *ensuite* and *après* to make sentences longer.
- Use connectives to make sentences more complex, *et*, *aussi*.
- Add opinions: *À mon avis, c'était …*
- Give reasons, using *parce que* and *car*.

A Look at the spider diagrams below. Add elements to each one and make them your own. Answer the questions: who, what, where, when, how, why?

1 Le weekend dernier et le weekend prochain

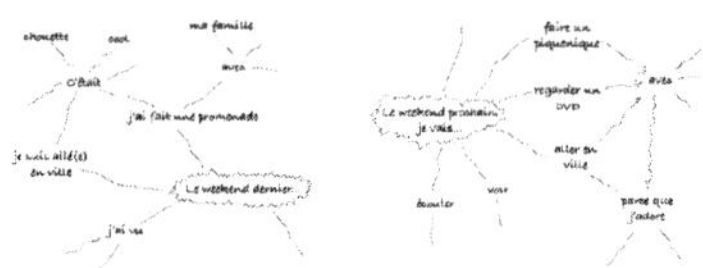

B With a partner, use your spider diagrams to talk about:

- **what you did last weekend and what it was like**
- **what you are going to do next weekend and why.**

Give your partner a mark out of 5 for confidence, fluency, pronunciation and the ability to talk without looking at his/her sheet.

C Write a paragraph, based on your spider diagrams, saying what you did last weekend and what you are going to do next weekend. Give opinions/reasons.

Page 1 of 1

Answers

(Answers will vary.)

Video

Episode 2: Le rendez-vous

Samira and Hugo go on a secret first date … followed closely by the rest of the team. Video worksheet 2 can be used in conjunction with this episode.

Answers to video worksheet (ActiveTeach)

1 A Probably well. We know that they are compatible from the previous episode.
– (Answers will vary.)
– Probably pleased and very curious. Maybe a bit jealous.

2 A Meeting in town for a date.
B Eavesdropping (listening in)!
C Hugo says he's going home. They want to put the others off the scent.
D To follow them.
E Mehdi.

3 A They are eating chocolate cake, which he loves.
B She's afraid Hugo and Samira might see Alex.
C For a walk in the park.
D Yes, they agree on everything, including which film to see.

4 A Samira says *Je suis restée chez moi* (I stayed at home). Hugo says *J'ai fait une promenade au parc* (I went for a walk in the park).
B Because they did not realise that the others had followed them.
C Yes. They got on really well and ended up holding hands.
D Speed dating works!

1 5 Fou de musique!

Learning objectives

- Describing a music event
- Using three tenses

Programme of Study references

GV1 Tenses (past, present and future)

GV4 Accuracy (grammar; spelling; punctuation)

LC1 Listening and responding

LC4 Expressing ideas (writing)

FCSE links

Unit 4: Leisure (Music)

Key language

un concert gratuit
en plein air
télécharger les nouveautés
une chanson
la rythmique
la mélodie
les paroles (f)
l'ambiance (f)
toute la soirée
son nouvel album

PLTS

R Reflective learners

Resources

Audio files:
09_Module1_Unit5_Ex1.mp3
10_Module1_Unit5_Ex4.mp3

Workbooks:
Cahier d'exercices Rouge, page 7

ActiveTeach:
Starter 1 resource
p.017 Class activity
p.017 Grammar skills

ActiveLearn:
Listening, Reading
Grammar

Starter 1

Aim

To introduce the topic of music

Write up the following. Give pupils two minutes to come up with a music artist in each category.

le R&B
le hip-hop
le reggae
le jazz
la pop
le rock
la techno

Hear answers. Take a vote by a show of hands on the most popular choice in each category.

1 Écoute et lis. Choisis le bon titre pour chaque paragraphe. (1–4) (Listening L5–6)

Listening. Pupils listen to Lucas talking about music, reading the text at the same time. For each section they choose the correct title from the list supplied.

Audioscript Track 9

1 *Salut, je m'appelle Lucas. Ma passion, c'est la musique! J'écoute un peu de tout: du R&B, du hip-hop, du reggae et même du jazz, quelquefois. Chaque semaine, je télécharge des chansons sur mon mp3, parce que j'adore écouter les nouveautés.*

2 *Tous les ans, le 21 juin, c'est la Fête de la Musique. Dans la ville où j'habite, il y a beaucoup de concerts gratuits où on peut écouter toutes sortes de musiques. C'est cool, ça! En général, je vais au concert en plein air avec mes copains.*

3 *L'année dernière, on est allés à un concert de ‹‹musiques du monde››. On a vu un groupe de salsa de Cuba, un chanteur de reggae de Jamaïque et un duo pop-rock de Russie! L'ambiance était fantastique et on a dansé toute la soirée. C'était le top du top!*

4 *Demain soir, je vais aller au concert d'Abd Al Malik qui est un de mes chanteurs préférés. Je le trouve vraiment génial! Donc, la semaine prochaine, je vais acheter son nouvel album. Je suis méga-fan de sa musique parce que j'adore la rythmique et les paroles.*

Answers

1 C **2** D **3** A **4** B

2 Qu'est-ce que c'est en anglais? Devine et puis cherche dans le Mini-dictionnaire. (Reading L4)

Reading. Pupils read the French words and find them in the text in exercise 1. They try to work out the meanings and then confirm their answers using the *Mini-dictionnaire* at the back of the Pupil Book.

Answers

1 every week **2** the latest/new things **3** free **4** open air **5** the atmosphere **6** all evening/night 7 the words

3 Trouve les verbes dans le texte. Copie et complète le tableau. (Reading L6)

Reading. Pupils copy out the table. They identify all the verbs in exercise 1 and complete the table, writing the verbs in the correct column. Draw their attention to the tip box on using time expressions to identify tenses.

Answers

présent	passé	futur
je m'appelle *c'est* *j'écoute* *je télécharge* *j'adore écouter* *j'habite* *c'est* *il y a* *on peut* *écouter* *je vais* *(qui) est* *je (le) trouve* *je suis* *j'adore*	*on est allés* *on a vu* *était* *on a dansé* *c'était*	*je vais aller* *je vais acheter*

4 Écoute. On parle du présent (pr), du passé (pa) ou du futur (f)? (1–6) (Listening L6)

Listening. Pupils listen to six people talking about music and note the tense used by each one: present (writing pr), past (writing pa) or future (writing f).

Audioscript Track 10

1 *En général, j'écoute du R&B, mais j'aime aussi le rap et quelquefois, j'écoute un peu de reggae. Chaque semaine, je télécharge les nouveautés de la semaine.*

2 *Demain, je vais acheter le dernier album de mon groupe préféré. Puis samedi soir, je vais aller à un concert de rock.*

3 *Le weekend dernier, c'était la Fête de la Musique. Je suis allé à un concert avec mes copains. L'ambiance était géniale et on a dansé toute la soirée!*

4 *Hier, j'ai téléchargé des nouvelles chansons sur mon mp3. Ensuite, j'ai regardé une émission de musique à la télé. Ce n'était pas trop mal.*

5 *Je suis méga-fan des chansons de Christophe Willem, parce que je le trouve sympa et j'adore ses mélodies.*

6 *En juin, je vais participer à un festival de musique à Paris. Je vais jouer du piano dans un orchestra de jeunes. On va jouer de la musique classique et de la musique pop.*

Answers

1 pr **2** f **3** pa **4** pa **5** pr **6** f

Starter 2

Aim

To review tense usage

Write up the following. Give pupils two minutes to write a verb in an appropriate tense for each time expression.

demain hier normalement vendredi dernier

Hear answers, asking pupils to identify the tense used each time and how it is formed.

Alternative Starter 2:

Use ActiveTeach p.017 Class activity to practise language from the module.

5 En tandem. Interviewe Lucas. Utilise les questions suivantes. Tu dois répondre au présent, au passé ou au futur? (Speaking L6)

Speaking. In pairs: pupils make up an interview with Lucas, taking it in turn to be Lucas/the interviewer. The questions to use are supplied. Pupils need to think carefully about which tense to use in replying to each one.

6 Refais l'interview. Change les détails. Utilise tes propres idées. (Speaking L6)

Speaking. Pupils put together another version of the interview in exercise 5, this time changing the details using their own ideas. A sample opening is given.

7 Écris un exposé au sujet d'un concert ou d'un festival de musique. Invente les détails si tu veux. (Writing L6)

Writing. Pupils write a report on a concert or music festival. If they haven't been to one recently, they can make up the details. A writing framework and a list of points to include are supplied.

8 Vérifie et corrige ton exposé. (Reading L6)

PLTS **R**

Reading. Pupils check and correct their report from exercise 7, using the checklist supplied. Ask pupils each to identify two areas in which they could improve (e.g. tense formation, vocabulary, adjective agreement, including connectives/intensifiers, using a wider variety of structures, etc.).

Plenary

Hear some pupils' reports. Ask the rest of the class to give constructive feedback.

Workbook, page 7

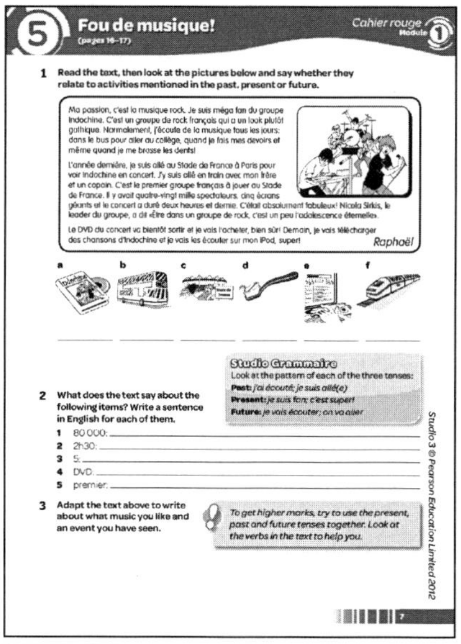

5 Fou de musique! (pages 16–17) *Cahier rouge* Module 1

1 Read the text, then look at the pictures below and say whether they relate to activities mentioned in the past, present or future.

Ma passion, c'est la musique rock. Je suis méga fan du groupe Indochine. C'est un groupe de rock français qui a un look plutôt gothique. Normalement, j'écoute de la musique tous les jours: dans le bus pour aller au collège, quand je fais mes devoirs et même quand je me brosse les dents!

L'année dernière, je suis allé au Stade de France à Paris pour voir Indochine en concert. J'y suis allé en train avec mon frère et un copain. C'est le premier groupe français à jouer au Stade de France. Il y avait quatre-vingt mille spectateurs, cinq écrans géants et le concert a duré deux heures et demie. C'était absolument fabuleux! Nicola Sirkis, le leader du groupe, a dit «Être dans un groupe de rock, c'est un peu l'adolescence éternelle».

Le DVD du concert va bientôt sortir et je vais l'acheter, bien sûr! Demain, je vais télécharger des chansons d'Indochine et je vais les écouter sur mon iPod, super!

Raphaël

a b c d e f

Studio Grammaire
Look at the pattern of each of the three tenses:
Past: *j'ai écouté; je suis allé(e)*
Present: *je suis fan; c'est super!*
Future: *je vais écouter; on va aller*

2 What does the text say about the following items? Write a sentence in English for each of them.
1 80 000: ______
2 2h30: ______
3 5: ______
4 DVD: ______
5 premier: ______

3 Adapt the text above to write about what music you like and an event you have seen.

To get higher marks, try to use the present, past and future tenses together. Look at the verbs in the text to help you.

Studio 3 © Pearson Education Limited 2012

7

Answers

1 a future **b** present **c** past **d** present
e future **f** past

2 1 80 000: This is the number of spectators that were at the concert.
2 2h30: This is how long the concert lasted.
3 5: There were five giant screens at the concert.
4 DVD: The DVD of the concert is coming out soon.
5 premier: Indochine were the first French group to play at the Stade de France.

3 (Answers will vary.)

Worksheet 1.7 Using three tenses

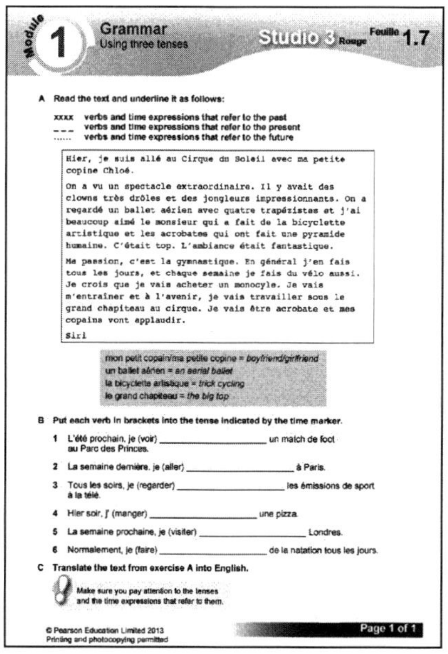

Module 1 **Grammar** Using three tenses — **Studio 3** Rouge Feuille **1.7**

A Read the text and underline it as follows:

xxxx verbs and time expressions that refer to the past
_ _ _ verbs and time expressions that refer to the present
...... verbs and time expressions that refer to the future

Hier, je suis allé au Cirque du Soleil avec ma petite copine Chloé.

On a vu un spectacle extraordinaire. Il y avait des clowns très drôles et des jongleurs impressionnants. On a regardé un ballet aérien avec quatre trapézistes et j'ai beaucoup aimé le monsieur qui a fait de la bicyclette artistique et les acrobates qui ont fait une pyramide humaine. C'était top. L'ambiance était fantastique.

Ma passion, c'est la gymnastique. En général j'en fais tous les jours, et chaque semaine je fais du vélo aussi. Je crois que je vais acheter un monocyle. Je vais m'entraîner et à l'avenir, je vais travailler sous le grand chapiteau au cirque. Je vais être acrobate et mes copains vont applaudir.

Siri

mon petit copain/ma petite copine = *boyfriend/girlfriend*
un ballet aérien = *an aerial ballet*
la bicyclette artistique = *trick cycling*
le grand chapiteau = *the big top*

B Put each verb in brackets into the tense indicated by the time marker.
1 L'été prochain, je (voir) ______ un match de foot au Parc des Princes.
2 La semaine dernière, je (aller) ______ à Paris.
3 Tous les soirs, je (regarder) ______ les émissions de sport à la télé.
4 Hier soir, j' (manger) ______ une pizza.
5 La semaine prochaine, je (visiter) ______ Londres.
6 Normalement, je (faire) ______ de la natation tous les jours.

C Translate the text from exercise A into English.

Make sure you pay attention to the tenses and the time expressions that refer to them.

© Pearson Education Limited 2013
Printing and photocopying permitted

Page 1 of 1

Answers

A Hier, je suis allé au Cirque du Soleil avec ma petite Copine Chloé.

On a vu un spectacle extraordinaire. Il y avait des clowns très drôles et des jongleurs impressionnants.

On a regardé un ballet aérien avec quatre trapézistes et j'ai beaucoup aimé le monsieur qui a fait de la bicyclette artistique et les acrobates qui ont fait une pyramide humaine. C'était top. L'ambiance était fantastique.

Ma passion, c'est la gymnastique. En général j'en fais tous les jours, et chaque semaine je fais du vélo aussi. Je crois que je vais acheter un monocyle, je vais m'entraîner et à l'avenir, je vais travailler sous le grand chapiteau au cirque. Je vais être acrobate et mes copains vont applaudir.

B 1 L'été prochain, je vais voir un match de foot au Parc des Princes.
2 La semaine dernière, je suis allé(e) à Paris.
3 Tous les soirs, je regarde les émissions de sport à la télé.
4 Hier soir, j'ai mangé une pizza.
5 La semaine prochaine, je vais visiter Londres.
6 Normalement, je fais de la natation tous les jours.

C Yesterday I went to the 'Cirque du Soleil' with my girlfriend Chloé.

We saw an extraordinary show. There were very funny clowns and impressive jugglers. We watched a ballet in the air with four trapeze artists and I liked the man who did the trick cycling very much and the acrobats who made a human pyramid. It was great.

The atmosphere was fantastic.

My passion is gymnastics. In general I do it every day, and each week I go bike riding too. I think I am going to buy a unicycle. I am going to practise and in the future I am going to work in the Big Top at the circus. I am going to be an acrobat and my friends are going to clap.

1 Bilan et Révisions

Bilan

Pupils use this checklist to review language covered in the module, working on it in pairs in class or on their own at home. Encourage them to follow up any areas of weakness they identify. There are Target Setting Sheets included in the Assessment Pack, and an opportunity for pupils to record their own levels and targets on the *J'avance* page in the Workbook, p. 12. You can also use the *Bilan* checklist as an end-of-module plenary option.

Révisions

These revision exercises can be used for assessment purposes or for pupils to practise before tackling the assessment tasks in the Assessment Pack.

Resources

Audio files:

11_Module1_Rev_Ex1.mp3

Workbooks:

Cahier d'exercices Rouge, pages 8 & 9

1 Qu'est-ce qu'ils font sur Facebook? Pour chaque personne, note (a) les deux activités et (b) la fréquence. (1–4) (Listening L4)

Listening. Pupils listen to four people talking about what they do on Facebook. For each person they note the two activities mentioned and how often they do them.

Audioscript Track 11

1 – *T'es sur Facebook?*
– *Ah oui, bien sûr.*
– *Qu'est-ce que tu fais sur Facebook?*
– *Alors … je lis mes messages …*
– *Tu fais ça souvent?*
– *Oui, je fais ça tous les jours. Et puis, quelquefois, je fais des quiz.*

2 – *Qu'est-ce que tu fais sur Facebook?*
– *Alors … Par exemple, je modifie mes préférences …*
– *Tu fais ça tous les jours?*
– *Ah non. Une fois par mois.*
– *Et tu envoies des invitations à tes copains?*
– *Ah oui, tous les weekends, j'invite mes copains chez moi.*

3 – *Que fais-tu sur Facebook?*
– *Je retrouve tous mes copains sur Facebook! On partage des photos …*
– *Vous faites ça souvent?*
– *Oh oui, on fait ça tout le temps.*
– *Qu'est-ce que vous faites, aussi?*
– *Ben, de temps en temps, on s'envoie des liens vers des vidéos, par exemple, sur YouTube.*

4 – *Tu aimes Facebook?*
– *Ah oui, j'adore ça! Je passe des heures sur Facebook!*
– *Et qu'est-ce que tu fais?*
– *Euh … je poste des messages sur le mur de mes copains … Je fais ça deux fois par jour.*
– *Et à part ça?*
– *À part ça, je commente les photos de mes copains.*
– *Tu fais ça souvent?*
– *Peut-être une fois par semaine.*

Answers

1 **a** reads messages **b** every day; **a** does quizzes **b** sometimes
2 **a** updates likes **b** once a month; **a** invites friends round **b** every weekend
3 **a** shares photos **b** all the time; **a** sends video links **b** from time to time
4 **a** posts messages **b** twice a day; **a** comments on friends' photos **b** once a week

2 En tandem. Fais un dialogue. Utilise les questions et les renseignements A ou B. (Speaking L5)

Speaking. In pairs: pupils choose a set of prompts (A or B) and make up a dialogue using the questions supplied.

3 Lis et choisis la bonne phrase. (Reading L6)

Reading. Pupils read Amélie's text and find the correct English sentence endings, choosing from the two options supplied each time.

Answers

1 The classical concert was last weekend.
2 Amélie doesn't usually listen to classical music.
3 Matthieu plays in the school orchestra.
4 Amélie likes Matthieu's personality.
5 Amélie has already bought tickets to see Jenifer in concert.
6 Matthieu likes Jenifer's looks.

4 Imagine que tu es sorti(e) avec une célébrité. Écris un paragraphe. (Writing L6)

Writing. Pupils imagine that they went out with a celebrity and write a paragraph saying what they normally do at weekends, how they spent time with their chosen celebrity and what they're going to do next weekend. A list of points to include is supplied, along with sample openings.

Workbook, pages 8 and 9

Révisions

Cahier rouge Module 1

1 Read the article about Facebook. Spend two minutes and note three or four things you can understand.

Try to get the gist of each question and answer, even if you don't understand the detail. The activities on page 9 will help you to understand the rest.

Quelques questions sur Facebook

On utilise Facebook pour partager de la musique, des vidéos, des événements et des photos, et aussi pour poser des questions et partager les réponses.

Qu'est-ce que je dois faire pour m'inscrire sur Facebook?
Il faut avoir une adresse e-mail, au moins treize ans et peut-être quelques photos pour mettre sur ta page perso.

Combien de temps est-ce que je peux passer sur Facebook?
Ça, c'est ta décision. Tu peux facilement passer des heures à tchatter avec tes copains sur Facebook, mais c'est peut-être mieux de sortir avec eux de temps en temps.

Je n'aime pas tous mes camarades de classe, est-ce que je dois les accepter tous comme amis?
Pas du tout! C'est ton choix. Il faut refuser si tu n'es pas sûr(e).

Ma mère veut être mon amie. Est-ce que je dois l'accepter?
C'est difficile à dire, mais ce n'est pas une mauvaise idée. Tu peux toujours limiter son accès et en réalité, elle ne veut pas savoir tous tes secrets.

Combien d'amis est-ce que je peux avoir?
C'est à toi de décider, mais ce n'est pas une bonne idée d'avoir 600 amis si tu n'as pas le temps de parler à tous.

Est-ce que je peux limiter les choses qu'on peut voir sur mon profil?
Oui, tu peux sélectionner ce que tu veux montrer (photos, etc.) et à qui (tout le monde, amis de mes amis, etc.). On te conseille de tout limiter à tes seul(e)s ami(e)s.

Studio 3 © Pearson Education Limited 2012

8

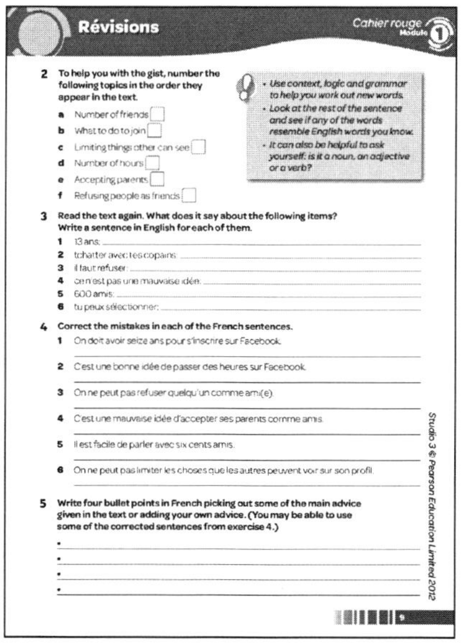

Révisions

Cahier rouge Module 1

2 To help you with the gist, number the following topics in the order they appear in the text.

a Number of friends
b What to do to join
c Limiting things other can see
d Number of hours
e Accepting parents
f Refusing people as friends

- *Use context, logic and grammar to help you work out new words.*
- *Look at the rest of the sentence and see if any of the words resemble English words you know.*
- *It can also be helpful to ask yourself: is it a noun, an adjective or a verb?*

3 Read the text again. What does it say about the following items? Write a sentence in English for each of them.

1 13 ans:
2 tchatter avec tes copains:
3 il faut refuser:
4 ce n'est pas une mauvaise idée:
5 600 amis:
6 tu peux sélectionner:

4 Correct the mistakes in each of the French sentences.

1 On doit avoir seize ans pour s'inscrire sur Facebook.
2 C'est une bonne idée de passer des heures sur Facebook.
3 On ne peut pas refuser quelqu'un comme ami(e).
4 C'est une mauvaise idée d'accepter ses parents comme amis.
5 Il est facile de parler avec six cents amis.
6 On ne peut pas limiter les choses que les autres peuvent voir sur son profil.

5 Write four bullet points in French picking out some of the main advice given in the text or adding your own advice. (You may be able to use some of the corrected sentences from exercise 4.)

Studio 3 © Pearson Education Limited 2012

9

Answers

2 a 5 **b** 1 **c** 6 **d** 2 **e** 4 **f** 3

3 **1** **13 ans:** You have to be 13 to subscribe to Facebook.
2 **tchatter avec tes copains:** You can easily spend hours chatting with your friends.
3 **il faut refuser:** Refuse someone as a friend if you're not sure.
4 **ce n'est pas une mauvaise idée:** It's not a bad idea to friend your mother.
5 **600 amis:** It's not a good idea to have six hundred friends if you don't have time to speak to all of them.
6 **tu peux sélectionner:** You can select what you want to show (photos, etc.) and to whom (everyone, friends of friends, etc.).

4 **1** On doit avoir **treize** ans pour s'inscrire sur Facebook.
2 **Ce n'est pas** une bonne idée de passer des heures sur Facebook.
3 **On peut refuser** quelqu'un comme ami(e).
4 **Ce n'est pas une** mauvaise idée d'accepter ses parents comme amis.
5 Il est **difficile** de parler avec six cents amis.
6 **On peut** limiter les choses que les autres peuvent voir sur son profil.

5 (Answers will vary.)

1 En plus: La Fête de la Musique

Learning objectives
- Finding out about music festivals around the world

Programme of Study references
LC3 Conversation
LC6 Reading comprehension
LC8 Writing creatively
LC8 Translation into French

FCSE links
Unit 4: Leisure (Music)
Unit 8: Celebrations (Various festivals, Carnival, Special celebrations)

Key language
Review of language from the module

PLTS
I Independent enquirers

Cross-curricular
Music: international music festivals
ICT: internet research

Resources
Audio files:
12_Module1_EnPlus_Ex1.mp3
13_Module1_EnPlus_Ex5.mp3
ActiveTeach:
p.021 Assignment 1
p.021 Assignment 1: prep

Starter

Aim

To introduce the topic

Ask the class about their experience of music festivals. Have they ever been to one? What kind of music did they hear? What else did they do there? What was it like?

1 Écoute et lis. Trouve la bonne photo pour chaque texte. (1–3) (Listening L6)

Listening. Pupils listen to three people talking about music festivals in their countries and read the text at the same time. They find the correct picture for each text. Draw their attention to the tip box on reading skills.

Audioscript Track 12

Le 21 juin, ça chante et ça danse, et pas seulement en France! Trois jeunes francophones nous expliquent comment la Fête de la Musique se passé dans leur pays.

– *À Tunis, la capitale de mon pays, vers vingt heures, tout le monde se retrouve au centre-ville où il y a du hip-hop pour faire danser tout le monde. Après, c'est la musique* live *qui commence. Cette année, il y avait d'abord un trio de rappeurs tunisiens. Je les ai trouvés sensationnels. Ensuite, c'était Cheb Khaled qui est très célèbre en Tunisie. Il chante du raï, un genre de musique pop chanté en arabe et en français. La musique a duré jusqu'à minuit!*

– *Chez nous, aux Antilles, la Fête de la Musique, c'est un vrai carnaval caribéen, plein de couleurs et de styles de musique différents. Et bien sûr, il y a toujours du soleil! Dans notre capitale, Pointe-à-Pitre, les gens dansent dans la rue au rythme du zouk (une musique de danse traditionnelle, avec des paroles en créole), du reggae, du jazz, du calypso … un peu de tout, quoi! L'année dernière, il y avait aussi un groupe d'environ cent musiciens qui jouaient du tambour, un instrument traditionnel de Guadeloupe. C'était vraiment impressionnant!*

– *Dans ma ville, Montréal, la Fête de la Musique dure trois jours! Cette année, on va diviser le vieux quartier de la ville en huit zones (des «scènes»). Chaque scène va avoir un genre de musique différent: rock, pop-rock, hip-hop/rhythm and blues, musiques du monde, électronique, jazz, classique et des musiques latines/reggae. Mon père va jouer du banjo dans un groupe de jazz, mais ce n'est pas mon truc: moi, je vais passer la journée à la scène rock!*

Answers

1 C **2** A **3** B

2 Relis les textes. Qui dit ça? Ousmane, Lola ou Édouard? (Reading L6)

Reading. Pupils read the texts in exercise 1 again and identify the speaker in each of the English sentences: Ousmane, Lola or Édouard.

Answers

1 Ousmane **2** Édouard **3** Lola **4** Édouard
5 Ousmane **6** Lola

3 Trouve les deux parties de chaque phrase. (Reading L4)

Reading. Pupils read the text in exercise 1 again and then find the correct ending for each sentence opening.

Answers

1 g **2** c **3** f **4** a **5** h **6** d **7** b **8** e

4 Lis et complète la traduction. Choisis les bons mots des cases. Attention! Il y a quatre mots de trop. (Reading L6)

Reading. Pupils read the French sentences and then complete the English translations, using the words supplied. There are four more words supplied than they need.

Answers

1 Then it was Cheb Khaled, who is very famous in Tunisia.
2 In our country, in the West Indies, it's a real Caribbean carnival, full of colour.
3 There was also a group of about a hundred musicians, who were playing the drums.
4 In my town, the music festival lasts three days!
5 Each stage will have a different kind of music.
6 My father is going to play in a jazz group, but that's not my thing.

5 Écoute. On parle de la Fête de la Musique en Tunisie (T), en Guadeloupe (G) ou au Québec (Q)? (1–4) (Listening L6)

Listening. Pupils listen to four conversations about different music festivals in Francophone countries and identify the location each time: Tunisia (writing T), Guadeloupe (writing G) or Québec (writing Q).

Audioscript Track 13

1
– On peut écouter quels genres de musique à la Fête de la Musique?
– Heu, un peu de tout: du reggae, du jazz, du calypso, du zouk …
– On chante en quelle langue? En français?
– Euh …ça dépend: certaines chansons sont en français, mais en général, le zouk est chanté en créole.
– Est-ce que beaucoup de gens dansent, aussi?
– Ah, oui, tout le monde danse dans la rue. C'est super, comme fête!

2
– Tu es allée à la Fête de la Musique, l'année dernière?
– Ah oui, bien sûr! J'ai écouté du hip-hop au centre-ville.
– C'était bien? Qu'est-ce qu'il y avait comme artistes?
– Il y avait un groupe de rap qui était vraiment génial.
– Il y avait aussi de la musique traditionnelle?
– Oui, j'ai écouté un groupe de raï qui n'était pas mal, mais ça, ce n'est pas trop mon truc. Je préfère le rap et le hip-hop.

3
– On va aller à la Fête de la Musique la semaine prochaine?
– Oui, mais tu vas y aller quand? Ça dure trios jours, tu sais.
– Je vais y aller le samedi. Tu viens?
– D'accord. Et c'est dans le vieux quartier, comme d'habitude?
– Oui, mais cette année, on va diviser le vieux quartier en huit scènes, avec un genre de musique différent sur chaque scène.
– C'est une bonne idée, ça. J'espère qu'il y aura une scène techno parce que j'adore ça!

4
– C'était comment, la Fête de la Musique, cette année?
– C'était cool! Il y avait toutes sortes de musiques.
– Qu'est-ce qu'il y avait comme musiques?
– Il y avait un énorme groupe d'environ cent musiciens qui jouaient du tambour …
– Tu rigoles! Cent tambours? Quel bruit!
– Ah oui, c'était vraiment impressionnant!
– Et il a fait beau?
– Ah oui, bien sûr! Il y a toujours du soleil aux Antilles!

Answers

1 G **2** T **3** Q **4** G

6 En tandem. Interviewe Ousmane, Lola ou Édouard. Utilise les questions suivantes. (Speaking L6)

Speaking. In pairs: pupils make up an interview with Ousmane, Lola or Édouard, taking it in turn to be the interviewer and person interviewed. They use the list of questions supplied.

7 Fais des recherches sur Internet sur la Fête de la Musique dans un autre pays. Imagine que tu habites dans ce pays. Décris la fête chez toi. (Writing L6)

PLTS I

Writing. Pupils do internet research on a music festival in a foreign country. They imagine that they live in that country and describe the festival. A list of points to cover is supplied.

Plenary

Ask some pupils to read out what they have found out in their internet research in exercise 7. Ask the class which of these festivals they would be most interested in visiting.

Worksheet 1.8 Mon blog
Assignment 1: Writing

Module 1 Défi
Mon blog
Assignment 1: writing
Studio 3 Rouge Feuille 1.8

A Complete the 'Prépa' worksheet.

B Write a blog entry of about 150 words. Mention the following:

- **an event you attended in the past**
- **an activity you do on a regular basis**
- **something you are going to do in the future.**

Make sure your text contains clear time markers.
Make sure your text contains clear opinions, which show how you feel.

C In pairs, read each other's text and suggest three improvements.

D Find another partner. Exchange texts and judge your new partner's text by completing the sentences below.

I was able to identify past / present / future events: very clearly / clearly / with difficulty.

I was able to identify opinions: very clearly / clearly / with difficulty.

I think the best sentence in your work was …

I think you could have given more examples of …

You can achieve levels 4–6 for this assignment

Level 4	Use your knowledge of grammar to adapt phrases. Include a personal response.
Level 5	Use varied language. Use the present tense and another tense, e.g. the near future or the perfect tense.
Level 6	Give information and opinions. Use descriptive language and a variety of structures. Show that you can use the present, the past and the future tenses.

Page 1 of 1

Worksheet 1.9 Mon blog: Prépa

Module 1 Défi
Mon blog
Prépa
Studio 3 Rouge Feuille 1.9

A Read Sarah's blog entry, then complete the sentences in English.

Je veux faire du rallye!

Le weekend dernier, je suis sortie avec mon petit copain, Valentin. On est allés voir une course de moto sur route. Les motos, ça ne m'intéresse pas du tout, mais Valentin adore ça, et il veut faire du rallye plus tard. L'ambiance de la course était sympa et c'était passionnant, mais pas du tout romantique! Après, Valentin nous a payé une pizza dans un petit restaurant très sympa. C'était délicieux.

Ensuite, Valentin m'a raccompagnée chez moi. Je le trouve vraiment amusant et extrêmement sympa.

Mais samedi prochain, on va aller voir le genre de spectacle que je préfère! J'ai acheté des billets pour un concert de Beyoncé qui est une de mes chanteuses préférées. Comme moi, Valentin aime beaucoup la musique de Beyoncé, et il la trouve très belle, alors il va oublier sa moto pour une fois!

Sarah

1 Last weekend, Sarah went to see ______________________
2 Sarah is not at all interested in motorbikes, but ______________________.
3 At the race, the atmosphere was ____________ and ____________ but not at all ______________.
4 Afterwards, Valentin paid for ______________________
5 Sarah finds Valentin ______________ and ______________________.
6 Sarah has bought tickets for ______________________.
7 Beyoncé is one of Sarah's ______________________.
8 Valentin thinks Beyoncé is ______________________.

B Underline all the phrases in the passage that give opinions and that you could reuse in your assignment.

C Make a separate list of the examples of the three different tenses and any time markers that you could reuse in your assignment.

Page 1 of 1

Answers

1 Last weekend, Sarah went to see a motorbike race.
2 Sarah is not at all interested in motorbikes, but her boyfriend loves it.
3 At the race, the atmosphere was friendly and exciting but not at all romantic.
4 Afterwards, Valentin paid for a pizza.
5 Sarah finds Valentin really funny and extremely nice.
6 Sarah has bought tickets for a concert next Saturday.
7 Beyoncé is one of Sarah's favourite singers.
8 Valentin thinks Beyoncé is very beautiful.

1 Je parle

The challenge

- Giving a 3-minute presentation: taking part in a 'blind date' speed-dating event in French

Overview

Explain how this section works.

- Pupils read the context and what they need to do to complete the challenge.
- They then read the list of suggested details to include. Explain that they should use this both to help structure their content and as a checklist as part of their final preparations.
- Explain that the exercises which follow in this section are structured to help them prepare for their presentation.
- Before starting, pupils read the POSM feature: this will help them to improve their performance. Encourage them to use this approach routinely in speaking tasks.

Programme of Study references

GV1 Tenses (past, present and future)
LC4 Expressing ideas (speaking)
LC5 Speaking coherently and confidently

Resources

Audio files:
14_Module1_Jeparle_Ex1.mp3
15_Module1_Jeparle_Ex4.mp3
16_Module1_Jeparle_Ex6.mp3

1 Listen to Florian. Which sentences could he use in his speed-dating presentation? There are two 'red herrings'! (1–10)

Pupils listen to Florian talking about himself. They identify the eight sentences which he could use in his speed-dating presentation (the other two sentences would not be useful).

Audioscript Track 14

1 *Je m'appelle Florian.*
2 *J'ai quatorze ans.*
3 *Je suis assez grand et mince.*
4 *J'ai les cheveux blonds et les yeux bleus.*
5 *Il y a une séance à trois heures vingt.*
6 *Ma passion, c'est le sport!*
7 *Je joue au rugby et je fais de la natation.*
8 *Je voudrais un coca, s'il vous plaît.*
9 *Je n'aime pas faire les magasins.*
10 *Mon caractère … je suis gentil et impatient.*

Answers

1 ✓ 2 ✓ 3 ✓ 4 ✓ 5 × 6 ✓ 7 ✓
8 × 9 ✓ 10 ✓

2 Write eight sentences like Florian's that you could use in your presentation. Use the prompts below.

Pupils write eight sentences about themselves for their own speed-dating presentation, using Florian's sentences in exercise 1 as a model. A list of prompts is also supplied for support.

3 Look back over the module and find connectives, qualifiers and time expressions you could use in your presentation. Make three lists.

Pupils look through Module 1 and list connectives, qualifiers and time expressions they could use in their presentation.

Example answers

connectives	qualifiers	time/frequency phrases
et	très	de temps en temps
mais	assez	quelquefois
ou	un peu	souvent
où	trop	tous les jours
aussi	carrément	tous les weekends
parce que	vraiment	tout le temps
alors		une/deux fois (etc.) par
qui		jour/semaine/mois
donc		en général
par exemple		normalement
		d'habitude
		ce matin/soir
		cet après-midi
		demain matin (etc.)
		samedi après-midi (etc.)
		dimanche soir (etc.)
		hier
		samedi (etc.) dernier
		le weekend dernier
		l'année dernière

4 Listen to Élodie and fill in the gaps.

Pupils listen to Élodie's speed-dating presentation and complete the written version by identifying the correct word to fill each of the gaps. (You could ask a good class to try to work out the missing words first, then use the recording to check their answers.)

Audioscript Track 15

Je m'appelle Élodie et j'ai treize ans. Je suis assez petite et très mince. J'ai les cheveux noirs et très longs et les yeux marron. Ma passion, c'est la danse, alors j'ai un cours de danse deux fois par semaine, mais j'aime aussi aller au cinéma. En général, je préfère les comédies ou les films romantiques, mais de temps en temps, je regarde des films d'action. Je n'aime pas faire du sport parce que je trouve ça ennuyeux. Maintenant, mon caractère. Alors … je suis très gentille, mais quelquefois, je suis un peu trop impatiente.

Answers
1 assez **2** alors **3** deux fois **4** aussi
5 ou **6** parce que **7** quelquefois **8** un peu

5 Note down any connectives, qualifiers and time expressions that Élodie uses which are not on your list.

Pupils note down any connectives, qualifiers and time expressions they have not already listed.

6 Listen and note down the memorable things these people have done and when. (1–6)

Pupils listen to six people talking about a memorable experience. They note what happened and when it took place. Some vocabulary is glossed for support. Draw pupils' attention to the tip box on using a range of tenses in order to achieve a higher level.

Audioscript Track 16

1. *L'année dernière, je suis allé à un match de football et j'ai rencontré David Beckham. C'était génial!*
2. *Le weekend dernier, j'ai participé à un concours de judo et j'ai gagné! C'était top!*
3. *Il y a deux ans, j'ai joué de la guitare à la télé. C'était terrifiant!*
4. *Il y a trois ans, j'ai chanté et dansé dans une comédie musicale au collège. C'était amusant.*
5. *La semaine dernière, je suis allé à Londres et j'ai vu Daniel Radcliffe dans un magasin de musique. C'était bizarre!*
6. *Il y a trois mois, j'ai joué au basket et mon équipe a gagné le championnat. C'était super!*

Answers
1. Met David Beckham – last year.
2. Won judo contest – last weekend.
3. Played guitar on TV – 2 years ago.
4. Sang and danced in a school musical – 3 years ago.
5. Saw Daniel Radcliffe in music shop (in London) – last week.
6. Won basketball championship – 3 months ago.

Studio Grammaire: *il y a*
Use the *Studio Grammaire* box to cover the two meanings of *il y a*.

7 Write a sentence about a memorable experience for your presentation and say what it was like. It doesn't have to be true!

Pupils write a sentence describing a memorable experience for their presentation, either from their own experience or making up the details.

8 Decipher these sentences in the near future tense, then write a similar sentence for your presentation. Try to link it to something you have already mentioned, such as a hobby or your memorable experience.

Pupils write out the wordsnakes as sentences. They use this as a model to write a sentence for their presentation.

Answers
1. Samedi prochain, je vais faire un match de foot au collège.
2. Demain soir, je vais aller à la patinoire avec mes copains.
3. La semaine prochaine, je vais participer à un concours de danse.
4. Le weekend prochain, je vais télécharger un nouvel album.
5. L'année prochaine, je vais participer au championnat de tennis.

9 Wow your audience with some 'fancy French'! Write three sentences for your presentation, using these ideas.

Pupils focus on writing a further three sentences, using the ideas supplied to enhance the content of their presentation.

10 Prepare what you are going to say for the speed-dating challenge. If it gives you more confidence, write it out in full first. (See the speaking tips on page 131.) Then check that what you are going to say is accurate and makes sense.

Pupils prepare their presentation. They can write it out in full first, then memorise it. Draw their attention to the tips on p. 131 of the Pupil Book and encourage them to follow the advice here. They should then check the accuracy and sense of what they have written, correcting and redrafting as necessary.

11 Now. memorise your presentation and rehearse it!

Pupils memorise and practise their presentation. They may also find it useful to make notes as an aide-mémoire when they are presenting. They then give their presentation to a partner, who makes suggestions for improving it. Pupils can then make a note of these suggestions for their next extended speaking task.

1 J'écris

The challenge

- Writing a 150-word report on a music festival for a music magazine

Overview

Explain how this section works.
- Pupils read the context and what they need to do to complete the challenge.
- They then read the list of suggested details to include. Explain that they should use this both to help structure their content and as a checklist as part of their final preparations.
- Explain that the exercises which follow in this section are structured to help them prepare for the extended writing task.
- Before starting, pupils read the POSM feature: this will help them to improve their performance. Encourage them to use this approach routinely in writing tasks.

Programme of Study references

GV3 Developing vocabulary
GV4 Accuracy (grammar; spelling; punctuation)
LC4 Expressing ideas (writing)
LC8 Writing creatively

1 Use phrases from the box to improve the variety of language in this very basic paragraph.

Pupils rewrite and improve the text, using the phrases supplied.

Example answer:
Normalement, j'écoute du rap, du hip-hop et du R&B. J'adore la musique de Dizzee Rascal et je suis méga-fan de Lady Gaga. Un de mes groupes préférés, c'est JLS.

2 Write two or three sentences about your musical tastes, using a variety of phrases.

Pupils write two or three sentences on their own musical tastes, using as wide a variety of phrases as they can.

3 Translate these phrases into French. Use the words in the guitar to help you.

Pupils translate the English phrases into French, using the expressions supplied.

Answers
1 parce que j'aime les paroles
2 parce que j'aime la rythmique
3 parce que j'aime la mélodie
4 parce qu'il a beaucoup de talent
5 parce qu'elle a une belle voix
6 parce que ça me donne envie de danser

4 Unjumble these sentences that talk about the past.

Pupils write out in the correct order the jumbled sentences. *il y avait* is glossed for support.

Answers
1 Le festival a commencé hier soir.
2 Je suis allé à un concert de musiques du monde.
3 Il y avait un excellent groupe de reggae.
4 Il a fait très beau.
5 L'ambiance était vraiment géniale.
6 On a dansé toute la soirée.

5 Complete the sentences below using your own ideas, then put them into whatever order you like using sequencers.

Pupils complete the sentence openings with their own ideas, then write them out in their preferred order, using the sequencers supplied appropriately.

6 Write three sentences saying what something was like, which you could use with some of your sentences from exercise 5.

Pupils write three sentences describing what something was like to use with their sentences from exercise 5.

7 What are you going to do next at the music festival? Complete the sentences with your own ideas. Use the verbs below to help you.

Pupils write sentences about what they're going to do next at the music festival, using the near future tense. Sentence openings and useful verbs are supplied.

8 There are two mistakes in each of the sentences below. Can you find and correct them?

Pupils rewrite the sentences, identifying and correcting the two errors in each of them. Draw their attention to the tip box on how to check text.

Answers

1 Je suis ici au Festival Megabeat **où** il y a **beaucoup** de fans de musique.

2 En **général**, j'**écoute** de la pop-rock et quelquefois, un peu de R&B.

3 Je suis méga-fan de **la** musique de Rihanna, parce que j'**adore** la rythmique.

4 **Hier**, il y avait un groupe de reggae et tout le monde a **dansé** toute la soirée.

5 Après, **j'ai** rencontré le chanteur Yannick Noah qui **est** une de mes idoles.

6 Je vais faire une interview avec **une** de mes chanteuses **préférées**, Jenifer Bartoli.

7 L'**après**-midi, je vais **écouter** un autre concert.

9 Now write your report about the music festival. When you have written it, check it carefully using the checklist on the right and correct any mistakes.

Pupils write their music festival report. They then check it using the checklist in the tip box and correct any errors. Draw their attention to the writing tips on p. 131 of the Pupil Book and encourage them to follow the advice here.

The class may find it helpful if you can create model answers together for this first module.

1 Studio Grammaire

The *Studio Grammaire* section provides a more detailed summary of the key grammar covered in the module, along with further exercises to practise these points. The activities on ActiveTeach pp.026 and 027 are repeated from elsewhere in the module.

Grammar topics
- the present tense
- direct object pronouns
- the near future tense
- the perfect tense

The present tense

1 Write out the present tense of these irregular verbs. Do as much from memory as possible. Then check with the verb tables on pages 128–130.

Pupils complete the present tense forms of *aller*, *avoir*, *être*, *faire* and *lire* and then check their answers using the verb tables at the back of the Pupil Book.

Answers

aller – je vais, tu vas, il/elle/on va, nous allons, vous allez, ils/elles vont

avoir – j'ai, tu as, il/elle/on a, nous avons, vous avez, ils/elles ont

être – je suis, tu es, il/elle/on est, nous sommes, vous êtes, ils/elles sont

faire – je fais, tu fais, il/elle/on fait, nous faisons, vous faites, ils/elles font

lire – je lis, tu lis, il/elle/on lit, nous lisons, vous lisez, ils/elles lisent

2 Translate these sentences into French, using the verbs in brackets.

Pupils translate the sentences into French. The verbs are supplied for support.

Answers

1 Je modifie mes préférences.
2 Nous partageons des photos.
3 Ils font des quiz.
4 Tu as beaucoup d'amis/de copains.
5 Il est sur Facebook.
6 Je lis mes messages.
7 Elle va sur sa page perso.
8 On joue à des jeux.

Direct object pronouns

3 Unjumble these sentences, then translate them into English.

Pupils write out the jumbled sentences in the correct order and then translate them into English.

Answers

1 Je la regarde. (I watch her/it.)
2 Je t'aime. (I love you.)
3 Elle nous adore. (She loves us.)
4 Tu les cherches? (Are you looking for them?)
5 Ils me détestent. (They hate me.)
6 Vous l'avez? (Do you have it?)
7 Je ne l'aime pas. (I don't like him/her/it.)
8 Il ne m'écoute pas. (He doesn't listen/isn't listening to me.)
9 Tu ne les regardes pas? (Don't you watch them?/Aren't you watching them?)
10 Nous ne l'avons pas. (We don't have/haven't got it.)

4 Rewrite these sentences, replacing the word(s) in bold with a direct object pronoun.

Pupils rewrite the sentences, replacing the nouns (given in bold for support) with the appropriate direct object pronouns.

Answers

1 Je l'aime.
2 Elle le déteste.
3 On les préfère.
4 Tu le cherches?
5 Vous l'avez?
6 Il ne les fait pas.
7 Nous ne l'avons pas.
8 Je ne l'aime pas.

The near future tense

5 Complete each sentence so that it makes sense. Then translate the sentences.

Pupils complete the gap-fill sentences with the most appropriate word. They then translate the sentences.

Answers

1 Demain matin, je **vais** faire les magasins. (Tomorrow morning, I'm going to go shopping.)

2 Samedi soir, **nous** allons manger une pizza. (On Saturday evening, we're going to eat a pizza.)

3 La semaine prochaine, on **va** jouer au basket. (Next week, we're going to play basketball.)

4 Ce soir, **tu** vas regarder un DVD? (This evening, are you going to watch a DVD?)

5 Demain à dix heures, ils vont **faire** du judo. (Tomorrow at ten o'clock, they're going to do judo.)

6 Cet après-midi, vous **allez** rester à la maison? (This afternoon, are you going to stay at home?)

The perfect tense

6 Put the verbs in brackets into the perfect tense. Then translate the sentences.

Pupils complete the sentences by writing out the perfect tense forms of the verbs given in brackets. They then translate the sentences into English.

Answers

1 J'**ai mangé** un hamburger avec Rémi et on **a bu** du coca. (I ate a burger with Rémi and we drank cola.)

2 Je **suis sorti(e)** avec Cassandra. Nous **avons fait** un piquenique. (I went out with Cassandra. We had a picnic.)

3 Tu **es allé(e)** au cinéma avec Damien? Vous **avez vu** quel film? (Did you go to the cinema with Damien? Which film did you see?)

4 Il **est resté** chez lui avec Julie. Ils **ont regardé** un DVD. (He stayed at home with Julie. They watched a DVD.)

5 Elles **ont joué** au bowling, puis elles **sont rentrées** à la maison. (They went bowling, then they went home.)

6 Nous **avons pris** le bus et nous **sommes arrivé(e)s** à deux heures. (We took the bus and arrived at two o'clock.)

7 Mon frère **a lu** un livre de science-fiction, puis il **est parti**. (My brother read a science fiction book, then he left.)

8 Elle **est entrée** dans la cuisine et elle **a parlé** avec Alex. (She came/went into the kitchen and she talked to Alex.)

7 Fill in each gap in the text with one of the verbs below. There are two verbs too many. Use the time expressions in the text to help you decide on the correct tense to use.

Pupils complete the gap-fill text using the verbs supplied (there are two verbs too many). They should use the time expressions in the text to help them work out the correct tenses.

Answers

1 écoute **2** télécharge **3** vais **4** est allés
5 a vu **6** a dansé **7** vais faire **8** vais acheter
9 vais aller **10** suis

1 À toi

Self-access reading and writing

A Reinforcement

1 Recopie ces invitations correctement. Fais correspondre les textes et les images. (Reading L5)

Reading. Pupils write out the mirror-version texts correctly and then match the texts and pictures.

Answers

1 Ça va, Clara? T'es invitée à sortir avec ma famille et moi cet après-midi. On va faire un piquenique sur la plage. Tu veux nous accompagner? **e**

2 Salut, Alyzée. Qu'est-ce que tu fais demain soir? On va aller à un match de volley. Ça t'intéresse? **d**

3 Coucou, Gabriel. Qu'est-ce que tu fais samedi matin? Je vais aller en ville. Tu viens avec moi? **a**

4 Salut, Lara. Je vais aller à la patinoire, dimanche soir. Ça t'intéresse? **f**

5 T'es libre, ce soir? Mon frère Rico et moi voulons aller au cinéma. Tu viens avec nous? **b**

6 Salut, Malik! Je vais aller à une fête d'anniversaire, demain soir. C'est la fête de ma meilleure copine, Lou-Anne. Tu veux m'accompagner? **c**

2 Écris deux invitations suivant les modèles de l'exercice 1. Change l'activité et le jour ou l'heure à chaque fois. (Writing L4)

Writing. Pupils write two invitations. They use the texts in exercise 1 as models, changing the activity and day or time in each one.

3 Lis le texte. Termine les phrases en anglais. (Reading L5)

Reading. Pupils read the text and complete the sentences in English.

Answers

1 Facebook is the most popular social network in the world with **600 million members in 2010.**

2 With Facebook, you can easily connect with your **friends**, **family** and **friends of friends**.

3 The average user has **130 friends**.

4 The average user spends more than **55 minutes per day on Facebook**.

5 Facebook has changed our way of **communicating**.

6 In 2008 Mark Zuckerberg was the youngest **billionaire in the world**.

B Extension

1 Lis le texte et réponds aux questions. C'est Thomas ou Adeline? Écris T, A ou T + A. (Reading L6)

Reading. Pupils read the text and answer the questions by identifying who is being described each time: Thomas (writing T), Adeline (writing A) or both of them (writing T + A). *les coordonnées* is glossed for support.

Answers

1 T **2** T **3** T + A **4** A **5** T **6** T + A

2 Relis le texte et trouve les verbes. (Reading L6)

Reading. Pupils read the text in exercise 1 again and identify the verbs: 13 in the present tense, 11 in the perfect and 7 in the near future.

Answers

au présent: je n'aime pas, tu trouves, je la trouve, elle est, elle aime, je le trouve, il est, nous avons, je n'aime pas, je pense, j'y vais, Thomas a, j'espère

au passé composé: vous avez fait, on est allés, j'ai (même) acheté, vous avez fait, on est allés, Thomas a acheté, on a mangé, j'ai adoré, on a (beaucoup) dansé, nous sommes allés, on a discuté, j'ai acheté

au futur proche: vous allez sortir, on va jouer, on va rigoler, vous allez sortir, on va jouer, on va rigoler, on va regarder

3 Invente deux interviews pour un «blind date». (Writing L6)

Writing. Pupils make up two interviews on the subject of their blind date. Draw pupils' attention to the tip box on where to look for content.

Module 2: Bien dans sa peau

2

Unit & Learning objectives	Programme of Study references	Key language	Grammar and other language features
1 Touché! (pp. 32–33) Learning the parts of the body Using *à* + the definite article	**GV2** Grammatical structures (*à* + definite article; *on*) **GV3** Developing vocabulary **LC2** Transcription **LC6** Reading comprehension	*la bouche, le bras, l'épaule* (f), *les oreilles,* etc.	**G** *à* + definite article **G** the nous form of the present tense – preparing for a conversation
2 Le sport et le fitness (pp. 34–35) Talking about sport Using *il faut*	**GV2** Grammatical structures (*il faut; depuis*) **GV3** Opinions and discussions **LC3** Conversation (dealing with the unexpected) **LC4** Expressing ideas (writing)	*Pour arriver en forme, il faut …* *avoir un bon programme/bien manger,* etc. *Le sport …* *diminue le stress/est bon pour le moral,* etc. *À mon avis, …,* etc.	**G** *il faut* **G** *depuis* + present tense – adapting text – developing reading strategies – developing writing skills
3 Mes résolutions pour manger sain (pp. 36–37) Learning about healthy eating Using the future tense	**GV1** Tenses (future) **GV2** Grammatical structures (negatives) **LC1** Listening and responding **LC8** Writing creatively	*les boissons gazeuses, l'eau* (f), *le pain, la viande, manger* *équilibré*	**G** talking about the future **G** negatives – *ne … pas* and *ne … jamais* – developing writing skills
4 Je serai en forme! (pp. 38–39) Making plans to get fit Practising the future tense	**GV1** Tenses (future) **LC1** Listening and responding **LC6** Reading comprehension **LC4** Expressing ideas (writing)	*Je ferai du sport.* *Je ferai trente minutes d'exercice par jour.* *J'irai au collège à vélo et pas en voiture.* *Je ne boirai jamais de boissons gazeuses.* *Je ne jouerai plus à des jeux vidéo.* etc.	**G** the future tense – adapting text
5 Es-tu en forme? (pp. 40–41) Describing levels of fitness Using three tenses together	**GV1** Tenses (past, present and future) **LC4** Expressing ideas (writing) **LC5** Speaking coherently and confidently **LC6** Reading comprehension	Review of language from the module	**G** using three tenses together – developing writing skills

Unit & Learning objectives	**Programme of Study references**	**Key language**	**Grammar and other language features**
Bilan et Révisions (pp. 42–43) Pupils' checklist and practice exercises			
En plus: La santé des jeunes (pp. 44–45) Talking about teenage health issues	**LC1** Listening and responding **LC4** Expressing ideas (speaking) **LC5** Speaking coherently and confidently **LC5** Accurate pronunciation and intonation	Review of language from the module	– developing reading skills – developing writing skills
J'écris (pp. 46–47) Extended writing practice	**GV1** Tenses (past, present and future) **GV3** Developing vocabulary **GV4** Accuracy (grammar; spelling; punctuation) **LC4** Expressing ideas (writing) **LC8** Writing creatively	Review of language from the module	– developing writing skills – checking your work
Studio Grammaire (pp. 48–49) Detailed grammar summary and practice exercises			**G** using *nous* in the present tense **G** *il faut* **G** the future tense **G** negatives **G** using three tenses together
À toi (pp. 120–121) Self-access reading and writing at two levels			

2 1 Touché!

Learning objectives

- Learning the parts of the body
- Using *à* + the definite article

Programme of Study references

GV2 Grammatical structures (*à* + definite article; *on*)
GV3 Developing vocabulary
LC2 Transcription
LC6 Reading comprehension

FCSE links

Unit 5: Healthy lifestyle (Sports)

Grammar

- *à* + definite article
- the *nous* form of the present tense

Key language

la bouche
le bras
le corps
le dos
l'épaule (f)
les fesses (fpl)
le front
le genou
la jambe
la main
le nez
les oreilles (fpl)
le pied
la tête
le visage
les yeux (mpl)
Qu'est-ce qui s'est passé?
Tu es touché(e)?
Où est-ce que tu es touché(e)?
le terrain
les billes (fpl)
le casque
le matériel
les règles (fpl)
le fairplay
le respect

PLTS

C Creative thinkers

Resources

Audio files:
17_Module2_Unit1_Ex1.mp3
18_Module2_Unit1_Ex2.mp3
Workbooks:
Cahier d'exercices Rouge, page 13
ActiveTeach:
p.032 Flashcards
p.032 Grammar
p.033 Grammar
p.033 Reading skills
ActiveLearn:
Listening, Reading
Grammar, Vocabulary

Starter 1

Aim

To introduce parts of the body

Touch your leg and say *la jambe*. Pupils copy you, repeating the word. Repeat with the other parts of the body featured in the unit. Once pupils are familiar with the words, say the words without touching the part of the body. Pupils touch the correct part of the body.

Alternative Starter 1:

Use ActiveTeach p.032 Flashcards to introduce parts of the body.

1 Écoute et écris la bonne lettre. (1–14) (Listening L2)

Listening. Pupils listen to the recording and note the letter of the correct picture for each part of the body mentioned.

Audioscript Track 17

1 *la jambe* **2** *la bouche* **3** *l'épaule*
4 *le bras* **5** *la main* **6** *le front* **7** *le dos*
8 *les fesses* **9** *le genou* **10** *le nez*
11 *la tête* **12** *les yeux* **13** *les oreilles* **14** *le pied*

Answers

1 h **2** l **3** e **4** f **5** b **6** j **7** g **8** c **9** d
10 n **11** a **12** m **13** k **14** i

2 On joue au paintball. Écoute et complète le tableau. (1–4) (Listening L5)

Listening. Pupils copy out the grid. They listen to four exchanges that take place during a paintballing session and complete the table with the details.

Audioscript Track 18

1 – *Aïe! Je suis touché.*
– *Ah non, Hélio, pas de chance. Qu'est-ce qui s'est passé? Où est-ce que tu es touché?*
– *Au bras et aussi à la jambe.*

2 – *Aïe!*
– *Ah non, pas possible, Odyssée est touchée. Qu'est-ce qui s'est passé? Où est-ce que tu es touchée, Odyssée? Montre-moi.*
– *Je suis touchée au dos et aussi à l'épaule. Et à la main. Oh là là. Je suis éliminée.*

3 – *Aïe!*
– *Ça va, Charles, t'as un problème? Qu'est-ce qui s'est passé?*
– *Je suis touché, je suis touché!*
– *Mince, où est-ce que tu es touché?*
– *Au genou et aux fesses.*

4 – *Ah non! Qu'est-ce qui s'est passé? … Fatima est touchée. Où est-ce que tu es touchée, Fatima?*
– *Aïe! Ça fait mal. Je suis touchée à la tête, au front.*

Answers

	touché(e)
1 Hélio	*au bras*, à la jambe
2 Odyssée	au dos, à l'épaule, à la main
3 Charles	au genou, aux fesses
4 Fatima	à la tête, au front

Studio Grammaire: *à* + definite article

Use the *Studio Grammaire* box to cover *à* + the definite article.

3 En tandem. Fais quatre dialogues. Utilise les renseignements suivants. (Speaking L5)

Speaking. In pairs: pupils make up four dialogues using the picture prompts supplied. Some vocabulary is glossed for support. A sample exchange is supplied.

4 À quatre. Invente un scénario de paintball. Utilise les phrases suivantes. (Speaking L5)

Speaking. In groups of four: pupils make up a paintballing scenario, including the phrases supplied. Draw their attention to the tip box on preparing for it.

Starter 2

Aim

To review vocabulary for parts of the body and the different forms of *à* + the definite article

Give pupils three minutes working in pairs to write down as many parts of the body as they can remember, each one with the correct form of *à* + the definite article. Tell them their target is 14.

Pupils swap answers with another pair to check, awarding 1 point for each correct body part and 2 points if the form of *à* is also correct. Reward the pair with the highest score.

5 Lis le texte et choisis les bons mots pour compléter chaque phrase. (Reading L6)

Reading. Pupils read the text on paintballing and then complete the sentences by choosing from the two options given each time. *la casque* is glossed for support.

R Translate the text orally round the class.

Answers

1 L'association de paintball de la Côte d'Opale joue tous les **dimanches**.
2 Leur terrain n'est pas loin de **Boulogne**.
3 Pour 30 euros, vous pouvez jouer pendant **120 minutes**.
4 Si vous êtes touché(e) à la jambe ou au bras, vous êtes **blessé(e)**.
5 Pour l'association de paintball de la Côte d'Opale, le fairplay est **très important**.
6 L'année dernière, il y a eu plus de **sept cents** visiteurs au centre.

Studio Grammaire: the *nous* form

Use the *Studio Grammaire* box to review the *nous* form of the verb. There is more information and further practice on Pupil Book p. 48.

6 Fais correspondre les phrases et les photos. (Reading L3)

Reading. Pupils match the sentences with the pictures by identifying each celebrity's body feature. Draw their attention to the tip box on the use of *de* to show possession.

Answers

1 e **2** a **3** b **4** d **5** c

7 En tandem. Ce sont les cheveux (etc.) de qui? Discute! (Speaking L4)

Speaking. In pairs: pupils discuss who the different body features pictured belong to.

Answers

a Ce sont les oreilles du prince Charles.
b C'est le pied de Wayne Rooney.
c C'est la main d'Arsène Wenger.
d Ce sont les cheveux de Lady Gaga.
e C'est la bouche de Jamie Oliver.

8 Décris ta personne idéale. (Writing L4)

PLTS **C**

Writing. Pupils write about their ideal person, describing him/her as having the body features of different celebrities. A sample opening is supplied.

Plenary

Review the different forms of *à* + the definite article. Go round the class. Pupil 1 says the name of and points to a part of the body, e.g. *épaule*, pointing to his/her shoulder; Pupil 2 responds, e.g. *Je suis touché(e) à l'épaule*. Continue in this way round the class.

Workbook, page 13

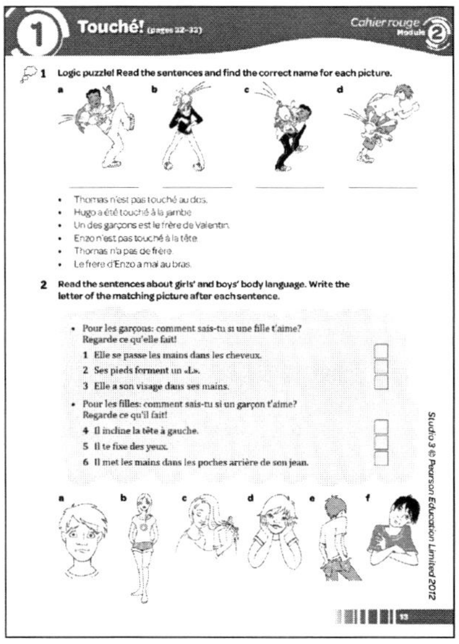

1 Touché! (pages 22–23) Cahier rouge Module 2

1 Logic puzzle! Read the sentences and find the correct name for each picture.

a b c d

- Thomas n'est pas touché au dos.
- Hugo a été touché à la jambe
- Un des garçons est le frère de Valentin.
- Enzo n'est pas touché à la tête.
- Thomas n'a pas de frère.
- Le frère d'Enzo a mal au bras.

2 Read the sentences about girls' and boys' body language. Write the letter of the matching picture after each sentence.

- Pour les garçons: comment sais-tu si une fille t'aime? Regarde ce qu'elle fait!
  1 Elle se passe les mains dans les cheveux.
  2 Ses pieds forment un «L».
  3 Elle a son visage dans ses mains.
- Pour les filles: comment sais-tu si un garçon t'aime? Regarde ce qu'il fait!
  4 Il incline la tête à gauche.
  5 Il te fixe des yeux.
  6 Il met les mains dans les poches arrière de son jean.

a b c d e f

Studio 3 © Pearson Education Limited 2012

13

Answers

1 a Enzo **b** Thomas **c** Valentin **d** Hugo

2 1 c **2** b **3** d **4** f **5** a **6** e

Worksheet 2.1 Reading unfamiliar texts

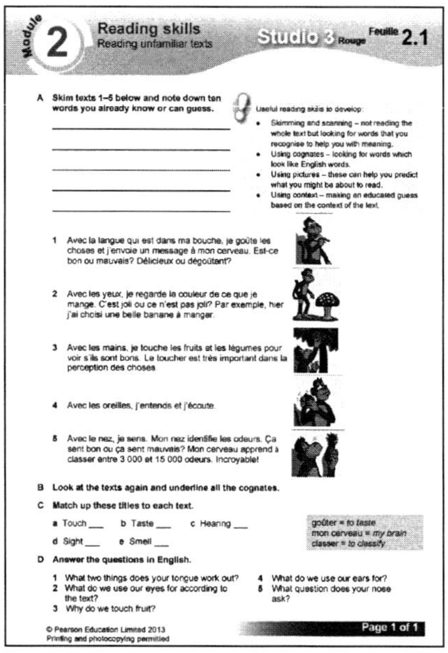

Module 2 Reading skills Reading unfamiliar texts Studio 3 Rouge Feuille 2.1

A Skim texts 1–5 below and note down ten words you already know or can guess.

Useful reading skills to develop:
- Skimming and scanning – not reading the whole text but looking for words that you recognise to help you with meaning.
- Using cognates – looking for words which look like English words.
- Using pictures – these can help you predict what you might be about to read.
- Using context – making an educated guess based on the context of the text.

1 Avec la langue qui est dans ma bouche, je goûte les choses et j'envoie un message à mon cerveau. Est-ce bon ou mauvais? Délicieux ou dégoûtant?

2 Avec les yeux, je regarde la couleur de ce que je mange. C'est joli ou ce n'est pas joli? Par exemple, hier j'ai choisi une belle banane à manger.

3 Avec les mains, je touche les fruits et les légumes pour voir s'ils sont bons. Le toucher est très important dans la perception des choses.

4 Avec les oreilles, j'entends et j'écoute.

5 Avec le nez, je sens. Mon nez identifie les odeurs. Ça sent bon ou ça sent mauvais? Mon cerveau apprend à classer entre 3 000 et 15 000 odeurs. Incroyable!

B Look at the texts again and underline all the cognates.

C Match up these titles to each text.

a Touch ___ b Taste ___ c Hearing ___
d Sight ___ e Smell ___

goûter = *to taste*
mon cerveau = *my brain*
classer = *to classify*

D Answer the questions in English.

1 What two things does your tongue work out?
2 What do we use our eyes for according to the text?
3 Why do we touch fruit?
4 What do we use our ears for?
5 What question does your nose ask?

© Pearson Education Limited 2013
Printing and photocopying permitted

Page 1 of 1

Answers

A (Answers will vary.)

B 1 Avec la langue qui est dans ma bouche, je goûte les choses et j'envoie un message à mon cerveau. Est-ce bon ou mauvais? Délicieux ou dégoûtant?

2 Avec les yeux, je regarde la couleur de ce que je mange. C'est joli ou ce n'est pas joli? Par exemple, hier, j'ai choisi une belle banane à manger.

3 Avec les mains, je touche les fruits et les legumes pour voir s'ils sont bons. Le toucher est très important dans la perception des choses.

4 Avec les oreilles, j'entends et j'écoute.

5 Avec le nez, je sens. Mon nez identifie les odeurs. Ça sent bon ou ça sent mauvais? Mon cerveau apprend à classer entre 3 000 et 15 000 odeurs. Incroyable!

C a 3 **b** 1 **c** 4 **d** 2 **e** 5

D 1 Whether something tastes good or bad.

2 To work out whether something looks good or not.

3 To see if it's good.

4 Listening and hearing.

5 Do things smell good or bad?

2 Le sport et le fitness

Learning objectives
- Talking about sport
- Using *il faut*

Programme of Study references
GV2 Grammatical structures (*il faut*; *depuis*)

GV3 Opinions and discussions

LC3 Conversation (dealing with the unexpected)

LC4 Expressing ideas (writing)

FCSE links
Unit 5: Healthy lifestyle (Exercise, Opinions)

Grammar
- *il faut*
- *depuis* + present ten

Key language
Pour arriver en forme, il faut …
avoir un bon programme
bien manger
bien dormir
être motivé(e)
faire du sport tous les jours
jouer dans une équipe
Le sport …
diminue le stress
est bon pour le moral
est important dans la vie
Ça me fatigue.
Il faut apprendre à suivre les règles.
À mon avis, …
Moi, je trouve ça très ennuyeux de … (+ inf).
Je crois fermement que …

PLTS
R Reflective learners

Resources
Audio files:
19_Module2_Unit2_Ex1.mp3
20_Module2_Unit2_Ex4.mp3

Workbooks:
Cahier d'exercices Rouge, page 14

ActiveTeach:
Starter 1 resource
Starter 2 resource
p.034 Grammar
p.034 Grammar practice
p.035 Video 3
p.035 Video worksheet 3
p.035 Thinking skills

ActiveLearn:
Listening, Reading

Starter 1
Aim

To review infinitives

Write up the following. Give pupils two minutes to write the infinitive form of each verb.

il aime j'ai je fais on mange je dors

ils gagnent nous sommes

Check answers. (**Answers:** *aimer, avoir, faire, manger, dormir, gagner, être*)

1 Écoute et lis le texte. (Listening L6)

Listening. Pupils listen to the feature on Renaud Lefèvre, a young French tennis player, and read the text at the same time. Some vocabulary is glossed for support.

Audioscript Track 19

Renaud Lefèvre est un jeune tennisman qui est passionné de sport.

Renaud a commencé à jouer quand il était tout petit, à l'âge de cinq ans. Il a maintenant quatorze ans, ce qui veut dire qu'il joue au tennis depuis neuf ans déjà.

Le samedi, il se lève tôt, à sept heures. Il a cours de huit heures à dix heures, et puis, après une petite pause, il joue un match qui peut durer entre une heure et trois heures. L'après-midi, il travaille sa technique avec son coach et son équipe; alors, il a encore deux heures d'entraînement. Le dimanche, c'est la même routine: il passe huit heures sur le court de tennis, c'est-à-dire toute la journée! Le weekend dernier, il a donc passé seize heures sur le court!

Son tennisman préféré est Gaël Monfils parce qu'il est le roi de la glisse. Renaud l'appelle «Sliderman». Pendant la semaine, Renaud fait des activités physiques tous les jours. Il fait du footing ou il joue au basket et, une fois par semaine, il fait de la natation.

Voici le credo sportif de Renaud pour être un bon joueur:

- *Il faut aimer la compétition.*
- *Il faut avoir un bon programme pour être en forme.*
- *Il faut bien manger.*
- *Il faut bien dormir parce qu'on ne peut pas gagner si on est fatigué.*
- *Il faut être motivé!*

Vous allez voir, Renaud Lefèvre va être un grand sportif!

2 Relis le texte et note: vrai (V) ou faux (F). (Reading L6)

Reading. Pupils read the text in exercise 1 again. They then read the sentences about it and note whether each one is true (writing V) or false (writing F).

Answers

1 F **2** V **3** V **4** F **5** V **6** F

Studio Grammaire: *il faut*

Use the *Studio Grammaire* box to review *il faut*. There is more information and further practice on Pupil Book p. 48.

Studio Grammaire: *depuis* + present tense

Use the *Studio Grammaire* box to cover *depuis* + the present tense.

Pupils write four sentences about themselves using *depuis* + present tense.

3 Choisis six phrases du texte. Change un élément dans chaque phrase. Compare tes phrases avec celles de ton/ta camarade. (Writing L5–6)

Writing. Pupils choose six sentences from the text in exercise 1. They change one element in each sentence. Draw their attention to the tip box on making the appropriate grammatical changes when adapting sentences. Pupils then compare their sentences with a friend's. A sample is given.

Starter 2

Aim

To review a range of verb structures

Write up the following. Give pupils two minutes to match the sentences halves.

1	*Il joue au foot*	**a**	*jouer un match samedi.*
2	*Il aime*	**b**	*avoir un bon programme.*
3	*Le dimanche, il ne joue*	**c**	*pas au foot.*
4	*Lundi, il a*	**d**	*depuis cinq ans.*
5	*Il va*	**e**	*a trois heures d'entraînement.*
6	*Chaque jour, il*	**f**	*beaucoup travaillé.*
7	*Pour être en forme, il faut*	**g**	*beaucoup jouer ses matchs.*

Check answers, asking pupils to explain how they worked each one out. (**Answers: 1** d, **2** g, **3** c, **4** f, **5** a, **6** e, **7** b)

Alternative Starter 2:

Use ActiveTeach p.034 Grammar practice to practise *il faut*.

4 Qui parle? Lis, écoute et écris le bon prénom. (1–5) (Listening L4)

Listening. Pupils read the magazine article. They then listen to five people talking about their attitude to sport and identify the speaker each time, using the information in the magazine text. Draw pupils' attention to the tip box on reading strategies. *courir sur un stade* is glossed for support.

Audioscript Track 20

1 – *Que penses-tu du sport?*
– *Moi, je trouve ça très ennuyeux de courir sur un stade ou d'aller dans une salle de sport. Je préfère surfer sur Internet ou regarder la télé.*

2 – *Que penses-tu du sport?*
– *J'adore le sport. J'aime beaucoup la sensation de bien-être qu'on ressent quand on fait du sport et j'aime aussi les valeurs que le sport représente: le respect de soi et des autres, le fairplay.*

3 – *Que penses-tu du sport?*
– *Si on veut être en forme, il faut faire un peu de sport. Pour moi, le sport diminue le stress et je crois fermement que c'est bon pour le moral. Ça booste le moral!*

4 – *Que penses-tu du sport?*
– *Moi, je n'aime pas trop le sport, ça me fatigue. Et s'il pleut ou s'il fait froid, je ne vais pas sortir faire du sport, je préfère rester chez moi à la maison avec des jeux vidéo!*

5 – *Que penses-tu du sport?*
– *Moi, j'adore la compétition, mais j'aime aussi jouer dans une équipe, travailler avec les gens, quoi. En sport, il faut apprendre à suivre les règles et c'est quelque chose qui est important dans la vie.*

Answers

1 Leïla **2** Fouad **3** Candice **4** Damien **5** Mattéo

5 Relis les textes de l'exercice 4 et écris le bon prénom. (Reading L4)

Reading. Pupils read the magazine article in exercise 4 again and then answer the questions in English by identifying who is being described each time.

Answers

1 Candice **2** Damien **3** Fouad **4** Mattéo **5** Leïla

6 En tandem. Tu es d'accord ou pas d'accord avec les jeunes de l'exercice 4? (Speaking L4)

Speaking. In pairs: pupils read the key language supplied. They discuss the attitudes of the people in the magazine article in exercise 4, saying with whom they agree and disagree. A sample opinion is given.

7 Tu es fou/folle de sport ou tu es anti-sport? Écris un paragraphe où tu donnes ton opinion sur le sport.
(Writing L4)

PLTS R

Writing. Pupils write a paragraph on their own opinion of sport. Draw their attention to the tip box on adapting what they know to improve their writing.

Plenary

Ask the class to summarise how *il faut* is used, giving as many examples as possible from the unit.

Ask some pupils to read out their paragraphs from exercise 7. The rest of the class give constructive feedback.

Workbook, page 14

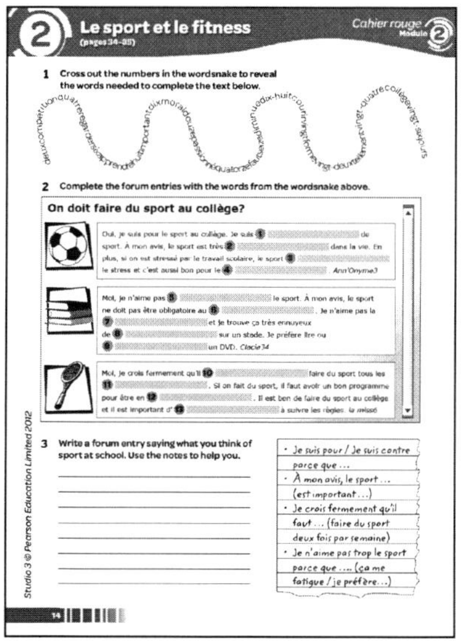

2 Le sport et le fitness (pages 34–35) Cahier rouge Module 2

1 Cross out the numbers in the wordsnake to reveal the words needed to complete the text below.

2 Complete the forum entries with the words from the wordsnake above.

On doit faire du sport au collège?

Oui, je suis pour le sport au collège. Je suis 1 ______ de sport. À mon avis, le sport est très 2 ______ dans la vie. En plus, si on est stressé par le travail scolaire, le sport 3 ______ le stress et c'est aussi bon pour le 4 ______. *Ann'Onyme3*

Moi, je n'aime pas 5 ______ le sport. À mon avis, le sport ne doit pas être obligatoire au 6 ______. Je n'aime pas la 7 ______ et je trouve ça très ennuyeux de 8 ______ sur un stade. Je préfère lire ou 9 ______ un DVD. *Clacie34*

Moi, je crois fermement qu'il 10 ______ faire du sport tous les 11 ______. Si on fait du sport, il faut avoir un bon programme pour être en 12 ______. Il est bon de faire du sport au collège et il est important d' 13 ______ à suivre les règles. *la missô*

3 Write a forum entry saying what you think of sport at school. Use the notes to help you.

- Je suis pour / Je suis contre parce que …
- À mon avis, le sport … (est important …)
- Je crois fermement qu'il faut … (faire du sport deux fois par semaine)
- Je n'aime pas trop le sport parce que …. (ça me fatigue / je préfère …)

Studio 3 © Pearson Education Limited 2012

14

Answers

1 compétition, regarder, apprendre, important, moral, passionné, faut, diminue, courir, forme, tellement, collège, jours

2 **1** passionné **2** important **3** diminue **4** moral **5** tellement **6** collège **7** compétition **8** courir **9** regarder **10** faut **11** jours **12** forme **13** apprendre

3 (Answers will vary.)

Worksheet 2.2 Odd one out!

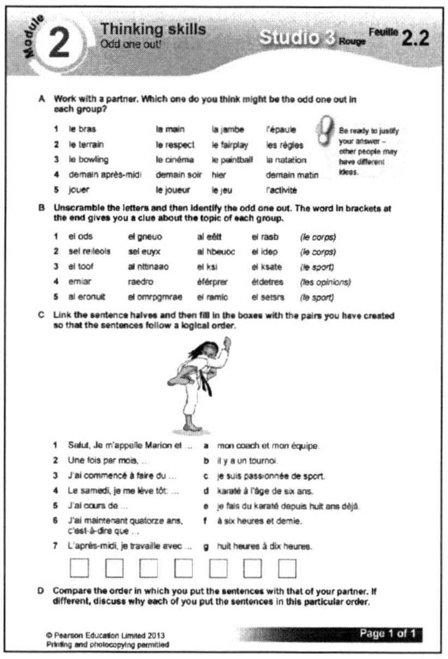

Module 2 Thinking skills
Odd one out!
Studio 3 Rouge Feuille 2.2

A Work with a partner. Which one do you think might be the odd one out in each group?

1	le bras	la main	la jambe	l'épaule
2	le terrain	le respect	le fairplay	les règles
3	le bowling	le cinéma	le paintball	la natation
4	demain après-midi	demain soir	hier	demain matin
5	jouer	le joueur	le jeu	l'activité

Be ready to justify your answer – other people may have different ideas.

B Unscramble the letters and then identify the odd one out. The word in brackets at the end gives you a clue about the topic of each group.

1	el ods	el gneuo	al eêtt	el rasb	*(le corps)*
2	sel reileols	sel euyx	al hbeuoc	el idep	*(le corps)*
3	el toof	al nttinaao	el ksi	el ksate	*(le sport)*
4	emiar	raedro	éférprer	étdetres	*(les opinions)*
5	al eronuit	el omrpgmrae	el ramlo	el setsrs	*(le sport)*

C Link the sentence halves and then fill in the boxes with the pairs you have created so that the sentences follow a logical order.

1 Salut, Je m'appelle Marion et …
2 Une fois par mois, …
3 J'ai commencé à faire du …
4 Le samedi, je me lève tôt: …
5 J'ai cours de …
6 J'ai maintenant quatorze ans, c'est-à-dire que …
7 L'après-midi, je travaille avec …

a mon coach et mon équipe.
b il y a un tournoi.
c je suis passionnée de sport.
d karaté à l'âge de six ans.
e je fais du karaté depuis huit ans déjà.
f à six heures et demie.
g huit heures à dix heures.

☐ ☐ ☐ ☐ ☐ ☐ ☐

D Compare the order in which you put the sentences with that of your partner. If different, discuss why each of you put the sentences in this particular order.

© Pearson Education Limited 2013
Printing and photocopying permitted

Page 1 of 1

Answers

A (Answers will vary.)

1 la jambe **2** les règles **3** la natation **4** hier **5** l'activité

B **1** le dos le genou **la tête** le bras
2 les oreilles les yeux la bouche **le pied**
3 le foot **la natation** le ski le skate
4 aimer adorer préférer détester
5 **la routine** le programme le moral le stress

C *There may be other possibilities for a logical order.*

1 c **3** d **6** e **4** f **5** g **7** a **2** b

D (Answers will vary.)

Video

Episode 3: La bataille d'eau

The team have a water fight, in which the last person to be hit on any part of the body is the winner. Video worksheet 3 can be used in conjunction with this episode.

Answers to video worksheet (ActiveTeach)

1 A (Answers will vary.)
B (Answers will vary.)

2 A The weather is hot.
B She is horrified.
C Water pistols.
D Boosting morale.
E Not really – three on one team and two on the other.
F It seems ideal – plenty of trees to hide behind.

3 A Eat well.
B Samira eats a lot of fruit and vegetables. Hugo eats too many crisps.

4 A Marielle dances every day.
B To be a good cameraman.

5 A She's been hit (on the leg/knee), so can't play any more.
B He misses Hugo at close range.
C Mehdi: forehead (*front*); Alex: stomach (*ventre*)

6 A Who got hit first.
B It was a draw (*match nul*).
C Marielle says they will have to start again. The others react with dismay ('oh no!') and turn on Marielle.
D *Les fesses*, because nobody got hit here.

2 3 Mes résolutions pour manger sain

Learning objectives

- Learning about healthy eating
- Using the future tense

Programme of Study references

GV1 Tenses (future)

GV2 Grammatical structures (negatives)

LC1 Listening and responding

LC8 Writing creatively

FCSE links

Unit 5: Healthy lifestyle (Food/ drink, Healthy/unhealthy eating, Fast food, Eating and drinking)

Unit 6: Food and drink (Food/ drink vocabulary, Opinions, Unhealthy/healthy food choices, Food and drink habits)

Grammar

- talking about the future
- negatives: ne … pas and ne … jamais

Key language

les boissons gazeuses
les céréales (fpl)
les chips (fpl)
l'eau (f)
les fruits (mpl)
les gâteaux (mpl)
les légumes (mpl)
les légumes secs
la nourriture salée
les oeufs (mpl)
le pain
le poisson
les pommes de terre (fpl)
les produits laitiers (mpl)
le repas
le sel
les sucreries (fpl)
la viande
manger équilibré

PLTS

I Independent enquirers

Cross-curricular

PSHE: healthy lifestyles

Resources

Audio files:
21_Module2_Unit3_Ex2.mp3
22_Module2_Unit3_Ex3.mp3
23_Module2_Unit3_Ex6.mp3

Workbooks:
Cahier d'exercices Rouge, page 15

ActiveTeach:
Starter 1 resource
Starter 2 resource
p.036 Flashcards
p.036 Flashcards
p.036 Grammar
p.036 Grammar practice
p.037 Grammar
p.037 Grammar practice
p.037 Class activity
p.037 Grammar skills

ActiveLearn:
Listening, Reading
Grammar, Vocabulary

Starter 1

Aim

To review food and drink vocabulary

Read out the following list. Ask pupils to note the numbers of the ones which are food or drink items.

1	*le pain*	**9**	*la comédie*
2	*la viande*	**10**	*le blouson*
3	*les yeux*	**11**	*les boissons gazeuses*
4	*l'œuf*		
5	*les magasins*	**12**	*les fraises*
6	*la page perso*	**13**	*la chanteuse*
7	*la fête*	**14**	*l'eau*
8	*les pommes de terre*	**15**	*le gâteau*

(**Answers:** 1, 2, 4, 8, 11, 12, 14, 15)

Check answers, asking pupils to say what the words mean.

Alternative Starter 1:

Use both sets of ActiveTeach p.036 Flashcards to introduce language for talking about healthy eating.

1 Fais correspondre les photos et les légendes. (Reading L4)

Reading. Pupils read the sentences and match them to the pictures.

Answers

For reference only: pupils check their answers using the exercise 2 recording.

1 c **2** a **3** g **4** d **5** f **6** e **7** h **8** i
9 b **10** j

2 Écoute et vérifie tes réponses. (1–10) (Listening L4)

Listening. Pupils listen to check their answers to exercise 1.

Audioscript Track 21

1. *Je mangerai trois produits laitiers par jour.* – **c**
2. *Je mangerai cinq portions de fruits ou de légumes par jour.* – **a**
3. *Je ne mangerai pas de chips.* – **g**
4. *Je mangerai du pain, des céréales, des pommes de terre ou des légumes secs à chaque repas.* – **d**
5. *Je mangerai équilibré.* – **f**
6. *Je mangerai de la viande, du poisson ou des oeufs une ou deux fois par jour.* – **e**

7 *Je ne mangerai pas trop de sucreries ou trop de gâteaux.* – **h**
8 *Je ne mangerai pas trop de sel.* – **i**
9 *Je boirai beaucoup d'eau.* – **b**
10 *Je ne boirai jamais de boissons gazeuses.* – *j*

Answers

See audioscript.

Studio Grammaire: talking about the future

Use the *Studio Grammaire* box to cover two ways of talking about the future: the near future tense and the future tense. There is more information and further practice on Pupil Book pp. 48–49.

R Pupils write out the je future tense forms of *pratiquer, attendre, jouer, se lever.*

3 Quelles sont leurs résolutions pour manger sain? Écoute et écris les bonnes lettres de l'exercice 1. (1–4)
(Listening L4)

Listening. Pupils listen to four conversations in which people talk about their resolutions to eat healthily. For each speaker they note the letters of the pictures in exercise 1.

Audioscript Track 22

1 – *Quelles sont tes résolutions pour manger sain, alors?*
– *Je mangerai cinq portions de fruits ou de légumes par jour et je ne boirai jamais de boissons gazeuses.*

2 – *Quelles sont tes résolutions pour manger sain, Clémence?*
– *Alors … Je mangerai de la viande, du poisson ou des oeufs une ou deux fois par jour, et je mangerai trois produits laitiers par jour, du fromage ou des yaourts, par exemple.*

3 – *Et toi, Delphine, quelles sont tes résolutions pour manger sain?*
– *Moi? Je mangerai du pain, des céréales, des pommes de terre ou des légumes secs à chaque repas. Je boirai beaucoup d'eau et je ne mangerai pas de chips.*

4 – *Quelles sont tes résolutions pour manger sain, Éric?*
– *Eh bien, premièrement, je mangerai équilibré. Deuxièmement, je ne mangerai pas trop de sucreries. Troisièmement, je ne mangerai pas trop de sel et puis quatrièmement, je boirai beaucoup d'eau.*

Answers

1 a, j **2** e, c **3** d, b, g **4** f, h, i, b

4 Fais un sondage dans la classe. Pose la question suivante à six personnes. Note les réponses. Chaque personne doit donner quatre résolutions.
(Speaking L4)

PLTS I

Speaking. Pupils do a class survey, asking six people the question supplied and noting their responses. When responding, pupils need to give four resolutions. A sample exchange is given.

Starter 2

Aim

To review negative structures

Write up the following. Give pupils two minutes to identify the negative expressions and how they are used.

Je ne mange pas très sain. Alors voici mes résolutions pour l'avenir.

- *Je ne mangerai jamais de hamburgers.*
- *Je ne boirai plus de boissons gazeuses.*

Check answers, asking pupils to translate the sentences into English. Point out that negative expressions go around the verb. With a good class, you could also get them to focus on what happens to *du*, *de la*, etc., after a negative (it changes to *de*).

Alternative Starter 2:

Use ActiveTeach p.037 Class activity to practise language for talking about healthy eating.

5 Lis les textes. Choisis les bons mots pour compléter chaque phrase.
(Reading L6)

Reading. Pupils read the two texts. They then complete the sentences about them by choosing the correct option from the two supplied each time.

Answers

1 Le coach de Gabriel pense que Gabriel doit manger **plus sain**.
2 Gabriel mangera beaucoup de **fruits**.
3 Gabriel ne boira pas **de coca**.
4 Gabriel ne mangera pas **de hamburgers**.
5 Léo mange **mal**.
6 Léo pense que c'est **agréable** d'aller au fastfood.
7 Léo **déteste** les produits laitiers.
8 À l'avenir, Léo continuera de boire **des boissons gazeuses**.

Studio Grammaire: negative expressions

Use the *Studio Grammaire* box to cover the negative expressions *ne … pas* and *ne … jamais*. There is more information and further practice on Pupil Book p. 49.

6 Écoute. Qu'est-ce qu'ils mangent et boivent? Copie et complète le tableau en anglais. (1–4) (Listening L6)

Listening. Pupils copy out the table. They then listen to four people talking about what they eat and drink and complete the table with the details in English.

Audioscript Track 23

1 **Élisa**
Normalement, je mange beaucoup de sucreries, et j'adore les gâteaux. Hier, j'ai mangé beaucoup de chocolat. Mais je veux être en forme, alors j'ai pris quelques résolutions: à l'avenir, je mangerai équilibré. Au revoir, les sucreries!

2 **Florian**
Moi, je suis très sportif, mais j'adore les hamburgers-frites. J'en mange tous les jours. Hier, j'en ai mangé deux! Mon coach m'a dit que je dois manger sain, alors j'ai pris des résolutions: à l'avenir, je ne mangerai pas trop de sel et je mangerai cinq portions de fruits ou de légumes par jour.

3 **Clarisse**
J'adore les fruits et j'en mange beaucoup. Hier, par exemple, j'ai mangé une banane, une pomme et des fraises. Mais je bois aussi beaucoup de boissons gazeuses et je sais que ce n'est pas sain. Alors, j'ai décidé qu'à l'avenir, je boirai de l'eau ou du lait. Je ne boirai plus de boissons gazeuses.

4 **Manu**
Moi, je bois beaucoup d'eau, je ne mange pas trop de sucreries et j'aime beaucoup les fruits, alors je mange assez sain. Mais j'adore les chips. Hier, j'ai mangé cinq paquets de chips et je crois que c'est un problème parce que je mange trop de sel. Alors, j'ai pris une résolution: à partir de demain, je mangerai seulement un paquet de chips par jour.

Answers

	normally	yesterday	in future
1 Élisa	eats lots of sweets, loves cakes	ate lot of chocolate	will eat a balanced diet (no more sweets)
2 Florian	loves hamburger and chips	ate two hamburgers and chips	won't eat too much salt, will eat five fruit/veg a day
3 Clarisse	loves fruit, drinks lots of fizzy drinks	ate banana, apple, strawberries	will drink water or milk, no more fizzy drinks
4 Manu	drinks a lot of water, doesn't eat too many sweets, likes fruit, eats quite healthily, loves crisps (eats too much salt)	ate five packets of crisps	will eat only one packet of crisps a day

7 Tu es un ange ou un diable? Écris un paragraphe sur tes résolutions pour manger sain ou pas sain! (Writing L5–6)

Writing. Pupils decide whether they are an angel (determined to eat healthily) or a devil (determined to eat unhealthily) and write a paragraph including the appropriate resolutions. Draw their attention to the tip box on including negatives and opinions to improve their writing. Key structures are supplied for support.

Plenary

Ask the class to summarise when the future tense is used and how it is formed.

Put the class into teams. Each team in turn comes up with an eating resolution. Award 1 point for a correct future tense verb and 1 point for a negative, with an extra point given for a completely correct answer.

Workbook, page 15

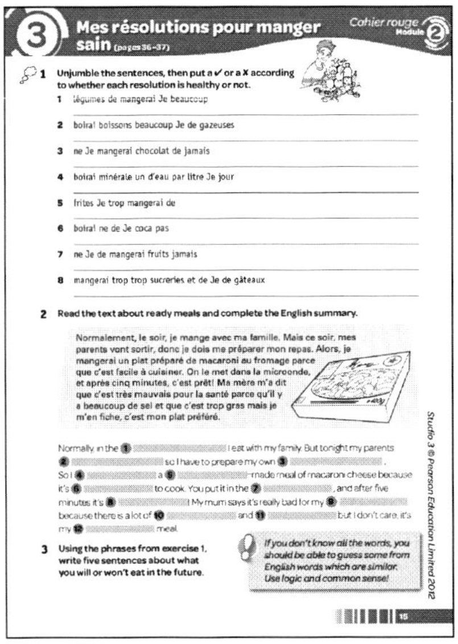

3 Mes résolutions pour manger sain (pages 36–37)

Cahier rouge Module 2

1 Unjumble the sentences, then put a ✓ or a ✗ according to whether each resolution is healthy or not.

1 légumes de mangerai Je beaucoup

2 boirai boissons beaucoup Je de gazeuses

3 ne Je mangerai chocolat de jamais

4 boirai minérale un d'eau par litre Je jour

5 frites Je trop mangerai de

6 boirai ne de Je coca pas

7 ne Je de mangerai fruits jamais

8 mangerai trop trop sucreries et de Je de gâteaux

2 Read the text about ready meals and complete the English summary.

Normalement, le soir, je mange avec ma famille. Mais ce soir, mes parents vont sortir, donc je dois me préparer mon repas. Alors, je mangerai un plat préparé de macaroni au fromage parce que c'est facile à cuisiner. On le met dans la microonde, et après cinq minutes, c'est prêt! Ma mère m'a dit que c'est très mauvais pour la santé parce qu'il y a beaucoup de sel et que c'est trop gras mais je m'en fiche, c'est mon plat préféré.

Normally, in the 1 ______ I eat with my family. But tonight my parents 2 ______ so I have to prepare my own 3 ______. So I 4 ______ a 5 ______-made meal of macaroni cheese because it's 6 ______ to cook. You put it in the 7 ______, and after five minutes it's 8 ______! My mum says it's really bad for my 9 ______ because there is a lot of 10 ______ and 11 ______ but I don't care, it's my 12 ______ meal.

3 Using the phrases from exercise 1, write five sentences about what you will or won't eat in the future.

If you don't know all the words, you should be able to guess some from English words which are similar. Use logic and common sense!

Studio 3 © Pearson Education Limited 2012

15

Answers

1 **1** Je mangerai beaucoup de légumes. ✓

2 Je boirai beaucoup de boissons gazeuses. ✗

3 Je ne mangerai jamais de chocolat. ✓

4 Je boirai un litre d'eau minérale par jour. ✓

5 Je mangerai trop de frites. ✗

6 Je ne boirai pas de coca. ✓

7 Je ne mangerai jamais de fruits. ✗

8 Je mangerai trop de sucreries et trop de gâteaux. ✗

2 **1** evening **2** are going out **3** meal **4** will eat **5** ready **6** easy **7** microwave **8** ready **9** health **10** salt **11** fat **12** favourite

Worksheet 2.3 Using negatives

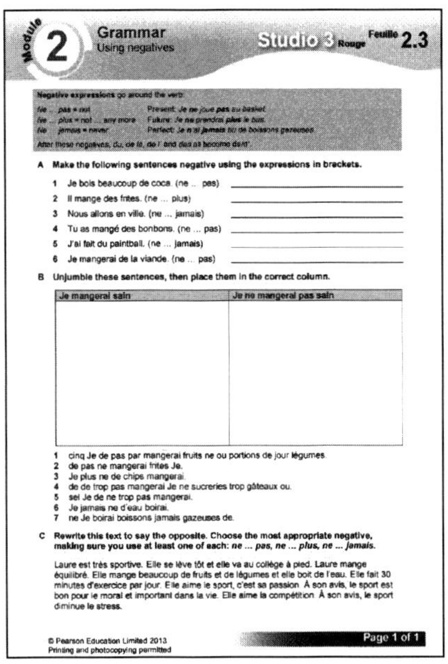

Module 2 Grammar Using negatives — Studio 3 Rouge — Feuille 2.3

Negative expressions go around the verb:

ne … pas = not — Present: Je ne joue pas au basket.

ne … plus = not … any more — Future: Je ne prendrai plus le bus.

ne … jamais = never — Perfect: Je n'ai jamais bu de boissons gazeuses.

After these negatives, du, de la, de l' and des all become de/d'.

A Make the following sentences negative using the expressions in brackets.

1 Je bois beaucoup de coca. (ne … pas)

2 Il mange des frites. (ne … plus)

3 Nous allons en ville. (ne … jamais)

4 Tu as mangé des bonbons. (ne … pas)

5 J'ai fait du paintball. (ne … jamais)

6 Je mangerai de la viande. (ne … pas)

B Unjumble these sentences, then place them in the correct column.

Je mangerai sain	Je ne mangerai pas sain

1 cinq Je de pas par mangerai fruits ne ou portions de jour légumes.

2 de pas ne mangerai frites Je.

3 Je plus ne de chips mangerai.

4 de de trop pas mangerai Je ne sucreries trop gâteaux ou.

5 sel Je de ne trop pas mangerai.

6 Je jamais ne d'eau boirai.

7 ne Je boirai boissons jamais gazeuses de.

C Rewrite this text to say the opposite. Choose the most appropriate negative, making sure you use at least one of each: *ne … pas, ne … plus, ne … jamais.*

Laure est très sportive. Elle se lève tôt et elle va au collège à pied. Laure mange équilibré. Elle mange beaucoup de fruits et de légumes et elle boit de l'eau. Elle fait 30 minutes d'exercice par jour. Elle aime le sport, c'est sa passion. À son avis, le sport est bon pour le moral et important dans la vie. Elle aime la compétition. À son avis, le sport diminue le stress.

© Pearson Education Limited 2013
Printing and photocopying permitted

Page 1 of 1

Answers

A **1** Je ne bois pas beaucoup de coca.

2 Il ne mange plus de frites.

3 Nous n'allons jamais en ville.

4 Tu n'as pas mangé de bonbons.

5 Je n'ai jamais fait de paintball.

6 Je ne mangerai pas de viande.

B **1** Je ne mangerai pas cinq portions de fruits ou de légumes par jour.

2 Je ne mangerai pas de frites.

3 Je ne mangerai plus de chips.

4 Je ne mangerai pas trop de sucreries ou trop de gâteaux.

5 Je ne mangerai pas trop de sel.

6 Je ne boirai jamais d'eau.

7 Je ne boirai jamais de boissons gazeuses.

je mangerai sain	je ne mangerai pas sain
2	1
3	6
4	
5	
7	

C Laure n'est pas très sportive. Elle ne se lève jamais tôt et elle ne va jamais au collège à pied. Laure ne mange pas équilibré. Elle ne mange pas beaucoup de fruits et de légumes et elle ne boit pas d'eau. Elle ne fait pas 30 minutes d'exercice par jour. Elle n'aime pas le sport, ce n'est pas sa passion.

À son avis, le sport n'est pas bon pour le moral et n'est pas important dans la vie. Elle n'aime pas la compétition. À son avis, le sport ne diminue pas le stress.

2 4 Je serai en forme!

Learning objectives
- Making plans to get fit
- Practising the future tense

Programme of Study references
GV1 Tenses (future)
LC1 Listening and responding
LC6 Reading comprehension
LC4 Expressing ideas (writing)

FCSE links
Unit 5: Healthy lifestyle (Healthy living, Healthy/unhealthy eating, Fast food, Exercise, Sports, Health farms, Activities, Eating and drinking)
Unit 6: Food and drink (Unhealthy/healthy food choices, Food and drink habits)

Grammar
- the future tense

Key language
Je ferai du sport.
Je ferai trente minutes d'exercice par jour.
J'irai au collège à vélo et pas en voiture.
Je jouerai au foot.
Je mangerai équilibré.
Je marcherai jusqu'au collège.
Je ne boirai jamais de boissons gazeuses.
Je ne jouerai plus à des jeux vidéo.
Je ne mangerai plus de frites/ hamburgers.
Je ne prendrai pas le bus.
Je prendrai les escaliers.
Je prendrai des cours d'arts martiaux.

PLTS
E Effective participators

Cross-curricular
PSHE: healthy lifestyles

Resources
Audio files:
24_Module2_Unit4_Ex1.mp3
25_Module2_Unit4_Ex3.mp3
Workbooks:
Cahier d'exercices Rouge, pages 16 & 17
ActiveTeach:
Starter 1 resource
p.038 Grammar
p.038 Grammar practice
p.039 Class activity
p.039 Video 4
p.039 Video worksheet 4
p.039 Grammar skills
p.039 Thinking skills
ActiveLearn:
Listening, Reading
Grammar

Starter 1
Aim

To work out meaning using context

Write up the following. Give pupils three minutes working in pairs to translate the sentences into English.

Pour être en forme …

1 *je ferai trente minutes d'exercices par jour.*
2 *j'irai au collège à vélo.*
3 *je ne mangerai pas de frites.*
4 *je prendrai des cours d'arts martiaux.*

Check answers, asking pupils how they worked them out. (**Answers: 1** I will do 30 minutes of exercise every day. **2** I will go to school by bike./ I will cycle to school. **3** I will not eat chips. **4** I will take martial arts classes.)

1 Écoute et lis l'histoire. (Listening L5)

Listening. Pupils listen to the celebrity fitness camp story, reading the text at the same time. Some vocabulary is glossed for support. Ask pupils whether they think the celebrities will stick to their resolutions.

Audioscript Track 24

– *Bienvenue au camp fitness, Simon, Jamel et Margot! Et voici les règles du camp: au camp fitness, on fera des activités physiques tous les jours sans exception et on sera en forme! Entendu?*
– *Oui, chef!*

– *Simon, quelles sont tes résolutions pour être en forme?*
– *Je ne mangerai pas de sucreries et je boirai beaucoup d'eau, chef. Je prendrai les escaliers et je ferai au moins trente minutes d'exercice par jour.*

– *Jamel, répète après moi: «Je mangerai sain, je ferai du sport régulièrement et je me coucherai de bonne heure!»*

– *Margot, quelles sont tes résolutions pour être en forme?*
– *Je ne mangerai pas de frites, chef. Je mangerai équilibré. C'est promis, chef!*
– *Est-ce que tu feras de l'exercice?*
– *Oui, chef! Je prendrai des cours d'arts martiaux!*

– *Je travaillerai avec vous, bien sûr! Ce sera difficile, mais l'échec n'est pas une option. Point final!*

2 Relis l'histoire et trouve les erreurs dans ces phrases. (Reading L5)

Reading. Pupils read the story in exercise 3 again. They then read and correct the errors in the sentences about it.

Answers

1 Au camp fitness, on fera des activités physiques **tous les jours (sans exception).**

2 Simon boira beaucoup **d'eau**.

3 Jamel fera **de l'exercice/du sport régulièrement**.

4 Margot **ne mangera pas de frites**.

3 Écoute. Quelles sont leurs résolutions au camp fitness? Copie et remplis le tableau en anglais. (1–3) (Listening L5)

Listening. Pupils copy out the table. They then listen to Nico, Coline and Axelle talking about their fitness camp resolutions and complete the table with the details.

Audioscript Track 25

1 – *Quelles sont tes résolutions au camp fitness, Nico?*
– *Alors … Je ferai du sport régulièrement, je boirai de l'eau et je me coucherai de bonne heure!*

2 – *Et toi, Coline, quelles sont tes résolutions au camp fitness?*
– *Je marcherai beaucoup pour être en forme. Je ne mangerai pas de sucreries et je prendrai aussi des cours d'arts martiaux.*

3 – *Quelles sont tes résolutions au camp fitness, Axelle?*
– *J'ai beaucoup de résolutions. D'abord, je mangerai équilibré, c'est-à-dire que je ne mangerai pas de frites et que je mangerai des fruits. Ensuite, je ferai au moins trente minutes d'exercice par jour. Voilà!*

Answers

	resolutions
1 Nico	will do sport regularly, will drink water, will go to bed early
2 Coline	will walk a lot, won't eat sweets, will take martial arts classes
3 Axelle	will eat a balanced diet, won't eat chips, will eat fruit, will do at least 30 minutes of exercise per day

Pupils work out/look up the future tense forms of six more verbs that they can use in their own writing/speaking.

Studio Grammaire: the future tense

Use the *Studio Grammaire* box to cover the future tense. There is more information and further practice on Pupil Book pp. 48–49.

Starter 2

Aim

To review the future tense

Give pupils three minutes working in pairs to identify, write down and translate into English all the future tense forms in the text in exercise 1, Pupil Book p. 38.

Check answers.
(**Answers:** *on fera* – we will do; *on sera* – we will be; *je ne mangerai pas* – I will not eat; *je boirai* – I will drink; *je prendrai* – I will take; *je ferai* – I will do; *je me coucherai* – I will go to bed; *tu feras* – you will do; *je tarvaillerai* – I will work; *ce sera* – it will be)

Alternative Starter 2:

Use ActiveTeach p.038 Grammar practice to practise the future tense.

4 Lis les textes et note vrai (V) ou faux (F). (Reading L5)

Reading. Pupils read the texts. They then read the sentences about them and note whether each one is true (writing V) or false (writing F). *c'est-à-dire* is glossed for support.

Answers

1 V **2** F **3** V **4** F **5** F **6** V **7** F **8** F

5 En tandem. Joue! Jette le dé et donne tes résolutions. (Speaking L4)

Speaking. In pairs: pupils take it in turn to throw the dice and make resolutions about what they will/will not do, using the pictures accompanying the number thrown. An example is given.

6 Écris huit règles pour un camp anti-fitness en utilisant le futur. (Writing L4–5)

Writing. Pupils write eight rules for an anti-fitness camp, using the future tense. A example is given. Draw pupils' attention to the tip box on extending their use of the future tense.

Plenary

PLTS E

Review the future tense by prompting in English to elicit different forms in French, e.g. *elle mangera, on fera*, etc.

Hear a selection of the rules for the anti-fitness camp that pupils wrote in exercise 6. Take a class vote by a show of hands on (1) whether they agree with each rule and (2) the best rule.

Workbook, pages 16 and 17

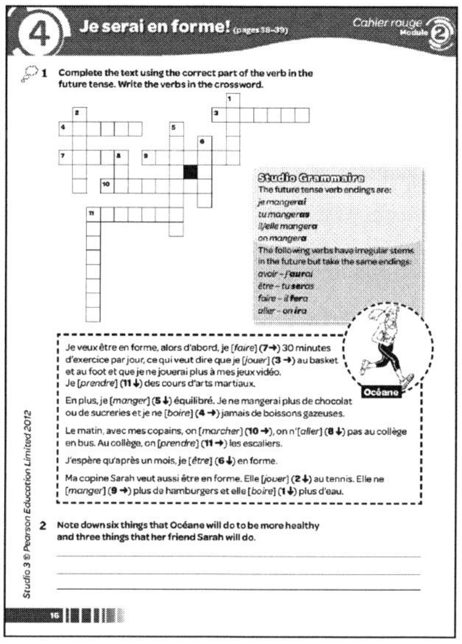
4 Je serai en forme! (pages 38–39) Cahier rouge Module 2

1 Complete the text using the correct part of the verb in the future tense. Write the verbs in the crossword.

Studio Grammaire

The future tense verb endings are:
je mangerai
tu mangeras
il/elle mangera
on mangera
The following verbs have irregular stems in the future but take the same endings:
avoir – j'aurai
être – tu seras
faire – il fera
aller – on ira

Je veux être en forme, alors d'abord, je [faire] (7 →) 30 minutes d'exercice par jour, ce qui veut dire que je [jouer] (3 →) au basket et au foot et que je ne jouerai plus à mes jeux vidéo. Je [prendre] (11 ↓) des cours d'arts martiaux.
En plus, je [manger] (5 ↓) équilibré. Je ne mangerai plus de chocolat ou de sucreries et je ne [boire] (4 →) jamais de boissons gazeuses.
Le matin, avec mes copains, on [marcher] (10 →), on n'[aller] (8 ↓) pas au collège en bus. Au collège, on [prendre] (11 →) les escaliers.
J'espère qu'après un mois, je [être] (6 ↓) en forme.
Ma copine Sarah veut aussi être en forme. Elle [jouer] (2 ↓) au tennis. Elle ne [manger] (9 →) plus de hamburgers et elle [boire] (1 ↓) plus d'eau.

Océane

2 Note down six things that Océane will do to be more healthy and three things that her friend Sarah will do.

Studio 3 © Pearson Education Limited 2012

16

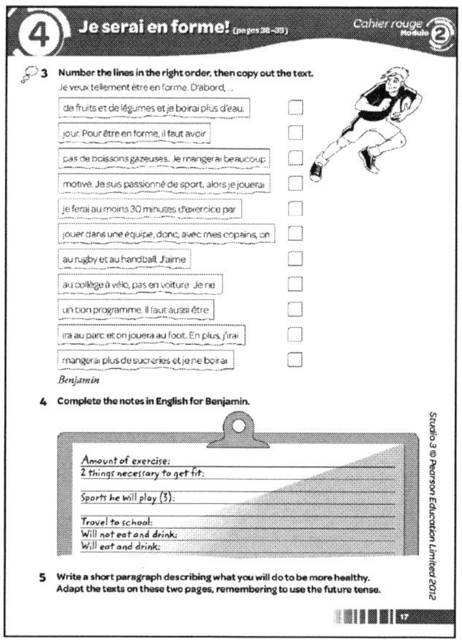
4 Je serai en forme! (pages 38–39) Cahier rouge Module 2

3 Number the lines in the right order, then copy out the text.
Je veux tellement être en forme. D'abord, ...
de fruits et de légumes et je boirai plus d'eau.
jour. Pour être en forme, il faut avoir
pas de boissons gazeuses. Je mangerai beaucoup
motivé. Je suis passionné de sport, alors je jouerai
je ferai au moins 30 minutes d'exercice par
jouer dans une équipe, donc, avec mes copains, on
au rugby et au handball. J'aime
au collège à vélo, pas en voiture. Je ne
un bon programme. Il faut aussi être
ira au parc et on jouera au foot. En plus, j'irai
mangerai plus de sucreries et je ne boirai
Benjamin

4 Complete the notes in English for Benjamin.
Amount of exercise:
2 things necessary to get fit:
Sports he will play (3):
Travel to school:
Will not eat and drink:
Will eat and drink:

5 Write a short paragraph describing what you will do to be more healthy. Adapt the texts on these two pages, remembering to use the future tense.

Studio 3 © Pearson Education Limited 2012

17

Answers

1 across: **3** jouerai **4** boirai **7** ferai **9** mangera **10** marchera **11** prendra
down: **1** boira **2** jouera **5** mangerai **6** serai **8** ira **11** prendrai

2 (Example answers:) **Océane:** 30 mins exercise per day; play basketball or football; take course in martial arts; eat a balanced diet; walk to school; take the stairs
Sarah: play tennis; won't eat hamburgers and will drink water

3 11, 2, 10, 4, 1, 6, 5, 8, 3, 6, 7, 9
Je veux tellement être en forme. D'abord, je ferai au moins 30 minutes d'exercice par jour. Pour être en forme, il faut avoir un bon programme. Il faut aussi être motivé. Je suis passionné de sport, alors je jouerai au rugby et au handball. J'aime jouer dans une équipe, donc, avec mes copains, on ira au parc et on jouera au foot. En plus, j'irai au collège à vélo, pas en voiture. Je ne mangerai plus de sucreries et je ne boirai pas de boissons gazeuses. Je mangerai beaucoup de fruits et de légumes et je boirai plus d'eau.

4 Amount of exercise: 30 minutes a day
2 things necessary to get fit: a good programme and motivation
Sports he will play: rugby, handball, football
Travel to school: by bike
Will not eat and drink: sweet things and fizzy drinks
Will eat and drink: lots of fruit and vegetables and more water

5 (Answers will vary.)

Worksheet 2.4 The future tense

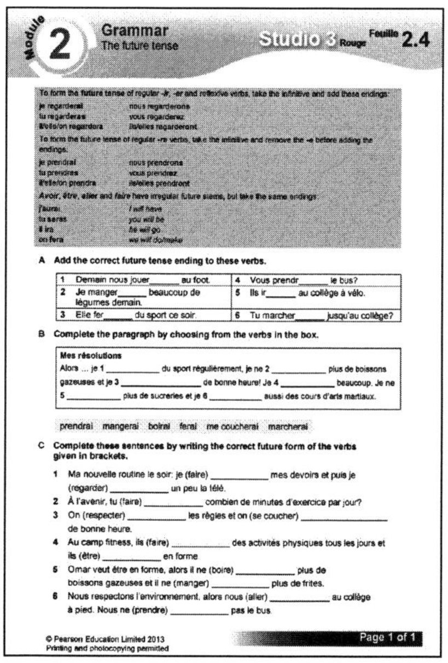
Module 2 Grammar The future tense Studio 3 Rouge Feuille 2.4

A Add the correct future tense ending to these verbs.

B Complete the paragraph by choosing from the verbs in the box.
prendrai mangerai boirai ferai me coucherai marcherai

C Complete these sentences by writing the correct future form of the verbs given in brackets.

© Pearson Education Limited 2013
Printing and photocopying permitted
Page 1 of 1

Answers

A 1 Demain, nous jouer**ons** au foot.

2 Je manger**ai** beaucoup de légumes demain.

3 Elle fer**a** du sport ce soir.

4 Vous prendr**ez** le bus?

5 Ils ir**ont** au collège à vélo.

6 Tu marcher**as** jusqu'au collège?

B 1 ferai **2** boirai **3** me coucherai **4** marcherai **5** mangerai **6** prendrai

C 1 nouvelle routine le soir: je **ferai** mes devoirs et puis je **regarderai** un peu la télé.

2 À l'avenir, tu **feras** combien de minutes d'exercice par jour?

3 On **respectera** les règles et **on se couchera** de bonne heure.

4 Au camp fitness, ils **feront** des activités physiques tous les jours et ils **seront** en forme.

5 Omar veut être en forme, alors il ne **boira** plus de boissons gazeuses et il ne **mangera** plus de frites.

6 Nous respectons l'environnement, alors nous **irons** au collège à pied. Nous ne **prendrons** pas le bus.

Worksheet 2.5 Making connections

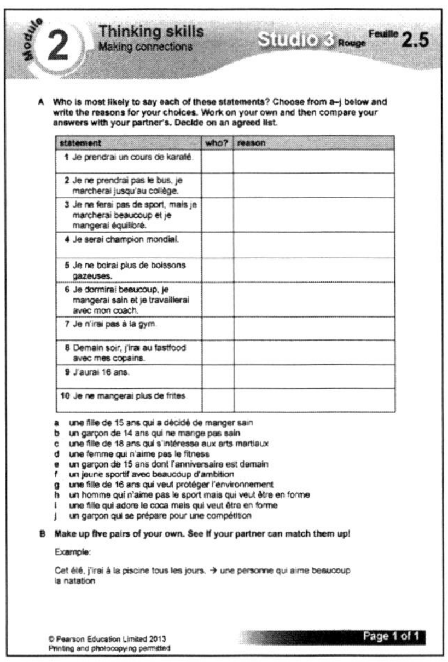

Module 2 Thinking skills
Making connections
Studio 3 Rouge Feuille 2.5

A Who is most likely to say each of these statements? Choose from a–j below and write the reasons for your choices. Work on your own and then compare your answers with your partner's. Decide on an agreed list.

statement	who?	reason
1 Je prendrai un cours de karaté.		
2 Je ne prendrai pas le bus, je marcherai jusqu'au collège.		
3 Je ne ferai pas de sport, mais je marcherai beaucoup et je mangerai équilibré.		
4 Je serai champion mondial.		
5 Je ne boirai plus de boissons gazeuses.		
6 Je dormirai beaucoup, je mangerai sain et je travaillerai avec mon coach.		
7 Je n'irai pas à la gym.		
8 Demain soir, j'irai au fastfood avec mes copains.		
9 J'aurai 16 ans.		
10 Je ne mangerai plus de frites.		

a une fille de 15 ans qui a décidé de manger sain
b un garçon de 14 ans qui ne mange pas sain
c une fille de 18 ans qui s'intéresse aux arts martiaux
d une femme qui n'aime pas le fitness
e un garçon de 15 ans dont l'anniversaire est demain
f un jeune sportif avec beaucoup d'ambition
g une fille de 16 ans qui veut protéger l'environnement
h un homme qui n'aime pas le sport mais qui veut être en forme
i une fille qui adore le coca mais qui veut être en forme
j un garçon qui se prépare pour une compétition

B Make up five pairs of your own. See if your partner can match them up!

Example:

Cet été, j'irai à la piscine tous les jours. → une personne qui aime beaucoup la natation

Page 1 of 1

Answers

1 c – She is interested in martial arts.

2 g – She wants to protect the environment.

3 h – He doesn't like sport but wants to be fit.

4 f – He is sporty and ambitious.

5 i – She loves Coca-Cola but wants to be fit.

6 j – A boy preparing for a competition.

7 d – She doesn't like keeping fit.

8 b – He is not a healthy eater.

9 e – His birthday is tomorrow.

10 a – The girl has decided to eat healthily.

Video

Episode 3: La danse

Marielle teaches the reluctant team to dance, in preparation for the Studio party. Video worksheet 4 can be used in conjunction with this episode.

Answers to video worksheet (ActiveTeach)

1 A The boys will probably not be keen, while the girls will be more enthusiastic.

B (Answers will vary.)

2 A A Studio party in two weeks.

B Here it means 'rehearse'.

C With horror.

D Do sport with him.

E He says he'll film rather than dance.

3 A *L'épaule, les bras, la tête, le dos, la main, les jambes.*

B Because he doesn't eat well.

C He reluctantly agrees that she's right. He's going to stop eating chips and hamburgers.

D He finds it boring and prefers judo and martial arts.

E He's dancing (badly) because he wants to get fit.

F She says he's going to be the best dancer. Judging by his performance, she's being sarcastic!

G They laugh and tell him to stop.

4 *oiseau* means 'bird', *carré* means 'square' and *soleil* means 'sun'. The words describe the movements.

(Pupil Book pp. 40–41)

2 5 Es-tu en forme?

Learning objectives
- Describing levels of fitness
- Using three tenses together

Programme of Study references
GV1 Tenses (past, present and future)
LC4 Expressing ideas (writing)
LC5 Speaking coherently and confidently
LC6 Reading comprehension

FCSE links
Unit 5: Healthy lifestyle (Exercise, Activities)

Grammar
- using three tenses together

Key language
Review of language from the module

PLTS
T Team workers

Cross-curricular
ICT: word-processing
PSHE: healthy lifestyles

Resources
Audio files:
26_Module2_Unit5_Ex1.mp3
27_Module2_Unit5_Ex4.mp3
Workbooks:
Cahier d'exercices Rouge, pages 18 & 19
ActiveTeach:
p.041 Grammar skills
ActiveLearn:
Listening, Reading
Grammar

Starter 1

PLTS T

Aim

To review different tenses and other verb structures

Give pupils three minutes working in pairs to identify in the first text in exercise 1 (Pupil Book p. 40) and write down the following structures:
- verb + infinitive
- two different negatives
- a perfect tense verb with *être*
- a perfect tense verb with *avoir*
- a future tense verb

Check answers.

1 Écoute et lis les textes. (Listening L6)

Listening. Pupils listen to two people talking about keeping in shape and read the text at the same time. Some vocabulary is glossed for support.

Audioscript Track 26

– *Moi, j'adore jouer à des jeux vidéo. Je n'aime pas beaucoup le sport, je trouve ça très ennuyeux de courir sur un stade.*

Mon problème, c'est que je veux être en forme, mais je ne suis pas très actif. Alors, j'ai pris des résolutions. D'abord, j'irai au collège à pied, je ne prendrai pas le bus. Comme ça, je ferai au moins trente minutes d'exercice par jour.

Ensuite, je mangerai équilibré. Je ne mangerai plus de frites et je ne mangerai pas de sucreries. Je boirai aussi beaucoup d'eau.

Hier, je suis allé au collège à pied et à midi, j'ai mangé une salade. L'après-midi, je suis allé au fastfood avec des copains mais j'ai bu un verre d'eau et je n'ai pas pris de hamburger!

– *Moi, j'adore le paintball. C'est génial! À mon avis, ça diminue le stress. Si on joue au paintball, il faut être en forme. Moi, je mange assez sain, j'adore les fruits et je bois beaucoup d'eau.*

Mon problème, c'est que je me couche tard. J'aime beaucoup surfer sur Internet jusqu'à minuit, et si on veut gagner au paintball, il faut bien dormir. On ne peut pas gagner si on est fatigué.

Alors, j'ai pris des résolutions: je me coucherai de bonne heure. J'irai dans ma chambre à neuf heures, je regarderai un peu la télé et puis dodo!

Hier, j'ai commencé ma nouvelle routine: je suis allée dans ma chambre, j'ai regardé un peu la télé et j'ai éteint la lumière à dix heures du soir. Je serai en forme pour le weekend!

2 Relis les textes. C'est vrai (V) ou faux (F)? (Reading L6)

Reading. Pupils read the texts in exercise 1 again. They then note whether the sentences about the text are true (writing V) or false (writing F).

Answers

1 F **2** V **3** F **4** V **5** V **6** F **7** V **8** V

3 Copie et remplis le tableau avec les verbes des textes de l'exercice 1. Écris chaque verbe dans la bonne colonne. (Reading L6)

Reading. Pupils copy out the table and complete it with the verbs from the texts in exercise 1, writing each verb in the correct tense column. Draw their attention to *Stratégie 2* on Pupil Book p. 51 and the tip box on using the three tenses together when writing.

Answers

passé	présent	futur	anglais
	j'adore		I love
	je n'aime pas		I don't like
	je trouve		I find
	je veux		I want
	je ne suis pas		I am not
j'ai pris			I took/made
		j'irai	I will go
		je ne prendrai pas	I won't take
		je ferai	I will do
		je mangerai	I will eat
		je ne mangerai pas/plus	I won't eat (any more)
		je boirai	I will drink
je suis allé(e)			I went
j'ai mangé			I ate
j'ai bu			I drank
je n'ai pas pris			I didn't take/have
	c'est		it's
	ça diminue		it reduces
	on joue		you/we play
	il faut		you must
	je mange		I eat
	j'adore		I love
	je bois		I drink
	je me couche		I go to bed
	j'aime		I like
	on veut		you/we want
	il faut		it's necessary
	on ne peut pas		you/we can't
	on est		you/we are
		je me coucherai	I will go to bed
		je regarderai	I will watch
j'ai commencé			I began
j'ai regardé			I watched
j'ai éteint			I switched off
		je serai	I will be

Starter 2

Aim

To practise using three tenses together

Give pupils three minutes to write a short text that uses the present, perfect and future tenses together.

Pupils swap with a partner and check each other's texts. Hear some examples.

4 Écoute Loïc et Estelle. Copie et remplis le tableau en anglais. (1–2) (Listening L6)

Listening. Pupils copy out the table. They then listen to Loïc and Estelle talking about keeping in shape and complete the table with the details in English.

Audioscript Track 27

1 Loïc

Moi, j'adore l'informatique. Je passe des heures à surfer sur Internet dans ma chambre. Mon problème, c'est que je n'aime pas du tout le foot. Je trouve ça très ennuyeux. Tous mes amis y jouent, mais moi, je n'aime pas du tout ça. Mais je veux être en forme. C'est important, je crois. Alors, j'ai pris des résolutions.

D'abord, j'irai au collège à pied, je ne prendrai plus le bus. Ensuite, je ne mangerai plus de frites. Je mangerai beaucoup de fruits et de légumes.

Hier, j'ai commencé ma nouvelle routine: je suis allé au collège à pied et à midi, j'ai pris une salade. Plus de frites pour moi!

2 Estelle

Moi, j'aime beaucoup aller en ville avec mes copines et j'adore danser. Je suis assez active. Mon problème, c'est que je veux manger sain, mais j'adore la nourriture de fastfood. Je trouve ça pratique et en plus, ce n'est pas cher. J'aime aller au fastfood. On mange et on discute. C'est sympa.

Alors, j'ai pris des résolutions: j'irai au fastfood, mais je ne mangerai pas de hamburgers. Je prendrai un smoothie ou un verre d'eau. Ensuite, je mangerai cinq fruits par jour.

Hier, j'ai mangé une pomme, deux bananes, des fraises et un kiwi.

Answers

	1 Loïc	**2** Estelle
passion	Computers, surfing the net.	Going into town with her friends, dancing.
problem	He doesn't like football, thinks it's boring. All his friends play, but he doesn't like it. But he wants to get fit.	Wants to eat healthily but loves fast food and likes going to fast-food restaurants.
resolutions	Will walk to school, won't take the bus. Won't eat chips any more, will eat lots of fruit and vegetables.	Will still go to fast food restaurants but will not eat hamburgers. Will have a smoothie or a glass of water. Will eat five pieces of fruit a day.
progress so far	Walked to school yesterday and ate salad for lunch.	Yesterday ate an apple, two bananas, strawberries and a kiwi fruit.

5 Tu es Jamel ou Noëlle. Prépare un exposé sur «mes résolutions». (Speaking L6)

Speaking. Pupils imagine they are Jamel or Noëlle. They prepare and give a presentation entitled *Mes résolutions*, using the appropriate set of prompts. Draw pupils' attention to the tip box on adding detail to personalise answers. A framework is supplied for support.

6 Écris le profil de Mélodie (Writing L6)

Writing. Pupils write a profile of Mélodie in French, using the English notes supplied.

Pupils could write their profile on computer, making it easier to correct and produce a second draft.

Plenary

Ask pupils to read sentences from the profile they wrote in exercise 6. Ask the rest of the class to give constructive feedback, encouraging them to pay particular attention to the use of tenses.

Remind pupils that it is necessary to use the three tenses in the same piece of work if aiming for a higher level.

Workbook, pages 18 and 19

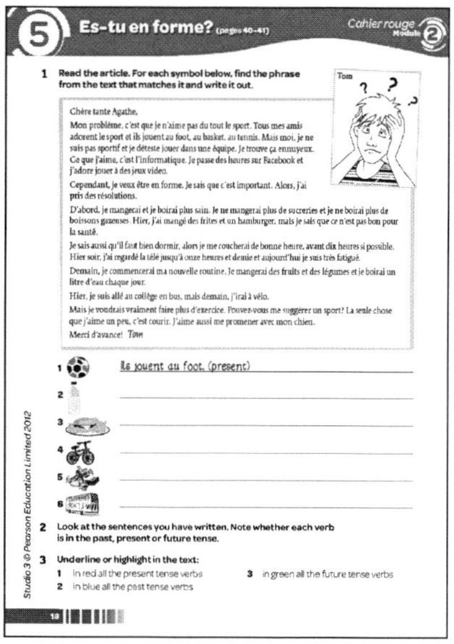

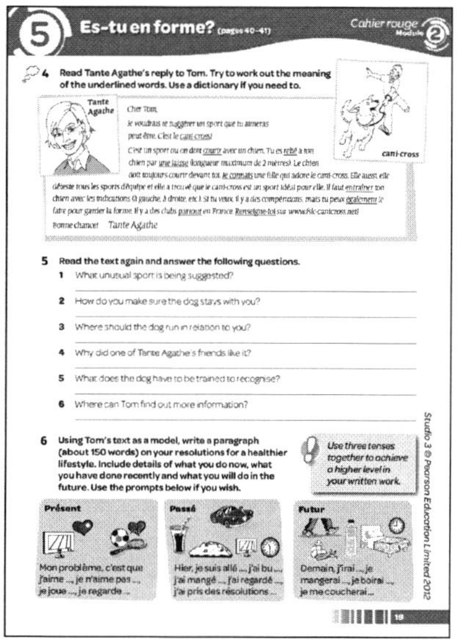

Answers

1 **1** Ils jouent au foot. (present)

2 Je boirai un litre d'eau chaque jour. (future)

3 Hier, j'ai mangé des frites et un hamburger. (past)

4 Demain j'irai à vélo. (future)

5 Je ne mangerai plus de sucreries. (future)

6 Je suis allé au collège en bus. (past)

2 (See above.)

3 **1** je n'aime pas, adorent, ils jouent, je ne suis pas, je déteste, Je trouve, j'aime, Je passe, j'adore, je veux, Je sais, je sais, Je sais, il faut, je suis, Pouvez-vous, j'aime, J'aime

2 j'ai pris, j'ai mangé, j'ai regardé, je suis allé

3 je mangerai, je boirai, Je ne mangerai plus, je ne boirai plus, je me coucherai, je commencerai, Je mangerai, je boirai, j'irai

4 cani-cross – cross-country with a dog
courir – to run
relié – tied
une laisse – lead
je connais – I know
entraîner – to train
également – equally
partout – everywhere
renseigne-toi – find out about

5 **1** Cani-cross – cross country with a dog

2 It's attached to you with a lead.

3 The dog should always run in front of you.

4 Because she hated team sports.

5 Directions such as left, right, etc.

6 On the suggested website.

6 (Example answer:)

Mon problème, c'est que j'aime regarder la télé tout le temps. Je n'aime pas le sport; je ne joue pas au foot et je déteste le tennis.

Mais je veux être en forme.

Hier, j'ai mangé de la pizza et j'ai bu du coca. Je suis allé au collège en voiture avec ma mère. J'ai regardé la télé jusqu'à onze heures et demie. Alors, j'ai pris des résolutions.

Demain, j'irai au collège à pied avec mes copains et je mangerai plus de légumes. Je ne boirai plus de coca mais je boirai de l'eau. Je me coucherai à neuf heures tous les soirs.

Worksheet 2.6 Using three tenses together

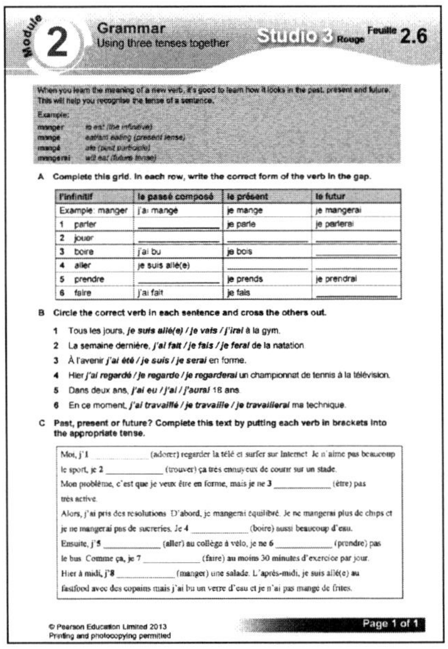

Module 2 Grammar
Using three tenses together
Studio 3 Rouge Feuille 2.6

When you learn the meaning of a new verb, it's good to learn how it looks in the past, present and future. This will help you recognise the tense of a sentence.

Example:
manger — *to eat (the infinitive)*
mange — *eat/am eating (present tense)*
mangé — *ate (past participle)*
mangerai — *will eat (future tense)*

A Complete this grid. In each row, write the correct form of the verb in the gap.

l'infinitif	le passé composé	le présent	le futur
Example: manger	j'ai mangé	je mange	je mangerai
1 parler	______	je parle	je parlerai
2 jouer	______	______	______
3 boire	j'ai bu	je bois	______
4 aller	je suis allé(e)	______	______
5 prendre	______	je prends	je prendrai
6 faire	j'ai fait	je fais	______

B Circle the correct verb in each sentence and cross the others out.

1 Tous les jours, ***je suis allé(e) / je vais / j'irai*** à la gym.
2 La semaine dernière, ***j'ai fait / je fais / je ferai*** de la natation
3 À l'avenir ***j'ai été / je suis / je serai*** en forme.
4 Hier ***j'ai regardé / je regarde / je regarderai*** un championnat de tennis à la télévision.
5 Dans deux ans, ***j'ai eu / j'ai / j'aurai*** 18 ans.
6 En ce moment, ***j'ai travaillé / je travaille / je travaillerai*** ma technique.

C Past, present or future? Complete this text by putting each verb in brackets into the appropriate tense.

Moi, j'**1** ______ (adorer) regarder la télé et surfer sur Internet. Je n'aime pas beaucoup le sport, je **2** ______ (trouver) ça très ennuyeux de courir sur un stade.
Mon problème, c'est que je veux être en forme, mais je ne **3** ______ (être) pas très active.
Alors, j'ai pris des résolutions. D'abord, je mangerai équilibré. Je ne mangerai plus de chips et je ne mangerai pas de sucreries. Je **4** ______ (boire) aussi beaucoup d'eau.
Ensuite, j'**5** ______ (aller) au collège à vélo, je ne **6** ______ (prendre) pas le bus. Comme ça, je **7** ______ (faire) au moins 30 minutes d'exercice par jour.
Hier à midi, j'**8** ______ (manger) une salade. L'après-midi, je suis allé(e) au fastfood avec des copains mais j'ai bu un verre d'eau et je n'ai pas mangé de frites.

Page 1 of 1

Answers

l'infinitif	le passé composé	le présent	le futur
manger	*j'ai mangé*	*je mange*	*je mangerai*
1 parler	j'ai parlé	je parle	je parlerai
2 jouer	j'ai joué	je joue	je jouerai
3 boire	j'ai bu	je bois	je boirai
4 aller	je suis allé(e)	je vais	j'irai
5 prendre	j'ai pris	je prends	je prendrai
6 faire	j'ai fait	je fais	je ferai

B **1** Tous les jours, **je vais** à la gym.

2 La semaine dernière, **j'ai fait** de la natation.

3 À l'avenir, **je serai** en forme.

4 Hier, **j'ai regardé** un championnat de tennis à la télévision.

5 Dans deux ans, **j'aurai** 18 ans.

6 En ce moment, **je travaille** ma technique.

C **1** adore **2** trouve
3 suis **4** boirai
5 irai **6** prendrai
7 ferai **8** ai mangé

2 Bilan et Révisions

Bilan

Pupils use this checklist to review language covered in the module, working on it in pairs in class or on their own at home. Encourage them to follow up any areas of weakness they identify. There are Target Setting Sheets included in the Assessment Pack, and an opportunity for pupils to record their own levels and targets on the *J'avance* page in the Workbook, p. 24. You can also use the *Bilan* checklist as an end-of-module plenary option.

Révisions

These revision exercises can be used for assessment purposes or for pupils to practise before tackling the assessment tasks in the Assessment Pack.

Resources

Audio files:

28_Module2_Rev_Ex1.mp3

Workbooks:

Cahier d'exercices Rouge, pages 20 & 21

1 Écoute et écris les bonnes lettres. (1–2) (Listening L5)

Listening. Pupils listen to two conversations. For each one they note the letters of the two pictures mentioned.

Audioscript Track 28

1 – *Aaaaaa!*
– *Ça va? T'as un problème? Qu'est-ce qui s'est passé?*
– *Aaaaaa, je suis touché, je suis touché!*
– *Mince, où est-ce que tu es touché?*
– *Au bras et à la jambe.*

2 – *Aïe!*
– *Ça va? T'as un problème? Qu'est-ce qui s'est passé?*
– *Aaaaa, je suis touchée!*
– *Ah non, où est-ce que tu es touchée?*
– *À l'épaule et au dos.*

Answers

1 a, d **2** e, b

2 En tandem. Réponds à ces questions. (Speaking L4–6)

Speaking. In pairs: pupils take it in turn to ask and answer the questions supplied.

3 Lis le texte et termine les phrases en anglais. (Reading L6)

Reading. Pupils read the text and supply the endings for the sentences about it in English.

Answers

1 … 9 years.
2 … 5.30 am.
3 … competitions.
4 … took part in two competitions but didn't win.
5 … be disciplined and like competition.

4 Écris une liste de six résolutions pour être en forme. Utilise les images. (Writing L4–6)

Writing. Pupils use the picture prompts to write six resolutions for keeping in shape.

Example answers

Je jouerai au foot (deux fois par semaine) et je ne jouerai plus à mes jeux vidéo.

J'irai au collège à pied et je ne prendrai pas le bus.

Je ferai (au moins) trente minutes d'exercice par jour.

J'irai au collège à vélo, pas en voiture.

Je ne mangerai plus de hamburgers.

Je ne mangerai plus de frites et je mangerai (tous les jours) des légumes.

Workbook, pages 20 and 21

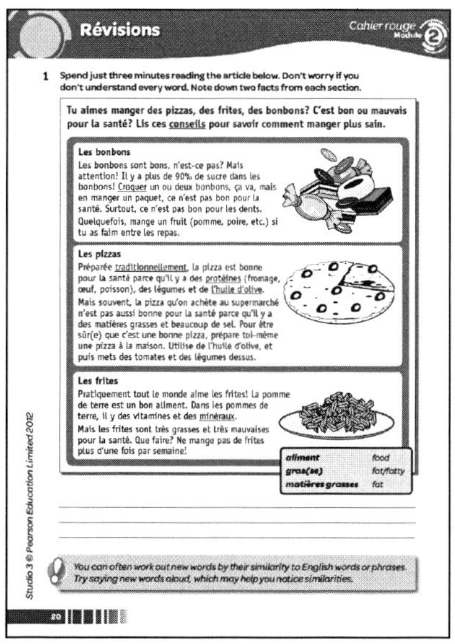
Révisions — Cahier rouge Module 2

1 Spend just three minutes reading the article below. Don't worry if you don't understand every word. Note down two facts from each section.

Tu aimes manger des pizzas, des frites, des bonbons? C'est bon ou mauvais pour la santé? Lis ces conseils pour savoir comment manger plus sain.

Les bonbons
Les bonbons sont bons, n'est-ce pas? Mais attention! Il y a plus de 90% de sucre dans les bonbons! Croquer un ou deux bonbons, ça va, mais en manger un paquet, ce n'est pas bon pour la santé. Surtout, ce n'est pas bon pour les dents.
Quelquefois, mange un fruit (pomme, poire, etc.) si tu as faim entre les repas.

Les pizzas
Préparée traditionnellement, la pizza est bonne pour la santé parce qu'il y a des protéines (fromage, œuf, poisson), des légumes et de l'huile d'olive.
Mais souvent, la pizza qu'on achète au supermarché n'est pas aussi bonne pour la santé parce qu'il y a des matières grasses et beaucoup de sel. Pour être sûr(e) que c'est une bonne pizza, prépare toi-même une pizza à la maison. Utilise de l'huile d'olive, et puis mets des tomates et des légumes dessus.

Les frites
Pratiquement tout le monde aime les frites! La pomme de terre est un bon aliment. Dans les pommes de terre, il y des vitamines et des minéraux.
Mais les frites sont très grasses et très mauvaises pour la santé. Que faire? Ne mange pas de frites plus d'une fois par semaine!

aliment	food
gras(se)	fat/fatty
matières grasses	fat

You can often work out new words by their similarity to English words or phrases. Try saying new words aloud, which may help you notice similarities.

Studio 3 © Pearson Education Limited 2012

20

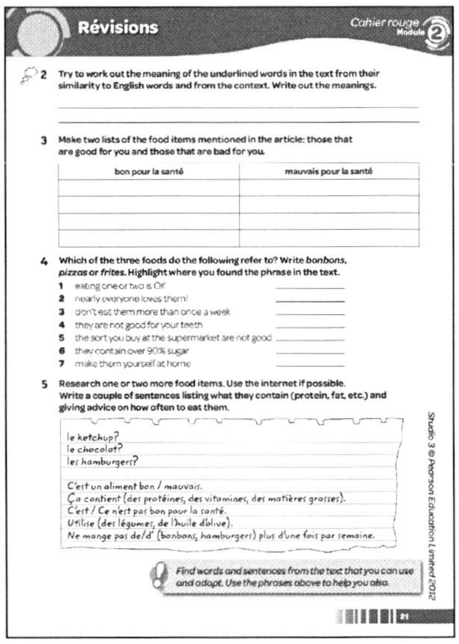

Révisions

Cahier rouge Module 2

2 Try to work out the meaning of the underlined words in the text from their similarity to English words and from the context. Write out the meanings.

3 Make two lists of the food items mentioned in the article: those that are good for you and those that are bad for you.

bon pour la santé	mauvais pour la santé

4 Which of the three foods do the following refer to? Write *bonbons*, *pizzas* or *frites*. Highlight where you found the phrase in the text.

1 eating one or two is OK
2 nearly everyone loves them!
3 don't eat them more than once a week
4 they are not good for your teeth
5 the sort you buy at the supermarket are not good
6 they contain over 90% sugar
7 make them yourself at home

5 Research one or two more food items. Use the internet if possible. Write a couple of sentences listing what they contain (protein, fat, etc.) and giving advice on how often to eat them.

le ketchup?
le chocolat?
les hamburgers?

C'est un aliment bon / mauvais.
Ça contient (des protéines, des vitamines, des matières grasses).
C'est / Ce n'est pas bon pour la santé.
Utilise (des légumes, de l'huile d'olive).
Ne mange pas de/d' (bonbons, hamburgers) plus d'une fois par semaine.

Find words and sentences from the text that you can use and adapt. Use the phrases above to help you also.

Answers

1 (Answers will vary.)

2 conseils – advice, pieces of advice
croquer – to crunch, crunching
traditionnellement – traditionally
protéines – proteins
l'huile d'olive – olive oil
minéraux – minerals

3

bon pour la santé	**mauvais pour la santé**
les fruits (pomme, poire)	les bonbons
une pizza avec proteins (fromage, oeuf, poisson)	une pizza qu'on achète
l'huile d'olive	au supermarché les frites
les pommes de terre	

4 **1** bonbons **2** frites **3** frites **4** bonbons **5** pizzas **6** bonbons **7** pizzas

5 (Answers will vary.)

2 En plus: La santé des jeunes

(Pupil Book pp. 44–45)

Learning objective

- Talking about teenage health issues

Programme of Study references

LC1 Listening and responding
LC4 Expressing ideas (speaking)
LC5 Speaking coherently and confidently
LC5 Accurate pronunciation and intonation

FCSE links

Unit 5: Healthy lifestyle (Healthy living, Exercise, State of health, Activities)

Key language

Review of language from the module

PLTS

S Self-managers

Cross-curricular

PSHE: healthy lifestyles
ICT: creating reference materials

Resources

Audio files:
29_Module2_EnPlus_Ex1.mp3
30_Module2_EnPlus_Ex5.mp3
ActiveTeach:
p.045 Assignment 2
p.045 Assignment 2: prep

Starter

Aim

To practise reading for gist

Give pupils one minute to skim-read the text in exercise 1.

Ask what the text was about and how they worked it out, e.g. reading the heading and opening sentences of paragraphs, scanning for key words, looking for special features (here, statistics), etc. Remind them that reading for gist in this way is a useful technique: it gives an overview of the topic, which makes the next stage of working out the detail in context much easier.

1 Écoute et lis le texte. (Listening L4)

Listening. Pupils listen to the feature on a health issue affecting young people, reading the text at the same time. Some vocabulary is glossed for support.

Audioscript Track 29

Alerte rouge chez les ados!

Près d'un adolescent sur deux ne pratique pas d'activité physique régulière.

Entre quinze et dix-sept ans, les filles ne sont que 24,4% à pratiquer une activité, contre 63,3% des garçons du même âge.

Différents facteurs expliquent la situation. Aujourd'hui, les moyens de transport ont remplacé la marche. La prédominance de l'écran (télévision, Internet, jeux vidéo) a bouleversé le mode de vie des jeunes. Chez les quinze à dix-sept ans, on passe plus de trois heures par jour devant un écran.

Un corps de rêve et une forme au top, ça se cultive très tôt. Un manque d'activité physique à l'adolescence peut être à l'origine de futures maladies.

Allez les ados, abandonnez l'ascenseur pour monter à pied, passez en mode vélo ou roller pour vous déplacer. Prenez des cours de danse ou d'arts martiaux. Bougez-vous!

2 Relis le texte et complète les phrases en anglais. (Reading L5)

Reading. Pupils read the text in exercise 1 again and then complete the gap-fill sentences about it in English. Draw pupils' attention to the tip box on reading skills.

Answers

1. Almost one adolescent in two does not **do any physical activity** on a regular basis.
2. Between the ages of 15 and 17, 24.4% of girls take part in a physical activity, undertake a physical activity as compared with **63.3% of boys**.
3. Where they used to walk, people now **use transport**.
4. 15–17 year olds spend more than three hours per day **in front of a screen**.
5. Inactivity can be the cause of **future diseases**.
6. Adolescents should walk upstairs rather than taking the lift and get about **by bike** or **on roller skates** rather than in vehicles.

3 Trouve des synonymes pour les expressions suivantes dans le texte. (Reading L4)

Reading. Pupils identify in the text in exercise 1 synonyms for the expressions listed.

PLTS S

Draw pupils' attention to the tip box on identifying language in reading passages that they can use in their own writing and speaking. Ask them to identify at least five phrases in the text in exercise 1 that they can use in this way. Suggest they keep a list of phrases like this (either in a notebook, on index cards or on computer), so that the language is easy to access, review and use.

Answers

1 pratiquer une activité (physique)
2 aujourd'hui
3 la marche
4 un corps de rêve
5 une forme au top
6 être à l'origine de
7 abandonner
8 se déplacer

4 Tu as lu l'article «Alerte rouge chez les ados!» et tu as pris certaines résolutions. Mets les mots dans le bon ordre. (Reading L4)

Reading. Pupils imagine that the article in exercise 1 has inspired them to make resolutions. They rewrite each series of jumbled words in the correct order to find the resolutions. *au lieu* de is glossed for support.

Answers

1 Je pratiquerai une activité physique régulièrement.
2 Je ne passerai pas tout mon temps devant un écran.
3 Je marcherai au lieu de prendre le bus ou la voiture/la voiture ou le bus.
4 J'aurai un corps de rêve.
5 J'abandonnerai l'ascenseur et je monterai à pied.
6 Je me déplacerai à vélo.

5 Thomas et Chloé discutent de l'article. Qui dit ça? Thomas ou Chloé? Écoute et lis. (Listening L6)

Listening. Pupils read the short texts. They listen to Thomas and Chloé discussing the article in exercise 1 and decide who said each one, Thomas or Chloé.

Audioscript Track 30

– *À mon avis, il faut prendre le problème du manque d'activité physique chez les jeunes au sérieux.*
– *Je suis d'accord. Je crois qu'il faut aussi examiner le problème de l'obésité chez les adolescents.*
– *Oui. Un adulte obèse ou inactif aura souvent de sérieux problèmes de santé, du diabète ou des maladies de coeur, par exemple.*
– *Les jeunes passent plus de trois heures par jour devant un écran. C'est trop!*
– *C'est vrai. Si on veut brûler des calories, si on veut être en forme, il faut être actif, il faut bouger.*
– *Tu as raison. Aujourd'hui, les ados prennent le bus au lieu de marcher. Moi, j'ai pris le bus hier pour venir au collège. Demain, je viendrai au collège à pied. Je ne veux pas être obèse!*
– *Je suis d'accord avec toi. Hier, au centre commercial, j'ai pris l'ascenseur. La prochaine fois, je monterai à pied.*
– *Si tu veux, on prendra des cours de danse ensemble. Ça te dit?*

Answers

a Chloé **b** Chloé **c** Chloé **d** Thomas
e Thomas **f** Thomas **g** Chloé **h** Thomas

6 Prépare un exposé sur la forme. (Speaking L6)

Speaking. Pupils prepare and give a presentation on fitness. A list of features to include is supplied.

When they listen to their friends' presentations, pupils award points using the guidelines supplied. Draw their attention to the tip box suggesting comments they can use in giving feedback.

Plenary

Ask pupils to think about the presentations they prepared for exercise 6 and identify two areas in which they could improve, e.g. tense formation, vocabulary, adjective agreement, including connectives/intensifiers, using a wider variety of structures, etc.

Worksheet 2.7 Le sport et le fitness Assignment 2: speaking

Module 2 Défi
Le sport et le fitness
Assignment 2: speaking
Studio 3 Rouge Feuille 2.7

You are going to create a podcast on healthy eating.

A Complete the 'Prépa' worksheet.

B Work in groups of three. Each of you must choose a role.

Roles

1 Broadcaster – he/she sets up the podcast by asking general questions to get people thinking and gives advice about what you should eat to stay healthy.

2 Case study 1 – a person who has a healthy diet and gives examples of food that they typically eat, and what they ate yesterday.

3 Case study 2 – an unhealthy person, with a terrible diet who wants to get fit and says what he/she will do to change his/her life.

Think about the content for each role together. To learn your own role by heart, follow these steps:

a Write out your role.
b Practise saying it aloud.
c Rehearse with your group and keep looking at your notes until you think you are ready to have a go without them.
d Try to perform your role without your notes, but keep them close by in case you need to sneak a look at them.
e Practise, practise, practise.

C Perform your podcast for your class. Judge the podcast of each of the other groups using the criteria below.

Give a mark out of 5 for each category:

- pronunciation
- confidence
- fluency
- range of structures.

You can achieve levels 4–6 for this assignment.

Level 4	Use your knowledge of grammar to adapt phrases. Include a personal response. Make your sentences longer by using connectives, and add opinions.
Level 5	Use varied language. Use the present tense and another tense, e.g. the near future or the perfect tense.
Level 6	Use descriptive language and a variety of structures. Show that you can use the present, the past and the future tenses.

Worksheet 2.8 Le sport et le fitness: Prépa

Module 2 Défi
Le sport et le fitness
Prépa
Studio 3 Rouge Feuille 2.8

A Unjumble these questions, then ask a partner the questions and note down his/her responses.

1 en Es- forme tu?
2 Est-ce assez que de tu légumes manges?
3 légumes comme aimes que tu Qu'est-ce?
4 Est-ce que ton tu tout devant passes un temps écran libre?
5 tu? Qu'est-ce mangé hier que soir as
6 fais Est-ce que au tu 30 minutes jour moins par d'activité?

B Read the text and answer true (T) or false (F) to the questions below.

Pour être en forme, il faut manger cinq portions de fruits ou de légumes par jour.

Il faut aussi manger trois produits laitiers, c'est-à-dire le fromage ou les yaourts.

Ensuite, il faut manger du pain, des céréales, des pommes de terre ou des légumes secs à chaque repas.

Il faut limiter les boissons gazeuses et il faut limiter aussi la consommation de matières grasses, de produits sucrés et de sel. Il faut faire 30 minutes d'activité physique par jour.

Enfin, il faut dormir huit heures par nuit et il faut éviter le stress. Et voilà!

légumes secs = *pulses*
matières grasses = *fatty foods*
éviter = *to avoid*

1 To be healthy, you have to eat six portions of fruit or vegetables per day ____
2 You have to eat three dairy products. ____
3 You have to eat bread, cereal, potatoes or pulses at each meal ____
4 You have to limit the amount of water you drink. ____
5 You can eat as much sugar or salt as you like. ____
6 You have to sleep ten hours a night. ____

C Use the text below as a model to write a speech as if you were an unhealthy person. Practise reading your text aloud.

Include the following points:

- Yesterday you ate a lot of sweets and cakes.
- You drank fizzy drinks.
- Normally you don't eat healthily.
- But in future you will eat five portions of fruit and vegetables.
- You will do 30 minutes of exercise per day.
- You will sleep eight hours per night.

Hier, j'ai mangé beaucoup de fruits, une banane, une pomme et des fraises et j'ai bu beaucoup d'eau. Normalement, je mange cinq portions de fruits ou de légumes par jour. Mon problème, c'est que je n'aime pas le sport, mais à l'avenir je ferai 30 minutes d'activité par jour. J'irai au collège à pied par exemple, au lieu de prendre le bus.

Answers

A 1 Es-tu en forme?
2 Est-ce que tu manges assez de légumes?
3 Qu'est-ce que tu aimes comme légumes?
4 Est-ce que tu passes tout ton temps libre devant un écran?
5 Qu'est-ce que tu as mangé hier soir?
6 Est-ce que tu fais au moins 30 minutes d'activité par jour?

B 1 F **2** T **3** T **4** F **5** F **6** F

2 J'écris

The challenge

- Writing a 150-word blog entry on a decision to adopt a healthier lifestyle

Overview

Explain how this section works.

– Pupils read the context and what they need to do to complete the challenge.

– They then read the list of suggested details to include. Explain that they should use this both to help structure their content and as a checklist as part of their final preparations.

– Explain that the exercises which follow in this section are structured to help them prepare for the extended writing task.

– Before starting, pupils read the POSM feature: this will help them to improve their performance. Encourage them to use this approach routinely in writing tasks.

Programme of Study references

GV1 Tenses (past, present and future)
GV3 Developing vocabulary
GV4 Accuracy (grammar; spelling; punctuation)
LC4 Expressing ideas (writing)
LC8 Writing creatively

1 Note down ten places you might have gone to last weekend.

Pupils brainstorm to list ten places they could have visited last weekend. Some suggestions are supplied.

2 Unjumble these verbs in the perfect tense. Add five verbs of your own.

Pupils write the correct forms of the jumbled perfect tense verbs. They then write fi ve different perfect tense verbs. Draw their attention to the tip box on using the verb tables at the end of the Pupil Book.

Answers

1 *je suis sorti* **2** j'ai mangé **3** j'ai regardé
4 on est allés **5** j'ai pris

3 Copy the table and put the time markers into the right column. Choose at least three to use in your own text.

Pupils copy out the table and complete it by writing the time expressions in the correct columns. They then choose three expressions to use in their writing.

Answers

past	present	future
le weekend dernier hier samedi dernier dimanche dernier	aujourd'hui ce matin	à l'avenir demain la semaine prochaine

4 Find five expressions with *il faut* in this word snake. Add four more of your own.

Pupils rewrite the word snake as sentences *with il faut*. They then write four sentences of their own using *il faut*.

Answers

Il faut manger équilibré.
Il ne faut pas manger trop de frites.
Il faut être actif.
Il ne faut pas manger trop de sucreries.
Il faut boire beaucoup d'eau.

5 Decode these sentences in the future tense. Choose three you could use in your blog entry.

Pupils write out the half-visible sentences. They then choose three of them to use in their blog entry.

Answers

a J'irai au collège à vélo et pas en voiture.
b Je mangerai équilibré.
c Je ferai au moins trente minutes d'exercice par jour.
d Je prendrai les escaliers.
e Je jouerai au foot au lieu de jouer à des jeux vidéo.
f Je ne mangerai plus de frites et je ne mangerai plus de hamburgers.

6 Find the correct sentence half to complete the sentences in this text. Think carefully about the context and the tense you need to look for.

Pupils complete the gap-fill text using the sentence endings supplied. Remind them to think about the context and appropriate tense each time. Draw their attention to the tip box on features to include to improve their writing.

Answers

1 c **2** e **3** a **4** d **5** f **6** b

7 Plan and write your blog entry.

Pupils plan and write their blog entry. Draw their attention to the tip box on how to check their work.

2 Studio Grammaire

The *Studio Grammaire* section provides a more detailed summary of the key grammar covered in the module, along with further exercises to practise these points. The activities on ActiveTeach pp.048 and 049 are repeated from elsewhere in the module.

Grammar topics

- using *nous* in the present tense
- *il faut*
- the future tense
- negatives
- using three tenses together

Using *nous* in the present tense

1 Translate these verbs into French.

Pupils translate the English verbs listed into French, using the *nous* form.

Answers

1 nous surfons **2** nous aimons **3** nous suivons
4 nous regardons **5** nous allons **6** nous avons

il faut

2 Choose the appropriate infinitive for each sentence. Then translate the sentences into English.

Pupils complete the *il faut* + infinitive sentences, selecting the correct verb from the infinitives supplied. They then translate the completed sentences into English.

Answers

1 Il faut **aimer** la compétition.
You must like competition.
2 Il faut **avoir** un bon programme pour être en forme.
You must have a good programme/schedule to get fit.
3 Il faut **apprendre** à suivre les règles.
You must learn to follow rules.
4 Il faut bien **dormir** parce qu'on ne peut pas gagner si on est fatigué.
You must sleep well because you can't win if you are tired.
5 Il faut **être** motivé.
You must be motivated.
6 Il faut **faire** de l'exercice.
You must do some exercise.
7 Il ne faut pas **manger** trop de sucreries.
You must not eat too many sweets.
8 Il ne faut pas **boire** trop de boissons gazeuses.
You must not drink too many fizzy drinks.

The future tense

3 Write out all the parts of the verbs *regarder* and *aller* in the future tense.

Pupils write out the complete paradigms of *regarder* and *aller* in the future tense.

Answers

regarder	**aller**
je regarderai	j'irai
tu regarderas	tu iras
il/elle/on regardera	il/elle/on ira
nous regarderons	nous irons
vous regarderez	vous irez
ils/elles regarderont	ils/elles iront

4 Put the verbs in brackets into the future tense.

Pupils rewrite the sentences putting the verbs in brackets into the future tense.

Answers

1 mangerai **2** irai **3** prendrai **4** ferai
5 jouerai **6** sera

5 Copy and complete the text using the correct forms of the future tense.

Pupils copy and complete the text, replacing the picture prompts with phrases using verbs in the future tense.

Answers

À l'avenir, je **ferai au moins trente minutes d'exercice par jour**. Je jouerai au volley avec mes copains. On **jouera au foot** après le collège et puis, après le match, **on prendra/mangera un sandwich** au café. Nous mangerons tous équilibré. Akim **ne mangera pas/plus de frites** et Mohamed **ne boira pas/plus de boissons gazeuses**. Et toi, qu'est-ce que tu **feras** pour être en forme?

6 Translate the text from exercise 5 into English.

Pupils translate the completed text from exercise 5 into English.

Example answer

In the future, I will do at least thirty minutes' exercise a day. I will play volleyball with my friends. We will play football after school and then, after the match, we will have/eat a sandwich at the café. We will all eat healthily. Akim will not eat (any more) chips and Mohamed will not drink (any more) fizzy drinks. And you, what will you do to get fit?

Negatives

7 Make these sentences negative using the construction in brackets. Translate the sentences into English.

Pupils rewrite the sentences, making them negative by using the negative expressions in brackets. They then translate the negative sentences into English.

Answers

1 Je n'aime pas la nourriture de fastfood.
I don't like fast food.

2 Elle ne fera pas trente minutes d'exercice par jour.
She won't do thirty minutes of exercise per day.

3 Tu ne mangeras plus de frites?
Won't you eat chips any more?

4 Nous n'allons jamais à la salle de gym.
We never go to the gym.

5 Je ne bois jamais de boissons gazeuses.
I never drink fizzy drinks.

6 Je n'irai plus au fastfood.
I won't go to the fast-food restaurant any more.

Using three tenses together

8 Copy this text and put the verbs in brackets into the correct tense.

Pupils copy and complete the text replacing the infinitives with verbs in the correct tense.

Answers

Hier soir, j'**ai regardé** la télévision avec mon frère. Nous **avons choisi** une émission de télé-réalité et ensuite, j'**ai surfé** un peu sur Internet. Mais je n'ai pas fait mes devoirs et j'**ai décidé** que je passe trop de temps devant un écran. Ce n'est pas sain. On ne **peut** pas être en forme si on ne bouge pas. Alors, hier, j'**ai pris** une résolution. À partir de demain, je **passerai** une heure à surfer sur Internet et je **regarderai** la télé pendant trente minutes, pas plus.

2 À toi

Self-access reading and writing

A Reinforcement

1 Lis les textes et note le bon prénom. (Reading L6)

Reading. Pupils read the texts and identify who is being described in each sentence, David or Serafino.

Answers

1 David **2** Serafino **3** Serafino **4** David
5 David **6** Serafino

2 Écris un paragraphe pour chaque personne. (Writing L5)

Writing. Pupils write a paragraph for each person (Axel, Sierra and Gilles), using the picture prompts supplied.

Example answers

Axel: *Je m'appelle Axel. Je n'aime pas trop le sport mais je veux être en forme, alors voici mes résolutions pour l'avenir.* Premièrement, j'irai dans la salle de sport deux fois par semaine. Deuxièmement, je ne mangerai pas de chips et troisièmement, je ne boirai pas de boissons gazeuses.

Sierra: Je m'appelle Sierra. Je n'aime pas trop le sport mais je veux être en forme, alors voici mes resolutions pour l'avenir. Premièrement, j'irai au collège à pied. Deuxièmement, je ne mangerai pas de sucreries et finalement j'arrêterai de manger des frites.

Gilles: Je m'appelle Gilles. Je n'aime pas trop le sport mais je veux être en forme, alors voici mes resolutions pour l'avenir. Premièrement, je ne prendrai pas le bus, j'irai au collège à pied. Deuxièmement, je ne mangerai plus de hamburgers. Troisièmement, je mangerai beaucoup de légumes et je boirai aussi beaucoup d'eau.

B Extension

1 Lis l'interview avec Mathilde Bergeron. Copie et complète la fiche. (Reading L6)

Reading. Pupils read the interview with Mathilde Bergeron. They then copy and complete the profile. Some vocabulary is glossed for support.

Answers

Sports pratiqués: l'escrime, la course, l'équitation, la natation et le tir au pistolet

Programme d'entraînement: tous les jours de 9h30 à 12h30 et de 15h45 à 19h, course et natation, l'escrime, quatre séances de musculation et de préparation physique, deux séances de tir et deux séances d'équitation par semaine

Se prépare pour: les championnats d'Europe

Discipline préférée: l'escrime

Ambitions pour l'année: se qualifier pour les Jeux olympiques

Choses à prouver: se donner à fond pour remplir ses objectifs

2 Écris une interview avec Djamel Monfils (un triathlète imaginaire). Utilise les renseignements suivants et invente d'autres choses si tu veux. (Writing L5)

Writing. Pupils write an interview with Djamel Monfils (an imaginary triathlete), using the details supplied and the interview in exercise 1 as a model, and adding further details if they want.

3 Module 3: À l'horizon

Unit & Learning objectives	Programme of Study references	Key language	Grammar and other language features
1 Es-tu fait pour ce métier? (pp. 54–55) Describing jobs Using masculine and feminine nouns	**GV2** Grammatical structures (gender) **GV3** Developing vocabulary **GV3** Opinions and discussions **LC3** Conversation	*Je veux être …* *avocat(e)* *botaniste* *chanteur/chanteuse,* etc. *Je suis accro à/aux …* *Je suis intéressé(e) par …* etc. *C'est mon rêve!* *Ce serait bien.* etc.	**G** nouns for jobs – developing speaking skills – developing writing skills
2 Le monde est un village (pp. 56–57) Learning languages Using modal verbs	**GV2** Grammatical structures (modal verbs) **LC1** Listening and responding **LC4** Expressing ideas (speaking) **LC5** Speaking coherently and confidently	*acheter, rencontrer, voir, voyager,* etc. *l'emploi, un stage, un candidat, créatif/créative, varié(e),* etc. *C'est un avantage.* *C'est essentiel.* *C'est un plus.*	**G** modal verbs *pouvoir, vouloir, devoir* – developing speaking skills
3 Quand j'étais plus jeune … (pp. 58–59) Saying what you used to do Using the imperfect tense	**GV1** Tenses (imperfect) **LC5** Accurate pronunciation and intonation **LC6** Reading comprehension **LC8** Writing creatively	*j'étais* *j'avais* *j'aimais* *je faisais* *je jouais* *je regardais* *je n'aimais pas*	**G** the imperfect tense – developing writing skills
4 Ta vie sera comment? (pp. 60–61) Discussing your future and your past Practising the future and imperfect tenses	**GV1** Tenses (future and imperfect) **GV4** Accuracy (grammar) **LC3** Conversation **LC4** Expressing ideas (writing)	*Je quitterai le collège.* *Je ferai un apprentissage.* *Je ferai le tour du monde.* *Je voyagerai.* *je travaillerai* *Je tomberai amoureux/amoureuse de quelqu'un.* *j'habiterai* *J'aurai une Ferrari.* *je serai*	**G** the future tense – developing speaking skills – developing writing skills

Unit & Learning objectives	Programme of Study references	Key language	Grammar and other language features
5 Mon boulot (pp. 62–63) Talking about your job Using different tenses together	**GV1** Tenses (using different tenses together) **LC3** Conversation **LC6** Reading comprehension **LC8** Writing creatively	*Qu'est-ce que tu fais dans la vie?* *Est-ce que tu as beaucoup d'expérience?* *Quelles sont les qualités requises pour ce métier?* *Quelles langues parles-tu?* *Que feras-tu à l'avenir?* etc. *communiquer, coordonner,* etc. *attentif/attentive, frustrant(e),* etc.	**G** question forms **G** using different tenses together – developing speaking skills – developing writing skills – developing listening skills
Bilan et Révisions (pp. 64–65) Pupils' checklist and practice exercises			
En plus: Un portrait professionnel (pp. 66–67) Investigating jobs using languages	**LC1** Listening and responding **LC3** Conversation (dealing with the unexpected) **LC6** Reading comprehension **LC8** Writing creatively	Review of language from the module	– developing writing skills – developing listening skills
Je parle (pp. 68–69) Extended speaking practice	**GV1** Tenses (past, present and future) **LC4** Expressing ideas (speaking) **LC5** Speaking coherently and confidently	Review of language from the module	– developing speaking skills – checking your work
Studio Grammaire (pp. 70–71) Detailed grammar summary and practice exercises			**G** modal verbs **G** the future tense **G** question forms **G** the imperfect tense **G** using three tenses together
À toi (pp. 122–123) Self-access reading and writing at two levels			

3 1 Es-tu fait pour ce métier?

Learning objectives

- Describing jobs
- Using masculine and feminine nouns

Programme of Study references

GV2 Grammatical structures (gender)
GV3 Developing vocabulary
GV3 Opinions and discussions
LC3 Conversation

FCSE links

Unit 2: Education and future plans (Future plans: after school, jobs and careers, further study)

Grammar

- nouns for jobs

Key language

Qu'est-ce que tu veux faire plus tard?
Je veux être …
avocat(e)
botaniste
chanteur/chanteuse
chauffeur de taxi/camion
comptable
diplomate
directeur/directrice de magasin
footballeur
guide touristique
infirmier/infirmière
ingénieur(e)
interprète
journaliste
juge
médecin généraliste
pilote
professeur
sociologue
vétérinaire
webdesigner
Je suis accro à/aux …
Je suis intéressé(e) par …
Ma passion, c'est …
… m'intéresse/me fascine
C'est mon rêve!
Ce serait bien.
Pas vraiment.
Ce serait ennuyeux.
Pourquoi pas?
Tu rigoles!
Ça ne m'intéresse pas du tout.
le métier
la profession

PLTS

C Creative thinkers

Cross-curricular

ICT: word-processing
PSHE: assessing interests in relation to options in learning and work, exploring options and choices in career contexts

Resources

Audio files:
31_Module3_Unit1_Ex1.mp3
32_Module3_Unit1_Ex3.mp3
33_Module3_Unit1_Ex6.mp3
Workbooks:
Cahier d'exercices Rouge, page 25
ActiveTeach:
Starter 1 resource
p.054 Flashcards
p.055 Reading skills
p.055 Learning skills
ActiveLearn:
Listening, Reading
Vocabulary

Starter 1

Aim

To use reading strategies to work out new vocabulary

Write up the following. Explain that they are jobs and give pupils two minutes to translate them into English.

avocat
infirmier
directeur de magasin
médecin généraliste
comptable
webdesigner
professeur
vétérinaire

Hear answers. Ask pupils how they worked out the words, reminding them as necessary of the various reading strategies (cognates, using what they know, guesswork/elimination, etc.).

Alternative Starter 1:

Use ActiveTeach p.054 Flashcards to introduce jobs.

1 Écoute et écris la bonne lettre. (1–8)
(Listening L4)

Listening. Pupils listen to eight conversations and identify the job mentioned in each one by writing the letter of the correct picture.

Audioscript Track 31

1 – *Qu'est-ce que tu veux faire plus tard?*
– *Je veux être avocate.*

2 – *Qu'est-ce que tu veux faire plus tard?*
– *Je veux être médecin généraliste.*

3 – *Qu'est-ce que tu veux faire plus tard?*
– *Je veux être comptable.*

4 – *Qu'est-ce que tu veux faire plus tard?*
– *Je voudrais être vétérinaire.*

5 – *Qu'est-ce que tu veux faire plus tard?*
– *Je veux être professeur.*

6 – *Qu'est-ce que tu veux faire plus tard?*
– *Je veux être webdesigner.*

7 – *Qu'est-ce que tu veux faire plus tard?*
– *Je voudrais être directrice de magasin.*

8 – *Qu'est-ce que tu veux faire plus tard?*
– *Je veux être infirmier.*

Answers

1 a **2** d **3** e **4** h **5** g **6** f **7** c **8** b

2 Fais correspondre les personnes et les professions de l'exercice 1. (Reading L4)

Reading. Pupils read what the people say about their interests and write the appropriate job for each one.

Answers

See exercise 3.

3 Écoute et vérifie tes réponses. (1–8) (Listening L4)

Listening. Pupils listen and check their answers to exercise 2.

Audioscript Track 32

1 – Je m'appelle Éva, je suis accro aux multimédias. Je veux être webdesigner.

2 – Bonjour! Je m'appelle Clarisse et je veux être directrice de magasin car ma passion, c'est la mode.

3 – Je suis Dimitri et j'adore les animaux. C'est pour ça que je voudrais être vétérinaire.

4 – Je m'appelle Jamel. La médecine m'intéresse, alors je veux être médecin généraliste.

5 – Et toi, Fatima?
– Moi, je suis intéressée par la justice. Je veux être avocate.

6 – Qu'est-ce que tu veux faire plus tard, Alexandra?
– Je voudrais être comptable parce que les chiffres me fascinent.

7 – Qu'est-ce que tu veux faire plus tard, Yann?
– Moi, j'aime travailler avec les enfants. Je veux être professeur! Je suis courageux, hein!

8 – Je m'appelle Albane. J'aime aider les autres. Je veux être infirmière.

Answers

Éva – webdesigner
Clarisse – directrice de magasin
Dimitri – vétérinaire
Jamel – médecin généraliste
Fatima – avocate
Alexandra – comptable
Yann – professeur
Albane – infirmière

R Pupils working in pairs take it in turn to read out one of the statements in exercise 2, e.g. *J'aime travailler avec les enfants.*, and to respond with the correct job, e.g. *Je veux être professeur.*

Studio Grammaire: nouns for jobs

Use the *Studio Grammaire* box to cover nouns for jobs.

4 En tandem. Fais une liste de dix emplois qui t'intéressent. Cherche les mots dans le dictionnaire, si nécessaire. (Writing L2)

Writing. In pairs: pupils make a list of ten jobs that interest them, looking up any words they don't know in a dictionary. Some ideas are supplied.

Starter 2

Aim

To review job vocabulary

Give pupils two minutes working in pairs to write down in French as many different jobs as they can. They then work with another pair. Each pair takes it in turn to read a job from their list.

If the other pair has it, both pairs cross it off. The winning pair is the one with the most jobs left on their list at the end.

5 Fais un sondage dans la classe. Pose cette question à dix personnes. Note les réponses. (Speaking L5)

Speaking. Pupils carry out a class survey, asking ten people what they want to do in the future. A sample exchange is supplied. Draw pupils' attention to the tip box on improving their speaking by including reasons for their choices. Remind them that *parce que* and *car* are useful words in this context.

6 Écoute. Que pensent-ils des professions? Copie et complète le tableau en anglais. (1–4). (Listening L6)

Listening. Pupils copy out the table. They listen to four conversations in which people say what they think about various jobs. They then complete the table with the details in English. Draw their attention to the list of expressions used to give opinions in this context.

Audioscript Track 33

1 – *Être avocate, ça t'intéresse?*
– *Oui, pourquoi pas? Ce serait bien. Moi, je suis intéressée par la justice. J'ai visité une cour de justice, une fois, et c'était fascinant.*

2 – *Être footballeur, ça t'intéresse?*
– *Oui, c'est mon rêve! Ce serait génial. Je m'entraîne tous les jours. Hier, j'ai joué au foot pendant trois heures.*

3 – *Être comptable, ça t'intéresse?*
– *Tu rigoles! Ça ne m'intéresse pas du tout. Ce serait nul. Je déteste les chiffres. J'ai toujours détesté les maths.*

4 – *Être professeur, ça t'intéresse?*
– *Pas vraiment. Ce serait ennuyeux. Être coureur automobile, par contre, c'est mon rêve, parce que j'ai une passion pour les voitures. La première fois que j'ai vu une Ferrari, c'était l'amour!*

Answers

	profession	opinion	other details
1	lawyer	✓	interested in justice, visited a court of justice (once), it was fascinating
2	footballer	✓✓	trains every day, played football for 3 hours yesterday
3	accountant	××	lousy, hates numbers and has always hated maths
4	teacher racing driver	× ✓✓	boring passion for cars, the first time he saw a Ferrari it was love

7 En tandem. Fais des dialogues. Utilise les professions de l'exercice 1. (Speaking L5)

Speaking. In pairs: pupils make up dialogues, in which they discuss the jobs in exercise 1. A sample exchange is given. *Ce serait bien* is glossed for support.

8 Choisis les bons mots pour compléter le texte. (Reading L6)

Reading. Pupils complete the gap-fill text by choosing from the three options supplied for each gap. Some vocabulary is glossed for support.

Answers

1 les voitures **2** parler **3** patience **4** dernière
5 voiture **6** chercher

9 Écris un paragraphe sur un métier que tu aimerais faire. (Writing L5)

PLTS C

Writing. Pupils write a paragraph on the job they'd like to do. A framework is supplied. Draw their attention to the tip box on improving their writing. You could suggest that pupils do this exercise on a computer, then read through all the tip boxes in the unit and check that they have implemented the advice given. They can then produce a second, improved version of their text.

Plenary

Review giving opinions on jobs. Ask a pupil to suggest a job. Another pupil then says why he/she would like to do that job; a third pupil disagrees, again explaining why. Repeat, giving as many people as possible the chance to speak.

Workbook, page 25

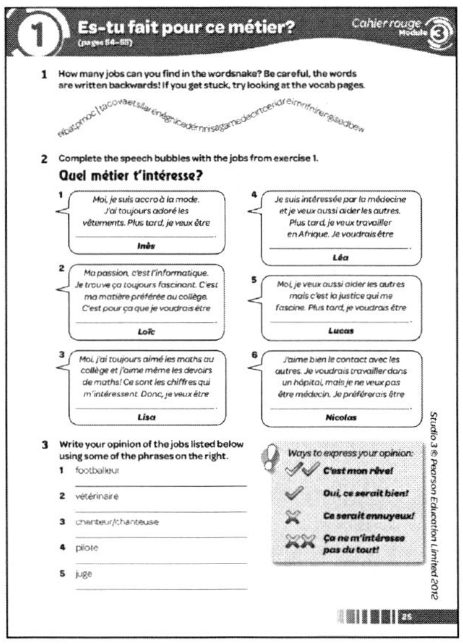
1 Es-tu fait pour ce métier?
Cahier rouge Module 3

1 How many jobs can you find in the wordsnake? Be careful, the words are written backwards! If you get stuck, try looking at the vocab pages.

2 Complete the speech bubbles with the jobs from exercise 1.

Quel métier t'intéresse?

1 *Moi, je suis accro à la mode. J'ai toujours adoré les vêtements. Plus tard, je veux être* ________. Inès

2 *Ma passion, c'est l'informatique. Je trouve ça toujours fascinant. C'est ma matière préférée au collège. C'est pour ça que je voudrais être* ________. Loïc

3 *Moi, j'ai toujours aimé les maths au collège et j'aime même les devoirs de maths! Ce sont les chiffres qui m'intéressent. Donc, je veux être* ________. Lisa

4 *Je suis intéressée par la médecine et je veux aussi aider les autres. Plus tard, je veux travailler en Afrique. Je voudrais être* ________. Léa

5 *Moi, je veux aussi aider les autres mais c'est la justice qui me fascine. Plus tard, je voudrais être* ________. Lucas

6 *J'aime bien le contact avec les autres. Je voudrais travailler dans un hôpital, mais je ne veux pas être médecin. Je préférerais être* ________. Nicolas

3 Write your opinion of the jobs listed below using some of the phrases on the right.
1 footballeur
2 vétérinaire
3 chanteur/chanteuse
4 pilote
5 juge

Ways to express your opinion:
✓✓ C'est mon rêve!
✓ Oui, ce serait bien!
× Ce serait ennuyeux!
×× Ça ne m'intéresse pas du tout!

Studio 3 © Pearson Education Limited 2012

25

Answers

1 comptable, avocat, médecin généraliste, directrice de magasin, infirmier, webdesigner

2 **1** directrice de magasin **2** webdesigner
3 comptable **4** médecin généraliste
5 avocat **6** infirmier

3 (Answers will vary.)

Worksheet 3.1 Reading a poem – 'The best jobs'

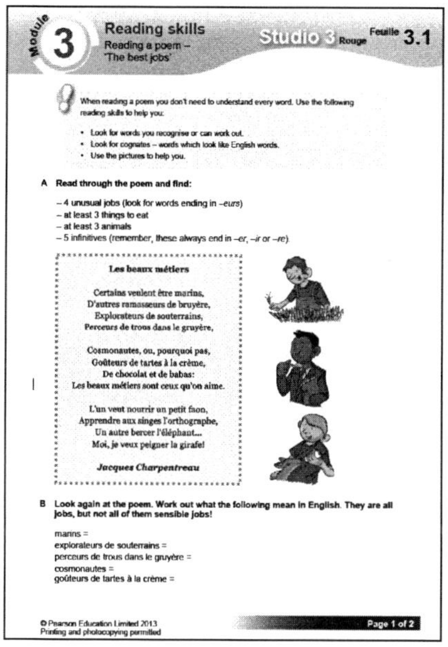
Module 3 Reading skills
Reading a poem – 'The best jobs'
Studio 3 Rouge Feuille 3.1

When reading a poem you don't need to understand every word. Use the following reading skills to help you:

- Look for words you recognise or can work out.
- Look for cognates – words which look like English words.
- Use the pictures to help you.

A Read through the poem and find:

– 4 unusual jobs (look for words ending in *–eurs*)
– at least 3 things to eat
– at least 3 animals
– 5 infinitives (remember, these always end in *–er*, *–ir* or *–re*)

Les beaux métiers

Certains veulent être marins,
D'autres ramasseurs de bruyère,
Explorateurs de souterrains,
Perceurs de trous dans le gruyère,

Cosmonautes, ou, pourquoi pas,
Goûteurs de tartes à la crème,
De chocolat et de babas:
Les beaux métiers sont ceux qu'on aime.

L'un veut nourrir un petit faon,
Apprendre aux singes l'orthographe,
Un autre bercer l'éléphant...
Moi, je veux peigner la girafe!

Jacques Charpentreau

B Look again at the poem. Work out what the following mean in English. They are all jobs, but not all of them sensible jobs!

marins =
explorateurs de souterrains =
perceurs de trous dans le gruyère =
cosmonautes =
goûteurs de tartes à la crème =

© Pearson Education Limited 2013
Printing and photocopying permitted
Page 1 of 2

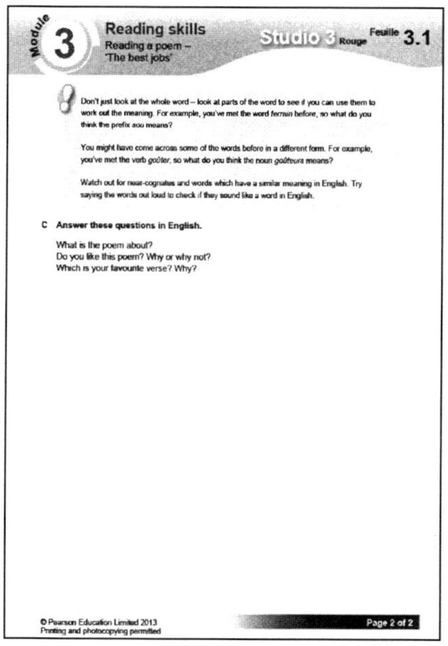
Module 3 Reading skills
Reading a poem – 'The best jobs'
Studio 3 Rouge Feuille 3.1

Don't just look at the whole word – look at parts of the word to see if you can use them to work out the meaning. For example, you've met the word *terrain* before, so what do you think the prefix *sou* means?

You might have come across some of the words before in a different form. For example, you've met the verb *goûter*, so what do you think the noun *goûteurs* means?

Watch out for near-cognates and words which have a similar meaning in English. Try saying the words out loud to check if they sound like a word in English.

C Answer these questions in English.

What is the poem about?
Do you like this poem? Why or why not?
Which is your favourite verse? Why?

© Pearson Education Limited 2013
Printing and photocopying permitted
Page 2 of 2

Answers

A

– **4 unusual jobs:** ramasseurs de bruyère, explorateurs de souterrains, perceurs de trous dans le gruyère, goûteurs de tartes à la crème

– **at least 3 things to eat:** (3 from:) gruyère, tartes, crème, chocolat, babas

– **at least 3 animals:** (3 from:) faon, singes, éléphant, giraffe

– **5 infinitives:** être, nourrir, apprendre, bercer, peigner

B

marins = *sailors, mariners*

explorateurs de souterrains = *underground explorers*

perceurs de trous dans le gruyère = *drillers or piercers of holes in gruyere cheese*

cosmonautes = *cosmonauts*

goûteurs de tartes à la crème = *cream tart tasters*

C

Answers will vary.

Worksheet 3.2 Looking up nouns in a dictionary

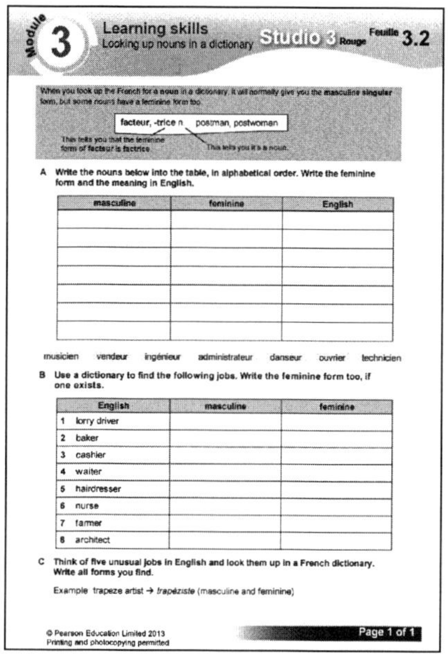
Module 3 Learning skills
Looking up nouns in a dictionary
Studio 3 Rouge Feuille 3.2

When you look up the French for a **noun** in a dictionary, it will normally give you the **masculine singular** form, but some nouns have a feminine form too.

facteur, -trice n. postman, postwoman

This tells you that the feminine form of **facteur** is **factrice**.
This tells you it's a noun.

A Write the nouns below into the table, in alphabetical order. Write the feminine form and the meaning in English.

masculine	feminine	English

musicien vendeur ingénieur administrateur danseur ouvrier technicien

B Use a dictionary to find the following jobs. Write the feminine form too, if one exists.

English	masculine	feminine
1 lorry driver		
2 baker		
3 cashier		
4 waiter		
5 hairdresser		
6 nurse		
7 farmer		
8 architect		

C Think of five unusual jobs in English and look them up in a French dictionary. Write all forms you find.

Example: trapeze artist → *trapéziste* (masculine and feminine)

© Pearson Education Limited 2013
Printing and photocopying permitted
Page 1 of 1

Answers

A

masculine	**feminine**	**English**
administrateur	administratrice	administrator
danseur	danseuse	dancer
ingénieur	ingénieure	engineer
musicien	musicienne	musician
ouvrier	ouvrière	worker
technicien	technicienne	technician
vendeur	vendeuse	salesperson

B

English	**masculine**	**feminine**
1 lorry driver	camionneur	camionneuse
2 baker	boulanger	boulangère
3 cashier	caissier	caissière
4 waiter	serveur	serveuse
5 hairdresser	coiffeur	coiffeuse
6 nurse	infirmier	infirmière
7 farmer	fermier	fermière
8 architect	architecte	architecte

3 2 Le monde est un village

Learning objectives

- Learning languages
- Using modal verbs

Programme of Study references

GV2 Grammatical structures (modal verbs)

LC1 Listening and responding

LC4 Expressing ideas (speaking)

LC5 Speaking coherently and confidently

Grammar

- modal verbs *pouvoir*, *vouloir*, *devoir*

Key language

acheter
aimer le contact avec
les gens/les autres
discuter
rencontrer
respecter
rigoler
vendre
voir
voyager
le travail
le boulot
l'emploi (m)
le métier
la profession
un stage
un poste
un candidat
créatif/créative
varié(e)
C'est un avantage.
C'est essentiel.
C'est un plus.

PLTS

S Self-managers

Resources

Audio files:
34_Module3_Unit2_Ex1.mp3
35_Module3_Unit2_Ex5.mp3

Workbooks:
Cahier d'exercices Rouge, page 26

ActiveTeach:
Starter 2 resource
p.056 Grammar
p.056 Grammar practice
p.057 Video 5
p.057 Video worksheet 5
p.057 Thinking skills
p.057 Grammar skills

ActiveLearn:
Listening, Reading
Grammar

Starter 1

Aim

To introduce the topic

Have a short class discussion in English on the usefulness of learning foreign languages. How important are they? What can you do with them? Ask pupils what countries they would like to visit and why. Elicit examples of jobs using foreign languages. Ask what the title of the unit means.

1 Écoute et lis les textes. (Listening L5)

Listening. Pupils listen to four people talking about different jobs and read the texts at the same time.

Audioscript Track 34

A *Si on veut travailler avec les gens, parler une langue étrangère, c'est un plus. Quand on parle d'autres langues, on peut rencontrer des personnes intéressantes de cultures différentes. On doit aimer le contact avec les autres et respecter les différences, c'est important dans la vie et le travail.*

B *Si on veut être commercial export, parler une langue étrangère, c'est essentiel, parce qu'on doit acheter et vendre des produits dans la langue du pays où on travaille. Quand on est commercial export, on doit beaucoup voyager et donc, on peut voir le monde.*

C *Si on veut découvrir le monde, parler une langue étrangère, c'est essentiel. On doit être curieux et ouvert, c'est important. Les employeurs aiment ces qualités. Si on parle une langue étrangère et si on a voyagé, c'est un plus. On peut trouver un bon emploi.*

D *Si on veut trouver un bon emploi, parler une langue étrangère, c'est un avantage. Si on parle une autre langue, on peut travailler dans un autre pays, on peut discuter avec les gens, et surtout, on peut rigoler avec eux.*

Studio Grammaire: modal verbs *pouvoir*, *vouloir*, *devoir*

PLTS S

Use the Studio Grammaire box to cover the modal verbs *pouvoir*, *vouloir*, *devoir*. Ask pupils to identify patterns in the verb forms that will help in memorising them, e.g. *je* and *tu* forms being the same; *nous* and *vous* forms having the same vowels in the stem as the infinitive, etc. They might find it useful to mark the patterns using different colours of highlighter pens. There is more information and further practice on Pupil Book p. 70.

R Put the class into groups. Allocate each group a modal verb and give them some time to memorise it. Get each group to chant their verb together.

2 Relis les textes et corrige les erreurs dans ces phrases. (Reading L5)

Reading. Pupils read the texts in exercise 1 again. They then read the sentences about the texts and correct the errors in the sentences.

Answers

1 Si on veut travailler avec les gens, parler une langue étrangère, **c'est un plus**.
2 On doit **aimer** le contact avec les autres.
3 Quand on est commercial export, on doit vendre des produits **dans la langue du pays où on travaille**.
4 Avec les langues étrangères, **on peut voyager/trouver un bon emploi**.
5 Si on veut trouver un bon emploi, parler une autre langue, **c'est un avantage**.

Translate the texts in exercise 1 round the class.

Starter 2

Aim

To review *pouvoir, vouloir, devoir*

Write up the following. Give pupils two minutes working in pairs to complete the grid.

pouvoir		
	je veux	
tu peux		
		il/elle/on doit
	nous voulons	
vous pouvez		
		ils/elles doivent

Check answers. Remind pupils that identifying patterns in verb forms will help them memorise them.

Alternative Starter 2:

Use ActiveTeach p.056 Grammar practice to practise modal verbs.

3 Écris ton opinion sur l'importance des langues étrangères pour les métiers ci-dessous. (Writing L4)

Writing. Pupils write their own opinion on the importance of foreign languages for the jobs shown. A framework is supplied.

4 En tandem. Compare tes réponses à celles de ton/ta camarade. (Speaking L4)

Speaking. In pairs: pupils discuss their answers to exercise 3, finding points of agreement and disagreement. A sample exchange is supplied. Draw their attention to the tip box on improving their speaking by including reasons.

5 Écoute Christine et Mahmoud. Écris le bon prénom pour compléter chaque phrase. (Listening L6)

Listening. Pupils listen to Christine and Mahmoud talking about their jobs and the importance of speaking foreign languages. They then complete the gap-fill sentences by writing the appropriate name (Christine or Mahmoud) for each one. Some vocabulary is glossed for support.

Audioscript Track 35

– *Je m'appelle Christine et je suis acheteuse habillement, c'est-à-dire que j'achète des vêtements pour une entreprise. Je dois trouver les meilleurs vêtements à la mode pour mon employeur, à un prix raisonnable. J'aime beaucoup mon travail parce que c'est très créatif.*

Si on veut être acheteur ou acheteuse habillement, parler une langue étrangère, c'est essentiel.

Je parle français, anglais et italien et je voyage beaucoup. En février, je suis allée à Milan et en novembre, je dois aller à Londres.

Pour devenir acheteuse habillement, j'ai fait cinq ans en école de commerce et puis j'ai trouvé mon poste. L'année prochaine, je vais faire un stage à Barcelone et je vais apprendre l'espagnol. Ce sera super!

– *Je m'appelle Mahmoud et je travaille pour un comparateur de prix sur Internet. Je dois parler avec des gens partout dans le monde pour comparer les prix de différents produits. J'aime beaucoup mon travail parce que c'est intéressant et très varié. J'ai aussi beaucoup de contact avec les gens. J'aime bien ça.*

Si on veut être comparateur de prix sur Internet, parler une autre langue, c'est vraiment un plus.

Je parle français, anglais et japonais. Mes journées sont intéressantes. Hier matin, par exemple, j'ai discuté avec nos ingénieurs en Inde, ensuite j'ai parlé avec mes collègues européens, et j'ai terminé avec les Américains. Je ne m'ennuie jamais!

À l'avenir, je voudrais travailler pour un site communautaire comme Facebook, par exemple. Ce serait génial.

Answers

1 Christine **2** Mahmoud **3** Christine
4 Mahmoud **5** Mahmoud **6** Christine
7 Christine **8** Mahmoud

6 Choisis un de ces jobs. Prépare et fais un mini-exposé. (Speaking L4)

Speaking. Pupils choose the job of interpreter or lorry driver and prepare and give a short presentation on what's required for the job. Draw their attention to the tip box on improving their presentation by including opinions, different tenses and negatives. They should also look at the tips on giving presentations on Pupil Book p. 131.

Plenary

Review the modal verbs *pouvoir*, *vouloir* and *devoir* by prompting with verb forms in English; pupils respond with the appropriate French verb.

Then put the class into teams. Give pupils the name of a job in French. The first team has to respond with a sentence on the importance of foreign languages to that job and must include a modal verb in their response. Continue, giving a different job as prompt to each team. Remind them that they can use negatives to add variety to their responses.

Workbook, page 25

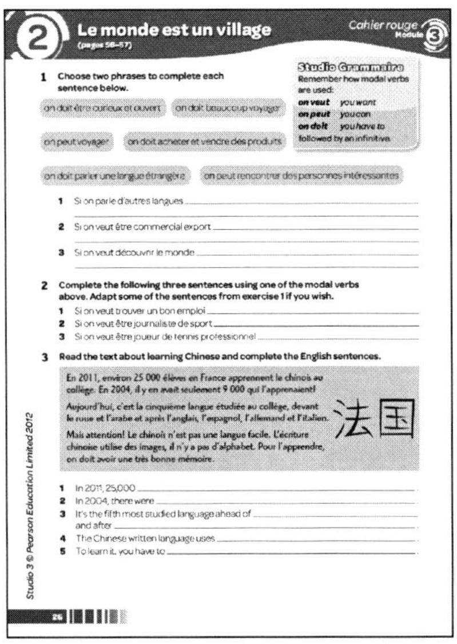

2 Le monde est un village
(pages 56–57)
Cahier rouge Module 3

1 Choose two phrases to complete each sentence below.

on doit être curieux et ouvert / on doit beaucoup voyager / on peut voyager / on doit acheter et vendre des produits / on doit parler une langue étrangère / on peut rencontrer des personnes intéressantes

Studio Grammaire
Remember how modal verbs are used:
on veut *you want*
on peut *you can*
on doit *you have to*
followed by an infinitive.

1 Si on parle d'autres langues ______
2 Si on veut être commercial export ______
3 Si on veut découvrir le monde ______

2 Complete the following three sentences using one of the modal verbs above. Adapt some of the sentences from exercise 1 if you wish.

1 Si on veut trouver un bon emploi ______
2 Si on veut être journaliste de sport ______
3 Si on veut être joueur de tennis professionnel ______

3 Read the text about learning Chinese and complete the English sentences.

En 2011, environ 25 000 élèves en France apprennent le chinois au collège. En 2004, il y en avait seulement 9 000 qui l'apprenaient!

Aujourd'hui, c'est la cinquième langue étudiée au collège, devant le russe et l'arabe et après l'anglais, l'espagnol, l'allemand et l'italien.

Mais attention! Le chinois n'est pas une langue facile. L'écriture chinoise utilise des images, il n'y a pas d'alphabet. Pour l'apprendre, on doit avoir une très bonne mémoire.

法国

1 In 2011, 25,000 ______.
2 In 2004, there were ______.
3 It's the fifth most studied language ahead of ______ and after ______.
4 The Chinese written language uses ______.
5 To learn it, you have to ______.

Studio 3 © Pearson Education Limited 2012

26

Answers

1 (Example answers:)

 1 … on peut voyager/on peut rencontrer des personnes intéressantes.

 2 … on doit acheter et vendre des produits/on doit parler une langue étrangère.

 3 … on doit beaucoup voyager/on doit être curieux et ouvert.

2 (Answers will vary.)

3 **1** pupils in France learned Chinese at school

 2 only 9,000

 3 Russian and Arabic; English, Spanish, German and Italian

 4 pictures, it doesn't have an alphabet

 5 have a very good memory

Worksheet 3.3 Cracking the code

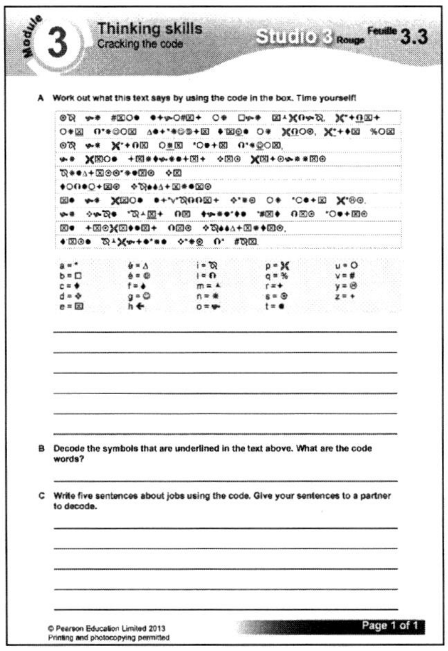

Module 3 Thinking skills
Cracking the code
Studio 3 Rouge Feuille 3.3

A Work out what this text says by using the code in the box. Time yourself!

a = ᐞ, b = □, c = ◆, d = ❖, e = ⊠, é = ∆, è = ◍, f = ♦, g = ☺, h ←, i = ☈, l = ∩, m = ▲, n = ✱, o = ✈, p = ✕, q = %, r = +, s = ⊙, t = ●, u = ○, v = #, y = ⊛, z = +

B Decode the symbols that are underlined in the text above. What are the code words?

C Write five sentences about jobs using the code. Give your sentences to a partner to decode.

© Pearson Education Limited 2013
Printing and photocopying permitted
Page 1 of 1

Answers

A Si on veut trouver un bon emploi, parler une langue étrangère c'est un plus,
parce que si on parle une autre langue, on peut rencontrer des personnes intéressantes de cultures différentes et on peut travailler dans un autre pays.
On doit aimer le contact avec les autres et respecter les différences, c'est important dans la vie.

B les langues

Worksheet 3.4 Using modal verbs

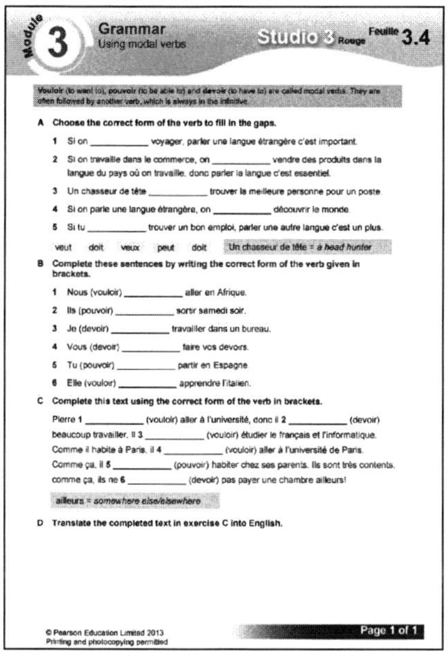
Module 3 Grammar
Using modal verbs
Studio 3 Rouge Feuille 3.4

Vouloir (to want to), *pouvoir* (to be able to) and *devoir* (to have to) are called modal verbs. They are often followed by another verb, which is always in the infinitive.

A Choose the correct form of the verb to fill in the gaps.

1 Si on __________ voyager, parler une langue étrangère c'est important.
2 Si on travaille dans le commerce, on __________ vendre des produits dans la langue du pays où on travaille, donc parler la langue c'est essentiel.
3 Un chasseur de tête __________ trouver la meilleure personne pour un poste.
4 Si on parle une langue étrangère, on __________ découvrir le monde.
5 Si tu __________ trouver un bon emploi, parler une autre langue c'est un plus.

veut doit veux peut doit

Un chasseur de tête = *a head hunter*

B Complete these sentences by writing the correct form of the verb given in brackets.

1 Nous (vouloir) __________ aller en Afrique.
2 Ils (pouvoir) __________ sortir samedi soir.
3 Je (devoir) __________ travailler dans un bureau.
4 Vous (devoir) __________ faire vos devoirs.
5 Tu (pouvoir) __________ partir en Espagne.
6 Elle (vouloir) __________ apprendre l'italien.

C Complete this text using the correct form of the verb in brackets.

Pierre **1** __________ (vouloir) aller à l'université, donc il **2** __________ (devoir) beaucoup travailler. Il **3** __________ (vouloir) étudier le français et l'informatique. Comme il habite à Paris, il **4** __________ (vouloir) aller à l'université de Paris. Comme ça, il **5** __________ (pouvoir) habiter chez ses parents. Ils sont très contents, comme ça, ils ne **6** __________ (devoir) pas payer une chambre ailleurs!

ailleurs = *somewhere else/elsewhere*

D Translate the completed text in exercise C into English.

© Pearson Education Limited 2013
Printing and photocopying permitted
Page 1 of 1

Answers

A 1 Si on **veut** voyager, parler une langue étrangère, c'est important.

2 Si on travaille dans le commerce, on **doit** vendre des produits dans la langue du pays où on travaille, donc parler la langue, c'est essentiel.

3 Un chasseur de tête **doit** trouver la meilleure personne pour un poste.

4 Si on parle une langue étrangère, on **peut** découvrir le monde.

5 Si tu **veux** trouver un bon emploi, parler une autre langue, c'est un plus.

B 1 Nous **voulons** aller en Afrique.

2 Ils **peuvent** sortir samedi soir.

3 Je **dois** travailler dans un bureau.

4 Vous **devez** faire vos devoirs.

5 Tu **peux** partir en Espagne.

6 Elle **veut** apprendre l'italien.

C Pierre **(1) veut** aller à l'université, donc il **(2) doit** beaucoup travailler. Il **(3) veut** étudier le français et l'informatique. Comme il habite à Paris, il **(4) veut** aller à l'université de Paris. Comme ça, il **(5) peut** habiter chez ses parents. Ils sont très contents, comme ça, ils ne **(6) doivent** pas payer une chamber ailleurs!

D Pierre wants to go to university, so he has to work a lot. He wants to study French and IT. As he lives in Paris, he wants to go to university in Paris. In this way, he will be able to live with his parents. They are very happy because this way, they will not have to pay for a room elsewhere!

Video

Episode 5: Les langues au travail

The team do a survey on the use of foreign languages in various professions, to help Hugo with his homework on the importance of languages at work. Video worksheet 5 can be used in conjunction with this episode.

Answers to video worksheet (ActiveTeach)

1 A Suggestions of what might be discussed:
- Languages enable you to talk and correspond with people from other countries. They provide the opportunity to work abroad and understand documents.
- Examples: teaching; anything export- or import-related; any job which involves foreign travel.
- Any European language, plus Mandarin, Japanese, Indonesian languages.
- It might be considered lazy and arrogant but many people do have this attitude. English is a world language.

2 A Hugo
B Marielle
C Mehdi
D Alex
E Samira

3 A (Answers will vary.)
B It's a cosmetics shop.
C *Que faites-vous dans la vie?*
D A diploma in commerce; you have to be capable of teamwork; *aimer le contact avec les clients* ('enjoy contact with customers').
E Speaking to foreign customers; ordering stock from abroad.

4 A They are going to the local tourist office.
B Samira.
C What is your typical working day like?
D Meeting tourists; organising tours; updating the website.
E A school exchange group from Spain.
F It's Flemish (spoken in Belgium).

5 A He's not sure.
B French.
C Her company has branches in 50 countries.

6 A Work and travel.
B He says it's essential to speak another language because we are in Europe.
C 'The language of love'. The others groan – typical Marielle!

3 Quand j'étais plus jeune …

(Pupil Book pp. 58–59)

Learning objectives

- Saying what you used to do
- Using the imperfect tense

Programme of Study references

GV1 Tenses (imperfect)

LC5 Accurate pronunciation and intonation

LC6 Reading comprehension

LC8 Writing creatively

FCSE links

Unit 2: Education and future plans (Future plans: Advantages and disadvantages of jobs)

Grammar

- the imperfect tense

Key language

j'étais
j'avais
j'aimais
je faisais
je jouais
je regardais
je n'aimais pas

PLTS

T Team workers

Resources

Audio files:

36_Module3_Unit3_Ex1.mp3
37_Module3_Unit3_Ex4.mp3

Workbooks:

Cahier d'exercices Rouge, page 27

ActiveTeach:

Starter 1 resource
Starter 2 resource
p.058 Grammar
p.058 Grammar practice
p.059 Class activity
p.059 Grammar skills

ActiveLearn:

Listening, Reading
Grammar

Starter 1

Aim

To introduce the concept of different past tenses

Write up the following. Give pupils two minutes to identify the verbs and translate both texts into English.

Le weekend dernier, je suis sorti avec mes copains. On a joué au bowling. C'était génial.

Le weekend dernier, je suis restée à la maison. J'ai regardé un DVD. C'était nul.

Check answers. Ask what tense is used for each verb. Ask if *était* is in the perfect tense. Encourage pupils to speculate on why a different tense is used here. Explain that *était* is in the imperfect tense and that one of the things the imperfect is used for is to say what things used to be like in the past.

1 Écoute et lis l'interview. (Listening L5)

Listening. Pupils listen to the journalist Salim Derechef talking about his childhood, and read the text at the same time.

Audioscript Track 36

Salim Derechef est journaliste. Dans cette interview, il nous parle de son enfance:

– *Est-ce que tu aimais le collège, Salim?*
– *Oui, j'aimais bien le collège. J'avais beaucoup d'amis. J'étais membre de plein de clubs. C'était génial.*
– *Quel genre d'élève étais-tu?*
– *J'étais bon élève. J'écoutais en classe, je faisais mes devoirs. J'aimais beaucoup l'histoire et le français. J'avais de bonnes notes!*
– *Quels étaient tes passetemps?*
– *Quand j'étais plus jeune, je faisais beaucoup de sport car j'adorais la compétition. Je jouais au volley et au foot, et je faisais du judo deux fois par semaine.*

2 Copie et complète le tableau pour Salim. (Reading L5)

Reading. Pupils copy out and complete the grid, using details from the interview in exercise 1.

Answers

Opinion sur les clubs (positive ou négative):	positive
Bon ou mauvais élève?	bon élève
Matières préférées:	l'histoire et le français
Passetemps:	le sport: le volley, le foot et le judo

3 Trouve l'équivalent de ces verbes dans le texte de l'exercice 1. (Reading L4)

Reading. Pupils find in the text in exercise 1 the French versions of the English verbs listed.

Answers

1 j'aimais **2** j'avais **3** j'étais **4** je faisais
5 j'adorais **6** je jouais

Studio Grammaire: imperfect tense

Use the *Studio Grammaire* box to cover the imperfect tense. There is more information and further practice on Pupil Book p. 71. Draw pupils' attention to the tip box on the pronunciation of imperfect tense verb endings.

R Pupils write out the full paradigm of *aimer* in the imperfect tense.

4 Écoute. Trouve les bonnes images pour chaque personne. Écris K pour Kevan ou M pour Madeleine. (Listening L5)

Listening. Pupils listen to Kevan and Madeleine being interviewed about their childhoods. They identify who the pictures (a–f) refer to, writing K (for Kevan) or M (for Madeleine) for each one.

Audioscript Track 37

- *Est-ce que tu aimais le collège, Kevan?*
- *Oui, j'adorais le collège. J'avais beaucoup d'amis et j'allais à beaucoup de clubs. C'était cool.*
- *Et toi, Madeleine, est-ce que tu aimais le collège?*
- *Non, je détestais le collège. Je n'avais pas beaucoup d'amis. J'étais très malheureuse. C'était affreux.*
- *Quel genre d'élève étais-tu, Kevan?*
- *J'étais bon élève. Je faisais mes devoirs. J'avais de très bonnes notes! J'aimais beaucoup les sciences.*
- *Et toi, Madeleine?*
- *Je n'étais pas très bonne élève. Je n'écoutais pas en classe, je ne faisais pas mes devoirs. J'avais de très mauvaises notes!*
- *Quels étaient tes passetemps, Madeleine?*
- *Quand j'étais petite, je lisais beaucoup et je regardais beaucoup de fi lms. Je ne faisais pas de sport. J'avais horreur de ça. Maintenant, j'aime jouer au squash.*
- *Et toi, Kevan, quels étaient tes passetemps?*
- *Quand j'étais petit, je faisais beaucoup de sport. Je jouais au foot et au tennis.*

Answers

a M **b** K **c** M **d** K **e** K **f** K

+ Pupils listen to the recording for exercise 4 again and answer the following questions.

1 Why didn't Madeleine like school?
2 Why wasn't she a good student?
3 What sports did she do at school?

Starter 2

Aim

To practise the imperfect tense

Write up the following. Give pupils three minutes working in pairs to copy and complete the text, replacing the infinitives with the correct imperfect tense forms.

Quand j'(être) ____________ *plus jeune,*
j'(aimer) ____________ *le collège. J'(avoir)*
____________ *beaucoup d'amis. Mais*
je n'(écouter) pas en classe. C'(être)
____________ *un peu ennuyeux. Je (faire)*
____________ *beaucoup de sport car*
j'(adorer) ____________ *la compétition.*
Je (jouer) ____________ *au tennis et au foot.*

(**Answers:** *étais, aimais, avais, écoutais, était, faisais, adorais, jouais*)

Check answers. Ask the class to summarise how the imperfect tense is formed (nous form of the verb + *–ais, –ais, –ait, –ions, –iez, –aient*) and which verb has an irregular stem in the imperfect tense (*être*: *ét–*)

Alternative Starter 2:

Use ActiveTeach p.058 Grammar practice or ActiveTeach p.059 Class activity to practise the imperfect tense.

5 En tandem. Fais trois dialogues. Fais des commentaires sur le travail de ton/ta camarade. (Speaking L4)

PLTS T

Speaking. In pairs: pupils make up three dialogues about their childhood, using the picture prompts supplied and the imperfect tense. The questions to use are also given. Pupils comment on each other's work: draw their attention to the list of key language that they can use to do this.

6 Lis les textes et écris le bon prénom. (Reading L5)

Reading. Pupils read the texts by Aline, Arthur and Alex. They then read the questions and identify who is being described in each one – Aline, Arthur or Alex.

Answers

1 Arthur **2** Aline **3** Alex **4** Arthur **5** Alex
6 Aline

7 Écris un paragraphe sur le passé d'une personne imaginaire. (Writing L4)

Writing. Pupils adopt a fictional persona and write a paragraph about their childhood, using the imperfect tense. A framework is supplied. Draw their attention to the tip box on improving their writing.

Plenary

Ask the class to summarise how the imperfect tense is formed. Then ask pupils to tell you about their own childhood, each person giving a sentence featuring the imperfect tense.

Workbook, page 27

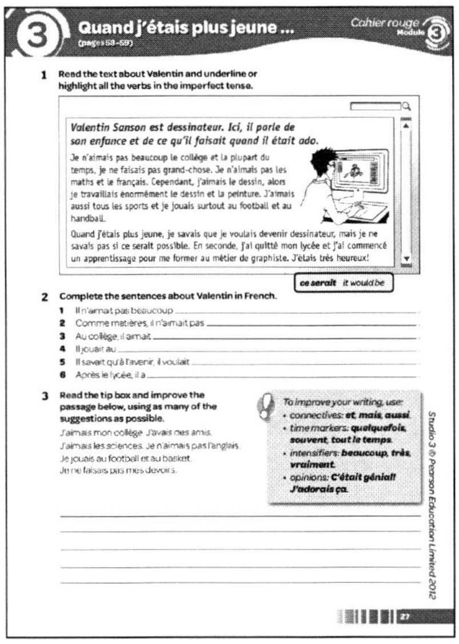

Quand j'étais plus jeune … (pages 58–59) Cahier rouge Module 3

1 Read the text about Valentin and underline or highlight all the verbs in the imperfect tense.

Valentin Sanson est dessinateur. Ici, il parle de son enfance et de ce qu'il faisait quand il était ado.

Je n'aimais pas beaucoup le collège et la plupart du temps, je ne faisais pas grand-chose. Je n'aimais pas les maths et le français. Cependant, j'aimais le dessin, alors je travaillais énormément le dessin et la peinture. J'aimais aussi tous les sports et je jouais surtout au football et au handball.

Quand j'étais plus jeune, je savais que je voulais devenir dessinateur, mais je ne savais pas si ce serait possible. En seconde, j'ai quitté mon lycée et j'ai commencé un apprentissage pour me former au métier de graphiste. J'étais très heureux!

ce serait *it would be*

2 Complete the sentences about Valentin in French.

1 Il n'aimait pas beaucoup ______.
2 Comme matières, il n'aimait pas ______.
3 Au collège, il aimait ______.
4 Il jouait au ______.
5 Il savait qu'à l'avenir, il voulait ______.
6 Après le lycée, il a ______.

3 Read the tip box and improve the passage below, using as many of the suggestions as possible.

J'aimais mon collège. J'avais des amis.
J'aimais les sciences. Je n'aimais pas l'anglais.
Je jouais au football et au basket.
Je ne faisais pas mes devoirs.

To improve your writing, use:
- *connectives:* ***et, mais, aussi***
- *time markers:* ***quelquefois, souvent, tout le temps***
- *intensifiers:* ***beaucoup, très, vraiment***
- *opinions:* ***C'était génial! J'adorais ça.***

Studio 3 © Pearson Education Limited 2012

27

Answers

1 Je n'aimais pas beaucoup le collège et la plupart du temps, je ne faisais pas grand-chose. Je n'aimais pas les maths ou le français. Cependant, j'aimais le dessin, alors je travaillais énormément le dessin et la peinture. J'aimais aussi tous les sports et je jouais surtout au football et au handball. Quand j'étais plus jeune, je savais que je voulais devenir dessinateur, mais je ne savais pas si ce serait possible. En seconde, j'ai quitté mon lycée et j'ai commencé un apprentissage pour me former au métier de graphiste. J'étais très heureux!

2 **1** le collège.
2 les maths et le français.
3 le dessin.
4 football et au handball.
5 devenir dessinateur.
6 commencé un apprentissage.

3 (Example answer:)
Quand j'étais plus jeune, j'aimais vraiment mon collège et j'avais beaucoup d'amis au collège. C'était génial! J'aimais bien les sciences mais je n'aimais pas du tout l'anglais.
Je jouais souvent au football et je jouais tous les jours au basket. Mais quand je rentrais chez moi le soir, je ne faisais pas mes devoirs. Je n'aimais pas ça!

Worksheet 3.5 The imperfect tense

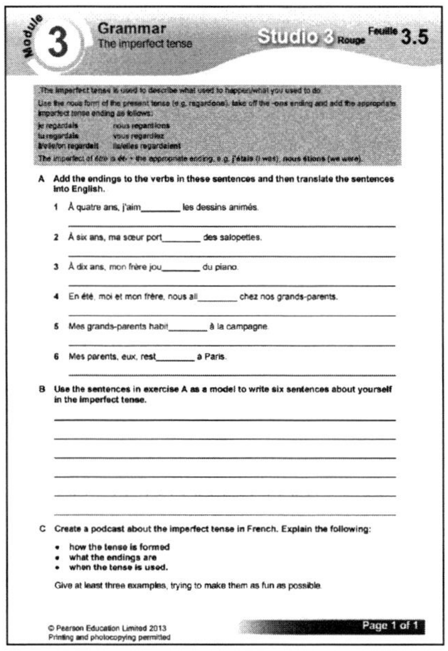

Module 3 **Grammar** The imperfect tense **Studio 3** Rouge Feuille 3.5

The imperfect tense is used to describe what used to happen/what you used to do.
Use the *nous* form of the present tense (e.g. regardons), take off the *-ons* ending and add the appropriate imperfect tense ending as follows:

je regardais	nous regardions
tu regardais	vous regardiez
il/elle/on regardait	ils/elles regardaient

The imperfect of *être* is *ét-* + the appropriate ending, e.g. **j'étais** (I was), **nous étions** (we were).

A Add the endings to the verbs in these sentences and then translate the sentences into English.

1 À quatre ans, j'aim______ les dessins animés.
2 À six ans, ma sœur port______ des salopettes.
3 À dix ans, mon frère jou______ du piano.
4 En été, moi et mon frère, nous all______ chez nos grands-parents.
5 Mes grands-parents habit______ à la campagne.
6 Mes parents, eux, rest______ à Paris.

B Use the sentences in exercise A as a model to write six sentences about yourself in the imperfect tense.

C Create a podcast about the imperfect tense in French. Explain the following:

- **how the tense is formed**
- **what the endings are**
- **when the tense is used.**

Give at least three examples, trying to make them as fun as possible.

© Pearson Education Limited 2013
Printing and photocopying permitted

Page 1 of 1

Answers

A **1** À quatre ans, j'aim**ais** les dessins animés.
When I was four, I used to like cartoons.

2 À six ans, ma soeur port**ait** des salopettes.
When she was six, my sister used to wear dungarees.

3 À dix ans, mon frère jou**ait** du piano.
When he was ten, my brother used to play the piano.

4 En été, moi et mon frère, nous all**ions** chez nos grands-parents.
In the summer, my brother and I used to go to our grandparents'.

5 Mes grands-parents habit**aient** à la campagne.
My grandparents used to live in the countryside.

6 Mes parents, eux, rest**aient** à Paris.
My parents used to stay in Paris.

B (Answers will vary.)

C (Answers will vary.)

(Pupil Book pp. 60–61)

3 4 Ta vie sera comment?

Learning objectives
- Discussing your future and your past
- Practising the future and imperfect tenses

Programme of Study references
GV1 Tenses (future and imperfect)

GV4 Accuracy (grammar)

LC3 Conversation

LC4 Expressing ideas (writing)

FCSE links
Unit 2: Education and future plans (Future plans: After school)

Grammar
- the future tense

Key language
Je quitterai le collège.
Je ferai un apprentissage.
Je ferai le tour du monde.
Je voyagerai.
je travaillerai
Je tomberai amoureux/ amoureuse de quelqu'un.
j'habiterai
J'aurai une Ferrari.
je serai

PLTS
E Effective participators

Cross-curricular
ICT: using spreadsheet or presentation software

PSHE: Recognising skills needed for employability

Resources
Audio files:
38_Module3_Unit4_Ex3.mp3

Workbooks:
Cahier d'exercices Rouge, pages 28 & 29

ActiveTeach:
Starter 1 resource
Starter 2 resource
p.060 Grammar
p.060 Grammar practice
p.061 Learning skills

ActiveLearn:
Listening, Reading
Grammar

Starter 1

Aim

To distinguish between tenses

Write up the following, omitting the underline (used to indicate the answers). Give pupils two minutes to work out the odd one out in each grouping.

1 vous avez joué   je suis allée   je mangerai   il a vu

2 je boirai   il ne jouait jamais   on détestait   c'était

3 on prépare   tu prendras   j'irai   nous ferons

4 elle mange   elle continuera   nous sommes   tu discutes

5 il va rester   je vais aller   elles vont danser   il sera

Check answers, asking pupils to explain their choices (in each group there is one verb in a different tense). Also accept plausible alternatives. Ask pupils to identify the tenses used and to translate the verbs into English.

1 Lis les textes et note vrai (V) ou faux (F). (Reading L5)

Reading. Pupils read the texts. They then read the sentences about them and note whether each sentence is true (writing V) or false (writing F). Some vocabulary is glossed for support.

Answers

1 V   **2** V   **3** F   **4** F   **5** V   **6** V   **7** V   **8** F

Pupils working in pairs take it in turn to make a statement as though they were Romain or Coralie. The statement must include an error for their partner to correct. e.g. *Je mangerai chez moi tous les soirs. – Non, je mangerai au restaurant tous les soirs.*

Studio Grammaire: the future tense

Use the *Studio Grammaire* box to cover the future tense. There is more information and further practice on Pupil Book p. 70.

2 Comment sera ta vie? Écris ton avenir en dix mots! (Writing L3)

Writing. Pupils write a ten-word sentence describing a future achievement.

3 Écoute et choisis la bonne fin pour chaque phrase. (Listening L6)

Listening. Pupils listen to Leïla talking about what she'll do in the future. They then complete the sentences by selecting from the two options given each time. Draw pupils' attention to the tip box on using fillers to help buy them thinking time in a speaking task.

Audioscript Track 38

- *Tu es en quelle classe, Leïla?*
- *Je suis en troisième.*
- *Et tu sais Leïla, qu'aujourd'hui, nous voulons te poser des questions sur ton avenir. Est-ce que tu pensais à ton avenir, quand tu étais petite?*
- *Quand j'étais petite, je ne pensais jamais à l'avenir, mais maintenant, je commence à avoir une petite idée.*
- *Comment sera ta vie, Leïla?*
- *Alors, l'année prochaine, je quitterai le collège et j'irai au lycée. Dans quatre ans, je crois que je ferai des études à la fac. Dans dix ans … voyons … dans dix ans, je serai peut-être professeur. Dans vingt ans … euh … j'aurai cinq enfants. Dans trente ans … je ne sais pas … ah oui, c'est ça … j'habiterai dans un petit village à la campagne.*
- *Et toi Matthieu, tu es en quelle classe?*
- *Je suis en troisième.*
- *Est-ce que tu pensais à l'avenir, quand tu étais plus jeune?*
- *Ben, je suis d'accord avec Leïla. C'est-à-dire que quand j'étais petit, je pensais très peu à mon avenir, mais maintenant, je commence à me demander où je serai dans vingt ans!*
- *Comment sera ta vie, alors?*
- *Alors, voyons, l'année prochaine, je quitterai le collège et je ferai un apprentissage, peut-être chez Peugeot. Dans quatre ans, je crois que je travaillerai comme mécanicien. Dans dix ans … euh … dans dix ans, je tomberai amoureux de quelqu'un. Dans vingt ans … je ne sais pas … dans vingt ans, je serai très riche. Dans trente ans … voyons … j'habiterai au bord de la mer et je crois que je serai très heureux!*

Answers

1 Leïla est en **troisième**.

2 L'année prochaine, Leïla ira **au lycée**.

3 Dans dix ans, Leïla sera **professeur**.

4 Dans vingt ans, Leïla aura **cinq** enfants.

5 Quand il était petit, Matthieu pensait **rarement** à son avenir.

6 L'année prochaine, Matthieu fera un apprentissage chez **Peugeot**.

7 Dans quatre ans, Matthieu travaillera comme **mécanicien**.

8 Dans vingt ans, Matthieu sera très **riche**.

Starter 2

Aim

To practise identifying which tense to use

Write up the following. Give pupils two minutes to identify in English which tense they would use to answer each question.

1 *Tu es en quelle classe?*

2 *Est-ce que tu pensais à ton avenir, quand tu étais petit?*

3 *Où iras-tu?*

4 *C'était comment?*

5 *Comment sera ta vie, à ton avis?*

6 *Est-ce que tu es intéressé par les animaux?*

Check answers.

4 En tandem. Fais deux dialogues. (Speaking L6)

Speaking. In pairs: pupils make up two dialogues about their future in which they take it in turn to ask and answer: whether they thought about it when they were little and what they will do. A framework is supplied. Point out that the framework includes examples of three different tenses and remind pupils of the importance of using a range of tenses confidently if they want to achieve a higher grade.

Draw pupils' attention to *Stratégie 3* on Pupil Book p. 73. Encourage them to practise forming the different tenses as briefed here so that they can use them confidently in their writing and speaking.

5 Lis le texte et termine les phrases en anglais. (Reading L6)

Reading. Pupils read Léna's description of her future plans. They then read and complete the sentences about it in English. les bases is glossed for support.

Answers

1 When she was little, Léna loved **comics/comic books.**

2 In two years she will leave **(high) school.**

3 and will go to Angoulême where **she will study the basics of the job (of comic book illustrator).**

4 In ten years, she will **perhaps be famous and will be very rich.**

5 Then she will **fall in love with someone (and live in Paris with him).**

6 She will **be very happy, because she will strike a good work–life balance.**

6 Écris un paragraphe pour décrire l'avenir de Pedro ou de Malika. Utilise il ou elle. (Writing L5)

Writing. Pupils choose Pedro or Malika and write about their future plans using the English notes supplied. Draw their attention to the tip box on checking that the grammar in their writing is correct.

7 Fais un sondage dans ta classe. Pose la question suivante et note les réponses. (Speaking L4)

PLTS E

Speaking. Pupils carry out a class survey, asking people what they will be doing in ten years' time. The question is supplied. Draw pupils' attention to the tip box on expressions you can use to express uncertainty. Pupils could collate the results of the survey on computer, using spreadsheet or presentation software.

Plenary

Ask the class to summarise how the future tense is formed and to tell you the four irregular future stems used in the unit. Then discuss the results of the survey in exercise 7, eliciting examples of what people will be doing in ten years' time.

Workbook, pages 28 and 29

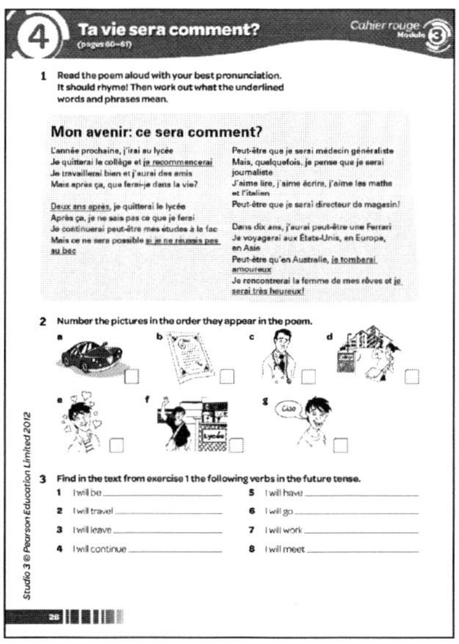

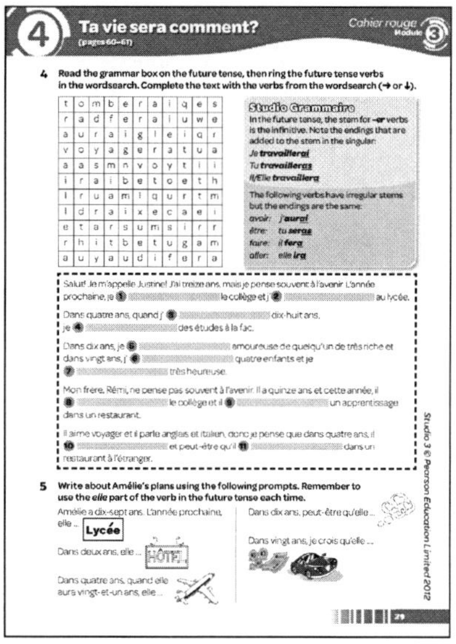

Answers

1 je recommencerai – I will start again
Deux ans après – two years later
si je ne réussis pas au bac – if I don't pass my bac
je tomberai amoureux – I will fall in love
je serai très heureux! – I will be very happy!

2 **a** 6 **b** 3 **c** 4 **d** 1 **e** 7 **f** 2 **g** 5

3 **1** je serai **2** je voyagerai **3** je quitterai **4** je continuerai **5** j'aurai **6** j'irai **7** je travaillerai **8** je rencontrerai

4

t	o	m	b	e	r	a	i	q	e	s
r	a	d	f	e	r	a	i	u	w	e
a	u	r	a	i	g	l	e	i	q	r
v	o	y	a	g	e	r	a	t	u	a
a	a	s	m	n	v	o	y	t	i	i
i	r	a	i	b	e	t	o	e	t	h
l	r	u	a	m	l	q	u	r	t	m
l	d	r	a	i	x	e	c	a	e	i
e	t	a	r	s	u	m	s	i	r	r
r	h	i	t	b	e	t	u	g	a	m
a	u	y	a	u	d	i	f	e	r	a

1 quitterai **2** irai **3** j'aurai **4** ferai **5** tomberai **6** aurai **7** serai **8** quittera **9** fera **10** voyagera **11** travaillera

5 (Example answer:)
Amélie a dix-sept ans. L'année prochaine, elle quittera le lycée. Dans deux ans, elle fera un apprentissage dans un hôtel.
Dans quatre ans, quand elle aura vingt-et-un ans, elle voyagera et travaillera à l'étranger.
Dans dix ans, peut-être qu'elle tombera amoureuse de quelqu'un de très beau et dans vingt ans, je crois qu'elle sera très riche et qu'elle aura une Ferrari! J'espère qu'elle sera très heureuse.

Worksheet 3.6 Using different tenses

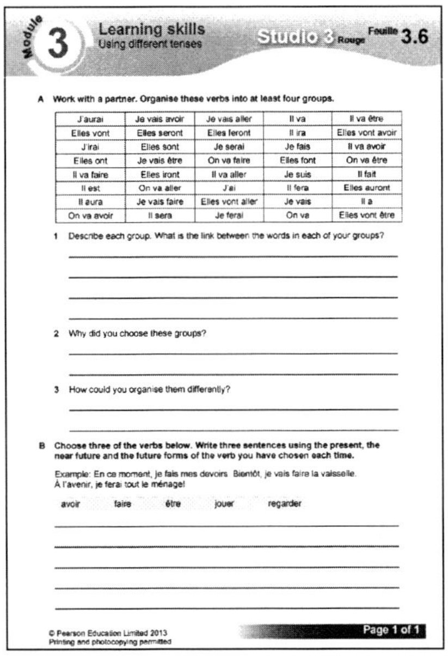

Module 3 **Learning skills**
Using different tenses

Studio 3 Rouge Feuille 3.6

A Work with a partner. Organise these verbs into at least four groups.

J'aurai	Je vais avoir	Je vais aller	Il va	Il va être
Elles vont	Elles seront	Elles feront	Il ira	Elles vont avoir
J'irai	Elles sont	Je serai	Je fais	Il va avoir
Elles ont	Je vais être	On va faire	Elles font	On va être
Il va faire	Elles iront	Il va aller	Je suis	Il fait
Il est	On va aller	J'ai	Il fera	Elles auront
Il aura	Je vais faire	Elles vont aller	Je vais	Il a
On va avoir	Il sera	Je ferai	On va	Elles vont être

1 Describe each group. What is the link between the words in each of your groups?

2 Why did you choose these groups?

3 How could you organise them differently?

B Choose three of the verbs below. Write three sentences using the present, the near future and the future forms of the verb you have chosen each time.

Example: En ce moment, je fais mes devoirs. Bientôt, je vais faire la vaisselle.
À l'avenir, je ferai tout le ménage!

avoir faire être jouer regarder

Page 1 of 1

Answers

A (Answers will vary.)

B (Answers will vary.)

C (Answers will vary.)

3 5 Mon boulot

Learning objectives

- Talking about your job
- Using different tenses together

Programme of Study references

GV1 Tenses (using different tenses together)

LC3 Conversation

LC6 Reading comprehension

LC8 Writing creatively

FCSE links

Unit 2: Education and future plans (Future plans: Jobs and careers)

Grammar

- question forms
- using different tenses together

Key language

le boulot
Qu'est-ce que tu fais dans la vie?
Est-ce que tu as beaucoup d'expérience?
Quelle est ta journée typique?
Quelles sont tes responsabilités?
Quelles sont les qualités requises pour ce métier?
Quelles langues parles-tu?
Que feras-tu à l'avenir?
communiquer
coordonner
créer
fonctionner
inventer
savoir
travailler en équipe
attentif/attentive
frustrant(e)
motivant(e)
poli(e)
rapide
solide
stimulant(e)
Côté formation, …
pour ma part
ma propre boîte

PLTS

R Reflective learners

Cross-curricular

All subjects: identifying areas for improvement and setting targets

PSHE: recognising skills needed for employability

Resources

Audio files:

39_Module3_Unit5_Ex1.mp3
40_Module3_Unit5_Ex5.mp3

Workbooks:

Cahier d'exercices Rouge, pages 30 & 31

ActiveTeach:

Starter 1 resource
Starter 2 resource
p.063 Class activity
p.063 Video 6
p.063 Video worksheet 6
p.063 Thinking skills

ActiveLearn:

Listening, Reading

Starter 1

Aim

To review the language for jobs

Write up the following. Give pupils two minutes to number them according to their order of preference (with 1 their favourite), then discuss in pairs why they would like to do the job they marked 1 and wouldn't like to do the job they marked 7.

acheteur/acheteuse habillement
chanteur/chanteuse
directeur/directrice de magasin
ingénieur(e)
journaliste
médecin généraliste
webdesigner

Alternative Starter 1:

Use ActiveTeach p.063 Class activity to review Module 3 language.

1 Écoute et lis le texte. (Listening L7)

Listening. Pupils listen to Vincent, a game designer, talking about the pros and cons of his job and his future plans. They read the text at the same time. Some vocabulary is glossed for support.

Audioscript Track 39

Quand j'étais petit, je jouais tout le temps à des jeux vidéo et j'inventais des jeux dans ma tête. J'adorais ça. Eh bien, maintenant, c'est mon job, puisque je suis game designer à Paris. J'adore mon boulot. C'est le top du top! Quand on veut créer un jeu, d'abord, on a une réunion où chacun peut donner ses idées. Pour ma part, je dois inventer les règles, les personnages et l'univers où les personnages vont habiter. Je dois rendre le jeu interactif et attractif. Je dois aussi coordonner toutes les équipes: les programmeurs, les animateurs, …

Si on veut être game designer, on doit aimer le contact avec les autres, il faut aimer travailler en équipe et savoir communiquer ses idées. C'est très stimulant et motivant mais, quelquefois, si les choses ne fonctionnent pas, ça peut être un peu frustrant. Côté formation, j'ai fait mes études à l'ENJMIN. Ensuite, j'ai travaillé à Annecy et puis je suis venu à Paris. L'année prochaine, je ferai un stage aux États-Unis. Je voudrais voir comment ça se passe dans la Silicon Valley. Après, j'irai en Inde parce que les informaticiens indiens sont des génies. Un jour, j'aurai peut-être ma propre boîte et ce sera la meilleure période de ma vie.

2 Copie et remplis la fiche pour Vincent. (Reading L7)

Reading. Pupils copy and complete the profile for Vincent, using the details in exercise 1.

Answers

Name: Vincent
Job: Games designer
Responsibilities/Tasks: Invents rules, characters and the world they will live in. Makes the game interactive and attractive. Coordinates all the teams.
Qualities needed: Must like contact with others, working in a team and know how to communicate ideas.
Training/Experience: Studied at ENJMIN, worked in Annecy, then came to Paris.
Future: Will do a training course in the USA, then will go to India. Will maybe have own company one day.

3 Relis le texte et corrige les erreurs dans ces phrases. (Reading L7)

Reading. Pupils read the text in exercise 1 again. They then read the sentences about it and correct them.

Answers

Accept plausible alternatives, e.g. génial *for* super.

1 Quand il était petit, Vincent jouait tout le temps **à des jeux vidéo**.
2 Vincent travaille **avec beaucoup de personnes/en équipe**.
3 Selon Vincent, le travail de game designer **est** très intéressant.
4 Vincent a travaillé **à Annecy, puis à Paris**.
5 Quand Vincent aura sa propre entreprise, ce sera **la meilleure période de sa vie**.

4 Trouve les synonymes pour ces mots dans le texte. (Reading L5)

Reading. Pupils find in the text in exercise 1 synonyms for the French words listed. Draw their attention to the tip box on techniques for improving their written and spoken French.

Answers

1 j'inventais **2** mon job/boulot **3** habiter **4** stimulant **5** boîte

Starter 2

Aim

To practise using synonyms

Write up the following. Give pupils three minutes working in pairs to come up with a French synonym for each one.

1 *j'invente*	**5** *elle n'aime pas du tout*
2 *aimer beaucoup*	**6** *il m'intéresse beaucoup*
3 *il faut*	**7** *mon boulot*
4 *une entreprise*	**8** *ensuite*

(**Answers: 1** *je crée* **2** *adorer* **3** *on doit* **4** *une boîte* **5** *elle déteste* **6** *il me fascine* **7** *mon emploi/travail* **8** *puis*)

Hear answers. Remind pupils that they can make their speaking and writing more interesting by varying the language they use.

5 Écoute l'interview avec Éva. Termine les phrases en anglais. (Listening L7)

Listening. Pupils listen to Éva being interviewed about her job and future plans. They then read and complete the sentences, summarising the interview in English. Draw pupils' attention to the tip box on listening skills.

Audioscript Track 40

– *Qu'est-ce que tu fais dans la vie?*
– *Je suis designer de chaussures. À mon avis, j'ai l'emploi idéal, fi gure-toi que je suis payée pour dessiner et j'adore ça! C'est ma passion.*
– *En quoi consiste ton travail?*
– *Alors, en principe, j'essaie de rajouter quelque chose d'extra aux baskets que je crée. Pour leur fabrication, je choisis les matériaux et les couleurs et je dois faire attention à toutes les tendances et aux nouvelles technologies.*
– *Quelles sont les qualités d'un bon designer de chaussures?*
– *Il faut aimer travailler en équipe et sur ordinateur. Il faut être fl exible et créatif.*
– *Tu as suivi quelle formation?*
– *J'ai fait cinq ans d'études dans une école des beaux-arts, c'était très intéressant et très utile. Actuellement, je travaille en Allemagne chez Adidas. Je travaille ici depuis deux ans. Avant cela, j'ai fait un stage chez Nike aux États-Unis et j'ai travaillé deux ans en Italie chez Fila.*
– *Que feras-tu à l'avenir?*
– *À l'avenir, je pense que je travaillerai à mon compte comme freelance. Comme ça, j'aurai plus de liberté. Un jour, j'aurai peut-être ma propre boutique, ça sera cool.*

Answers

1 Éva works as a **shoe designer**.
2 In her opinion, it's her **ideal** job.
3 She chooses the **materials** and the **colours**.
4 To do her job well, she has to work in a team and needs to be **flexible** and **creative**.
5 She studied for **five years** at a fine art school.

6 She is currently working for Adidas in **Germany**.
7 Before that she worked in the USA and spent two years in **Italy**.
8 In the future she would like to **work for herself/as a freelance and have her own shop**.

Pupils summarise in French what Éva does, her experience and her future plans.

6 Fais correspondre le français et l'anglais. (Reading L7)

Reading. Pupils match the French and English versions of the questions Éva is asked in her interview.

Answers

1 b **2** c **3** e **4** a **5** d

7 En tandem. Imagine que tu es Florence. Fais une interview. Utilise les questions de l'exercice 6. (Speaking L7)

Speaking. In pairs: pupils take it in turn to be interviewed as Florence, using the details supplied and the questions in exercise 6. Remind pupils to try to work in some of the new words they identified in the text in exercise 4.

8 Écris une interview avec Alain. (Writing L7)

Writing. Pupils write an interview with Alain Saad, using the details supplied. Remind them to try to work in some of the new words they identified in the text in exercise 4. Draw their attention to the tip box on including the imperfect tense, which is not prompted by the details supplied. trier is glossed for support.

Plenary

PLTS R

Ask pupils to work in pairs. They swap and check the interview they wrote for exercise 8, focusing on the following:
- How many tenses are used?
- Is the imperfect included?
- Does the text include examples of new words from exercise 4?

Then ask pupils to look again at their own interviews and identify two ways in which they could improve their writing.

Point out that reviewing work and identifying ways to improve is a useful technique to use for other school subjects too.

Workbook, pages 30 and 31

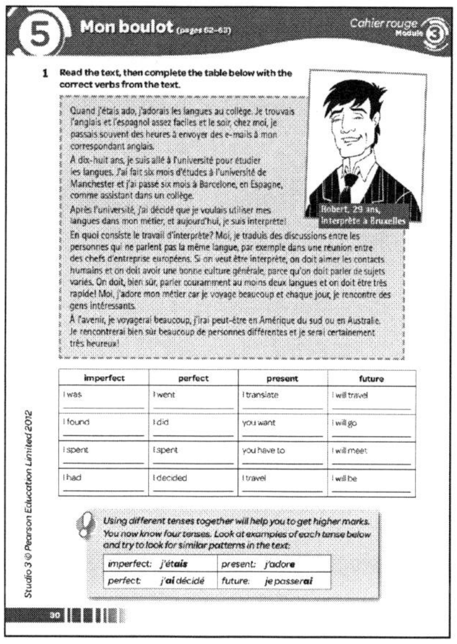
5 Mon boulot (pages 62–63) Cahier rouge Module 3

1 Read the text, then complete the table below with the correct verbs from the text.

Quand j'étais ado, j'adorais les langues au collège. Je trouvais l'anglais et l'espagnol assez faciles et le soir, chez moi, je passais souvent des heures à envoyer des e-mails à mon correspondant anglais.

À dix-huit ans, je suis allé à l'université pour étudier les langues. J'ai fait six mois d'études à l'université de Manchester et j'ai passé six mois à Barcelone, en Espagne, comme assistant dans un collège.

Après l'université, j'ai décidé que je voulais utiliser mes langues dans mon métier, et aujourd'hui, je suis interprète!

En quoi consiste le travail d'interprète? Moi, je traduis des discussions entre les personnes qui ne parlent pas la même langue, par exemple dans une réunion entre des chefs d'entreprise européens. Si on veut être interprète, on doit aimer les contacts humains et on doit avoir une bonne culture générale, parce qu'on doit parler de sujets variés. On doit, bien sûr, parler couramment au moins deux langues et on doit être très rapide! Moi, j'adore mon métier car je voyage beaucoup et chaque jour, je rencontre des gens intéressants.

À l'avenir, je voyagerai beaucoup, j'irai peut-être en Amérique du sud ou en Australie. Je rencontrerai bien sûr beaucoup de personnes différentes et je serai certainement très heureux!

Robert, 29 ans, interprète à Bruxelles

imperfect	perfect	present	future
I was	I went	I translate	I will travel
I found	I did	you want	I will go
I spent	I spent	you have to	I will meet
I had	I decided	I travel	I will be

Using different tenses together will help you to get higher marks. You now know four tenses. Look at examples of each tense below and try to look for similar patterns in the text:

*imperfect: j'ét**ais***	*present: j'ador**e***
*perfect: j'**ai** décidé*	*future: je passer**ai***

Studio 3 © Pearson Education Limited 2012

30

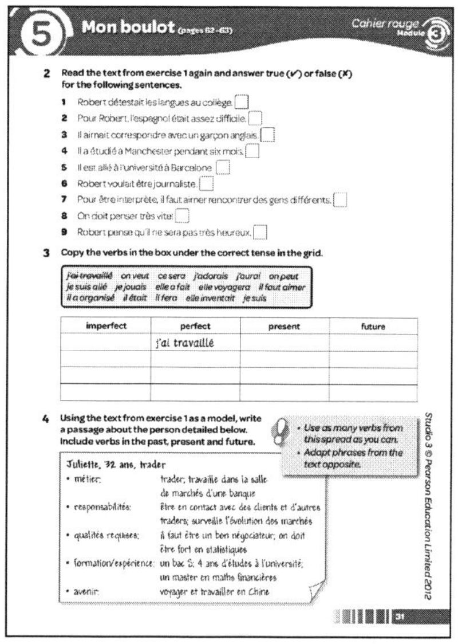
5 Mon boulot (pages 62–63) Cahier rouge Module 3

2 Read the text from exercise 1 again and answer true (✓) or false (✗) for the following sentences.
1 Robert détestait les langues au collège.
2 Pour Robert, l'espagnol était assez difficile.
3 Il aimait correspondre avec un garçon anglais.
4 Il a étudié à Manchester pendant six mois.
5 Il est allé à l'université à Barcelone.
6 Robert voulait être journaliste.
7 Pour être interprète, il faut aimer rencontrer des gens différents.
8 On doit penser très vite!
9 Robert pense qu'il ne sera pas très heureux.

3 Copy the verbs in the box under the correct tense in the grid.

~~j'ai travaillé~~ on veut ce sera j'adorais j'aurai on peut je suis allé je jouais elle a fait elle voyagera il faut aimer il a organisé il était il fera elle inventait je suis

imperfect	perfect	present	future
	j'ai travaillé		

4 Using the text from exercise 1 as a model, write a passage about the person detailed below. Include verbs in the past, present and future.

- *Use as many verbs from this spread as you can.*
- *Adapt phrases from the text opposite.*

Juliette, 32 ans, trader
- métier: trader; travaille dans la salle de marchés d'une banque
- responsabilités: être en contact avec des clients et d'autres traders; surveille l'évolution des marchés
- qualités requises: il faut être un bon négociateur; on doit être fort en statistiques
- formation/expérience: un bac S; 4 ans d'études à l'université; un master en maths financières
- avenir: voyager et travailler en Chine

Studio 3 © Pearson Education Limited 2012

31

Answers

1

imperfect	perfect	present	future
I was j'étais	*I went* je suis allé	*I translate* je traduis	*I will travel* je voyagerai
I found je trouvais	*I did* j'ai fait	*You want* on veut	*I will go* j'irai
I spent je passais	*I spent* j'ai passé	*You have to* on doit	*I will meet* je rencontrerai
I had j'avais	*I decided* j'ai décidé	*I travel* je voyage	*I will be* je serai

2 1 × 2 × 3 ✓ 4 ✓ 5 × 6 × 7 ✓ 8 ✓ 9 ×

3

imperfect	perfect	present	future
j'adorais	*j'ai travaillé*	on veut	j'aurai
je jouais	je suis allé	on peut	ce sera
il était	elle a fait	il faut aimer	elle voyagera
elle inventait	il a organisé	je suis	il fera

4 (Example answer:) *Juliette, 32 ans, trader*

Quand j'étais ado j'adorais les maths au collège. Je trouvais les maths et les statistiques assez faciles et chez moi, le soir, je passais souvent des heures à faire mes devoirs et des quiz de maths.

À dix-huit ans, je suis allée à l'université pour étudier les maths.

Après l'université, j'ai décidé que je voulais utiliser les maths dans un métier et aujourd'hui, je suis trader!

En quoi consiste le travail d'un trader? Moi, je travaille dans la salle de marchés d'une banque. Je suis en contact avec des clients et d'autres traders et je surveille l'évolution des marchés.

Si on veut être trader, il faut être un bon négociateur et on doit être fort en statistiques. Moi, j'adore mon métier car chaque jour, je rencontre des gens intéressants. Comme formation, tout d'abord, il faut avoir un bac S. Après ça, moi, j'ai fait quatre ans d'études à l'université puis, j'ai fait un master en maths financières.

À l'avenir, je voyagerai beaucoup. J'irai peut-être en Chine ou à Hong Kong. Je rencontrerai bien sûr beaucoup de personnes différentes et je serai certainement très heureuse!

Worksheet 3.7 Logic puzzle

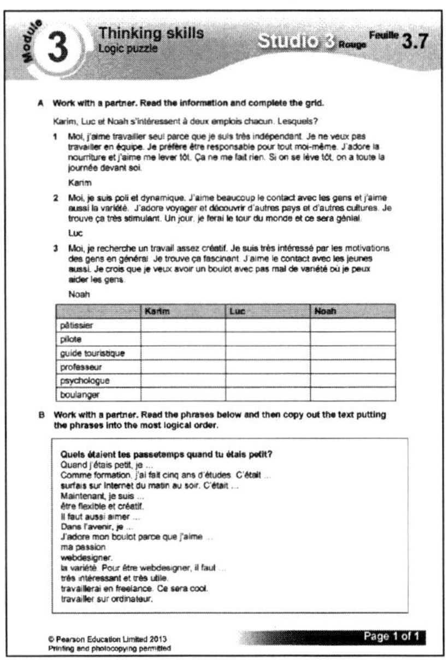

Module 3 Thinking skills
Logic puzzle
Studio 3 Rouge Feuille 3.7

A Work with a partner. Read the information and complete the grid.

Karim, Luc et Noah s'intéressent à deux emplois chacun. Lesquels?

1 Moi, j'aime travailler seul parce que je suis très indépendant. Je ne veux pas travailler en équipe. Je préfère être responsable pour tout moi-même. J'adore la nourriture et j'aime me lever tôt. Ça ne me fait rien. Si on se lève tôt, on a toute la journée devant soi.

Karim

2 Moi, je suis poli et dynamique. J'aime beaucoup le contact avec les gens et j'aime aussi la variété. J'adore voyager et découvrir d'autres pays et d'autres cultures. Je trouve ça très stimulant. Un jour, je ferai le tour du monde et ce sera génial.

Luc

3 Moi, je recherche un travail assez créatif. Je suis très intéressé par les motivations des gens en général. Je trouve ça fascinant. J'aime le contact avec les jeunes aussi. Je crois que je veux avoir un boulot avec pas mal de variété où je peux aider les gens.

Noah

	Karim	Luc	Noah
pâtissier			
pilote			
guide touristique			
professeur			
psychologue			
boulanger			

B Work with a partner. Read the phrases below and then copy out the text putting the phrases into the most logical order.

Quels étaient tes passetemps quand tu étais petit?
Quand j'étais petit, je ...
Comme formation, j'ai fait cinq ans d'études. C'était ...
surfais sur Internet du matin au soir. C'était ...
Maintenant, je suis ...
être flexible et créatif.
Il faut aussi aimer ...
Dans l'avenir, je ...
J'adore mon boulot parce que j'aime ...
ma passion.
webdesigner.
la variété. Pour être webdesigner, il faut ...
très intéressant et très utile.
travaillerai en freelance. Ce sera cool.
travailler sur ordinateur.

Page 1 of 1

Answers

A

	Karim	Luc	Noah
pâtissier	✓		
pilote		✓	
guide touristique		✓	
professeur			✓
psychologue			✓
boulanger	✓		

B Quand j'étais petit, je ...
surfais sur Internet du matin au soir. C'était ...
ma passion.
Maintenant, je suis ...
webdesigner.
J'adore mon boulot parce que j'aime ...
la variété. Pour être webdesigner, il faut ...
être flexible et créatif.
Il faut aussi aimer ...
travailler sur ordinateur.
Comme formation, j'ai fait cinq ans d'études.
C'était ...
très intéressant et très utile.
À l'avenir, je ...
travaillerai en freelance. Ce sera cool.

Video

Episode 6: Le judo

Alex films Mehdi's day of work experience as a judo instructor, and they learn more about the qualities needed for the job. Video worksheet 6 can be used in conjunction with this episode.

Answers to video worksheet (ActiveTeach)

1 A It definitely has to be Mehdi, as he is the sporty one.
B (Answers will vary.)

2 A He's a bit nervous (*nerveux*).
B Attentive (*attentif*) and quick (*rapide*).
C To see what it is like to be a judo instructor.

3 A For ten years.
B Judo and Japan.
C He wants to be a judo teacher.
D *La politesse, le respect, l'honneur* – politeness, respect, honour.
E Afternoon (*après-midi*).
F Hop.
G Fifteen (*quinze pompes*).

4 A The different levels of skill.
B Yellow.
C He has a brown belt, meaning he is nearly an expert.

5 A He thinks he has done well.
B Mehdi was a bit too serious at the beginning.
C To become a sports journalist.
D He takes on Mehdi, with little success!

3 Bilan et Révisions

Bilan

Pupils use this checklist to review language covered in the module, working on it in pairs in class or on their own at home. Encourage them to follow up any areas of weakness they identify. There are Target Setting Sheets included in the Assessment Pack, and an opportunity for pupils to record their own levels and targets on the *J'avance* page in the Workbook, p. 36. You can also use the *Bilan* checklist as an end-of-module plenary option.

Révisions

These revision exercises can be used for assessment purposes or for pupils to practise before tackling the assessment tasks in the Assessment Pack.

Resources

Audio files:

41_Module3_Rev_Ex1.mp3

Workbooks:

Cahier d'exercices Rouge, pages 32 & 33

1 Copie le tableau. Écoute et mets les activités dans la bonne colonne. (1–4) (Listening L5)

Listening. Pupils copy out the table. They then listen to four adults talking about their childhood and what they do now. They complete the table by writing the letter of each picture in the correct column.

Answers

	past	**present**
1 Adnan	b	f
2 Malika	c	h
3 Gabriel	d	g
4 Clémentine	a	e

Audioscript Track 41

1 – *Adnan, quels étaient tes passetemps quand tu étais petit?*
– *Quand j'étais petit, j'adorais la musique. Je jouais de la guitare du matin au soir.*
– *Qu'est-ce que tu fais dans la vie, maintenant?*
– *Eh bien maintenant, je suis prof de musique et j'adore ça!*

2 – *Malika, quels étaient tes passetemps quand tu étais petite?*
– *Quand j'étais petite, j'adorais travailler dans le jardin, je trouvais ça très cool.*
– *Et qu'est-ce que tu fais dans la vie, maintenant?*
– *Je suis botaniste, alors je passe tout mon temps parmi les plantes!*

3 – *Gabriel, quels étaient tes passetemps quand tu étais petit?*
– *Quand j'étais petit, je surfais sur Internet du matin au soir. C'était ma passion.*
– *Qu'est-ce que tu fais dans la vie maintenant?*
– *Maintenant, j'ai beaucoup de chance, parce que je suis webdesigner.*

4 – *Et toi, Clémentine, quel genre d'élève étais-tu?*
– *J'étais bonne élève. J'adorais la biologie et les sciences.*
– *Qu'est-ce que tu fais dans la vie, maintenant?*
– *Maintenant, je suis vétérinaire.*

2 En tandem. Prépare et donne une réponse à ces questions. (Speaking L6)

Speaking. In pairs: pupils prepare and practise answering the questions.

3 Lis l'interview avec Tom. C'est vrai (V) ou faux (F)? (Reading L6)

Reading. Pupils read the interview with Tom. They then read the sentences and decide whether each is true (writing V) or false (writing F).

Answers

1 F **2** F **3** V **4** F **5** V

4 Tu es Jamel. Décris tes projets d'avenir en français. (Writing L6)

Writing. Pupils pretend they are Jamel and write a short text on their future projects, using the English prompts supplied.

Workbook, pages 32 and 33

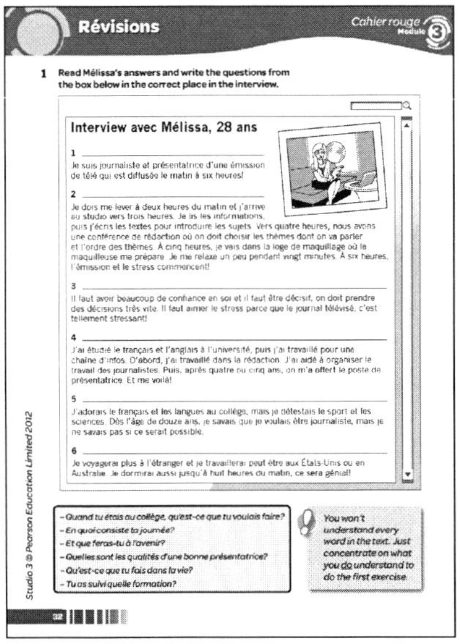

Révisions

Cahier rouge Module 3

1 **Read Mélissa's answers and write the questions from the box below in the correct place in the interview.**

Interview avec Mélissa, 28 ans

1 ______
Je suis journaliste et présentatrice d'une émission de télé qui est diffusée le matin à six heures!

2 ______
Je dois me lever à deux heures du matin et j'arrive au studio vers trois heures. Je lis les informations, puis j'écris les textes pour introduire les sujets. Vers quatre heures, nous avons une conférence de rédaction où on doit choisir les thèmes dont on va parler et l'ordre des thèmes. À cinq heures, je vais dans la loge de maquillage où la maquilleuse me prépare. Je me relaxe un peu pendant vingt minutes. À six heures, l'émission et le stress commencent!

3 ______
Il faut avoir beaucoup de confiance en soi et il faut être décisif, on doit prendre des décisions très vite. Il faut aimer le stress parce que le journal télévisé, c'est tellement stressant!

4 ______
J'ai étudié le français et l'anglais à l'université, puis j'ai travaillé pour une chaîne d'infos. D'abord, j'ai travaillé dans la rédaction. J'ai aidé à organiser le travail des journalistes. Puis, après quatre ou cinq ans, on m'a offert le poste de présentatrice. Et me voilà!

5 ______
J'adorais le français et les langues au collège, mais je détestais le sport et les sciences. Dès l'âge de douze ans, je savais que je voulais être journaliste, mais je ne savais pas si ce serait possible.

6 ______
Je voyagerai plus à l'étranger et je travaillerai peut être aux États-Unis ou en Australie. Je dormirai aussi jusqu'à huit heures du matin, ce sera génial!

– Quand tu étais au collège, qu'est-ce que tu voulais faire?
– En quoi consiste ta journée?
– Et que feras-tu à l'avenir?
– Quelles sont les qualités d'une bonne présentatrice?
– Qu'est-ce que tu fais dans la vie?
– Tu as suivi quelle formation?

You won't understand every word in the text. Just concentrate on what you do understand to do the first exercise.

Studio 3 © Pearson Education Limited 2012

32

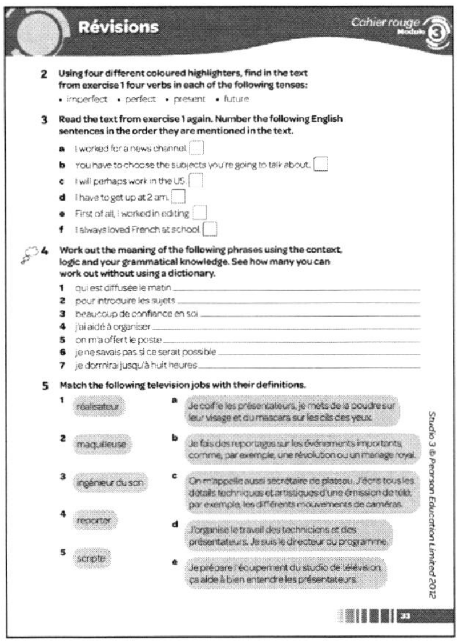

Révisions

Cahier rouge Module 3

2 **Using four different coloured highlighters, find in the text from exercise 1 four verbs in each of the following tenses:**
• imperfect • perfect • present • future

3 **Read the text from exercise 1 again. Number the following English sentences in the order they are mentioned in the text.**
a I worked for a news channel. ☐
b You have to choose the subjects you're going to talk about. ☐
c I will perhaps work in the US. ☐
d I have to get up at 2 am. ☐
e First of all, I worked in editing. ☐
f I always loved French at school. ☐

4 **Work out the meaning of the following phrases using the context, logic and your grammatical knowledge. See how many you can work out without using a dictionary.**
1 qui est diffusée le matin ______
2 pour introduire les sujets ______
3 beaucoup de confiance en soi ______
4 j'ai aidé à organiser ______
5 on m'a offert le poste ______
6 je ne savais pas si ce serait possible ______
7 je dormirai jusqu'à huit heures ______

5 **Match the following television jobs with their definitions.**
1 réalisateur
2 maquilleuse
3 ingénieur du son
4 reporter
5 scripte

a Je coiffe les présentateurs, je mets de la poudre sur leur visage et du mascara sur les cils des yeux.
b Je fais des reportages sur les événements importants, comme, par exemple, une révolution ou un mariage royal.
c On m'appelle aussi secrétaire de plateau. J'écris tous les détails techniques et artistiques d'une émission de télé, par exemple, les différents mouvements de caméras.
d J'organise le travail des techniciens et des présentateurs. Je suis le directeur du programme.
e Je prépare l'équipement du studio de télévision, ça aide à bien entendre les présentateurs.

Studio 3 © Pearson Education Limited 2012

33

Answers

1 **1** Qu'est-ce que tu fais dans la vie?
2 En quoi consiste ta journée?
3 Quelles sont les qualités d'une bonne présentatrice?
4 Tu as suivi quelle formation?
5 Quand tu étais au collège, qu'est-ce que tu voulais faire?
6 Et que feras-tu à l'avenir?

2 **present (any four of):** je suis, (qui) est (diffusée), Je dois, j'arrive, Je lis, j'écris, nous avons, on doit, je vais (la maquilleuse) me prépare, Je me relaxe, (l'émission et le stress) commencent, il faut, Il faut, on doit, c'est
perfect (any four of): J'ai étudié, j'ai travaillé, j'ai travaillé, J'ai aidé, on m'a offert
imperfect (any four of): j'adorais, je détestais, je savais, je voulais, je ne savais
future: Je voyagerai, je travaillerai, Je dormirai, ce sera

3 **a** 3 **b** 2 **c** 6 **d** 1 **e** 4 **f** 5

4 **1** which is broadcast in the morning
2 to introduce the subjects
3 a lot of self-confidence
4 I helped to organise
5 I was offered the job/they offered me the job
6 I didn't know if it would be possible
7 I will sleep until 8 o'clock

5 **1** d **2** a **3** e **4** b **5** c

3 En plus: Un portrait professionnel

(Pupil Book pp. 66–67)

Learning objective

- Investigating jobs using languages

Programme of Study references

LC1 Listening and responding

LC3 Conversation (dealing with the unexpected)

LC6 Reading comprehension

LC8 Writing creatively

Key language

Review of language from the module

PLTS

I Independent enquirers

Cross-curricular

ICT: internet research

PSHE: recognising skills needed for employability, exploring options and choices in career contexts

Resources

Audio files:

42_Module3_EnPlus_Ex1.mp3

43_Module3_EnPlus_Ex5.mp3

ActiveTeach:

Starter resource

p.067 Assignment 3

p.067 Assignment 3: prep

Starter

Aim

To review language for talking about jobs and future plans

Write up the following. Give pupils three minutes to think up a job and complete the profile in French with the appropriate details. They then swap and check each other's work in pairs. Collect in the profiles to use for the Plenary at the end of the unit.

Nom: ______________________

Emploi: ______________________

Responsabilités: ______________________

Qualités requises: ______________________

Formation/Expérience: ______________________

Avenir: ______________________

____

1 Écoute et lis le texte. (Listening L7)

Listening. Pupils listen to the feature on Declan and his career, and read the text at the same time. *en tant que* is glossed for support.

Audioscript Track 42

La passion de Declan, c'est le snowboard. Son père Mark est fan de ski, et quand Declan était petit, ils partaient ensemble en France pour s'amuser dans les Alpes car ils adoraient ça tous les deux. Declan était bon élève. Il a étudié le français au collège, mais il préférait l'EPS et l'informatique. Pourtant, il a passé son examen de français à l'âge de 16 ans et a eu un B.

Lorsqu'il avait dix-huit ans, Declan a décidé de devenir moniteur de ski. Il est donc parti à Val Thorens en Savoie, le plus haut village d'Europe. Son père était furieux parce qu'il pensait que son fils devait aller à l'université. Declan a fait les études nécessaires et puis a travaillé pendant trois saisons à Val Thorens.

En tant que moniteur de ski, il doit enseigner le ski à ses élèves. Il doit être très patient. En été, Declan travaille comme moniteur de VTT. Il aime bien ça, mais il préfère son travail d'hiver!

Il y a deux ans, Declan a décidé d'apprendre l'italien et il est parti à San Martino di Castrozza en Italie. Il a très vite appris la langue. Aujourd'hui, il la parle parfaitement parce qu'il a une petite amie italienne, Rossella.

Dans deux ans, Declan ira faire un stage au Canada et ensuite, il préparera un diplôme de management et de marketing en France. Son ambition, c'est de voir «Declan Armstrong, directeur d'école de ski» inscrit sur sa porte! Rossella n'aime pas trop l'idée de voir son petit ami partir au Canada, mais elle comprend son ambition.

Mark, le père de Declan, n'est plus en colère contre son fils et il lui rend visite dans les Alpes tous les ans. Ils rigolent bien ensemble sur les pistes.

2 Mets ces titres dans l'ordre du texte. (Reading L7)

Reading. Pupils read the headings in French and put them in the order the topics are mentioned in the text in exercise 1. Draw their attention to the tip box on reading skills.

Answers

h, c, f, g, d, b, e, a

3 Relis le texte et réponds aux questions en anglais. (Reading L7)

Reading. Pupils read the text in exercise 1 again and answer the questions about it in English.

Answers

1 Declan **2** his dad 3 Declan **4** Rossella **5** Declan

4 En tandem. Prépare et fais une interview entre Declan et un reporter. (Speaking L7)

Speaking. In pairs: pupils prepare and practise an interview, taking it in turn to be Declan and a reporter and using the details in exercise 1. The questions and answer openings are supplied. Draw pupils' attention to the tip box on how to adapt a model text and improve their writing.

5 Écoute Olivia, qui est trader, et réponds aux questions en anglais. (Listening L7)

Listening. Pupils listen to Olivia, a financial trader, talking about her job. They then answer the questions about her in English. Draw their attention to the tip box on listening skills.

Audioscript Track 43

Je m'appelle Olivia Gareton et je travaille pour une banque sur le marché financier. Je suis trader. Je travaille avec 200 à 300 personnes. Sur mon bureau, j'ai trois ordinateurs et un micro. Je dois faire très attention parce que je dois contacter des clients ou d'autres traders si nécessaire. Mon travail est intense car je dois réagir vite. Je ne peux pas hésiter quand je dois prendre des décisions. Sinon, on est perdu!

Ce que j'aime dans mon travail, c'est qu'on ne passe pas des heures en réunion. Je suis responsable de mes décisions et j'aime ça. On me juge sur mes résultats. Chaque soir, je discute avec mon chef. Si j'ai de bons résultats, je gagne plus d'argent; si mes résultats ne sont pas bons, je peux perdre mon job!

Côté formation, j'ai fait un bac S et un master en maths financières. Il faut absolument être fort en maths. C'est très important, ça! Avant, il fallait surtout être un bon négociateur, mais aujourd'hui, on doit être fort en statistiques, en probabilités, en maths, quoi.

Answers

1 200 to 300.
2 Three computers and a microphone.
3 Clients or other traders.
4 She doesn't spend hours in meetings and she is responsible for her own decisions.
5 She gets more money.
6 It's very important to be good at maths in her job.

6 Invente un portrait comme celui de Declan. Fais des recherches sur un job ou utilise les idées suivantes. (Writing L7)

PLTS I

Writing. Pupils write a profile of a person, giving details of his/her job and future plans. They can use the notes supplied or research a job they are interested in, using the internet, newspapers/magazines or career literature at your school to find out about it. *une fouille* is glossed for support.

Plenary

Review the language for talking about jobs with a game. Put the class into teams. Use the profiles the pupils wrote for the Starter. Read out the information from one category, e.g. *Formation/Expérience*. The teams compete to name the job. Award 2 points for each correct answer. Repeat, varying the category and information. The team with the most points at the end wins.

Worksheet 3.8 Mon CV. Assignment 3: writing

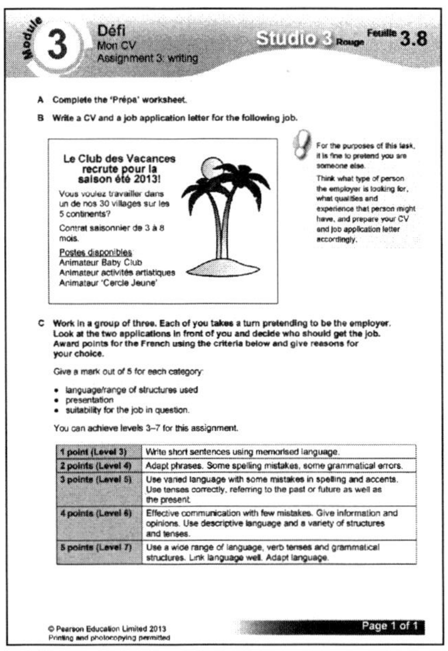
Module 3 Défi
Mon CV
Assignment 3: writing
Studio 3 Rouge Feuille 3.8

A Complete the 'Prépa' worksheet.

B Write a CV and a job application letter for the following job.

Le Club des Vacances recrute pour la saison été 2013!
Vous voulez travailler dans un de nos 30 villages sur les 5 continents?
Contrat saisonnier de 3 à 8 mois.
Postes disponibles
Animateur Baby Club
Animateur activités artistiques
Animateur 'Cercle Jeune'

For the purposes of this task, it is fine to pretend you are someone else.
Think what type of person the employer is looking for, what qualities and experience that person might have, and prepare your CV and job application letter accordingly.

C Work in a group of three. Each of you takes a turn pretending to be the employer. Look at the two applications in front of you and decide who should get the job. Award points for the French using the criteria below and give reasons for your choice.

Give a mark out of 5 for each category:
- language/range of structures used
- presentation
- suitability for the job in question.

You can achieve levels 3–7 for this assignment.

1 point (Level 3)	Write short sentences using memorised language.
2 points (Level 4)	Adapt phrases. Some spelling mistakes, some grammatical errors.
3 points (Level 5)	Use varied language with some mistakes in spelling and accents. Use tenses correctly, referring to the past or future as well as the present.
4 points (Level 6)	Effective communication with few mistakes. Give information and opinions. Use descriptive language and a variety of structures and tenses.
5 points (Level 7)	Use a wide range of language, verb tenses and grammatical structures. Link language well. Adapt language.

© Pearson Education Limited 2013
Printing and photocopying permitted
Page 1 of 1

Worksheet 3.9 Mon CV: Prépa

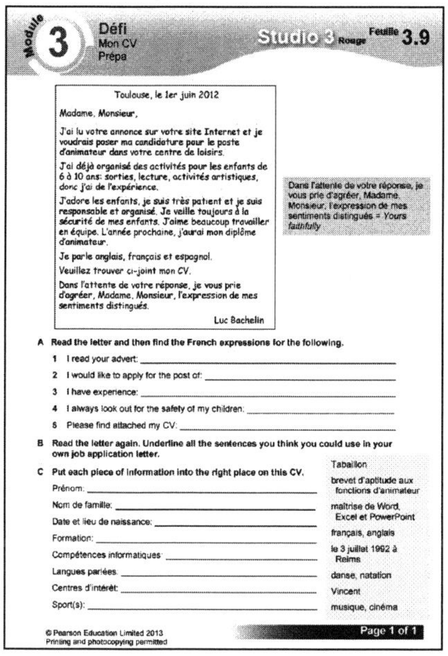
Module 3 Défi
Mon CV
Prépa
Studio 3 Rouge Feuille 3.9

Toulouse, le 1er juin 2012

Madame, Monsieur,

J'ai lu votre annonce sur votre site Internet et je voudrais poser ma candidature pour le poste d'animateur dans votre centre de loisirs.

J'ai déjà organisé des activités pour les enfants de 6 à 10 ans: sorties, lecture, activités artistiques, donc j'ai de l'expérience.

J'adore les enfants, je suis très patient et je suis responsable et organisé. Je veille toujours à la sécurité de mes enfants. J'aime beaucoup travailler en équipe. L'année prochaine, j'aurai mon diplôme d'animateur.

Je parle anglais, français et espagnol.

Veuillez trouver ci-joint mon CV.

Dans l'attente de votre réponse, je vous prie d'agréer, Madame, Monsieur, l'expression de mes sentiments distingués.

Luc Bachelin

Dans l'attente de votre réponse, je vous prie d'agréer, Madame, Monsieur, l'expression de mes sentiments distingués = *Yours faithfully*

A Read the letter and then find the French expressions for the following.

1 I read your advert: ____
2 I would like to apply for the post of: ____
3 I have experience: ____
4 I always look out for the safety of my children: ____
5 Please find attached my CV: ____

B Read the letter again. Underline all the sentences you think you could use in your own job application letter.

C Put each piece of information into the right place on this CV.

Prénom: ____
Nom de famille: ____
Date et lieu de naissance: ____
Formation: ____
Compétences informatiques: ____
Langues parlées: ____
Centres d'intérêt: ____
Sport(s): ____

Tabaillon
brevet d'aptitude aux fonctions d'animateur
maîtrise de Word, Excel et PowerPoint
français, anglais
le 3 juillet 1992 à Reims
danse, natation
Vincent
musique, cinéma

© Pearson Education Limited 2013
Printing and photocopying permitted
Page 1 of 1

Answers

A 1 J'ai lu votre annonce

2 je voudrais poser ma candidature pour le poste d'

3 j'ai de l'expérience.

4 Je veille toujours à la sécurité de mes enfants.

5 Veuillez trouver ci-joint mon CV.

C Prénom: Vincent

Nom de famille: Tabaillon

Date et lieu de naissance: le 3 juillet 1992 à Reims

Formation: brevet d'aptitude aux fonctions d'animateur

Compétences informatiques: maîtrise de Word, Excel et PowerPoint

Langues parlées: français, anglais

Centres d'intérêt: musique, cinéma

Sport(s): danse, natation

3 Je parle

The challenge

- Delivering a podcast about your career path and experience

Overview

Explain how this section works.

- Pupils read the context and what they need to do to complete the challenge.
- They then read the English questions supplied. Explain that they should use these both to help structure their content and as a checklist as part of their final preparations.
- Explain that the exercises which follow in this section are structured to help them prepare for their presentation.
- Before starting, pupils read the POSM feature: this will help them to improve their performance. Encourage them to use this approach routinely in speaking tasks.

Programme of Study references

GV1 Tenses (past, present and future)
LC4 Expressing ideas (speaking)
LC5 Speaking coherently and confidently

Resources

Audio files:
44_Module3_Jeparle_Ex2.mp3
45_Module3_Jeparle_Ex8.mp3

1 Unjumble the questions you'll be asked.

Pupils write out each jumbled question in the correct order.

Answers

1. Qu'est-ce que tu aimais faire quand tu étais petit(e)?
2. Quelle est ta journée typique?
3. Quelles sont les qualités requises pour ce métier?
4. Tu as suivi quelle formation?
5. Que feras-tu à l'avenir?

2 Listen to Nicole. She is a surgeon. Which sentences could she use in her podcast? There are two 'red herrings'. (1–8)

Pupils listen to Nicole, a surgeon, and identify which of the sentences she says could be included in her podcast. Two sentences are not relevant.

Audioscript Track 44

1 *Quand j'étais au collège, j'étais bonne élève. J'adorais la biologie.*
2 *Je rêvais d'être chirurgienne.*
3 *Je me lève tôt parce que je dois être à l'hôpital de bonne heure.*
4 *Je me prépare pour la salle d'opération.*
5 *L'année dernière, j'ai passé mes vacances en Espagne.*
6 *Pour faire ce métier, il faut être calme parce que c'est difficile et très intense.*
7 *Comme formation, j'ai fait onze ans d'études médicales.*
8 *J'ai aussi fait de la natation.*

Answers

1 ✓ 2 ✓ 3 ✓ 4 ✓ 5 ✗ 6 ✓ 7 ✓ 8 ✗

3 Note down five activities you used to do when you were little.

Pupils think up a list of five activities they used to do when they were little. Some picture prompts are supplied to get them started.

4 Make a list of six things you do in a typical day in your job.

Pupils write six short sentences describing what they do in a typical day in their dream job. Draw their attention to the tip box on using what you know, rather than trying to invent details that require complicated language.

5 Work in pairs. Find five adjectives in the snake on the right. Now come up with five more for your job. Write five sentences using your own adjectives.

Pupils identify the five adjectives in the word snake and then think up five more adjectives that they could use when talking about their dream job. They then write five sentences using the adjectives they thought up.

Answers

patient débrouillard indépendant rapide flexible

6 Decode these sentences in the future tense. Write three sentences of your own that you can use in your podcast.

Pupils decode and write out correctly the sentences featuring the future tense. They then write three more sentences with the future tense that they can use in their podcast.

Answers

1 Dans deux ou trois ans, j'irai aux États-Unis.

2 Je doublerai les acteurs d'Hollywood.

3 Je tomberai amoureuse de quelqu'un.

4 J'aurai un ou deux enfants.

5 Je trouverai un très bon équilibre entre ma vie professionnelle et ma vie privée.

7 Put the infinitives into the correct tense. The verb will always be in the same tense as the question!

Pupils complete the gap-fill text, replacing each infinitive prompt with the correct tense.

Answers

See exercise 8.

8 Now listen to the model answer to check your tenses.

Pupils listen and check their answers to exercise 7. Draw their attention to the tip box on using the full range of language they know to add variety to their speaking.

Audioscript Track 45

- *Qu'est-ce que tu aimais faire, quand tu étais petit?*
- *Quand j'étais petit, j'adorais la gymnastique. Je faisais tout le temps des acrobaties. Je voulais conduire des voitures de course. Je regardais ça à la télé et c'était passionnant. Je rêvais d'être cascadeur.*
- *Quelle est ta journée typique?*
- *Ça dépend. Tous les jours, je me lève tôt et je bouge! Je prends mon petit déjeuner. Je mange sain. Je fais de l'escalade, ou bien je fais de l'équitation ou des arts martiaux. Ça dépend de mon rôle. C'est très varié. Je trouve ça génial.*
- *Quelles sont les qualités requises pour ce métier?*
- *Pour faire ce métier, il faut être en forme. Il faut être discipliné parce qu'on doit suivre des ordres. Il faut être à la fois indépendant et flexible.*
- *Tu as suivi quelle formation?*
- *Moi, j'ai fait l'école du cirque et ensuite, j'ai suivi des cours d'art dramatique. Il n'y a pas vraiment de formation officielle.*
- *Que feras-tu à l'avenir?*
- *Dans deux ou trois ans, j'irai en Angleterre. Je travaillerai à Pinewood où je doublerai l'acteur qui joue James Bond.*

Answers

1 étais **2** adorais **3** faisais **4** voulais
5 regardais **6** était **7** rêvais **8** me lève
9 bouge **10** prends **11** mange **12** fais
13 fais **14** dépend **15** trouve **16** doit
17 ai fait **18** ai suivi **19** irai **20** travaillerai
21 doublerai

9 Look up some vocabulary that is specific to the job you have chosen.

Pupils use a dictionary to look up words that relate to their dream job.

10 Write out what you are going to say for the job challenge.

Pupils write out the complete text of their podcast, using the text in exercise 8 as a model and adapting this to include the language they have developed in the course of the challenge. They then check their texts, making sure that they are accurate and logical.

11 Now memorise your podcast and rehearse it!

Pupils memorise and practise their podcast. Draw their attention to the tip box on presentation skills. They might also find it useful to look again at the tips on p. 131.

Pupils can then record or deliver their podcasts. They send the recorded podcast to a partner, and the partner gives suggestions on how they could improve it. Pupils make a note of these suggestions for the next extended speaking task they do.

3 Studio Grammaire

The *Studio Grammaire* section provides a more detailed summary of the key grammar covered in the module, along with further exercises to practise these points. The interactive activities on ActiveTeach pp.070 and 071 are repeated from elsewhere in the module.

Grammar topics

- modal verbs
- the future tense
- question forms
- the imperfect tense
- using three tenses together

Modal verbs

1 Find the eight errors in this text, then write it out correctly.

Pupils identify the eight errors in the text, then write the text out correcting the errors.

Answers

Si on **veut** vendre des produits, on doit d'abord les **acheter**. Ensuite, si on parle des langues étrangères, on **peut** vendre dans la langue du client. C'est un grand avantage. Dans mon travail, je **dois** écouter mes clients et je dois **comprendre** exactement ce qu'ils **veulent**. Je **dois** aussi bien connaître mes produits si je veux **réussir**.

Future tense

2 Match up the verbs to the correct person then translate them into English.

Pupils match each subject pronoun to the correct part of the verb. They then translate the verbs into English.

Answers

je travaillerai	I will work
tu voyageras	you will travel
il/elle/on tombera	he/she/we will fall
nous vendrons	we will sell
vous discuterez	you will discuss
ils/elles mangeront	they will eat

3 Match up these irregular verbs to their future stems.

Pupils match each infinitive to the correct future stem.

Answers

1 e **2** a **3** b **4** c **5** d

Question forms

4 Unjumble these questions, then write whether they are in the present (PR), the future (F) or the past (P) tense.

Answers

1 Est-ce que tu aimais le basket? **P**

2 Qu'est-ce que tu fais dans la vie? **PR**

3 Tu jouais au foot tous les jours? **P**

4 Que feras-tu à l'avenir? **F**

5 Quels sont tes passetemps? **PR**

6 Quelle est ta journée typique? **PR**

7 Est-ce que tu iras à l'université? **F**

8 Tu as suivi quelle formation? **P**

Imperfect tense

5 Write out the verb *travailler* in the imperfect tense.

Pupils write out the full paradigm of *travailler* in the imperfect tense.

Answers

je travaillais
tu travaillais
il/elle/on travaillait
nous travaillions
vous travailliez
ils/elles travaillaient

6 Write the verbs in brackets in the imperfect tense. Then translate the sentences into English.

Pupils change the infinitive prompt in each sentence to the correct part of the imperfect tense. They then translate the sentences into English.

Answers

1 J'**aimais** le collège.
I used to like school.

2 Tu **avais** beaucoup d'amis?
Did you use to have a lot of friends?

3 Il **était** membre de beaucoup de clubs.
He was a member of lots of clubs.

4 Elle **faisait** ses devoirs.
She used to do her homework.

5 Nous **aimions** beaucoup les maths.
We used to like maths a lot.

6 Ils **faisaient** beaucoup de sport.
They used to do a lot of sport.

7 Vous **jouiez** au volley ou au foot?
Did you used to play volleyball or football?

8 On **adorait** aller en ville.
We used to love going into town.

7 Translate this short text into French. The infinitives of the verbs you will need are next to the text.

Pupils translate the text into French. The infinitives of the verbs they need to use are supplied for support.

Answers

Quand j'étais petit, j'étais bon élève. Je faisais mes devoirs et j'écoutais en classe. J'aimais beaucoup le collège. C'était génial/super. J'adorais la géographie parce que j'avais de bonnes notes.

Using three tenses together

8 Copy and complete this text using the appropriate tense of the verbs in brackets.

Pupils copy and complete the gap-fill text, replacing the infinitives with verbs in the appropriate tense.

Answers

1 étais **2** étais **3** avais **4** jouais **5** ai **6** suis
7 veux **8** irai **9** ferai **10** travaillerai
11 habiterai **12** sera **13** trouverai

3 À toi

Self-access reading and writing

A Reinforcement

1 Lis les textes et réponds aux questions. Utilise un dictionnaire, si nécessaire. (Reading L6)

Reading. Pupils read the texts and then identify who is being described in each of the questions that follow. They can use a dictionary to help them.

Answers

1 Jade **2** Maëlys **3** Abdoul **4** Jade **5** Maëlys **6** Abdoul

2 Écris un paragraphe pour Vincent, en utilisant les renseignements suivants. (Writing L4–6)

Writing. Pupils write a paragraph for Vincent, using the picture prompts supplied. Draw pupils' attention to the tip box on what to include if aiming for a higher level.

Example answer

Plus tard dans la vie, je veux être vétérinaire, car j'aime les animaux et la médecine m'intéresse. Je ne veux pas être mécanicien, puisque je ne suis pas intéressé par les voitures et je n'aime pas travailler avec mes mains. Ce serait ennuyeux.

3 Lis et copie le texte dans le bon ordre. Puis traduis le texte. (Reading L4)

Reading. Pupils write out the text, putting the words in each sentence in the correct order. They then translate the text into English.

Answers

Si on veut travailler dans le tourisme ou l'hôtellerie en Grande-Bretagne, parler une langue étrangère, c'est important. Par exemple, si on veut être guide touristique à Londres ou dans une autre grande ville, on doit souvent parler avec des touristes de différentes nationalités. Ou si on veut travailler comme réceptionniste dans un hôtel où il y a des visiteurs internationaux, parler une autre langue, c'est un plus. Et bien sûr, si on veut être steward ou stewardess à bord d'un avion, parler une langue étrangère, c'est essentiel.

If you want to work in tourism or the hotel industry in Great Britain, it's important to speak a foreign language. For example, if you want to be a tourist guide in London or another big city, you often have to speak to people of different nationalities. Or if you want to work as a receptionist in a hotel where there are international visitors, speaking another language is a plus. And of course, if you want to be a steward or stewardess on an aeroplane, it's essential to speak a foreign language.

B Extension

1 Lis le texte et choisis les bonnes réponses. Utilise un dictionnaire, si nécessaire. (Reading L7)

Reading. Pupils read the text and complete each sentence by choosing from the three options given. They can use a dictionary. *le bac* is glossed for support.

Answers

1 interprète
2 des conversations
3 des chefs d'entreprise
4 gens
5 les langues
6 voyagé

2 Lis le texte et note vrai (V) ou faux (F). (Reading L6)

Reading. Pupils read the text and note whether each sentence is true (writing V) or false (writing F). EICAR is glossed for support.

Answers

1 F **2** V **3** V **4** F **5** F **6** V

3 Imagine que tu es Antoine. Adapte le texte de l'exercice 2, en utilisant les idées suivantes. (Writing L7)

Writing. Pupils imagine they are Antoine and write about themselves, adapting the text in exercise 2 using the prompts supplied.

Example answer

Quand j'étais plus jeune, j'aimais le collège. Je trouvais ça intéressant et j'avais de bonnes notes. En dehors du collège, ma passion, c'était la musique. J'allais à des concerts de rock une ou deux fois par mois. Puis, quand j'avais treize ans, mes parents m'ont acheté une guitare et j'ai commencé à jouer. L'année dernière, j'ai gagné le premier prix dans un concours de talent, donc j'ai décidé que je veux être guitariste professionnel. Dans trois ans, j'irai à l'Académie de Musique pour étudier la musique. Ce serait mon rêve de travailler à New York, un jour.

4 Module 4: Spécial vacances

Unit & Learning objectives	Programme of Study references	Key language	Grammar and other language features
1 Question de vacances (pp. 76–77) Discussing holidays Asking questions using inversion	**GV2** Grammatical structures (questions with inversion; *y*) **LC1** Listening and responding **LC2** Transcription **LC3** Conversation (dealing with the unexpected)	*Je vais en vacances …* *au bord de la mer* *J'y reste …* *une semaine/quinze jours/ un mois* *On fait du camping.* etc. *Je fais …* *du canoë-kayak* *du VTT/de la plongée sous-marine/de l'escalade,* etc.	**G** the pronoun *y* **G** question forms – developing writing skills
2 J'adore les sensations fortes! (pp. 78–79) Imagining adventure holidays Using the conditional	**GV1** Tenses (conditional) **GV3** Developing vocabulary **GV3** Opinions and discussions **LC3** Conversation	*Je voudrais …/ J'aimerais …* *descendre l'Amazone en canoë* *essayer des sports extrêmes* etc. *Ce serait génial/super.* *Quelle horreur!* etc.	**G** the conditional
3 C'est indispensable! (pp. 80–81) Talking about what you take with you on holiday Using reflexive verbs	**GV2** Grammatical structures (reflexive verbs) **GV3** Developing vocabulary **LC4** Expressing ideas (speaking) **LC5** Speaking coherently and confidently	*Je me douche.* *Je me fais bronzer.* *Je me fais piquer.* *Je m'amuse.* *Je m'ennuie.* etc. *un adaptateur* *un chargeur (pour mon mp3)* *des tongs* (fpl) etc.	**G** reflexive verbs – using reference resources
4 Mes vidéos de vacances (pp. 82–83) Describing what happened on holiday Combining different tenses	**GV1** Tenses (combining different tenses) **LC1** Listening and responding **LC3** Conversation (dealing with the unexpected) **LC8** Writing creatively	*Pas vraiment.* *C'était un désastre.* *Je suis resté(e) trop longtemps au soleil.* *Il a plu tout le temps.* *C'est dommage.* etc.	**G** the perfect tense (irregular past participles & verbs taking *être*) – techniques for memorising verb forms

Unit & Learning objectives	Programme of Study references	Key language	Grammar and other language features
5 À la base de loisirs (pp. 84–85) Visiting a tourist attraction Using emphatic pronouns	**GV2** Grammatical structures (emphatic pronouns) **LC2** Transcription **LC6** Reading comprehension **LC8** Writing creatively	*J'ai …/On a …* *fait du trampoline* *fait de la baignade* *fait une balade en barque* *joué aux boules* *joué sur des structures gonflables* *loué un pédalo* etc.	**G** emphatic pronouns **G** using three tenses – developing listening skills – developing speaking skills
Bilan et Révisions (pp. 86–87) Pupils' checklist and practice exercises			
En plus: Des vacances au collège! (pp. 88–89) Debating the idea of 'open school' in the holidays	**LC1** Listening and responding **LC3** Conversation (dealing with the unexpected) **LC6** Reading comprehension (adapted from authentic) **LC6** Translation into English	Review of language from the module	– developing speaking skills
J'écris (pp. 90–91)	**GV1** Tenses (past, present and future) **GV4** Accuracy (grammar; spelling; punctuation) **LC4** Expressing ideas (writing) **LC8** Writing creatively	Review of language from the module	– developing writing skills – checking work
Studio Grammaire 1 (pp. 92–93) Detailed grammar summary and practice exercises			**G** the pronoun y **G** forming questions **G** the conditional **G** reflexive verbs
Studio Grammaire 2 (pp. 94–95) Detailed grammar summary and practice exercises			**G** more perfect tense verbs **G** emphatic pronouns **G** using three tenses (past, present and future)
À toi (pp. 124–125) Self-access reading and writing at two levels			

(Pupil Book pp. 76–77)

4 1 Question de vacances

Learning objectives

- Discussing holidays
- Asking questions using inversion

Programme of Study references

GV2 Grammatical structures (questions with inversion; *y*)

LC1 Listening and responding

LC2 Transcription

LC3 Conversation (dealing with the unexpected)

FCSE links

Unit 3: Holidays and travel (Holidays, Activities, Accommodation, Destination)

Grammar

- the pronoun *y*
- question forms

Key language

Je vais en vacances …
au bord de la mer
à la campagne
à la montagne
J'y vais …
avec ma famille
J'y reste …
une semaine/quinze jours/ un mois
Je pars en colo.
Je pars en classe de neige.
On fait du camping.
Je fais …
du canoë-kayak
du VTT
du ski nautique
du snowboard
de la plongée sous-marine
de la voile
de la planche à voile
de l'équitation
de l'escalade
des randonnées dans la forêt
Je vais à la pêche.
Je prends des cours de ski.
J'ai fait un stage (de voile).
Il n'y a pas grand-chose à faire.

PLTS

C Creative thinkers

Cross-curricular

ICT: word-processing
English: pronouns

Resources

Audio files:
46_Module4_Unit1_Ex2.mp3
47_Module4_Unit1_Ex3.mp3
48_Module4_Unit1_Ex5.mp3

Workbooks:
Cahier d'exercices Rouge, page 37

ActiveTeach:
Starter 1 resource
Starter 2 resource
p.076 Grammar
p.076 Grammar practice
p.077 Grammar
p.077 Grammar practice
p.077 Grammar skills
p.077 Listening skills

ActiveLearn:
Listening, Reading
Grammar

Starter 1

Aim

To review question words

Write up the following. Give pupils three minutes to translate the words into English. If necessary, supply the English words in random order for support.

Où? Quand? Combien? Pourquoi? Qui?

Qu'est-ce que? Que? Comment?

Check answers. (**Answers:** Where? When? How much?/How many? Why? Who? What? What? How?)

1 Fais correspondre les questions et les réponses. (Reading L5)

Reading. Pupils read and match the questions and answers. Some vocabulary is glossed for support.

Answers

See exercise 2.

2 Écoute et vérifie tes réponses. (Listening L5)

Listening. Pupils listen and check their answers to exercise 1.

Audioscript Track 46

– *Aurélie, où vas-tu en vacances?*
– *En général, je vais au bord de la mer, en Bretagne.*
– *Avec qui vas-tu en vacances?*
– *J'y vais avec ma famille.*
– *Combien de temps y restes-tu?*
– *J'y reste quinze jours.*
– *Que fais-tu pendant les vacances?*
– *Je vais à la plage tous les jours. Je me fais bronzer et je me baigne dans la mer.*
– *Pourquoi aimes-tu ou n'aimes-tu pas ce style de vacances?*
– *J'aime bien ça parce que j'adore le soleil.*
– *Où es-tu allée en vacances l'année dernière?*
– *Je suis allée à la Baule, en Bretagne.*
– *Qu'est-ce que tu as fait?*
– *J'ai fait un stage de voile. C'était super!*

Answers

1 e **2** g **3** d **4** f **5** b **6** c **7** a

Studio Grammaire: the pronoun *y*

Use the *Studio Grammaire* box to cover the pronoun *y*. Explain that it is used to avoid having to repeat expressions like *en Bretagne/à la plage*. Point out that it is used in French even when 'there' might be omitted in English, e.g. 'I go to Brittany. I go (there) with my family.' There is more information and further practice on Pupil Book p. 92.

➕ Pupils write four phrases in French that could be replaced by the pronoun *y*.

3 Écoute et lis. Trouve l'équivalent des phrases en anglais dans le texte. (Listening L5)

Listening. Pupils listen to three teenagers talking about their holidays, and read the text at the same time. They then find in the text the French versions of the English phrases/sentences listed. Some vocabulary is glossed for support.

Audioscript Track 47

- *Tous les ans, en février, je pars en classe de neige, dans les Alpes. J'y vais avec mes copains de classe et j'y reste une semaine. Nous prenons des cours de ski et on fait aussi du snowboard. Je trouve ça génial parce que j'adore les sports d'hiver. D'habitude, on skie en France, mais l'année dernière, on est allés en Suisse.*
- *Normalement, je vais en vacances à la campagne. J'y vais avec mes parents. Nous y passons un mois. Nous faisons du camping et des randonnées dans la forêt. C'est ennuyeux pour moi parce qu'il n'y a pas grand-chose à faire. Pourtant, l'année dernière, j'ai rencontré un garçon sympa et on est devenus bons amis.*
- *Chaque été, je pars en colo. J'y vais avec mon frère. On y reste dix jours. On fait toutes sortes d'activités: par exemple, du VTT, de l'équitation et du canoë-kayak. J'aime ça parce que je préfère les vacances actives. L'année dernière, je suis allé en colo en Alsace où j'ai fait de l'escalade. C'était top!*

Answers

1 J'y vais avec mes copains de classe
2 Nous prenons des cours de ski
3 on est allés en Suisse
4 je vais en vacances à la campagne
5 Nous y passons un mois.
6 Nous faisons du camping et des randonnées dans la forêt.
7 il n'y a pas grand-chose à faire
8 on est devenus bons amis
9 Chaque été, je pars en colo.
10 j'ai fait de l'escalade

R Pupils identify in the texts in exercise 3 the phrases being replaced by the pronoun *y*.

Starter 2

Aim

To review questions

Write up the following. Give pupils three minutes to write out the questions in the correct order.

1 *avec vacances vas-tu en ? qui*
2 *restes-tu de temps y ? combien*
3 *pendant vacances fais-tu que les ?*
4 *? de pourquoi vacances style aimes-tu ce*

Check answers. (**Answers: 1** *Avec qui vas-tu en vacances?* **2** *Combien de temps y restes-tu?* **3** *Que fais-tu pendant les vacances?* **4** *Pourquoi aimes-tu ce style de vacances?*)

Alternative Starter 2:

Use ActiveTeach p.076 Grammar practice to practise *y* or ActiveTeach p.077 Grammar practice to practise forming questions.

4 En tandem. Interviewe une personne de l'exercice 3. Utilise les questions de l'exercice 1. (Speaking L5)

Speaking. In pairs: pupils take it in turn to be interviewed, adopting the persona of one of the people in exercise 3. The interviewer uses the questions from exercise 1. A sample opening is supplied. Ask pupils to monitor each other's intonation when using questions.

Studio Grammaire: forming questions

Use the *Studio Grammaire* box to cover how to form questions. There is more information and further practice on Pupil Book p. 92.

5 Écoute. Copie le tableau et note les reseignements. (1–2) (Listening L6)

Listening. Pupils copy out the table. They listen to two dialogues about holidays and complete the table with the details. *faire du ski nautique* is glossed for support.

Audioscript Track 48

1 – *Aïcha, où vas-tu en vacances?*
– *Je vais au bord de la mer. D'habitude, nous allons en Espagne, mais l'année dernière, nous sommes allés au Portugal.*
– *Avec qui vas-tu en vacances?*
– *J'y vais avec mes parents et ma grand-mère.*
– *Combien de temps y restes-tu?*
– *Nous louons une villa au mois d'août et nous y restons un mois.*
– *Que fais-tu pendant les vacances?*
– *Alors … je me baigne dans la mer ou à la piscine de la villa, je lis des livres ou des magazines …*
– *Pourquoi aimes-tu ou n'aimes-tu pas ce style de vacances?*
– *C'est un peu ennuyeux pour moi, parce qu'il y a trois adultes … et moi! Je suis la seule ado, et mes copines me manquent.*
– *Où iras-tu en vacances, l'année prochaine?*
– *J'irai en Espagne. Mais cette fois, ce sera un peu différent parce que je ferai un stage de ski nautique. Ce sera génial!*

2 – *Julien, où vas-tu en vacances?*
– *Pendant les grandes vacances, je pars toujours en colo. J'adore ça, parce qu'on peut faire toutes sortes d'activités. Par exemple, l'année dernière, j'ai fait de l'équitation pour la première fois. C'était fabuleux!*
– *Avec qui vas-tu en vacances?*
– *J'y vais avec un groupe de trois copains.*
– *Combien de temps y restes-tu?*
– *J'y reste quinze jours.*
– *Que fais-tu pendant les vacances?*
– *Il y a une rivière et un lac, alors on peut pratiquer des sports nautiques: le canoë-kayak, le rafting, la voile, le ski nautique …*
– *Pourquoi aimes-tu ou n'aimes-tu pas ce genre de vacances?*
– *Moi, j'adore ça parce que je suis très sportif et je préfère partir en vacances avec mes copains qu'avec mes parents!*
– *Où iras-tu l'année prochaine?*
– *J'irai en colo dans les Alpes. Ce sera super, parce qu'on fera de l'escalade!*

Answers

	1	2
où?	*bord de la mer*, Espagne	colo
l'année dernière	Portugal	equitation
avec qui?	parents, grandmère	3 copains
combien de temps?	un mois	15 jours
activités?	se baigne, lit livres ou magazines	canoë-kayak, rafting, voile, ski nautique
opinion ☺ ☹ **et raison?**	☹ ennuyeux, seule ado, copines lui manquent	☺ sportif, vacances avec copains
l'année prochaine	Espagne, stage de ski nautique	(colo) Alpes, escalade

6 En tandem. Fais trois interviews. Complète les questions et utilise les images ou tes propres idées. (Speaking L5–6)

Speaking. In pairs: pupils prepare and perform three interviews using the framework and sets of picture prompts supplied. They take it in turn to ask and answer. Draw pupils' attention to the tip box on including a question about the past and/or the future in order to reach a higher level.

7 Imagine que tu es une célébrité. Écris un paragraphe sur tes vacances. (Writing L5–6)

PLTS C

Writing. Pupils imagine that they are a celebrity and write a paragraph about their holiday. A list of features to include is supplied. Draw pupils' attention to the tip box on including the future tense in order to improve their writing.

Pupils could write the text on computer, to facilitate the production of a second draft. They could also include photographs.

Plenary

Ask pupils to summarise the different ways of forming questions.

Put the class into teams. The teams take it in turn to ask each other a question about a holiday. They should aim to use the various different question types and a range of tenses in their questions and responses. Award extra points if they manage to do so.

Workbook, page 37

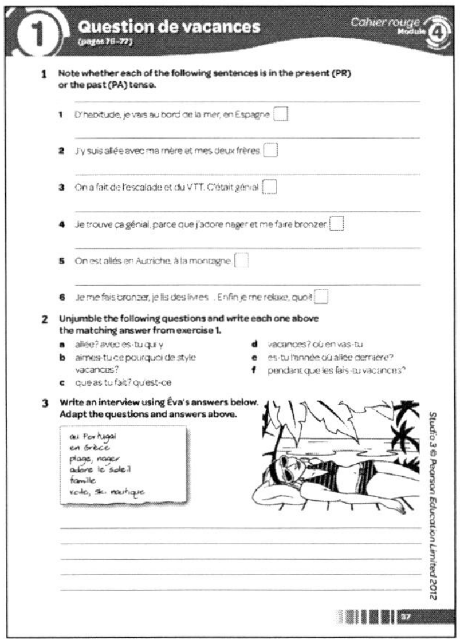

1 Question de vacances (pages 76–77) Cahier rouge Module 4

1 Note whether each of the following sentences is in the present (PR) or the past (PA) tense.

1 D'habitude, je vais au bord de la mer, en Espagne. ☐

2 J'y suis allée avec ma mère et mes deux frères. ☐

3 On a fait de l'escalade et du VTT. C'était génial. ☐

4 Je trouve ça génial, parce que j'adore nager et me faire bronzer. ☐

5 On est allés en Autriche, à la montagne. ☐

6 Je me fais bronzer, je lis des livres… Enfin je me relaxe, quoi! ☐

2 Unjumble the following questions and write each one above the matching answer from exercise 1.

a allée? avec es-tu qui y

b aimes-tu ce pourquoi de style vacances?

c que as tu fait? qu'est-ce

d vacances? où en vas-tu

e es-tu l'année où allée dernière?

f pendant que les fais-tu vacances?

3 Write an interview using Éva's answers below. Adapt the questions and answers above.

Studio 3 © Pearson Education Limited 2012

37

Answers

1 **1** PR **2** PA **3** PA **4** PR **5** PA **6** PR

2 **a** Avec qui y es-tu allée? 2

b Pourquoi aimes-tu ce style de vacances? 4

c Qu'est-ce que tu as fait? 3

d Où vas-tu en vacances? 1

e Où es-tu allée l'année dernière? 5

f Que fais-tu pendant les vacances? 6

3 (Example answer:)

– Où vas-tu en vacances?
– Normalement, nous allons au Portugal.
– Que fais-tu pendant les vacances?
– Je me fais bronzer à la plage et je nage dans la mer.
– Pourquoi aimes-tu ce style de vacances?
– Parce que j'adore le soleil.
– Où es-tu allée l'année dernière?
– On est allés en Grèce.
– Avec qui y es-tu allée?
– J'y suis allée avec ma famille.
– Qu'est-ce que tu as fait?
– J'ai fait de la voile et du ski nautique.

Worksheet 4.1 Asking questions

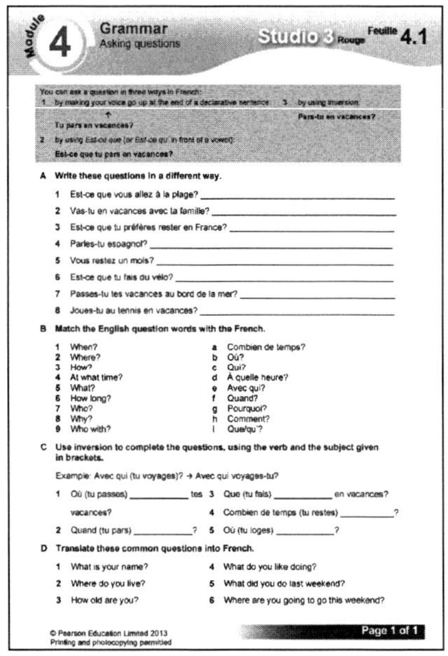

Module 4 Grammar Asking questions Studio 3 Rouge Feuille 4.1

You can ask a question in three ways in French:
1 by making your voice go up at the end of a declarative sentence: Tu pars en vacances?
2 by using Est-ce que (or Est-ce qu' in front of a vowel): Est-ce que tu pars en vacances?
3 by using inversion: Pars-tu en vacances?

A Write these questions in a different way.

1 Est-ce que vous allez à la plage? ______
2 Vas-tu en vacances avec ta famille? ______
3 Est-ce que tu préfères rester en France? ______
4 Parles-tu espagnol? ______
5 Vous restez un mois? ______
6 Est-ce que tu fais du vélo? ______
7 Passes-tu tes vacances au bord de la mer? ______
8 Joues-tu au tennis en vacances? ______

B Match the English question words with the French.

1 When?	a Combien de temps?
2 Where?	b Où?
3 How?	c Qui?
4 At what time?	d À quelle heure?
5 What?	e Avec qui?
6 How long?	f Quand?
7 Who?	g Pourquoi?
8 Why?	h Comment?
9 Who with?	i Que/qu'?

C Use inversion to complete the questions, using the verb and the subject given in brackets.

Example: Avec qui (tu voyages)? → Avec qui voyages-tu?

1 Où (tu passes) ______ tes vacances?
2 Quand (tu pars) ______?
3 Que (tu fais) ______ en vacances?
4 Combien de temps (tu restes) ______?
5 Où (tu loges) ______?

D Translate these common questions into French.

1 What is your name?
2 Where do you live?
3 How old are you?
4 What do you like doing?
5 What did you do last weekend?
6 Where are you going to go this weekend?

© Pearson Education Limited 2013 Printing and photocopying permitted

Page 1 of 1

Answers

A **1** Allez-vous à la plage?

2 Est-ce que tu vas en vacances avec ta famille?

3 Préfères-tu rester en France?

4 Tu parles espagnol?

5 Est-ce que vous restez un mois?

6 Fais-tu du vélo?

7 Tu passes tes vacances au bord de la mer?

8 Est-ce que tu joues au tennis en vacances?

B **1** f **2** b **3** h **4** d **5** I **6** a **7** c **8** g **9** e

C **1** Où passes-tu tes vacances?

2 Quand pars-tu?

3 Que fais-tu en vacances?

4 Combien de temps restes-tu?

5 Où loges-tu?

D *All question forms are acceptable.*

1 Comment t'appelles-tu?

2 Où habites-tu?

3 Quel âge as-tu?

4 Qu'est-ce que tu aimes faire?

5 Qu'est-ce que tu as fait le weekend dernier?

6 Où vas-tu aller ce weekend?

Worksheet 4.2 Listening for gist and detail

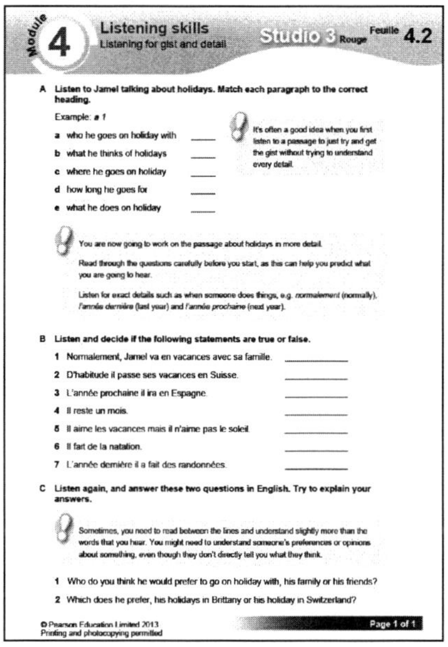

Module 4 Listening skills
Listening for gist and detail
Studio 3 Rouge Feuille 4.2

A Listen to Jamel talking about holidays. Match each paragraph to the correct heading.

Example: *a 1*

a who he goes on holiday with ____
b what he thinks of holidays ____
c where he goes on holiday ____
d how long he goes for ____
e what he does on holiday ____

It's often a good idea when you first listen to a passage to just try and get the gist without trying to understand every detail.

You are now going to work on the passage about holidays in more detail.

Read through the questions carefully before you start, as this can help you predict what you are going to hear.

Listen for exact details such as when someone does things, e.g. *normalement* (normally), *l'année dernière* (last year) and *l'année prochaine* (next year).

B Listen and decide if the following statements are true or false.

1 Normalement, Jamel va en vacances avec sa famille. ________
2 D'habitude il passe ses vacances en Suisse. ________
3 L'année prochaine il ira en Espagne. ________
4 Il reste un mois. ________
5 Il aime les vacances mais il n'aime pas le soleil. ________
6 Il fait de la natation. ________
7 L'année dernière il a fait des randonnées. ________

C Listen again, and answer these two questions in English. Try to explain your answers.

Sometimes, you need to read between the lines and understand slightly more than the words that you hear. You might need to understand someone's preferences or opinions about something, even though they don't directly tell you what they think.

1 Who do you think he would prefer to go on holiday with, his family or his friends?
2 Which does he prefer, his holidays in Brittany or his holiday in Switzerland?

Page 1 of 1

Answers

A

a 1
b 4
c 2
d 3
e 5

B

1 True
2 False
3 True
4 False
5 False
6 True
7 True

C

1 His friends, because he misses them when he's away.

2 His holidays in Brittany because he said that his holiday in Switzerland was boring and there wasn't much to do.

4

2 J'adore les sensations fortes!

Learning objectives

- Imagining adventure holidays
- Using the conditional

Programme of Study references

GV1 Tenses (conditional)
GV3 Developing vocabulary
GV3 Opinions and discussions
LC3 Conversation

FCSE links

Unit 3: Holidays and travel (Types of holiday, Camping, Activities)

Grammar

- the conditional

Key language

Je voudrais …/J'aimerais …
descendre l'Amazone en canoë
essayer des sports extrêmes
faire un safari en Afrique
passer des vacances sur une île déserte
traverser le Sahara à dos de chameau
visiter tous les parcs d'attractions du monde
voir des gorilles en liberté
Oua-a-a-is! Cool!
Bonne idée!
Ce serait génial/super.
Quelle horreur!
Tu rigoles!
Ce serait trop …
dangereux/tranquille pour moi
Ce n'est pas mon truc.

PLTS

T Team workers

Cross-curricular

Geography: location of places and environments

Resources

Audio files:
49_Module4_Unit2_Ex2.mp3
Workbooks:
Cahier d'exercices Rouge, page 38
ActiveTeach:
p.078 Flashcards
p.078 Grammar
p.078 Grammar practice
p.079 Grammar skills
ActiveLearn:
Listening, Reading
Grammar, Vocabulary

Starter 1

Aim

To introduce the topic

Do exercise 1 on Pupil Book p. 78 as the Starter.

Alternative Starter 1:

Use ActiveTeach p.078 Flashcards to introduce adventure holiday activities.

1 Trouve la bonne photo pour chaque texte. (Reading L4)

Reading. Pupils read the chatroom texts and find the correct photo for each one. Some vocabulary is glossed for support.

Answers

1 E **2** D **3** A **4** B **5** C

R Ask pupils to find the places mentioned in exercise 1 in an atlas.

\+ Pupils read the texts in exercise 1 again and rate the adventure holidays in their personal order of preference (1–6, with 1 their favourite). They then tell the class which activity they would most like to do, giving reasons.

Studio Grammaire: the conditional

Use the *Studio Grammaire* box to cover the conditional. There is more information and further practice on Pupil Book p. 93.

2 Écoute. Note la lettre de la bonne photo de l'exercice 1. Note aussi si la réaction est positive 🙂 ou négative ☹ .(1–5) (Listening L5–6)

Listening. Pupils listen to five people talking about what they'd like to do on a dream holiday and for each note the letter of the correct picture in exercise 1. They also note whether the response in each conversation is positive (drawing a smiley face) or negative (drawing a sad face).

Audioscript Track 49

1 – *Comment aimerais-tu passer tes vacances de rêve?*
– *e voudrais essayer les sports extrêmes, par exemple, le parapente ou la chute libre.*
– *Ah bon? Tu as déjà essayé?*
– *Non, mais mon frère a fait du parapente.*
– *Je n'aimerais pas faire ça, moi. À mon avis, c'est trop dangereux.*

2 – *Tu sais, un jour, je voudrais aller aux Antilles.*
– *Ah bon, pourquoi?*
– *Parce que je voudrais faire de la plongée sous-marine. J'aimerais voir tous les poissons tropicaux et le corail.*

- *Tu rigoles! Ce serait vraiment ennuyeux! Moi, je préfère les sensations fortes!*

3 – *Où voudrais-tu aller en vacances, un jour?*
- *Moi, j'aimerais faire un voyage extraordinaire.*
- *Quoi, par exemple?*
- *Par exemple, traverser le Sahara à dos de chameau ou descendre l'Amazone en canoë.*
- *Ah oui, j'aimerais aussi faire ça. Ce serait génial! On le fera ensemble, un jour, d'accord?*
- *D'accord! J'ai trouvé un site web sur les vacances d'aventure comme ça, hier. Tu veux voir?*
- *Oui, je veux bien.*
- *Attends que je trouve l'adresse. Ah oui, la voilà.*

4 – *Comment aimerais-tu passer tes vacances de rêve?*
- *Moi, je voudrais faire un safari en Afrique. J'aimerais surtout voir des gorilles en liberté au Congo.*
- *Bonne idée! Ce serait sympa, comme vacances. Je peux venir aussi?*
- *Mais bien sûr! Tu es déjà allé en Afrique, toi?*
- *Non, mais j'ai une correspondante au Cameroun et elle a vu des gorilles. Elle a dit que c'était une expérience inoubliable.*

5 – *Un jour, je voudrais passer des vacances sur une île déserte.*
- *Quoi? Tu voudrais y aller toute seule?*
- *Oui, pourquoi? Tu voudrais venir aussi?*
- *Ah non, ce n'est pas mon truc. Ce serait trop tranquille pour moi!*
- *Ce serait parfait pour moi. Je pourrais bouquiner en paix: pas de portable, pas de télé … et surtout, pas de petit frère avec sa PlayStation! OK, c'est décidé: j'irai là-bas dès demain.*
- *Tu iras là-bas dès demain … dans tes rêves!*

Answers

1 A ☹ 2 B ☹ 3 C ☺ 4 E ☺ 5 D ☹

Pupils listen again and note two additional details mentioned in each conversation.

3 En tandem. Discute avec ton/ta camarade. Utilise les phrases de l'exercice 1. (Speaking L5)

PLTS T

Speaking. In pairs: pupils discuss their dream holidays. A sample opening is supplied, along with a list of key language, covering activities and opinions.

Starter 2

Aim

To review the conditional; To review language for adventure holidays

Write up the following. Give pupils three minutes to translate the sentence openings into French and complete them with their own examples.

I would like to …	*I wouldn't like to …*
It would be …	*It wouldn't be …*

Hear answers. Ask how the conditional is formed and when it is used.

Alternative Starter 2:

Use ActiveTeach p.078 Grammar practice to practise the conditional.

4 Écris un court paragraphe. Utilise les conseils suivants. (Writing L5)

Writing. Pupils write a short paragraph about a dream holiday. A list of features to include is supplied.

5 Lis le quiz. Cherche les mots inconnus dans le dictionnaire. (Reading L5)

Reading. Pupils read the quiz. Some vocabulary is glossed for support. They should look up any other unknown words in a dictionary.

6 En tandem. Fais le quiz avec ton/ta camarade. (Speaking L5)

Speaking. In pairs: pupils do the quiz. A sample exchange is supplied.

7 Calcule ton score et lis les résultats. Tu es d'accord ou pas d'accord avec ça? (Reading L5)

Reading. Pupils work out their quiz score and read the results to find out how daring they are. They say whether or not they agree with the results.

Plenary

Ask the class to summarise how the conditional is formed and when it is used.

Challenge the class to come up with as many different daring holiday activities as they can, forming sentences with *je voudrais*. Encourage them to add their own ideas to the ones already in the Pupil Book.

Workbook, page 38

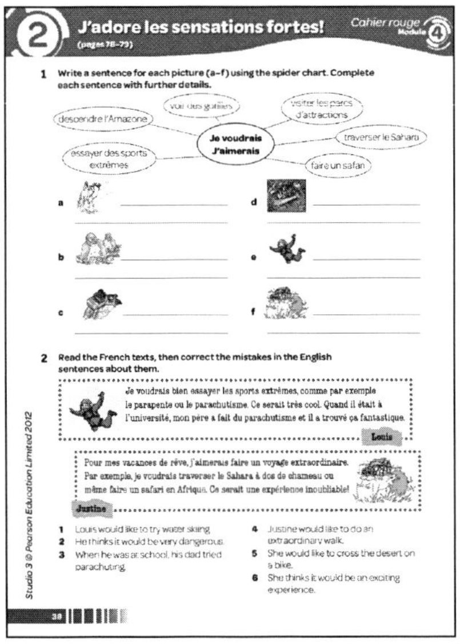

2 J'adore les sensations fortes! (pages 78–79) *Cahier rouge* Module 4

1 Write a sentence for each picture (a–f) using the spider chart. Complete each sentence with further details.

Je voudrais / J'aimerais: descendre l'Amazone; voir des gorilles; visiter les parcs d'attractions; traverser le Sahara; essayer des sports extrêmes; faire un safari

a ______ d ______
b ______ e ______
c ______ f ______

2 Read the French texts, then correct the mistakes in the English sentences about them.

Je voudrais bien essayer les sports extrêmes, comme par exemple le parapente ou le parachutisme. Ce serait très cool. Quand il était à l'université, mon père a fait du parachutisme et il a trouvé ça fantastique. **Louis**

Pour mes vacances de rêve, j'aimerais faire un voyage extraordinaire. Par exemple, je voudrais traverser le Sahara à dos de chameau ou même faire un safari en Afrique. Ce serait une expérience inoubliable! **Justine**

1 Louis would like to try water skiing.
2 He thinks it would be very dangerous.
3 When he was at school, his dad tried parachuting.
4 Justine would like to do an extraordinary walk.
5 She would like to cross the desert on a bike.
6 She thinks it would be an exciting experience.

Studio 3 © Pearson Education Limited 2012

38

Answers

1 (Example answers:)

a J'aimerais traverser le Sahara à dos de chameau.

b Je voudrais voir des gorilles en liberté.

c J'aimerais visiter les parcs d'attractions du monde entier.

d Je voudrais descendre l'Amazone en canoë.

e J'aimerais essayer des sports extrêmes comme la chute libre, par exemple.

f Je voudrais faire un safari en Afrique.

2 **1** Louis would like to try parachuting.

2 He thinks it would be very cool.

3 When he was at university, his dad tried parachuting.

4 Justine would like to make an extraordinary trip.

5 She would like to cross a desert on a camel.

6 She thinks it would be an unforgettable experience.

Worksheet 4.3 Using the conditional

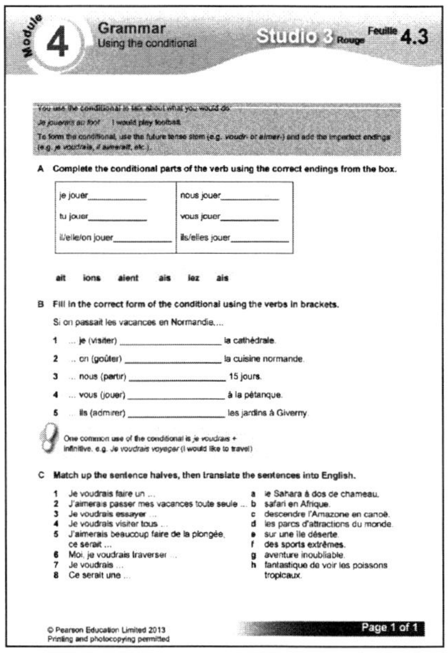

Module 4 **Grammar** Using the conditional — Studio 3 Rouge Feuille 4.3

You use the conditional to talk about what you would do.
Je jouerais au foot I would play football.
To form the conditional, use the future tense stem (e.g. *voudr-* or *aimer-*) and add the imperfect endings (e.g. *je voudrais, il aimerait,* etc.).

A Complete the conditional parts of the verb using the correct endings from the box.

je jouer______	nous jouer______
tu jouer______	vous jouer______
il/elle/on jouer______	ils/elles jouer______

ait ions aient ais iez ais

B Fill in the correct form of the conditional using the verbs in brackets.

Si on passait les vacances en Normandie,...

1 ... je (visiter) ______ la cathédrale.
2 ... on (goûter) ______ la cuisine normande.
3 ... nous (partir) ______ 15 jours.
4 ... vous (jouer) ______ à la pétanque.
5 ... ils (admirer) ______ les jardins à Giverny.

One common use of the conditional is *je voudrais* + infinitive. e.g. *Je voudrais voyager* (I would like to travel)

C Match up the sentence halves, then translate the sentences into English.

1 Je voudrais faire un ...
2 J'aimerais passer mes vacances toute seule ...
3 Je voudrais essayer ...
4 Je voudrais visiter tous ...
5 J'aimerais beaucoup faire de la plongée, ce serait ...
6 Moi, je voudrais traverser ...
7 Je voudrais ...
8 Ce serait une ...

a le Sahara à dos de chameau.
b safari en Afrique.
c descendre l'Amazone en canoë.
d les parcs d'attractions du monde.
e sur une île déserte.
f des sports extrêmes.
g aventure inoubliable.
h fantastique de voir les poissons tropicaux.

© Pearson Education Limited 2013
Printing and photocopying permitted
Page 1 of 1

Answers

A

je joue**rais**	nous joue**rions**
tu joue**rais**	vous joue**riez**
il/elle/on joue**rait**	ils/elles joue**raient**

B **1** … je **visiterais** la cathédrale.

2 … on **goûterait** la cuisine normande.

3 … nous **partirions** 15 jours.

4 … vous **joueriez** à la pétanque.

5 … ils **admireraient** les jardins à Giverny.

C **1** b – I would like to go on a safari in Africa.

2 e – I would like to spend my holidays alone on a desert island.

3 f – I would like to try extreme sports.

4 d – I would like to visit all the theme parks in the world.

5 h – I would really like to go diving, it would be fantastic to see the tropical fish.

6 a – I would like to cross the Sahara on camel's back.

7 c – I would like to go down the Amazon in a canoe.

8 g – It would be an unforgettable adventure.

4 3 C'est indispensable!

Learning objectives

- Talking about what you take with you on holiday
- Using reflexive verbs

Programme of Study references

GV2 Grammatical structures (reflexive verbs)

GV3 Developing vocabulary

LC4 Expressing ideas (speaking)

LC5 Speaking coherently and confidently

FCSE links

Unit 3: Holidays and travel (Activities)

Grammar

- reflexive verbs

Key language

Je me baigne.
Je me coiffe.
Je me couche.
Je me douche.
Je me fais bronzer.
Je me fais piquer.
Je m'amuse.
Je m'ennuie.
un adaptateur
un chargeur (pour mon mp3)
un chapeau de paille
un tuba
un sac à dos
une bombe anti-insectes
une lampe de poche
de la crème solaire
du gel coiffant
des lunettes de plongée (fpl)
des palmes (fpl)
des tongs (fpl)
plein de bouquins (mpl)

PLTS

S Self-managers

Cross-curricular

Humanities subjects: dictionary use

Resources

Audio files:
50_Module4_Unit3_Ex1.mp3
51_Module4_Unit3_Ex4.mp3

Workbooks:
Cahier d'exercices Rouge, page 39

ActiveTeach:
Starter 1 resource
Starter 2 resource
p.080 Flashcards
p.080 Grammar
p.080 Grammar practice
p.081 Video 7
p.081 Video worksheet 7
p.081 Class activity
p.081 Learning skills

ActiveLearn:
Listening, Reading
Grammar, Vocabulary

Starter 1

Aim

To review reflexive verbs

Write up the following, jumbling the order of the second column. Give pupils three minutes to match the French and English verbs. With a good class, you could omit the English versions and ask pupils to work in pairs to translate the French verbs.

je me baigne	I swim
je me coiffe	I do my hair
je me douche	I have a shower
je me fais bronzer	I sunbathe
je me fais piquer	I get stung
je m'amuse	I have fun
je m'ennuie	I get bored

Check answers. Ask pupils how these verbs differ from those that appear earlier in the module. Remind them that reflexive verbs always include an extra (reflexive) pronoun before the verb.

Alternative Starter 1:

Use ActiveTeach p.080 Flashcards to introduce reflexive verbs.

1 Écoute et lis. Regarde les photos et trouve le vocabulaire dans les textes (A–M). (1–3) (Listening L5)

Listening. Pupils listen to three young people talking about their holidays and read the text at the same time. They then find the French for each of the items pictured (A–M).

Audioscript Track 50

1 *Normalement, nous louons une villa avec piscine en Grèce. Je me baigne tous les jours dans la piscine, donc je prends des lunettes de plongée. Après, je me fais bronzer, alors je prends aussi de la crème solaire. Mais je n'oublie pas de mettre un chapeau de paille et des tongs pour me protéger la tête et les pieds, parce qu'il fait très chaud, là-bas.*

2 *Chaque année, nous allons faire du camping en Écosse. Pendant le voyage, je m'amuse avec mon mp3, alors je prends un chargeur pour ça. Je prends aussi un adaptateur, parce que les prises de courant sont différentes, là-bas. À part ça, je prends une lampe de poche et, cette année, je prendrai une bombe anti-insectes, car je me fais toujours piquer!*

3 *Cette année, nous partirons en vacances sur la Côte d'Azur. Nous irons tous les jours à la plage, donc je prendrai un sac à dos pour mes affaires et plein de bouquins, parce que je m'ennuie facilement. J'aime faire de la plongée, donc je prendrai un tuba et des palmes. Après la plongée, je me douche et je me coiffe, alors je prends toujours du gel coiffant.*

Answers

A la crème solaire	**H** un chargeur
B un chapeau de paille	**I** un sac à dos
C des lunettes de plongée	**J** plein de bouquins
D des tongs	**K** des palmes
E une lampe de poche	**L** un tuba
F un adaptateur	**M** du gel coiffant
G une bombe anti-insectes	

PLTS S

R Pupils identify a technique for memorising the vocabulary for essential holiday items. Elicit different approaches for noting the vocabulary (e.g. listing alphabetically, arranging by gender, drawing labelled pictures, etc.), then ideas for learning the words (e.g. asking a friend/family member to test, self-testing by covering up the French and looking at the English, then vice versa, etc.). Encourage pupils to try out the ideas and identify the approach that works best for them.

Studio Grammaire: reflexive verbs

Use the *Studio Grammaire* box to cover reflexive verbs. There is more information and further practice on Pupil Book p. 93.

2 Trouve la bonne phrase pour chaque image. (Reading L5)

Reading. Pupils choose the correct reflexive verb for each of the activities pictured.

Answers

A je me douche	**E** je me fais piquer
B je me coiffe	**F** je me baigne
C je m'amuse	**G** je m'ennuie
D je me fais bronzer	

Starter 2

Aim

To review reflexive verbs; To review language for holiday routines

Write up the following. Give pupils three minutes working in pairs to translate the verbs into French.

1 *she does her hair*	**4** *we get bored*
2 *I sunbathe*	**5** *they have fun*
3 *he swims*	**6** *you have a shower*

Check answers. Ask what is special about reflexive verbs (extra pronoun before the verb). (**Answers*:* 1** *elle se coiffe* **2** *je me fais bronzer* **3** *il se baigne* **4** *on s'ennuie/nous nous ennuyons* **5** *ils/elles s'amusent* **6** *tu te douches/vous vous douchez*)

Alternative Starter 2:

Use ActiveTeach p.081 Class activity to practise holiday activities or ActiveTeach p.080 Grammar practice to practise reflexive verbs.

3 En tandem. Jeu de mémoire. Fais une liste aussi longue que possible! (Speaking L4)

Speaking. In pairs: pupils play a memory game, aiming to create the longest list possible. A sample exchange is given.

4 Écoute et note (1) la lettre de l'activité de l'exercice 2 et (2) l'objet essentiel. (1–6) (Listening L5–6)

Listening. Pupils listen to six people talking about their holidays. For each one, they note the activity using the pictures A–G in exercise 2 (NB not exercise 1) and the essential item mentioned. One of the picture letters isn't needed.

Audioscript Track 51

1 *Là où nous allons en vacances, il n'y a pas grand-chose à faire et je m'ennuie. Alors, cette année, je prendrai plein de bouquins et de magazines.*

2 *Nous allons tous les jours à la plage. Il fait toujours soleil et donc, bien sûr, je me fais bronzer. Mais il faut faire attention, alors je mets beaucoup de crème solaire. L'année dernière, j'ai oublié de mettre de la crème et j'ai pris un coup de soleil terrible.*

3 *On va en vacances en voiture et le voyage est assez long, mais je m'amuse avec mon mp3. Je prends toujours un chargeur quand je pars*

en vacances parce que j'écoute tout le temps de la musique.

4 *Quand nous allons en vacances, je me baigne tous les jours dans la piscine. Mais je n'aime pas avoir de l'eau dans les yeux, donc je prends toujours mes lunettes de plongée.*

5 *Je me fais souvent piquer et l'année dernière, aux Antilles, il y avait plein de moustiques, alors cette année, je prendrai une grosse bombe anti-insectes!*

6 *J'adore nager dans la mer. Puis le soir, avant de sortir, je me lave toujours les cheveux et je me coiffe. Donc, je prendrai beaucoup de gel coiffant.*

Answers

1 **G** *bouquins*
2 **D** crème solaire
3 **C** chargeur
4 **F** lunettes de plongée
5 **E** bombe anti-insectes
6 **B** gel coiffant

5 Copie et complète les phrases. Utilise tes propres idées. (Writing L6)

Writing. Pupils copy and complete the sentences about essential holiday items, using their own ideas.

Example answers

1 *Je me baigne tous les jours, alors je prendrai avec moi* **des lunettes de plongée**.
2 Après, je me douche et je me coiffe, donc je prends toujours **du gel coiffant**.
3 Tous les jours, je me fais bronzer sur la plage, alors j'ai pris **de la crème solaire**.
4 Je me fais toujours piquer par des moustiques, **alors je prends/je prendrai/j'ai pris une bombe anti-insectes**.
5 Pendant le voyage, je m'amuse avec ma PlayStation portable, **alors je prends/je prendrai/j'ai pris un chargeur**.
6 Je m'ennuie souvent en vacances, **alors je prends/je prendrai/j'ai pris plein de bouquins**.

6 Choisis une des destinations suivantes. Imagine que tu y vas tous les ans. Qu'est-ce que tu prends et pourquoi? Fais un mini-exposé oral. (Speaking L4)

Speaking. Pupils choose one of the holiday destinations listed. Imagining that they go there every year, they prepare and give a short presentation on what they take with them, giving reasons. A sample opening is given. Draw pupils' attention to the tip box on using a dictionary to extend the scope of what they can talk about.

Remind pupils that using a dictionary in this way when doing extended writing tasks in other subjects, such as English and History, can also improve their writing there.

7 Lis le texte et réponds aux questions en anglais. (Reading L7)

Reading. Pupils read Lucie's blog and answer the questions on it in English. *des moucherons* is glossed for support.

Answers

1 She got sunburnt.
2 sun cream, swimming costume, towel, flip-flops
3 about 11.30 pm.
4 (mountains in) Wales
5 about ten hours
6 gel because he likes to make his hair spiky, adaptor because the electric plugs are different, hair-dryer because he can't do without it

Pupils do an oral summary in French of Lucie's blog.

Plenary

Ask the class to explain how reflexive verbs work, giving you examples of different verbs in a range of different persons.

Then challenge the class to remember (with Pupil Books closed) all 13 of the essential holiday items mentioned in the unit. They can earn bonus points for any additional items they can think of.

Workbook, page 39

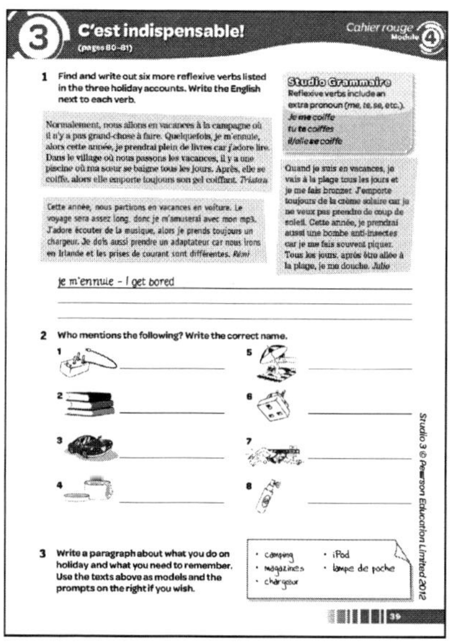
3 C'est indispensable!
Cahier rouge
1 Find and write out six more reflexive verbs listed in the three holiday accounts. Write the English next to each verb.
je m'ennuie - I get bored
2 Who mentions the following? Write the correct name.
3 Write a paragraph about what you do on holiday and what you need to remember. Use the texts above as models and the prompts on the right if you wish.

Answers

1. je *m'ennuie – I get bored*
   ma soeur se baigne – my sister swims
   elle se coiffe – she does her hair
   je m'amuse – I enjoy myself
   je me fais bronzer – I sunbathe
   je me fais souvent piquer – I often get stung
   je me douche – I have a shower
2. **1** Rémi **2** Tristan **3** Rémi **4** Tristan
   5 Julie **6** Rémi **7** Tristan **8** Julie
3. (Example answer:)
   Normalement, nous allons en vacances à la campagne où on fait du camping. Quelquefois, je m'ennuie, alors cette année, je prendrai plein de magazines car j'adore lire. Le voyage sera assez long, donc je m'amuserai avec mon iPod. J'adore écouter de la musique tout le temps, alors je prends toujours un chargeur pour mon mp3. J'emporte aussi une lampe de poche.

Worksheet 4.4 Learning by heart

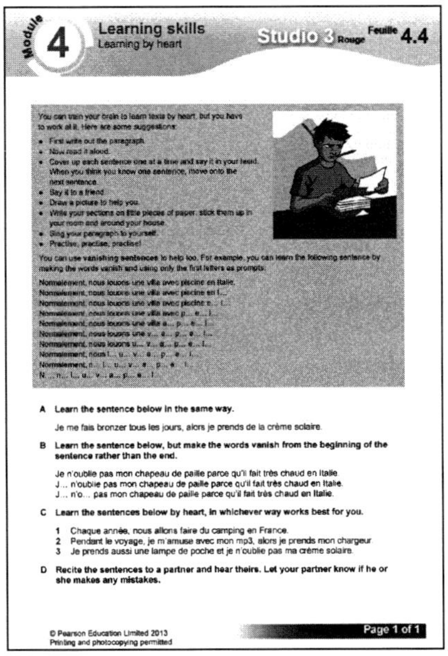

Module 4 Learning skills
Learning by heart
Studio 3 Rouge Feuille 4.4

You can train your brain to learn texts by heart, but you have to work at it. Here are some suggestions:

- First write out the paragraph.
- Now read it aloud.
- Cover up each sentence one at a time and say it in your head. When you think you know one sentence, move onto the next sentence.
- Say it to a friend.
- Draw a picture to help you.
- Write your sections on little pieces of paper: stick them up in your room and around your house.
- Sing your paragraph to yourself.
- Practise, practise, practise!

You can use **vanishing sentences** to help too. For example, you can learn the following sentence by making the words vanish and using only the first letters as prompts:

Normalement, nous louons une villa avec piscine en Italie.
Normalement, nous louons une villa avec piscine en I...
Normalement, nous louons une villa avec piscine e... I...
Normalement, nous louons une villa avec p... e... I...
Normalement, nous louons une villa a... p... e... I...
Normalement, nous louons une v... a... p... e... I...
Normalement, nous louons u... v... a... p... e... I...
Normalement, nous l... u... v... a... p... e... I...
Normalement, n... l... u... v... a... p... e... I...
N... n... l... u... v... a... p... e... I...

A Learn the sentence below in the same way.

Je me fais bronzer tous les jours, alors je prends de la crème solaire.

B Learn the sentence below, but make the words vanish from the beginning of the sentence rather than the end.

Je n'oublie pas mon chapeau de paille parce qu'il fait très chaud en Italie.
J... n'oublie pas mon chapeau de paille parce qu'il fait très chaud en Italie.
J... n'o... pas mon chapeau de paille parce qu'il fait très chaud en Italie.

C Learn the sentences below by heart, in whichever way works best for you.

1 Chaque année, nous allons faire du camping en France.
2 Pendant le voyage, je m'amuse avec mon mp3, alors je prends mon chargeur.
3 Je prends aussi une lampe de poche et je n'oublie pas ma crème solaire.

D Recite the sentences to a partner and hear theirs. Let your partner know if he or she makes any mistakes.

© Pearson Education Limited 2013
Printing and photocopying permitted
Page 1 of 1

Answers

(Answers will vary.)

Video

Episode 7: On part

Samira has arranged a mystery holiday for the team, who each reveal what they have decided to pack. Video worksheet 7 can be used in conjunction with this episode.

Answers to video worksheet (ActiveTeach)

1 A The French summer holidays are longer. Most families head for the coast, causing massive traffic jams.
B (Answers will vary.)
C (Answers will vary.)

2 A To film reports for StudioFR.
B She'd like to go on a safari in Africa.
C He'd like to go down the Amazon in a canoe and go fishing.
D *Je voudrais …/j'aimerais …*
E It would be too quiet for him.
F A desert island.
G No, it's a surprise.
H Nine o'clock the next morning.

3 A Some items are suitable (anti-insect spray, binoculars, torch). Others, such as a hair-dryer and an mp3 player, aren't.
B Fishing gear: rod, straw hat; also camera, matches and clothes.
C Extreme sports (climbing, horse riding, mountain biking).
D A quiet beach holiday (on a desert island).
E Because the holiday she has planned covers everyone's wishes.
F Marielle, because she had been hoping to go somewhere more exotic.
G It's great (*génial*).
H Go fishing.

4 Mes vidéos de vacances

Learning objectives

- Describing what happened on holiday
- Combining different tenses

Programme of Study references

GV1 Tenses (combining different tenses)

LC1 Listening and responding

LC3 Conversation (dealing with the unexpected)

LC8 Writing creatively

FCSE links

Unit 3: Holidays and travel (Problems on holiday, Holiday experiences)

Grammar

- the perfect tense (irregular past participles & verbs taking *être*)

Key language

Pas vraiment.
C'était un désastre.
Je suis resté(e) trop longtemps au soleil.
J'ai pris un coup de soleil.
Il a plu tout le temps.
L'eau est entrée dans la tente.
Je suis tombé(e) à l'eau.
J'ai été malade.
On a tous été malades.
C'est dommage.
C'est pas drôle, ça.

PLTS

R Reflective learners

Cross-curricular

ICT: creating learning materials; word-processing

Resources

Audio files:
52_Module4_Unit4_Ex1.mp3
53_Module4_Unit4_Ex3.mp3

Workbooks:
Cahier d'exercices Rouge, pages 40 & 41

ActiveTeach:
Starter 1 resource
p.082 Grammar
p.082 Grammar practice
p.083 Video 8
p.083 Video worksheet 8
p.083 Thinking skills

ActiveLearn:
Listening, Reading
Grammar

Starter 1

Aim

To review the perfect tense

Write up the following. Give pupils three minutes working in pairs to complete the grid.

subject	infinitive	present	perfect
il		*il reste*	
je			*j'ai joué*
on	*faire*		
ils			*ils sont entrés*
elle			*elle a mis*
je	*prendre*		

Check answers. Ask how the perfect tense is formed. (**Answers: infinitive:** *rester, jouer, faire, entrer, mettre, prendre;* **present:** *il reste, je joue, on fait, ils entrent, elle met, je prends; perfect: il est resté, j'ai joué, on a fait, ils sont entrés, elle a mis, j'ai pris*)

1 Écoute et lis. Qui parle? (1–3) (Listening L6)

Listening. Pupils listen to three people talking about disastrous holidays. They read the text at the same time and identify who is speaking each time.

Audioscript Track 52

1 *Normalement, quand on fait du camping, il fait beau. Mais cette année, il a plu tout le temps et l'eau est entrée dans la tente! Quelle horreur! L'année prochaine, c'est décidé: on logera à l'hôtel.*

2 *Tous les ans en vacances, je joue au beach-volley. Mais cette année, j'ai fait un stage de planche à voile. C'était très difficile et je suis tombée à l'eau au moins cent fois! Alors, la prochaine fois, je choisirai un sport plus facile, comme le tennis.*

3 *Quand je suis en vacances, je me fais toujours bronzer sur la plage. Mais l'année dernière, je suis restée trop longtemps au soleil et j'ai pris un coup de soleil. C'était horrible. La prochaine fois, je mettrai plus de crème solaire!*

Answers

1 Samuel **2** Yasmina **3** Romane

Studio Grammaire: the perfect tense (irregular past participles & verbs taking *être*)

Use the *Studio Grammaire* box to cover the perfect tense (irregular past participles and key verbs using *être* in the perfect). There is more information and further practice on Pupil Book p. 94.

2 Relis les textes et complète le tableau en anglais. (Reading L6)

Reading. Pupils copy out the table. They read the texts in exercise 1 again and complete the table with the details in English. Draw pupils' attention to the tip box on learning the main tenses of key verbs and any new verbs they learn. Encourage them to keep a verb notebook for this or to create files on computer to help them memorise and review verb forms.

Answers

	1 Romane	**2** Samuel	**3** Yasmina
usually/ always	sunbathes on beach	has good weather when camping	plays beach volleyball
this year/ last year	stayed in sun too long, got sunburnt	rained all the time, water came into tent	did windsurfing course, fell in water a lot
next time/ next year	will put on more sun cream	will stay in a hotel	will choose an easier sport, like tennis

3 Écoute et choisis la bonne réponse. (1–4) (Listening L6)

Listening. Pupils listen to four people talking about their holidays and complete the sentences by choosing the correct option from the two supplied each time.

Audioscript Track 53

1 – *Salut, Rémi! T'as passé de bonnes vacances?*
– *Non, pas trop!*
– *Ah bon, pourquoi?*
– *Normalement, on va en Espagne. Mais cette année, on est allés en Angleterre.*
– *Ce n'était pas intéressant, l'Angleterre?*
– *Le temps était horrible! Il a plu tout le temps!*
– *Ah, c'est dommage, ça.*
– *L'année prochaine, on ira en Espagne!*

2 – *Alors, Léa, ça s'est bien passé, les vacances?*
– *Pas vraiment.*
– *Dis-donc, t'es un peu rouge, tu sais!*
– *Oui, je sais! Quand je suis en vacances, tu sais bien que j'aime me faire bronzer …*
– *Et alors?*
– *Un jour, je suis restée trop longtemps au soleil. Quelle idiote!*
– *Ah, je vois. C'est pas drôle, ça.*
– *La prochaine fois, je mettrai plein de crème solaire, et en plus, je porterai un chapeau de paille!*

3 – *Salut, Arthur! C'était comment, tes vacances au Portugal?*
– *C'était un désastre!*
– *Ah bon, pourquoi?*
– *Normalement, on mange à l'hôtel, parce qu'il y a un bon restaurant.*
– *Mais cette fois …?*
– *Cette fois, on est sortis manger dans un petit restaurant en ville. On a mangé du poisson …*
– *Il n'était pas bon, le poisson?*
– *Non. On a tous été malades! J'ai vomi toute la nuit!*
– *Quelle horreur!*
– *L'année prochaine, on mangera tous les jours au restaurant de l'hôtel!*

4 – *Alors, Sophie, t'as passé de bonnes vacances?*
– *Mouais, ce n'était pas mal, mais …*
– *Mais quoi?*
– *Tu sais, normalement, je ne fais pas grand -chose: on va à la plage, je bouquine un peu …*
– *Oui, et alors?*
– *Cette année, j'ai essayé quelque chose de nouveau. J'ai fait un stage de ski nautique.*
– *C'était comment?*
– *C'était vachement difficile! Je suis tombée à l'eau je ne sais pas combien de fois!*
– *Ah bon?*
– *En plus, mon père a tout fi lmé avec son caméscope et il a posté la vidéo sur YouTube!*
– *Ah bon?*
– *C'est pas drôle, tu sais! La prochaine fois, je resterai sur la plage!*

Answers

1 a Normalement, Rémi va en vacances en **Espagne**.
b Cette année, **il a plu**.
c L'année prochaine, il ira en **Espagne**.
2 a Quand Léa va en vacances, elle **se fait bronzer**.
b Un jour, elle **est restée trop longtemps au soleil**.
c La prochaine fois, elle mettra **un chapeau**.
3 a D'habitude, la famille d'Arthur mange **à l'hôtel**.
b Le poisson **n'était pas bon**.
c L'année prochaine, ils mangeront **à l'hôtel**.
4 a Cette année, Sophie a fait un stage de **ski nautique**.
b Son père a tout filmé avec **son caméscope**.
c La prochaine fois, elle restera **sur la plage**.

Starter 2

Aim

To review the perfect tense; To review talking about past holidays

Give pupils three minutes to write four different endings to this sentence opening:

L'année dernière, je n'ai pas passé de bonnes vacances parce que …

In pairs, pupils check each other's answers. Hear some sentences.

Alternative Starter 2:

Use ActiveTeach p.082 Grammar practice to practise the perfect tense.

4 En tandem. Fais un dialogue. Utilise les images et les phrases suivantes. (Speaking L6)

Speaking. In pairs: pupils make up a conversation about their holidays, using the pictures and framework supplied. They take it in turn to ask and answer. Some vocabulary is glossed for support.

5 Lis et complète le texte avec les verbes dans les cases. (Reading L6)

Reading. Pupils complete the gap-fill text using the verbs supplied. Some vocabulary is glossed for support.

Answers

1 suis allée **2** se baigne **3** est tombé

4 ai posté **5** restera **6** passe **7** a fait **8** a mis

9 ai pris **10** mangera

6 Écris un résumé des textes de l'exercice 5 en anglais. Utilise 70 mots au maximum. (Reading L6)

Reading. Pupils write a summary in English of the texts in exercise 5, using a maximum of 70 words.

Example answer

Manon's family went to Greece. One day, they hired a boat. Her father stood up to take a photo and fell in the water. Manon filmed it on her mobile and posted the video on YouTube.

Dimitri's family went to Gibraltar. They had a picnic and some monkeys/apes turned up. One of them grabbed his sister's hat and put it on its head. Dimitri filmed it with the camcorder.

(= 69 words)

7 Écris l'histoire d'un incident amusant ou désastreux en vacances. (Writing L7)

Writing. Pupils write about an amusing or disastrous holiday incident, including details of what they usually do on holiday and what their future plans are. It can be real or fictional. A list of features to include and techniques to bear in mind is supplied. Pupils could write the story on computer, to facilitate the production of a second draft.

Plenary

PLTS R

Ask pupils to read out sentences from the texts they wrote in exercise 7. Ask the rest of the class to give constructive feedback on the accuracy of the French and encourage pupils to identify areas where they can improve. Reward the most imaginative sentences.

Workbook, pages 40 and 41

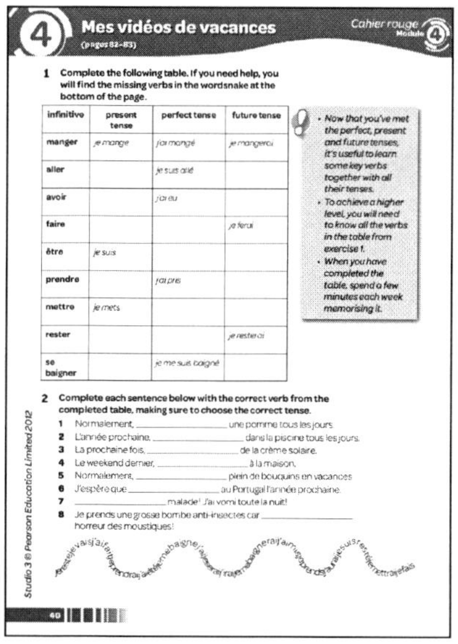

4 Mes vidéos de vacances (pages 82–83) Cahier rouge Module 4

1 Complete the following table. If you need help, you will find the missing verbs in the wordsnake at the bottom of the page.

infinitive	present tense	perfect tense	future tense
manger	je mange	j'ai mangé	je mangerai
aller		je suis allé	
avoir		j'ai eu	
faire			je ferai
être	je suis		
prendre		j'ai pris	
mettre	je mets		
rester			je resterai
se baigner		je me suis baigné	

- Now that you've met the perfect, present and future tenses, it's useful to learn some key verbs together with all their tenses.
- To achieve a higher level, you will need to know all the verbs in the table from exercise 1.
- When you have completed the table, spend a few minutes each week memorising it.

2 Complete each sentence below with the correct verb from the completed table, making sure to choose the correct tense.

1 Normalement, ______ une pomme tous les jours.
2 L'année prochaine, ______ dans la piscine tous les jours.
3 La prochaine fois, ______ de la crème solaire.
4 Le weekend dernier, ______ à la maison.
5 Normalement, ______ plein de bouquins en vacances.
6 J'espère que ______ au Portugal l'année prochaine.
7 ______ malade! J'ai vomi toute la nuit!
8 Je prends une grosse bombe anti-insectes car ______ horreur des moustiques!

Studio 3 © Pearson Education Limited 2012

40

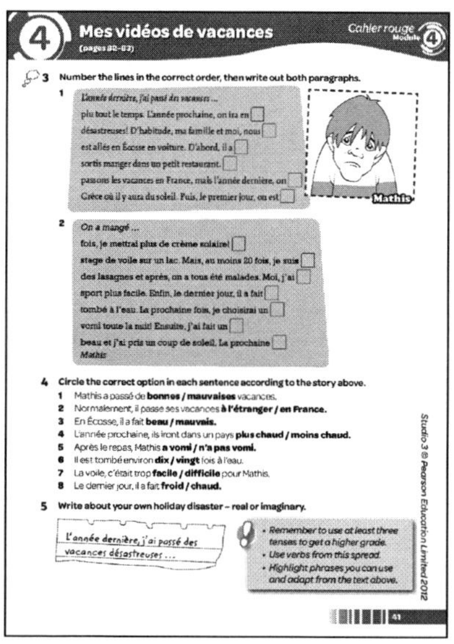

4 Mes vidéos de vacances (pages 82–83) Cahier rouge Module 4

3 Number the lines in the correct order, then write out both paragraphs.

1 *L'année dernière, j'ai passé des vacances …*
plu tout le temps. L'année prochaine, on ira en
désastreuses! D'habitude, ma famille et moi, nous
est allés en Écosse en voiture. D'abord, il a
sortis manger dans un petit restaurant.
passons les vacances en France, mais l'année dernière, on
Grèce où il y aura du soleil. Puis, le premier jour, on est

Mathis

2 *On a mangé …*
fois, je mettrai plus de crème solaire!
stage de voile sur un lac. Mais, au moins 20 fois, je suis
des lasagnes et après, on a tous été malades. Moi, j'ai
sport plus facile. Enfin, le dernier jour, il a fait
tombé à l'eau. La prochaine fois, je choisirai un
vomi toute la nuit! Ensuite, j'ai fait un
beau et j'ai pris un coup de soleil. La prochaine
Mathis

4 Circle the correct option in each sentence according to the story above.

1 Mathis a passé de **bonnes / mauvaises** vacances.
2 Normalement, il passe ses vacances **à l'étranger / en France.**
3 En Écosse, il a fait **beau / mauvais.**
4 L'année prochaine, ils iront dans un pays **plus chaud / moins chaud.**
5 Après le repas, Mathis **a vomi / n'a pas vomi.**
6 Il est tombé environ **dix / vingt** fois à l'eau.
7 La voile, c'était trop **facile / difficile** pour Mathis.
8 Le dernier jour, il a fait **froid / chaud.**

5 Write about your own holiday disaster – real or imaginary.

L'année dernière, j'ai passé des vacances désastreuses …

- Remember to use at least three tenses to get a higher grade.
- Use verbs from this spread.
- Highlight phrases you can use and adapt from the text above.

Studio 3 © Pearson Education Limited 2012

41

Answers

1

infinitive	present tense	perfect tense	future tense
manger	*je mange*	*j'ai mangé*	*je mangerai*
aller	je vais	*je suis allé*	j'irai
avoir	j'ai	*j'ai eu*	j'aurai
faire	je fais	j'ai fait	*je ferai*
être	*je suis*	j'ai été	je serai
prendre	je prends	*j'ai pris*	je prendrai
mettre	*je mets*	j'ai mis	je mettrai
rester	je reste	je suis resté	*je resterai*
se baigner	je me baigne	*je me suis baigné*	je me baignerai

2 **1** Normalement, **je mange** une pomme tous les jours.

2 L'année prochaine, **je me baignerai** tous les jours dans la piscine.

3 La prochaine fois, **je mettrai** de la crème solaire.

4 Le weekend dernier, **je suis resté** à la maison.

5 Normalement, **je prends** plein de bouquins en vacances.

6 J'espère que **j'irai** au Portugal l'année prochaine.

7 **Je suis** malade! J'ai vomi toute la nuit!

8 Je prend une grosse bombe anti-insectes car **j'ai** horreur des moustiques!

3 **1** 4, 1, 3, 7, 2, 5, 6

L'année dernière, j'ai passé des vacances … désastreuses! D'habitude, ma famille et moi, nous passons les vacances en France, mais l'année dernière, on est allés en Écosse en voiture. D'abord, il a plu tout le temps! L'année prochaine, on ira en Grèce où il y aura du soleil! Puis, le premier jour, on est sorti manger dans un petit restaurant.

2 7, 3, 1, 5, 4, 2, 6

On a mangé … des lasagnes et après, on a tous été malades! Moi, j'ai vomi toute la nuit! Ensuite, j'ai fait un stage de voile sur un lac. Mais, au moins 20 fois, je suis tombé à l'eau! La prochaine fois, je choisirai un sport plus facile. Enfin, le dernier jour, il a fait beau et j'ai pris un coup de soleil. La prochaine fois, je mettrai plus de crème solaire!
Mathis

4 **1** mauvaises **2** en France **3** mauvais **4** plus chaud **5** a vomi **6** vingt **7** difficile **8** chaud

5 (Answers will vary.)

Worksheet 4.5 Logic puzzle

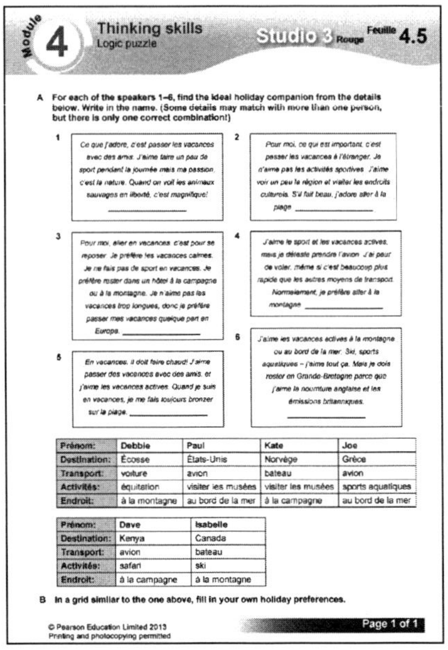
Module 4 Thinking skills
Logic puzzle
Studio 3 Rouge Feuille 4.5

A For each of the speakers 1–6, find the ideal holiday companion from the details below. Write in the name. (Some details may match with more than one person, but there is only one correct combination!)

1 *Ce que j'adore, c'est passer les vacances avec des amis. J'aime faire un peu de sport pendant la journée mais ma passion, c'est la nature. Quand on voit les animaux sauvages en liberté, c'est magnifique!* ________

2 *Pour moi, ce qui est important, c'est passer les vacances à l'étranger. Je n'aime pas les activités sportives. J'aime voir un peu la région et visiter les endroits culturels. S'il fait beau, j'adore aller à la plage* ________

3 *Pour moi, aller en vacances, c'est pour se reposer. Je préfère les vacances calmes. Je ne fais pas de sport en vacances. Je préfère rester dans un hôtel à la campagne ou à la montagne. Je n'aime pas les vacances trop longues, donc je préfère passer mes vacances quelque part en Europe.* ________

4 *J'aime le sport et les vacances actives, mais je déteste prendre l'avion. J'ai peur de voler, même si c'est beaucoup plus rapide que les autres moyens de transport. Normalement, je préfère aller à la montagne* ________

5 *En vacances, il doit faire chaud! J'aime passer des vacances avec des amis, et j'aime les vacances actives. Quand je suis en vacances, je me fais toujours bronzer sur la plage.* ________

6 *J'aime les vacances actives à la montagne ou au bord de la mer. Ski, sports aquatiques – j'aime tout ça. Mais je dois rester en Grande-Bretagne parce que j'aime la nourriture anglaise et les émissions britanniques.* ________

Prénom:	Debbie	Paul	Kate	Joe
Destination:	Écosse	États-Unis	Norvège	Grèce
Transport:	voiture	avion	bateau	avion
Activités:	équitation	visiter les musées	visiter les musées	sports aquatiques
Endroit:	à la montagne	au bord de la mer	à la campagne	au bord de la mer

Prénom:	Dave	Isabelle
Destination:	Kenya	Canada
Transport:	avion	bateau
Activités:	safari	ski
Endroit:	à la campagne	à la montagne

B In a grid similar to the one above, fill in your own holiday preferences.

© Pearson Education Limited 2013
Printing and photocopying permitted
Page 1 of 1

Answers

1 Dave **2** Paul **3** Kate **4** Isabelle **5** Debbie **6** Joe

Video

Episode 8: Les vacances (1)

The boys begin their holiday with a fishing trip, while the girls discover the wildlife on a nature trail. Video worksheet 8 can be used in conjunction with this episode.

Answers to video worksheet (ActiveTeach)

1 **A** They are going on a camping holiday.

B It could be things like fishing, riding, walking, sailing, etc. Mehdi and Hugo would be up for active things, Alex for practical things, etc.

C (Answers will vary.)

2 **A** The boys are going fishing and the girls will be walking.

B Samira.

C Yes, they seem to be.

3 **A** Water, sky, nature.

B Boring; there's nothing to do.

C Semi-successful. Alex was happy but Mehdi wasn't.

4 **A** She thinks the walk will be like a safari.

B Sort of. They will be observing animals and plants in their natural environment, just not in Africa.

C Water birds.

D They smell it (it's mint).

E They are pretending to be looking for lions.

F Hold the frog in their hands.

(Pupil Book pp. 84–85)

4 5 À la base de loisirs

Learning objectives

- Visiting a tourist attraction
- Using emphatic pronouns

Programme of Study references

GV2 Grammatical structures (emphatic pronouns)

LC2 Transcription

LC6 Reading comprehension

LC8 Writing creatively

FCSE links

Unit 3: Holidays and travel (Activities)

Grammar

- emphatic pronouns
- using three tenses

Key language

J'ai …/On a …
fait du tir à l'arc
fait de la planche à voile
fait du trampoline
fait de la baignade
fait une balade en barque
joué aux boules
joué sur des structures gonflables
loué un pédalo

PLTS

I Independent enquirers

Resources

Audio files:

54_Module4_Unit5_Ex2.mp3
55_Module4_Unit5_Ex3.mp3

Workbooks:

Cahier d'exercices Rouge, pages 42 & 43

ActiveTeach:

Starter 2 resource
p.084 Flashcards
p.084 Grammar
p.084 Grammar practice
p.085 Video 9
p.085 Video worksheet 9
p.085 Class activity
p.085 Thinking skills
p.085 Reading skills

ActiveLearn:

Listening, Reading
Grammar, Vocabulary

Starter 1

Aim

To practise reading for gist

Give pupils one minute to look at the text in exercise 1 on Pupil Book p. 84. Ask them to summarise in a sentence what the text is and who it is aimed at.

(**Example answer:** It's a brochure for a holiday activity centre aimed at families looking for a fun, active holiday.)

Alternative Starter 1:

Use ActiveTeach p.084 Flashcards to introduce holiday activities.

1 Lis le texte. Utilise un dictionnaire et note le nouveau vocabulaire. (Reading L4)

PLTS I

Reading. Pupils read the holiday brochure. Using a dictionary, they note any new vocabulary in French and English.

2 Écoute. Thomas et sa famille ont fait quelles activités? Complète le tableau en français. (Listening L7)

Listening. Pupils copy out the table. They listen to Thomas talking about his family trip to the leisure park and complete the table with the details.

Audioscript Track 54

– *Salut, Thomas! Qu'est-ce que t'as fait pendant les vacances?*
– *Je suis allé à la Base de Loisirs de Jonzac avec ma famille.*
– *Ah bon? Qu'est-ce qu'on peut faire, là-bas?*
– *On peut faire toutes sortes d'activités. D'abord, on a loué des canoës.*
– *Alors, il y a un lac ou une rivière?*
– *Il y a un grand lac. On a fait du canoë sur le lac. C'était marrant parce que ma soeur est tombée à l'eau. Elle n'était pas contente!*
– *Ah oui, c'est marrant, ça. À part ça, qu'est-ce que t'as fait?*
– *Ensuite, on a joué aux boules au boulodrome. J'ai trouvé ça un peu ennuyeux parce que moi, je préfère les activités plus dynamiques.*
– *Ah oui, moi aussi.*
– *Oui, mais après, j'ai fait un parcours acrobatique qui était vraiment super!*
– *Un parcours acrobatique? Qu'est-ce que c'est?*
– *Ben, c'est comme l'accrobranche, tu sais? Tu mets un casque, t'es attaché à un fi l, tu montes en haut d'un arbre, puis tu glisses d'arbre en arbre.*
– *Ouais! Co-o-o-ol! Je voudrais bien faire ça!*
– *Oui, c'était le top du top!*
– *Tes parents aussi en ont fait?*
– *Tu rigoles! Mon père est allé à la pêche.*
– *Ah oui, il aime bien faire ça, lui. Il a attrapé des poissons?*

- *Ah non, il n'a rien attrapé, mais il s'est bien amusé quand même.*
- *Et ta mère, qu'est-ce qu'elle a fait?*
- *Elle, elle a fait du tir à l'arc. Elle a trouvé ça un peu difficile parce qu'il faut avoir pas mal de force dans les bras.*
- *Ah oui, c'est pas facile, le tir à l'arc. Et ta soeur, qu'est-ce qu'elle a fait, comme activités?*
- *Elle, elle adore les chevaux. Il y a un centre équestre là-bas, alors elle a fait du cheval.*
- *Et ton petit frère, il s'est bien amusé, lui?*
- *Bien sûr, il est trop petit pour beaucoup d'activités, mais il a joué sur des structures gonflables. Il a trouvé ça super.*
- *Ah oui, c'est très drôle pour les petits.*

Answers

toute la famille	*canoë*, boules
Thomas	parcours acrobatique
père	pêche
mère	tir à l'arc
soeur	cheval/équitation
petit frère	structures gonflables

3 Écoute à nouveau. Note les opinions sur chaque activité et les raisons. (Listening L7)

Listening. Pupils listen to the exercise 2 recording again. This time they note in English the opinions Thomas's family expressed on each activity and their reasons. Draw pupils' attention to the tip box on the listening skill of identifying viewpoints and reasons, and the importance of doing so if aiming for a higher level.

Audioscript Track 55

As exercise 1.

Answers

canoeing: *funny, sister fell in water*
boules: boring, prefers more exciting activities
ziplining: great, parents don't like it
fishing: didn't catch anything, had fun
archery: difficult, need strong arms
horse riding: great, loves horses/riding centre there
bouncy castle: great, funny for little ones

4 En tandem. Imagine que tu as visité la Base de Loisirs de Jonzac avec ta famille. Ton/Ta camarade pose des questions. (Speaking L7)

Speaking. In pairs: pupils imagine that they visited the Jonzac Leisure Park with their own family. They take it in turn to ask and answer questions about the visit. The questions are supplied. Encourage pupils to include emphatic pronouns in their responses. Draw pupils' attention to the tip box on developing speaking skills.

Studio Grammaire: emphatic pronouns

Use the *Studio Grammaire* box to cover emphatic pronouns. There is more information and further practice on Pupil Book p. 95.

Starter 2

Aim

To review tense usage; To practise using questions as part of a response

Write up the following. Give pupils three minutes to write an answer opening to each of the questions – make it clear that they **do not** have to write complete sentences.

1 *Où es-tu allé(e), quand et avec qui?*
2 *Qu'est-ce que vous avez fait comme activités?*
3 *C'était comment?*
4 *Est-ce que tu voudrais y retourner?*
5 *Quelles activités voudrais-tu faire, la prochaine fois?*

Check answers. Remind pupils how important it is to listen to/look at questions very carefully and use the information in them to help structure a response.

(**Answers**

1 *Je suis allé(e) à/à la/ à l'/en* [+ place] … *Je suis allé(e)* [+ time phrase] … *Je suis allé(e) avec* [+ person/people] …
2 *J'ai fait/joué/loué* [+ activity] …
3 *C'était* [+ opinion] …
4 *Oui, je voudrais y retourner …/Non, je ne voudrais pas y retourner …*
5 *La prochaine fois, je voudrais faire/jouer/louer* [+ activity] …)

Alternative Starter 2:

Use ActiveTeach p.085 Class activity to review Module 4 language or ActiveTeach p.085 Grammar practice to practise emphatic pronouns.

5 Lis le texte. Puis trouve les trois phrases qui sont vraies. (Reading L7)

Reading. Pupils read the text and then identify which three of the sentences about it are true. *soit … soit* is glossed for support.

Answers

Sentences 1, 2 and 6 are true.

6 Écris une description de ta visite imaginaire à la Base de Loisirs de Jonzac. (Writing L7)

Writing. Pupils write a description of their imaginary visit to the Jonzac Leisure Park. A framework is supplied, plus a key language box. Encourage pupils to include emphatic pronouns.

Plenary

Ask pupils when emphatic pronouns are used. Elicit the different forms by prompting with the subject pronoun. Ask for examples of sentences featuring emphatic pronouns.

Workbook, pages 42 and 43

5 À la base de loisirs (pages 84–85) Cahier rouge Module 4

1 Spend one minute looking at the outdoor activities centre brochure and find four activities that you can do there.

Base de Réals

Sports et nature pour tous

La Base de Réals vous offre une aventure sportive!

Escalade
À partir de huit ans, découvrez l'escalade avec notre équipe de moniteurs.

Accro roc
Venez essayer Accro roc: une aventure forte en sensations!

Canoë-kayak
Une activité amusante et rafraîchissante. Descente de rivière: une expérience inoubliable!

Randonnée
Pour les randos aventures ou sportives, notre accompagnateur vous guidera dans le parc naturel du Haut-Languedoc.

Exemples de séjours groupe:
- Stage Kayak
Enfants et ados; 5 jours, 4 nuits incluant 5 séances de kayak et logement sous marabouts:
149€ par personne
- Formule multisports
Enfants et ados; 5 jours + 4 nuits incluant 5 séances d'activités sportives (canoë, escalade, etc.):
À partir de 121€ par personne
- Formule weekend
2 jours + 1 nuit; incluant 2 séances d'activités sportives (escalade, canoë).
À partir de 50€ par personne

2 Imagine you've just visited this centre. Complete the French sentences below.

1 La semaine dernière, je suis allé(e) … *(where you went)* ______
2 À la Base de Réals, j'ai fait … *(what you did)* ______
3 C'était … *(your opinion)* ______
4 Je voudrais / Je ne voudrais pas y retourner, parce que … *(go back there? why?)* ______
5 La prochaine fois, je voudrais … *(what to do next time)* ______

Studio 3 © Pearson Education Limited 2012

42

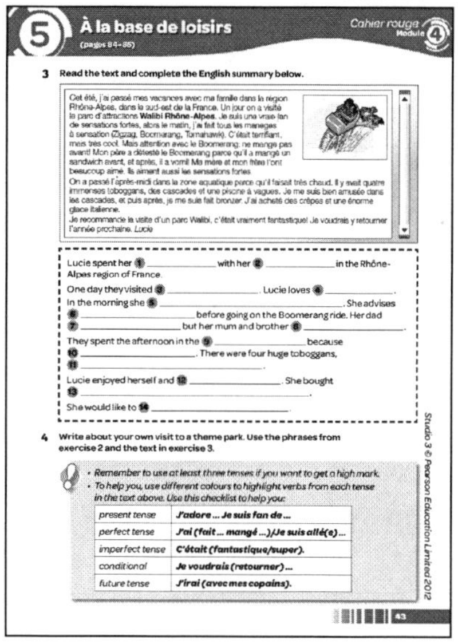

5 À la base de loisirs (pages 84–85) Cahier rouge Module 4

3 Read the text and complete the English summary below.

Cet été, j'ai passé mes vacances avec ma famille dans la région Rhône-Alpes, dans le sud-est de la France. Un jour on a visité le parc d'attractions **Walibi Rhône-Alpes**. Je suis une vraie fan de sensations fortes, alors le matin, j'ai fait tous les manèges à sensation (Zigzag, Boomerang, Tomahawk). C'était terrifiant, mais très cool. Mais attention avec le Boomerang: ne mange pas avant! Mon père a détesté le Boomerang parce qu'il a mangé un sandwich avant, et après, il a vomi! Ma mère et mon frère l'ont beaucoup aimé. Ils aiment aussi les sensations fortes.
On a passé l'après-midi dans la zone aquatique parce qu'il faisait très chaud. Il y avait quatre immenses toboggans, des cascades et une piscine à vagues. Je me suis bien amusée dans les cascades, et puis après, je me suis fait bronzer. J'ai acheté des crêpes et une énorme glace italienne.
Je recommande la visite d'un parc Walibi, c'était vraiment fantastique! Je voudrais y retourner l'année prochaine. *Lucie*

Lucie spent her 1 ______ with her 2 ______ in the Rhône-Alpes region of France.
One day they visited 3 ______. Lucie loves 4 ______.
In the morning she 5 ______. She advises 6 ______ before going on the Boomerang ride. Her dad 7 ______ but her mum and brother 8 ______.
They spent the afternoon in the 9 ______ because 10 ______. There were four huge toboggans, 11 ______.
Lucie enjoyed herself and 12 ______. She bought 13 ______.
She would like to 14 ______.

4 Write about your own visit to a theme park. Use the phrases from exercise 2 and the text in exercise 3.

- *Remember to use at least three tenses if you want to get a high mark.*
- *To help you, use different colours to highlight verbs from each tense in the text above. Use this checklist to help you:*

present tense	***J'adore … Je suis fan de …***
perfect tense	***J'ai (fait … mangé …)/Je suis allé(e) …***
imperfect tense	***C'était (fantastique/super).***
conditional	***Je voudrais (retourner) …***
future tense	***J'irai (avec mes copains).***

Studio 3 © Pearson Education Limited 2012

43

Answers

1 escalade (mountain climbing), accroc roc (ziplining), canoë-kayak (kayaking), randonnée (hill-walking)

2 (Example answers:)

1 La semaine dernière, je suis allé(e) **à la Base de Réals.**

2 À la Base de Réals, j'ai fait **de l'accro roc. J'ai aussi fait des randonnées et j'ai fait un stage de kayak.**

3 C'était **vraiment fantastique.**

4 Je voudrais y retourner, parce **que j'adore les sensations fortes.**

5 La prochaine fois, je voudrais **faire un stage de canoë.**

3 **1** holiday **2** family **3** a theme park **4** thrills **5** went on all the big rides **6** not to eat **7** hated it **8** really liked it **9** water area **10** it was very hot **11** waterfalls and a wave pool **12** sunbathed **13** some pancakes and an enormous Italian ice-cream **14** go back next year.

4 (Answers will vary.)

Worksheet 4.6 Drawing from text

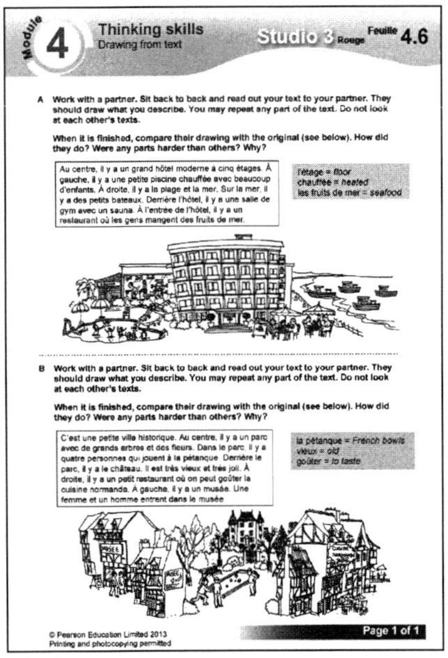

Module 4 Thinking skills
Drawing from text
Studio 3 Rouge Feuille 4.6

A Work with a partner. Sit back to back and read out your text to your partner. They should draw what you describe. You may repeat any part of the text. Do not look at each other's texts.

When it is finished, compare their drawing with the original (see below). How did they do? Were any parts harder than others? Why?

Au centre, il y a un grand hôtel moderne à cinq étages. À gauche, il y a une petite piscine chauffée avec beaucoup d'enfants. À droite, il y a la plage et la mer. Sur la mer, il y a des petits bateaux. Derrière l'hôtel, il y a une salle de gym avec un sauna. À l'entrée de l'hôtel, il y a un restaurant où les gens mangent des fruits de mer.

l'étage = *floor*
chauffée = *heated*
les fruits de mer = *seafood*

B Work with a partner. Sit back to back and read out your text to your partner. They should draw what you describe. You may repeat any part of the text. Do not look at each other's texts.

When it is finished, compare their drawing with the original (see below). How did they do? Were any parts harder than others? Why?

C'est une petite ville historique. Au centre, il y a un parc avec de grands arbres et des fleurs. Dans le parc, il y a quatre personnes qui jouent à la pétanque. Derrière le parc, il y a le château. Il est très vieux et très joli. À droite, il y a un petit restaurant où on peut goûter la cuisine normande. À gauche, il y a un musée. Une femme et un homme entrent dans le musée

la pétanque = *French bowls*
vieux = *old*
goûter = *to taste*

© Pearson Education Limited 2013
Printing and photocopying permitted
Page 1 of 1

Answers

(Answers will vary.)

Worksheet 4.7 Reading complicated texts

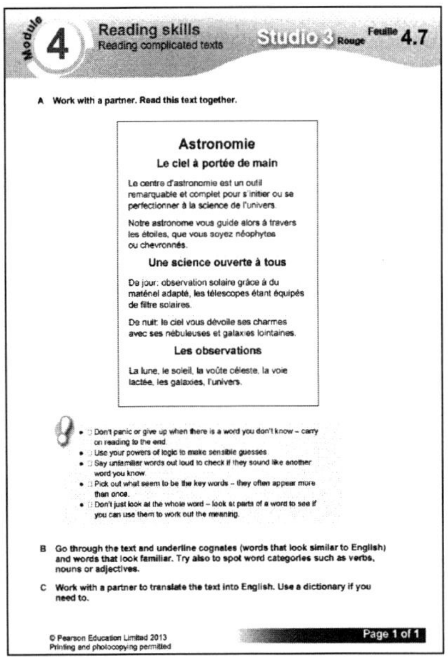

Module 4 Reading skills
Reading complicated texts
Studio 3 Rouge Feuille 4.7

A Work with a partner. Read this text together.

Astronomie

Le ciel à portée de main

Le centre d'astronomie est un outil remarquable et complet pour s'initier ou se perfectionner à la science de l'univers.

Notre astronome vous guide alors à travers les étoiles, que vous soyez néophytes ou chevronnés.

Une science ouverte à tous

De jour: observation solaire grâce à du matériel adapté, les télescopes étant équipés de filtre solaires.

De nuit: le ciel vous dévoile ses charmes avec ses nébuleuses et galaxies lointaines.

Les observations

La lune, le soleil, la voûte céleste, la voie lactée, les galaxies, l'univers.

- Don't panic or give up when there is a word you don't know – carry on reading to the end.
- Use your powers of logic to make sensible guesses.
- Say unfamiliar words out loud to check if they sound like another word you know.
- Pick out what seem to be the key words – they often appear more than once.
- Don't just look at the whole word – look at parts of a word to see if you can use them to work out the meaning.

B Go through the text and underline cognates (words that look similar to English) and words that look familiar. Try also to spot word categories such as verbs, nouns or adjectives.

C Work with a partner to translate the text into English. Use a dictionary if you need to.

© Pearson Education Limited 2013
Printing and photocopying permitted
Page 1 of 1

Answers

(Answers will vary.)

Video

Episode 9: Les vacances (2)

The team continue their camping trip with a mountain-bike ride and a sailing lesson. Video worksheet 9 can be used in conjunction with this episode.

Answers to video worksheet (ActiveTeach)

1 A (Answers will vary.)
B Probably mixed. Mehdi was bored, Marielle would have preferred a real safari.
C (Answers will vary.)

2 A She got sunburnt.
B Lions!
C A frog and lots of birds.
D Cook the fish that he caught.
E He's already got her bike ready for her.

3 A Hugo and Samira.
B Sailing. They are all pleased.

4 A Kévin.
B They get the boat ready and put on their lifejackets.
C She has fallen in.
D Yes, because earlier she was dangling her feet in the water.

4 Bilan et Révisions

Bilan

Pupils use this checklist to review language covered in the module, working on it in pairs in class or on their own at home. Encourage them to follow up any areas of weakness they identify. There are Target Setting Sheets included in the Assessment Pack, and an opportunity for pupils to record their own levels and targets on the *J'avance* page in the Workbook, p. 48. You can also use the *Bilan* checklist as an end-of-module plenary option.

Révisions

These revision exercises can be used for assessment purposes or for pupils to practise before tackling the assessment tasks in the Assessment Pack.

Resources

Audio files:

56_Module4_Rev_Ex1.mp3

Workbooks:

Cahier d'exercices Rouge, pages 44 & 45

1 Écoute. On parle de quelle activité? Quelle est la réaction? Complète le tableau. (1–5) (Listening L5)

Listening. Pupils copy out the table. They listen to five people telling friends about their dream holidays and complete the table with the details.

Audioscript Track 56

1 – *Comment aimerais-tu passer tes vacances de rêve?*

– *Je voudrais visiter tous les parcs d'attractions du monde.*

– *Ah bon, pourquoi?*

– *Parce que je voudrais trouver la montagne russe la plus terrifiante!*

– *Quelle horreur! Moi, je n'aimerais pas faire ça!*

2 – *Un jour, je voudrais faire de la plongée aux Antilles.*

– *h bon? Tu as déjà fait de la plongée, toi?*

– *Oui, j'ai fait un stage l'année dernière. Ce serait super de voir tous les poissons tropicaux aux Antilles, non?*

– *Ah oui, ce serait trop cool. Je pourrais t'accompagner?*

3 – *Tu sais, moi, j'aimerais passer mes vacances sur une île déserte!*

– *Une île déserte! Pourquoi?*

– *Parce que, chez moi, il y a toujours mon petit frère qui joue avec la Wii ou ma soeur qui met sa musique trop fort.*

– *Tu cherches de la tranquillité, alors?*

– *Oui, c'est ça. Tu voudrais venir avec moi?*

– *Tu rigoles! Ce serait trop calme pour moi!*

4 – *Comment aimerais-tu passer tes vacances de rêve?*

– *Moi, j'aimerais partir à l'aventure en vacances.*

– *Comme quoi, par exemple?*

– *Par exemple, je voudrais descendre l'Amazone en canoë.*

– *Ah oui! Ce serait une aventure inoubliable, ça!*

– *Si tu veux, on pourrait faire ça ensemble.*

– *Bonne idée! Ce serait trop cool. On le fera quand?*

5 – *Un jour, je voudrais essayer des sports extrêmes!*

– *Quels sports extrêmes voudrais-tu faire, alors?*

– *La chute libre, par exemple.*

– *Tu rigoles! La chute libre!*

– *Ah oui, ce serait top de faire ça, non?*

– *Ah non, à mon avis, ce serait trop dangereux.*

Answers

	activité	réaction positive ✓ ou négative ✗?
1	C	✗
2	A	✓
3	D	✗
4	E	✓
5	B	✗

2 En tandem. Interviewe ton/ta camarade au sujet des vacances. Utilise les questions suivantes. (Speaking L5)

Speaking. In pairs: pupils interview each other on the subject of holidays. They take it in turn to ask and answer, using the questions supplied. Draw their attention to the tip box on also including the future tense (not prompted by a question) in order to aim for a higher level.

3 Lis le texte et complète les phrases en anglais. (Reading L6)

Reading. Pupils read the blog and complete the sentences in English.

Answers

1 Usually, Louis and his family **go camping in Brittany**.

2 Every day, he and his father **go fishing**.

3 Last year, they went **to Guadeloupe**.

4 Louis' sister **got sunburnt**.

5 His father broke his leg when **he went water skiing**.

6 Louis got sick because **he ate some bad fish**.

7 Next year, three of the things they will do are **stay in France, take lots of sun cream, go fishing, eat chicken and chips**. (*any three of these*)

4 Décris des vacances désastreuses. Adapte le texte de Louis. Utilise les renseignements suivants. (Writing L6–7)

Writing. Pupils write a description of a disastrous holiday, using the English prompts supplied to adapt Louis' text in exercise 3.

Workbook, pages 44 and 45

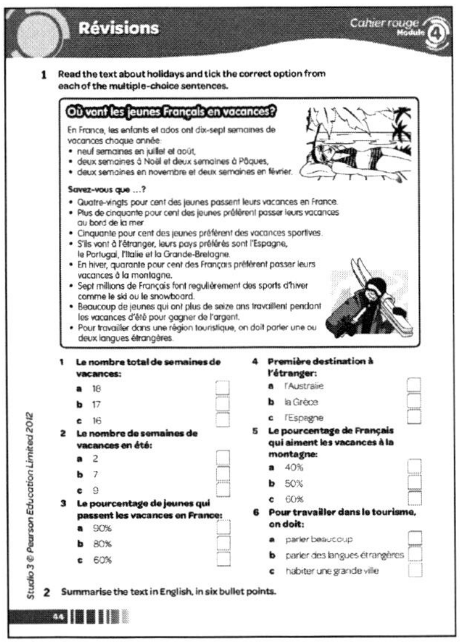
Révisions *Cahier rouge* Module 4

1 Read the text about holidays and tick the correct option from each of the multiple-choice sentences.

Où vont les jeunes Français en vacances?

En France, les enfants et ados ont dix-sept semaines de vacances chaque année:
- neuf semaines en juillet et août,
- deux semaines à Noël et deux semaines à Pâques,
- deux semaines en novembre et deux semaines en février.

Savez-vous que ...?
- Quatre-vingts pour cent des jeunes passent leurs vacances en France.
- Plus de cinquante pour cent des jeunes préfèrent passer leurs vacances au bord de la mer
- Cinquante pour cent des jeunes préfèrent des vacances sportives.
- S'ils vont à l'étranger, leurs pays préférés sont l'Espagne, le Portugal, l'Italie et la Grande-Bretagne.
- En hiver, quarante pour cent des Français préfèrent passer leurs vacances à la montagne.
- Sept millions de Français font regulièrement des sports d'hiver comme le ski ou le snowboard.
- Beaucoup de jeunes qui ont plus de seize ans travaillent pendant les vacances d'été pour gagner de l'argent.
- Pour travailler dans une région touristique, on doit parler une ou deux langues étrangères.

1 **Le nombre total de semaines de vacances:** a 18 b 17 c 16

2 **Le nombre de semaines de vacances en été:** a 2 b 7 c 9

3 **Le pourcentage de jeunes qui passent les vacances en France:** a 90% b 80% c 60%

4 **Première destination à l'étranger:** a l'Australie b la Grèce c l'Espagne

5 **Le pourcentage de Français qui aiment les vacances à la montagne:** a 40% b 50% c 60%

6 **Pour travailler dans le tourisme, on doit:** a parler beaucoup b parler des langues étrangères c habiter une grande ville

2 Summarise the text in English, in six bullet points.

Studio 3 © Pearson Education Limited 2012

44

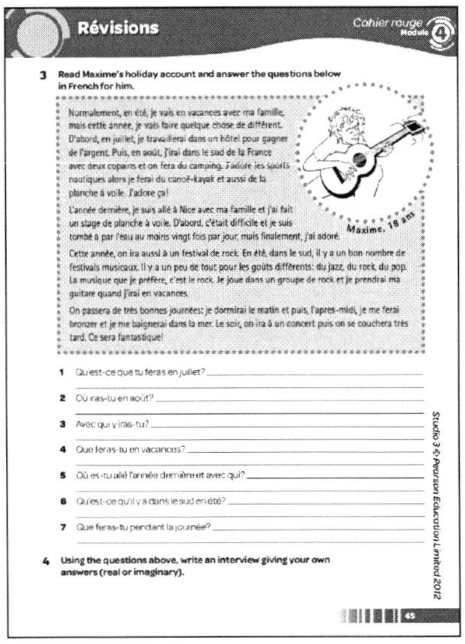
Révisions *Cahier rouge* Module 4

3 Read Maxime's holiday account and answer the questions below in French for him.

Normalement, en été, je vais en vacances avec ma famille, mais cette année, je vais faire quelque chose de différent. D'abord, en juillet, je travaillerai dans un hôtel pour gagner de l'argent. Puis, en août, j'irai dans le sud de la France avec deux copains et on fera du camping. J'adore les sports nautiques alors je ferai du canoë-kayak et aussi de la planche à voile. J'adore ça!

L'année dernière, je suis allé à Nice avec ma famille et j'ai fait un stage de planche à voile. D'abord, c'était difficile et je suis tombé à par l'eau au moins vingt fois par jour, mais finalement, j'ai adoré.

Cette année, on ira aussi à un festival de rock. En été, dans le sud, il y a un bon nombre de festivals musicaux. Il y a un peu de tout pour les goûts différents: du jazz, du rock, du pop. La musique que je préfère, c'est le rock. Je joue dans un groupe de rock et je prendrai ma guitare quand j'irai en vacances.

On passera de très bonnes journées: je dormirai le matin et puis, l'après-midi, je me ferai bronzer et je me baignerai dans la mer. Le soir, on ira à un concert puis on se couchera très tard. Ce sera fantastique!

Maxime, 18 ans

1 Qu'est-ce que tu feras en juillet?

2 Où iras-tu en août?

3 Avec qui y iras-tu?

4 Que feras-tu en vacances?

5 Où es-tu allé l'année dernière et avec qui?

6 Qu'est-ce qu'il y a dans le sud en été?

7 Que feras-tu pendant la journée?

4 Using the questions above, write an interview giving your own answers (real or imaginary).

Studio 3 © Pearson Education Limited 2012

45

Answers

1 **1** b **2** c **3** b **4** a **5** c **6** b

2 (Example answers:)
- French children have 17 weeks holiday each year.
- 80% of young people spend their holidays in France.
- More than 50% of young people spend their holidays by the sea.
- 50% of young people prefer sporty holidays.
- In winter, 40% of French people prefer to go to the mountains.
- 7 million French people regularly do winter sports.
- A lot of young people over 16 work during holidays.
- To work in tourist regions, you should speak one or two foreign languages.

3 **1** Je travaillerai dans un hôtel pour gagner de l'argent.

2 J'irai dans le sud de la France et on fera du camping.

3 J'irai avec deux copains.

4 Je ferai du canoë-kayak et aussi de la planche à voile.

5 L'année dernière, je suis allé à Nice avec ma famille.

6 En été dans le sud, il y a un bon nombre de festivals musicaux.

7 Je dormirai le matin et puis, l'après-midi, je me ferai bronzer et je me baignerai dans la mer.

4 (Answers will vary.)

4 En plus: Des vacances au collège!

(Pupil Book pp. 88–89)

Learning objective
- Debating the idea of 'open school' in the holidays

Programme of Study references

LC1 Listening and responding
LC3 Conversation (dealing with the unexpected)
LC6 Reading comprehension (adapted from authentic)
LC6 Translation into English

FCSE links

Unit 2: Education and future plans (Education: School)

Key language

Review of language from the module

PLTS

E Effective participators

Cross-curricular

Citizenship: the role of school in the broader community

Resources

Audio files:
57_Module4_EnPlus_Ex1.mp3
58_Module4_EnPlus_Ex5.mp3
59_Module4_EnPlus_Ex6.mp3

ActiveTeach:
p.089 Assignment 4
p.089 Assignment 4: prep

Starter

Aim

To introduce the topic.

PLTS E

Have a class discussion in French on what pupils do in the summer holidays when they don't go away. Ask *Vous vous amusez ou vous vous ennuyez?* to elicit a range of opinions.

1 Écoute et lis le texte. Il s'agit de quoi? (Listening L7)

Listening. Pupils listen to the feature about holiday activities at schools in France, reading the text at the same time. They summarise very briefly in English what it is about. Before they start, ask pupils to read *Stratégie 4* on Pupil Book p. 97 and to implement these strategies when they read the text.

Audioscript Track 57

Et si on passait les vacances au collège?

Tu t'ennuies un peu pendant les vacances scolaires? En France, beaucoup de collèges restent ouverts … même pendant les grandes vacances. Au lieu des cours traditionnels, les profs proposent un programme d'activités gratuites aux élèves qui ne partent pas en vacances.

Mais pas question de rester assis devant le tableau! Par exemple, dans certains collèges, on peut faire un stage avec des pilotes d'avion, visiter les studios d'une chaîne de télévision, suivre un cours de survie ou même enregistrer une chanson avec l'aide de musiciens professionnels! Et à part tout cela, on fait aussi quelques révisions pour la rentrée.

Éloïse, quinze ans, a surtout apprécié «d'être avec d'autres jeunes et d'apprendre plein de choses».

Quant à Najim, quatorze ans, il a dit: «J'ai beaucoup aimé apprendre de nouvelles choses, au lieu de rester chez moi à m'ennuyer.» Qui a dit que ce n'était pas intéressant, le collège?

Example answer

Schools in France staying open in the holidays to offer pupils different activities.

2 Lis et complète la traduction sans utiliser de dictionnaire. Devine! (Reading L7)

Reading. Pupils complete the translation of the sentences into French without using a dictionary.

Answers

Pupils check their answers in exercise 3.

3 Vérifie tes réponses à l'exercice 2 dans un dictionnaire. (Reading L7)

Reading. Pupils use a dictionary to check their answers to exercise 2.

Answers

1 free, pupils
2 course, channel
3 survival, record
4 return to school/new school term
5 especially, learning
6 new, getting bored

4 En tandem. Une personne est Éloïse ou Najim. L'autre personne pose les questions. (Speaking L7)

Speaking. In pairs: pupils take it in turn to be Éloïse or Najim from exercise 1 and to be the interviewer, asking the questions supplied. Draw pupils' attention to the tip box on using the language in the text to frame natural responses.

5 Écoute. On parle de l'article de l'exercice 1. Pour chaque personne, note si son opinion est positive (P) ou négative (N). (1–6) (Listening L7)

Listening. Pupils listen to six people talking about summer-holiday activities at school and note whether each person's opinion is positive (writing P) or negative (writing N). *en avoir marre de* is glossed for support.

Audioscript Track 58

1 – *Que penses-tu de l'idée des collèges qui restent ouverts pendant les vacances?*
– *Personnellement, je m'ennuie pendant les grandes vacances, alors à mon avis, c'est une bonne idée.*

2 – *Et toi, tu es d'accord?*
– *Pas du tout. Moi, je n'aimerais pas faire ça. Si je m'ennuie pendant les vacances, je vais au centre sportif avec mes copains ou au parc d'attractions avec ma famille.*

3 – *Et toi, tu penses que c'est une bonne chose, les «écoles ouvertes»?*
– *ui, c'est une bonne chose parce que c'est gratuit! En ce moment, mon père ne travaille pas, alors je n'ai pas beaucoup d'argent. Je voudrais bien faire des activités gratuites!*

4 – *Et toi, tu aimerais aller au collège pendant les vacances?*
– *C'est-à-dire que moi, j'ai de la chance parce que tous les ans, je pars en vacances avec mes parents. Mais je pense que c'est une bonne chose pour les élèves qui ne partent pas en vacances.*

5 – *Et toi, qu'est-ce que tu en penses?*
– *Je pense que c'est ridicule, comme idée! À la fin de l'année scolaire, j'en ai marre du collège.*

6 – *Quelle est ton opinion? Tu voudrais aller au collège pour faire des activités comme ça?*
– *Non, ça ne m'intéresse pas du tout. Moi, je préfère rester chez moi, jouer à la PlayStation ou regarder des DVD.*

Answers

1 P 2 N 3 P 4 P 5 N 6 N

6 Écoute à nouveau. Tu entends les phrases suivantes dans quel ordre? Écris les lettres dans le bon ordre. (Listening L7)

Listening. Pupils listen to the exercise 5 recording again. This time they note the sentences listed (a–i) in the order they are mentioned.

Audioscript Track 59

As exercise 5.

Answers

b, d, e, a, g, f, i, c, h

7 En tandem. Imagine une dispute avec ton/ta camarade au sujet des «collèges ouverts». Utilise les phrases de l'exercice 6. (Speaking L7)

Speaking. In pairs: pupils debate the subject of 'Open schools' (i.e. schools open for summer-holiday activities), using the sentences from exercise 6. A sample exchange is supplied. Draw pupils' attention to the tip box on giving reasons to support opinions.

8 Imagine que ton collège restera ouvert pendant les vacances. Écris un programme d'activités pour deux semaines. Utilise un dictionnaire, si nécessaire. (Writing L4)

Writing. Pupils imagine that their own school will stay open during the holidays and write a programme of activities covering two weeks. They can use a dictionary if they wish.

Plenary

Ask some pupils to read the programme of activities they wrote for exercise 8. Take a class vote by a show of hands on the most appealing programme.

Worksheet 4.8 Le centre de vacances Assignment 4: speaking

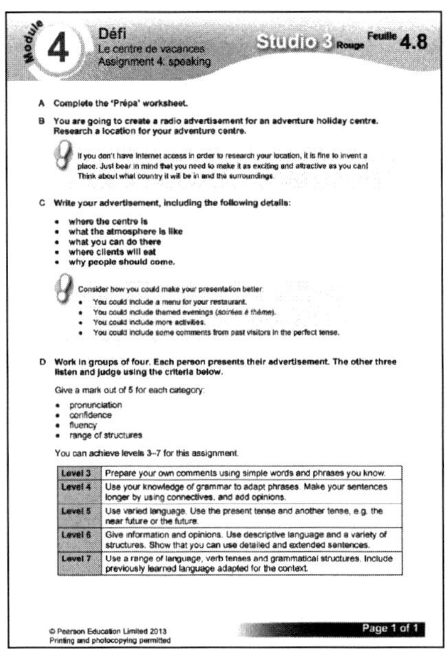

Module 4 Défi
Le centre de vacances
Assignment 4: speaking
Studio 3 Rouge Feuille 4.8

A Complete the 'Prépa' worksheet.

B You are going to create a radio advertisement for an adventure holiday centre. Research a location for your adventure centre.

If you don't have internet access in order to research your location, it is fine to invent a place. Just bear in mind that you need to make it as exciting and attractive as you can! Think about what country it will be in and the surroundings.

C Write your advertisement, including the following details:

- where the centre is
- what the atmosphere is like
- what you can do there
- where clients will eat
- why people should come.

Consider how you could make your presentation better:

- You could include a menu for your restaurant.
- You could include themed evenings (*soirées à thème*).
- You could include more activities.
- You could include some comments from past visitors in the perfect tense.

D Work in groups of four. Each person presents their advertisement. The other three listen and judge using the criteria below.

Give a mark out of 5 for each category:

- pronunciation
- confidence
- fluency
- range of structures

You can achieve levels 3–7 for this assignment.

Level 3	Prepare your own comments using simple words and phrases you know.
Level 4	Use your knowledge of grammar to adapt phrases. Make your sentences longer by using connectives, and add opinions.
Level 5	Use varied language. Use the present tense and another tense, e.g. the near future or the future.
Level 6	Give information and opinions. Use descriptive language and a variety of structures. Show that you can use detailed and extended sentences.
Level 7	Use a range of language, verb tenses and grammatical structures. Include previously learned language adapted for the context.

© Pearson Education Limited 2013
Printing and photocopying permitted
Page 1 of 1

Worksheet 4.9 Le centre de vacances: Prépa

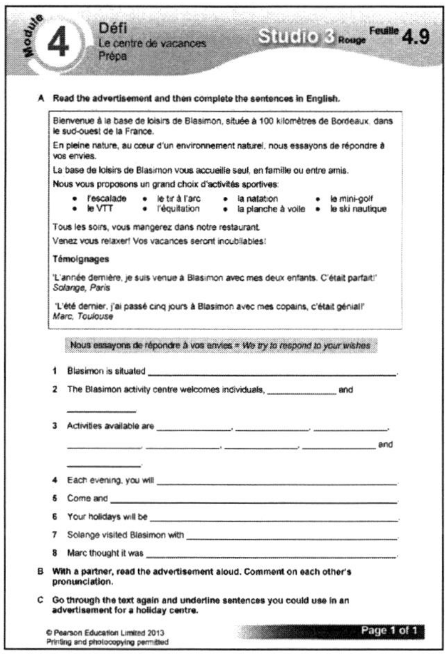

Module 4 Défi
Le centre de vacances
Prépa

Studio 3 Rouge Feuille 4.9

A Read the advertisement and then complete the sentences in English.

Bienvenue à la base de loisirs de Blasimon, située à 100 kilomètres de Bordeaux, dans le sud-ouest de la France.

En pleine nature, au cœur d'un environnement naturel, nous essayons de répondre à vos envies.

La base de loisirs de Blasimon vous accueille seul, en famille ou entre amis.

Nous vous proposons un grand choix d'activités sportives:

- l'escalade
- le VTT
- le tir à l'arc
- l'équitation
- la natation
- la planche à voile
- le mini-golf
- le ski nautique

Tous les soirs, vous mangerez dans notre restaurant.

Venez vous relaxer! Vos vacances seront inoubliables!

Témoignages

'L'année dernière, je suis venue à Blasimon avec mes deux enfants. C'était parfait!'
Solange, Paris

'L'été dernier, j'ai passé cinq jours à Blasimon avec mes copains, c'était génial!'
Marc, Toulouse

Nous essayons de répondre à vos envies = *We try to respond to your wishes*

1 Blasimon is situated ______________________.
2 The Blasimon activity centre welcomes individuals, __________ and __________
3 Activities available are __________, __________, __________, __________, __________, __________, __________ and __________.
4 Each evening, you will ______________________.
5 Come and ______________________.
6 Your holidays will be ______________________.
7 Solange visited Blasimon with ______________________.
8 Marc thought it was ______________________.

B With a partner, read the advertisement aloud. Comment on each other's pronunciation.

C Go through the text again and underline sentences you could use in an advertisement for a holiday centre.

Page 1 of 1

Answers

A 1 Blasimon is situated in southwest France.

2 The Blasimon activity centre welcomes individuals, families and friends.

3 Activities available are climbing, archery, swimming, mini-golf, mountain biking, horse riding, windsurfing and water skiing.

4 Each evening, you will eat in their restaurant.

5 Come and relax.

6 Your holidays will be unforgettable.

7 Solange visited Blasimon with her two children.

8 Marc thought it was great.

4 J'écris

The challenge

- Writing a 150-word blog entry on a dream holiday

Overview

Explain how this section works.

– Pupils read the context and what they need to do to complete the challenge.
– They then read the list of suggested details to include. Explain that they should use this both to help structure their content and as a checklist as part of their final preparations.
– Explain that the exercises which follow in this section are structured to help them prepare for the extended writing task.
– Before starting, pupils read the POSM feature: this will help them to improve their performance. Encourage them to use this approach routinely in writing tasks.

Programme of Study references

GV1 Tenses (past, present and future)
GV4 Accuracy (grammar; spelling; punctuation)
LC4 Expressing ideas (writing)
LC8 Writing creatively

1 Write four present–tense sentences you could use in your blog.

Using the example as a model, pupils write four sentences in the present tense about what they normally do on holiday.

2 Change any two of your sentences from exercise 1 into the *nous* form. Make sure they still make sense!

Pupils choose two of their sentences from exercise 1 and adapt them to use the *nous* form, making sure that the sentences are still logical. Draw pupils' attention to the tip box on checking verb forms in the verb tables on pp. 128–130 of the Pupil Book.

3 Write six sentences in the perfect tense by taking one phrase from each shape. Then use your own ideas to write four more perfect–tense sentences that you could use in your blog entry.

Pupils create six sentences, for each sentence taking one phrase from each shape. They then use their own ideas to write four more sentences featuring the perfect tense that they could use in their blog entry.

Answers

Any of the past tense time phrases can be used with any of the verbs.

4 Write these sentences correctly. Note which are in the future tense (F) and which are in the conditional (C).

Pupils write out the wordsnake sentences. They then identify the verb form used in each: future tense (writing F) or conditional (writing C).

Answers

1 Je resterai sur la plage. (F)
2 Je ferai de la planche à voile. (F)
3 Je voudrais visiter un parc d'attractions. (C)
4 J'irai à la campagne. (F)
5 J'aimerais faire une randonnée. (C)
6 Je mangerai au restaurant. (F)

5 Copy the opinions into the correct column of the grid. Then add at least one more of your own to each column.

Pupils copy out and complete the table by writing the opinion phrases supplied in the correct columns. They then add at least one more appropriate item to each column.

Answers

present	je trouve ça ennuyeux à mon avis, c'est nul
past	c'était genial j'ai beaucoup aimé ça c'était très difficile
future	ce sera intéressant
conditional	ce serait fantastique

Plus pupils' own answers.

6 Read the text and find examples from the list below.

Pupils read Nathan's blog entry and find in the text examples of the language features listed. *il n'y a pas grand-chose* is glossed for support.

Answers

1 **connectives:** et, mais, parce que, par exemple, puis, puisque, car, comme

2 **intensifiers:** un peu, beaucoup de, assez, très

3 **time and frequency expressions:** normalement, cette année, lundi matin, hier après-midi, demain, un jour

4 **opinions:** je trouve ça ..., moi, je préfère ..., c'est fantastique, j'ai trouvé ça ..., c'était ..., ce serait ...

5 **reasons:** parce qu'il n'y a pas grand-chose à faire, parce qu'on peut faire toutes sortes d'activités, puisqu'il fait très chaud, car j'aimerais prendre des photos

6 **different tenses:** (Present tense) je vais, nous faisons, je trouve, il n'y a pas, je préfère, c'est, on peut, il fait, je ne veux pas.
(Perfect tense) j'ai gagné, j'ai fait, j'ai vu, j'ai trouvé, je suis tombé
(Imperfect tense) c'était
(Future tense) j'irai, nous louerons, nous passerons, je mettrai
(Conditional) je voudrais, j'aimerais, ce serait

7 Find the longest three sentences in the text. How has Nathan linked different ideas to create these? Write an extended sentence like this for your blog entry.

Pupils read the text in exercise 6 again and find the three longest sentences in it. They identify how Nathan has linked ideas to make the sentences longer and then write an extended sentence like these for use in their own blog entry.

Answers

J'ai trouvé ça assez difficile **et** je suis tombé à l'eau beaucoup de fois, **mais** c'était quand même marrant. Je mettrai beaucoup de crème solaire **puisqu**'il fait très chaud **et** je ne veux pas prendre un coup de soleil! Un jour, je voudrais faire un safari en Afrique, **car** j'aimerais prendre des photos de tous les animaux sauvages, **comme** les girafes et les lions.

Plus pupils' own answers.

8 Now plan and write your blog entry.

Pupils plan and write their blog entry. Draw their attention to the tip box on features to include and techniques to use in order to improve their writing.

9 Ask your partner to read your blog entry and award you a score out of 5 for the following.

Pupils work in pairs. They read and assess each other's blog entry, awarding it a score out of 5. A list of features to assess is supplied.

4 Studio Grammaire 1

The *Studio Grammaire* section provides a more detailed summary of the key grammar covered in the module, along with further exercises to practise these points. There are two parts, *Studio Grammaire 1* and *Studio Grammaire 2*. The interactive activities on ActiveTeach pp.092 and 093 are repeated from elsewhere in the module.

Grammar topics

- the pronoun *y*
- forming questions
- the conditional
- reflexive verbs

The pronoun *y*

1 Rewrite these sentences, replacing the underlined words with *y*. Remember to put y in front of the verb.

Pupils rewrite the sentences using *y*, correctly positioned, instead of the underlined words.

Answers

1 J'y vais avec mes parents.
2 Nous y passons quinze jours.
3 Ma soeur y va en bus.
4 Tu y restes toute la journée?
5 Ils y mangent parce qu'il y a un bon restaurant.
6 On y arrive vers dix heures.

Forming questions

2 Rewrite these questions, using inversion in numbers 1–4 and *est-ce que* in numbers 5–8.

Pupils rewrite questions 1–4 using inversion and questions 5–8 using *est-ce que*.

Answers

1 Normalement, où passes-tu tes vacances?
2 Avec qui êtes-vous allés en Espagne?
3 Que feras-tu cette année?
4 Pourquoi aimez-vous ce style de vacances?
5 Où est-ce que tu iras l'année prochaine?
6 Avec qui est-ce que vous avez fait du camping?
7 Pourquoi est-ce que tu prends toujours un chargeur?
8 Combien de temps est-ce que tu as passé en Alsace?

The conditional

3 What would people do if they were very rich? Put the verb in brackets into the conditional.

Answers

1 J'acheterais une grande voiture.
2 Tu mangerais tous les jours au restaurant.
3 On passerait un mois en Espagne.
4 Ils regarderaient la télé tout le temps.
5 Vous habiteriez dans une belle villa.
6 serais très content.
7 Elle aurait beaucoup d'amis.
8 Nous voudrions aller aux Antilles.

Reflexive verbs

4 Put the reflexive verbs into the correct form, using the subject pronoun given. Then translate them.

Pupils rewrite the verbs, replacing the infinitive prompts with the correct form of the reflexive verbs. Some vocabulary is glossed for support.

Answers

1 je me coiffe (I do my hair)
2 je me baigne (I swim/bathe)
3 tu t'ennuies (you get bored)
4 on se fait bronzer (we sunbathe)
5 nous nous amusons (we have fun)
6 vous vous couchez (you go to bed)
7 ils se reposent (they rest)
8 elles s'habillent (they get dressed)

4 Studio Grammaire 2

This is the second *Studio Grammaire* section for Module 4, which again provides a more detailed summary of the key grammar covered in the module, along with further exercises to practise these points. The interactive activities on ActiveTeach pp.094 and 095 are repeated from elsewhere in the module.

Grammar topics
- more perfect tense verbs
- emphatic pronouns
- using three tenses (past, present and future)

More perfect tense verbs

1 Copy and complete the text, putting the verb in brackets into the perfect tense.

Pupils copy and complete the gap-fi ll text, replacing the infinitive prompts with the correct perfect tense verb forms.

Answers

1 suis parti(e) **2** suis allé(e) **3** a fait
4 avons joué **5** avons fait **6** sommes allé(e)s
7 est tombée **8** a fait **9** ai mis **10** avons pris
11 avons visité **12** a mangé **13** ai été
14 ai vomi **15** (ne) suis (pas) sorti(e)
16 suis resté(e) **17** ai dormi

2 Translate these sentences into French. Use the verb tables on pages 128–130 to check the past participles if you need to.

Pupils translate the sentences into French, using the perfect tense. They can check past participle forms using the verb tables on pp. 128–130 of the Pupil Book.

Answers

1 Elle a été malade.
2 On a fait une pizza.
3 J'ai mis un chapeau.
4 Ils ont pris le train.
5 Il est tombé à l'eau.
6 Elle est restée sur la plage.
7 Nous sommes sorti(e)s à sept heures.
8 Elles sont parties hier.
9 Je suis arrivé(e) à l'hôtel.
10 Tu es rentré(e) à dix heures.

Emphatic pronouns

3 Complete each sentence with the correct emphatic pronoun. Then translate the sentences into English.

Pupils copy and complete the sentences using the correct emphatic pronouns. They then translate the sentences into English.

Answers

1 **Moi**, je voudrais aller en Espagne.
2 **Lui**, il n'aime pas se faire bronzer.
3 **Nous**, on mangera à l'hôtel.
4 **Toi**, tu as fait de la voile?
5 **Eux**, ils ont loué une villa.
6 **Elle**, elle se baigne tous les jours.
7 **Vous**, vous allez où en vacances?
8 **Elles**, elles ont fait du ski nautique.

Using three tenses (past, present and future)

4 Each of these sentences contains two verbs, but one of them is in the wrong tense. Correct the tense of the verbs, using the time expression in each sentence as a guide.

Pupils identify the two verbs in each sentence. They use the time expression in the sentence to help them decide which verb is in the wrong tense and then write it in the correct tense.

Answers

1 Normalement, je **vais** en vacances en Écosse et je fais du camping.
2 L'année dernière, **on est allés** au Portugal, mais j'ai pris un coup de soleil.
3 La prochaine fois, je mettrai une casquette et je **ne resterai pas** au soleil.
4 Hier, on **a loué** un bateau, mais on est tombés à l'eau!
5 L'année prochaine, mon frère partira en colo, où il **fera** du canoë-kayak.
6 En général, ma famille et moi passons un mois en France et nous **sortons** tous les soirs.

5 Copy and complete the text, putting the verb in brackets into the correct tense.

Pupils copy and complete the gap-fill text, replacing the infinitive prompts with the correct verb forms.

Answers

1 vais **2** passe **3** fait **4** ai fait **5** est allés
6 mangeons **7** jouons **8** irai **9** louera **10** ferons

4 À toi

Self-access reading and writing

A Reinforcement

1 Lis les textes et regarde les images. Copie et complète le tableau avec les bonnes lettres. (Reading L6)

Reading. Pupils read the texts. They copy and complete the table by writing the letters of the pictures (a–k) in the appropriate columns.

Answers

	present	passé	futur
Solène	*b*	e, d	g
Alban	f	i	k
Jérémy	j, a	h	c

2 Écris des cartes postales pour Tariq et Cassandra. Invente les destinations et utilise les idées dans le tableau. (Writing L6)

Writing. Pupils write postcards from Tariq and Cassandra, making up details of the destinations and using the picture prompts supplied for the activities. Draw pupils' attention to the tip box on how to improve their writing.

Example answers

Salut! Je suis en vacances au Portugal. Tous les jours, je fais du ski nautique et de la plongée, mais hier, j'ai fait un stage de voile. J'ai aussi fait du canoë-kayak. C'était super! Demain, je prendrai des photos et jeudi, je ferai de l'escalade.
Tariq

Me voici en vacances en Bretagne. Tous les matins, je me baigne dans la mer. Lundi, je suis allée à la pêche et j'ai rencontré un garçon sympa. Il est anglais. Demain, on fera du camping et on fera des randonnées dans la forêt. Ce sera marrant!
Cassandra

B Extension

1 Lis le texte et note vrai (V) ou faux (F). (Reading L7)

Reading. Pupils read the text and decide whether each sentence is true (writing V) or false (writing F).

Answers

1 F **2** F **3** V **4** V **5** V **6** F **7** V **8** F

2 Imagine que tu es en vacances à la colo «Ma belle Corse». Décris ton séjour. (Writing L6–7)

Writing. Pupils imagine that they are on holiday at the *Ma belle Corse* holiday camp and describe their stay. A list of features to include and techniques to use are supplied.

3 Écris de la publicité pour une autre colonie de vacances. Utilise les renseignements suivants. Adapte le texte de l'exercice 1. (Writing L7)

Writing. Pupils write an advert for another holiday camp, adapting the exercise 1 text and using the details supplied.

Example answer

Si tu as entre 14 et 18 ans et que tu aimes les activités sportives, voici la colo idéale pour toi!

Tu seras hébergé(e) dans l'auberge de jeunesse «L'Aigle d'or». L'auberge est équipée d'une cantine et d'une grande salle de jeux.

Grâce à la situation géographique de l'auberge à la montagne/dans les Alpes, tu pourras pratiquer au choix: l'escalade, le tir à l'arc et le canoë (séance d'une heure).

Tu feras aussi un stage de ski avec nos moniteurs professionnels. Tout le matériel nécessaire (bottes, skis) te sera fourni gratuitement.

À la fin de ton séjour, tu passeras une journée entière à la patinoire «La grande Glisse». Le soir, tu ne manqueras pas d'occasions de t'amuser: on ira au cinéma, on fera un quiz musical et il y aura une soirée fondue. Alors, à bientôt dans les Alpes!

5 Module 5: Moi dans le monde

Unit & Learning objectives	Programme of Study references	Key language	Grammar and other language features
1 Mes droits (pp. 100–101) Discussing what you are allowed to do Using expressions with *avoir*	**GV2** Grammatical structures (expressions with *avoir*, the imperative) **GV3** Opinions and discussions **LC3** Conversation (dealing with the unexpected) **LC6** Reading comprehension	*J'ai le droit de/d' …* *aller sur des forums* *jouer à des jeux vidéo* *sortir seul(e)* *si j'ai aidé à la maison* *si j'ai fini mes devoirs* etc. *Mais ce n'est pas juste!* *C'est tout à fait normal.* etc. *avoir faim/avoir envie de/en* *avoir marre de*, etc.	**G** expressions with *avoir* **G** the informal imperative – developing speaking skills – developing writing skills
2 Mes priorités (pp. 102–103) Explaining what's important to you Using direct object pronouns	**GV2** Grammatical structures (direct object pronouns) **GV3** Opinions and discussions **LC1** Listening and responding **LC4** Expressing ideas (writing)	*Ce qui est important pour moi, c'est …* *mes études* (fpl)*/ma santé*, etc. *Ce qui me préoccupe, c'est …* *l'argent* (m), *la cruauté envers les animaux, la faim dans le monde*, etc. *consommer, exploiter, fabriquer*, etc.	**G** direct object pronouns (*me, te, nous, vous*) – developing writing skills
3 Tu vas l'acheter? (pp. 104–105) Talking about things you buy Using *si* in complex sentences	**GV2** Grammatical structures (*si*; direct object pronouns) **LC1** Listening and responding **LC2** Transcription **LC4** Expressing ideas (writing)	*bon marché* *le commerce équitable* *les conditions de travail* *écolo* *l'éthique sur l'étiquette* *l'ouvrier/ouvrière* *le produit*	**G** direct object pronouns (*le/la/l', les*) **G** *si* … sentences – developing writing skills – developing speaking skills

Unit & Learning objectives	Programme of Study references	Key language	Grammar and other language features
4 Le bonheur, c'est … (pp. 106–107) Describing what makes you happy Using complex structures	**GV3** Developing vocabulary **GV3** Opinions and discussions **LC1** Listening and responding **LC3** Conversation	*Ce qui me rend heureux, c'est de/d'* (+ infin) *Ce qui me rend heureux, c'est le/la/les* (+ noun) *Le bonheur, c'est quand …* *accro* *l'amitié (f)* *apprécier* *déprimé(e)* *rester au lit* *réussir* etc.	**G** *meilleur* **G** using different time frames – developing writing skills – developing speaking skills
Bilan et Révisions (pp. 108–109) Pupils' checklist and practice exercises			
En plus: Les jeunes contre l'injustice (pp. 110–111) Learning about human rights issues	**GV2** Grammatical structures (*ce qui* and *ce que*) **LC4** Expressing ideas (speaking) **LC4** Expressing ideas (writing) **LC6** Reading comprehension (adapted from authentic)	Review of language from the module	**G** questions with question words **G** *ce qui, ce que* – developing reading strategies
Je parle (pp. 112–113) Extended speaking practice	**GV1** Tenses (past, present and future) **GV3** Developing vocabulary **LC4** Expressing ideas (speaking) **LC5** Speaking coherently and confidently	Review of language from the module	– developing speaking skills – checking your work
Studio Grammaire (pp. 114–115) Detailed grammar summary and practice exercises			**G** using different time frames **G** direct object pronouns
À toi (pp. 126–127) Self-access reading and writing at two levels			

5 1 Mes droits

Learning objectives
- Discussing what you are allowed to do
- Using expressions with *avoir*

Programme of Study references
GV2 Grammatical structures (expressions with *avoir*, the imperative)

GV3 Opinions and discussions

LC3 Conversation (dealing with the unexpected)

LC6 Reading comprehension

FCSE links
Unit 1: Relationships, family and friends (good and bad relations, issues, taking sides)

Grammar
- expressions with *avoir*
- the informal imperative

Key language
J'ai le droit de/d' …
aller au MacDo avec mes copains
aller sur des forums
aller sur Facebook
jouer à des jeux vidéo
regarder la télé jusqu'à onze heures du soir
sortir avec mes copains le weekend
sortir seul(e)
surfer sur Internet une heure par jour
si j'ai aidé à la maison
si j'ai fi ni mes devoirs
si j'ai mon portable sur moi
si je rentre avant dix heures du soir
si je veux
si mes parents savent avec qui je suis
si mes parents savent où je vais
Mais ce n'est pas juste!
C'est tout à fait normal.
Ce n'est pas du tout normal.
C'est fou!
On te traite comme un enfant.
Mais révolte-toi!
Tes parents exagèrent!
avoir faim
avoir envie de
avoir le droit de
avoir raison
avoir soif
avoir tort
en avoir marre de

PLTS
S Self-managers

Cross-curricular
ICT: using a presentation package

PSHE: personal well-being

Resources
Audio files:
60_Module5_Unit1_Ex1.mp3
61_Module5_Unit1_Ex3.mp3
62_Module5_Unit1_Ex5.mp3

Workbooks:
Cahier d'exercices Rouge, page 49

ActiveTeach:
Starter 1 resource
p.100 Flashcards
p.100 Grammar
p.100 Grammar practice
p.101 Grammar
p.101 Video 10
p.101 Video worksheet 10
p.101 Class activity
p.101 Thinking skills

ActiveLearn:
Listening, Reading

Starter 1
Aim

To introduce language for expressing what you are allowed to do

Write up the following. Give pupils two minutes to identify what they are personally allowed to do.

1 *le droit de sortir avec mes copains le weekend*
2 *le droit de jouer à des jeux vidéo*
3 *le droit d'aller au MacDo avec mes copains*
4 *le droit de sortir seul(e)*
5 *le droit d'aller sur des forums en ligne*
6 *le droit d'aller sur Facebook*
7 *le droit de regarder la télé dans ma chambre*
8 *le droit de surfer sur Internet une heure par jour*

Find out how many pupils are allowed to do each thing by asking for a show of hands. Ask pupils to explain in English why they aren't allowed to do some things and whether they think the restrictions are justified.

Alternative Starter 1:
Use ActiveTeach p.100 Flashcards to introduce the expression *J'ai le droit de …*

1 Écoute et lis les textes. (Listening L6)
Listening. Pupils listen to four teenagers talking about what they're allowed to do, and read the text at the same time. Some vocabulary is glossed for support.

Audioscript Track 60
– *Moi, j'ai le droit de sortir avec mes copains le weekend si je rentre avant dix heures du soir, mais je n'ai pas le droit de jouer à des jeux vidéo le soir, même si j'ai fini mes devoirs.*
– *Moi, j'ai le droit de sortir seule si mes parents savent où je vais, mais je n'ai pas le droit d'aller sur Facebook parce que mon père n'aime pas Facebook.*
– *Moi, j'ai le droit d'aller au MacDo avec mes copains si j'ai mon portable sur moi et si mes parents savent avec qui je suis. Hier, par exemple, je voulais aller en ville avec mes*

copines, alors j'ai envoyé un SMS à ma mère et elle était d'accord. Mais je n'ai pas le droit d'aller sur des forums en ligne parce que ma mère pense que ça peut être dangereux.

– *J'ai le droit de surfer sur Internet une heure par jour si j'ai aidé à la maison et j'ai le droit de regarder la télé dans ma chambre jusqu'à onze heures du soir si je veux.*

2 Relis les textes. Copie et complète le tableau. (Reading L6)

Reading. Pupils copy out the table. They read the texts in exercise 1 again and complete the table with the details.

Answers

	is allowed to …	**is not allowed to …**	**conditions**
1 Jamel	go out with his friends at the weekend	play video games even if he has finished his homework	if he comes home before 10 pm
2 Manon	go out by herself	go onto Facebook because her dad doesn't like it	if her parents know where she is going
3 Astrid	go to McDonald's (with her friends)	go onto forums because her mum thinks it's dangerous	if she has her phone with her and if her parents know who she is with
4 Charles	surf the net one hour per day watch TV in his room until 11 pm		if he has helped in the house if he wants to

Studio Grammaire: expressions with *avoir*

Use the *Studio Grammaire* box to cover expressions with *avoir*. Draw pupils' attention to the tip box on including these expressions in different tenses in order to improve their speaking and writing.

R Pupils write three complex sentences, each featuring a different expression with *avoir* and a different tense – present, imperfect or future.

3 Écoute et corrige les erreurs dans ces phrases. (1–6) (Listening L4)

Listening. Pupils listen to six teenagers talking about what they are allowed to do and correct the error in each sentence.

Audioscript Track 61

1 – *Tu as le droit d'aller sur des forums, Alexis?*
– *Oui, j'ai le droit d'aller sur des forums, mais je dois donner l'adresse des forums que j'aime à ma mère.*

2 – *Jonathan, tu as le droit de surfer sur Internet tous les soirs?*
– *Si j'ai aidé à la maison et si j'ai fait mes devoirs, j'ai le droit de surfer sur Internet si je veux.*

3 – *Sarah, tu as le droit de sortir avec tes copains le weekend?*
– *Euh oui, j'ai le droit de sortir avec mes copains le weekend si je rentre avant onze heures du soir, mais je n'ai pas le droit d'aller au MacDo avec mes copains parce que ma mère pense que je dois manger sain.*

4 – *Nassim, tu as le droit de jouer à des jeux vidéo le soir?*
– *Moi, je n'ai le droit ni de jouer à des jeux vidéo le soir ni de regarder la télé, même si j'ai fini mes devoirs.*

5 – *Simon, tu as le droit de sortir seul?*
– *Non, je n'ai pas le droit de sortir seul, même si mes parents savent où je vais.*

6 – *Samira, tu as le droit d'aller sur Facebook?*
– *Oui, j'ai le droit d'aller sur Facebook parce que ma mère est aussi sur Facebook.*

Answers

1. Alexis a le droit d'aller sur **des forums**.
2. Jonathan a le droit de surfer sur Internet **s'il a aidé à la maison et s'il a fait ses devoirs**.
3. Sarah **n'a pas le droit** d'aller au MacDo avec ses copains./Sarah a le droit **de sortir** avec ses copains **le weekend**.
4. Nassim n'a pas le droit de jouer à des jeux vidéo **le soir**.
5. Simon n'a pas **le droit** de sortir seul.
6. Samira a le droit d'aller sur **Facebook**.

4 Fais un sondage en classe. Écris cinq questions. Pose les questions à cinq personnes et note les réponses. (Speaking L4)

Speaking. Pupils do a class survey. They write five questions. They ask five people the questions and note their responses. A sample question is supplied.

Pupils could compile their results on computer using a presentation package.

Starter 2

Aim

To review the language for expressing what you are allowed to do

Write up the following. Give pupils three minutes working in pairs to write four sentences (two positive and two negative) about what they are allowed/not allowed to do, using the verbs supplied.

sortir surfer aller regarder

Hear answers.

Alternative Starter 2:

Use ActiveTeach p.101 Class activity to practise expressions with *avoir*.

5 Écoute et écris la lettre de l'opinion que tu entends. (1–5) (Listening L4)

Listening. Pupils listen to five conversations and note the opinion expressed in each, choosing from statements a–e.

Audioscript Track 62

1 – *Tu as le droit de sortir seule?*
– *on, je n'ai pas le droit de sortir seule.*
– *Ben, à mon avis, c'est tout à fait normal, à ton âge.*

2 – *Tu as le droit d'aller sur Facebook?*
– *Non, je n'ai pas le droit d'aller sur Facebook.*
– *Mais ce n'est pas juste!*

3 – *Tu as le droit de jouer à des jeux vidéo le soir?*
– *Je n'ai pas le droit de jouer à des jeux vidéo, point final. Pas le soir, pas le weekend, jamais!*
– *Mais, franchement, c'est fou! On te traite comme un enfant!*

4 – *Tu as le droit d'aller sur des forums?*
– *Non, je n'ai même pas le droit d'utiliser l'ordi à la maison. J'en ai marre.*
– *Mais révolte-toi! Il est temps! Tes parents exagèrent!*

5 – *Tu as le droit de sortir avec tes copains le weekend?*
– *Non, je n'ai pas le droit de sortir avec mes copains le weekend. Ma mère ne veut pas. Je dois rester à la maison.*
– *Mais ce n'est pas du tout normal!*

Answers

1 b **2** a **3** d **4** e **5** c

6 À trois. Une personne pose les questions. La deuxième personne répond et la troisième personne doit réagir. (Speaking L4)

Speaking. Pupils work in threes. One person asks the questions. The second person answers and the third person responds to the answer with an opinion. The questions to use and a sample exchange are supplied. Pupils should swap so that everyone gets a turn in each role.

7 Lis les textes et note vrai (V) ou faux (F). (Reading L5)

Reading. Pupils read the letter and the reply and note whether the sentences are true (writing V) or false (writing F). Some vocabulary is glossed for support.

Answers

1 F **2** V **3** V **4** V **5** V **6** V

+ Pupils working in pairs give their opinions of Sylvie's advice in exercise 7.

Studio Grammaire: the informal imperative

Use the *Studio Grammaire* box to review the informal imperative.

8 Écris un paragraphe sur tes droits. (Writing L5)

PLTS S

Writing. Pupils write a paragraph on what they're allowed to do and not allowed to do. Draw their attention to the tip box on improving writing skills.

Pupils swap texts with a partner and check their work, marking any errors but not correcting them. Pupils then do a second draft. They also identify three areas in which they could improve and use this information to set targets in areas that they need to revise. Tell pupils that using this approach routinely will help them raise their levels.

Plenary

Challenge pupils to recall all the expressions with *avoir* used in the unit. They then take it in turn to prompt in English (e.g. 'I will be hungry') and to respond in French (e.g. *j'aurai faim*), using the present, perfect or future tense as appropriate.

Workbook, page 49

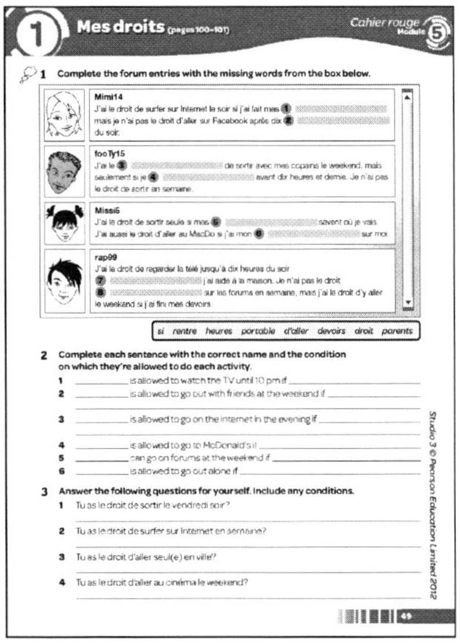

1 Mes droits (pages 100–101) Cahier rouge Module 5

1 Complete the forum entries with the missing words from the box below.

Mimi14
J'ai le droit de surfer sur Internet le soir si j'ai fait mes (1) ______ mais je n'ai pas le droit d'aller sur Facebook après dix (2) ______ du soir.

fooTy15
J'ai le (3) ______ de sortir avec mes copains le weekend, mais seulement si je (4) ______ avant dix heures et demie. Je n'ai pas le droit de sortir en semaine.

Missi5
J'ai le droit de sortir seule si mes (5) ______ savent où je vais. J'ai aussi le droit d'aller au MacDo si j'ai mon (6) ______ sur moi.

rap99
J'ai le droit de regarder la télé jusqu'à dix heures du soir (7) ______ j'ai aidé à la maison. Je n'ai pas le droit (8) ______ sur les forums en semaine, mais j'ai le droit d'y aller le weekend si j'ai fini mes devoirs.

si rentre heures portable d'aller devoirs droit parents

2 Complete each sentence with the correct name and the condition on which they're allowed to do each activity.

1 ______ is allowed to watch the TV until 10 pm if ______
2 ______ is allowed to go out with friends at the weekend if ______
3 ______ is allowed to go on the internet in the evening if ______
4 ______ is allowed to go to McDonald's if ______
5 ______ can go on forums at the weekend if ______
6 ______ is allowed to go out alone if ______

3 Answer the following questions for yourself. Include any conditions.

1 Tu as le droit de sortir le vendredi soir?
2 Tu as le droit de surfer sur Internet en semaine?
3 Tu as le droit d'aller seul(e) en ville?
4 Tu as le droit d'aller au cinéma le weekend?

Studio 3 © Pearson Education Limited 2012

49

Answers

1 **1** devoirs **2** heures **3** droit **4** rentre **5** parents **6** portable **7** si **8** d'aller

2
- **1** rap99 (he has helped in the house)
- **2** fooTy15 (he comes back before 10.30 pm)
- **3** Mimi14 (she has done her homework)
- **4** Missi5 (she has her mobile)
- **5** rap99 (he has finished his homework)
- **6** Missi5 (her parents know where she is)

3 (Answers will vary.)

Worksheet 5.1 Unravelling texts

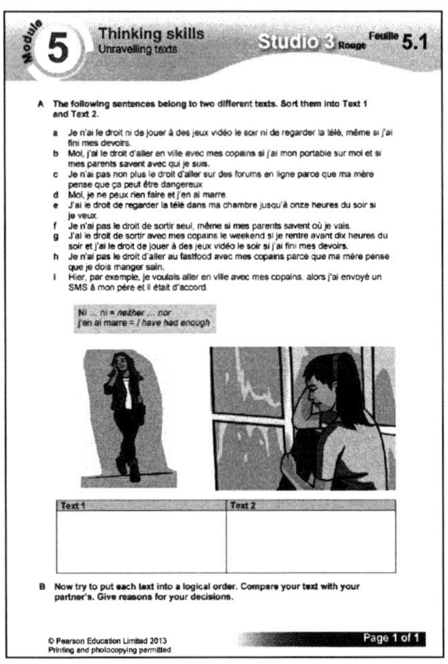

Module 5 Thinking skills Unravelling texts Studio 3 Rouge Feuille 5.1

A The following sentences belong to two different texts. Sort them into Text 1 and Text 2.

a Je n'ai le droit ni de jouer à des jeux vidéo le soir ni de regarder la télé, même si j'ai fini mes devoirs.
b Moi, j'ai le droit d'aller en ville avec mes copains si j'ai mon portable sur moi et si mes parents savent avec qui je suis.
c Je n'ai pas non plus le droit d'aller sur des forums en ligne parce que ma mère pense que ça peut être dangereux
d Moi, je ne peux rien faire et j'en ai marre.
e J'ai le droit de regarder la télé dans ma chambre jusqu'à onze heures du soir si je veux.
f Je n'ai pas le droit de sortir seul, même si mes parents savent où je vais.
g J'ai le droit de sortir avec mes copains le weekend si je rentre avant dix heures du soir et j'ai le droit de jouer à des jeux vidéo le soir si j'ai fini mes devoirs.
h Je n'ai pas le droit d'aller au fastfood avec mes copains parce que ma mère pense que je dois manger sain.
i Hier, par exemple, je voulais aller en ville avec mes copains, alors j'ai envoyé un SMS à mon père et il était d'accord.

Ni … ni = *neither … nor*
j'en ai marre = *I have had enough*

Text 1	Text 2

B Now try to put each text into a logical order. Compare your text with your partner's. Give reasons for your decisions.

© Pearson Education Limited 2013
Printing and photocopying permitted

Page 1 of 1

Answers

A and **B** (*the order may vary*)

Text 1: b, e, g, i

Moi, j'ai le droit d'aller en ville avec mes copains si j'ai mon portable sur moi et si mes parents savent avec qui je suis. Hier, par exemple, je voulais aller en ville avec mes copains, alors j'ai envoyé un SMS à mon père et il était d'accord. J'ai le droit de regarder la télé dans ma chambre jusqu'à onze heures du soir si je veux. J'ai le droit de sortir avec mes copains le weekend si je renter avant dix heures du soir et j'ai le droit de jouer à des jeux vidéo le soir si j'ai fini mes devoirs.

Text 2: a, c, d, f, h

Moi, je ne peux rien faire et j'en ai marre. Je n'ai pas le droit de sortir seul, même si mes parents savent où je vais. Je n'ai le droit ni de jouer à des jeux vidéo le soir ni de regarder la télé, même si j'ai fi ni mes devoirs. Je n'ai pas le droit d'aller au fastfood avec mes copains parce que ma mère pense que je dois manger sain. Je n'ai pas non plus le droit d'aller sur des forums en ligne parce que ma mère pense que ça peut être dangereux.

Video

Episode 10: Mes droits

The team remember the time when they carried out a survey of local adolescents, to discover what they were allowed to do in their free time. Video worksheet 10 can be used in conjunction with this episode.

Answers to video worksheet (ActiveTeach)

1 **A** Suggestions may include: going out, having friends round, bedtimes, using phones and computers, etc.
B (Answers will vary.)

2 **A** How great the holiday is.
B Marielle says she can sunbathe and Samira says she can eat ice cream three times a day.

3 **A** At the weekend but not in the evening.
B She thinks that's normal.
C Hugo.
D He's allowed to watch TV and surf the internet.
E No. One girl refuses to be interviewed.
F She's not allowed to go out on her own.
G A mobile phone.
H They think her parents shouldn't be so protective.

4 **A** That her parents know where she is.
B Play video games.
C Cinema, music, laughing with friends. *vivre* – 'to live'.
D For asking a different question from what she's supposed to ask.
E Marielle goes off with Guillaume.

5 **A** She's in love with him. He's *l'amour de ma vie* – 'the love of my life'.
B To have an ice cream.

5 2 Mes priorités

Learning objectives

- Explaining what's important to you
- Using direct object pronouns

Programme of Study references

GV2 Grammatical structures (direct object pronouns)
GV3 Opinions and discussions
LC1 Listening and responding
LC4 Expressing ideas (writing)

FCSE links

Unit 7: Local area and environment (Preferences, Environment, Recycling)

Grammar

- direct object pronouns (*me, te, nous, vous*)

Key language

Ce qui est important pour moi, c'est …
Qu'est-ce qui te préoccupe dans la vie?
Ce qui me préoccupe, c'est …
l'argent (m)
la cruauté envers les animaux
l'état de la planète
mes études (fpl)
la faim dans le monde
l'injustice (f)
la musique
la pauvreté dans le monde
ma santé
la violence
le racisme
acheter
adopter
agir
consommer
énerver
exploiter
fabriquer
faire attention
devenir membre
participer (à)
penser
protéger
respecter

PLTS

E Effective participators

Cross-curricular

English: direct object pronouns
PSHE: diverse values in society; personal well-being

Resources

Audio files:
63_Module5_Unit2_Ex1.mp3
64_Module5_Unit2_Ex5.mp3
Workbooks:
Cahier d'exercices Rouge, page 50
ActiveTeach:
p.102 Flashcards
p.102 Flashcards
p.102 Grammar
p.102 Grammar practice
p.103 Class activity
p.103 Learning skills
ActiveLearn:
Listening, Reading
Grammar, Vocabulary

Starter 1

Aim

To predict vocabulary in a new topic

Tell the class that this unit is about the priorities of young people: what is important to them and what they are concerned about. Ask pupils what kind of language they think will come up. Explain that predicting is a useful strategy in language learning as it puts learners in a stronger position to work out new words in context.

Alternative Starter 1:

Use both sets of ActiveTeach p.102 Flashcards to introduce language for saying what's important to you.

1 Qui est-ce? Écoute et écris le bon prénom. (1–4) (Listening L4)

Listening. Pupils listen to four conversations in which teenagers talk about what is important to them. They use the labelled pictures to identify who is speaking each time. Some vocabulary is glossed for support.

Audioscript Track 63

1 – *Qu'est-ce qui est important pour toi dans la vie?*
– *Voyons … Ce qui est important pour moi, c'est … alors … d'abord, c'est ma famille, ensuite, mes amis et puis aussi mon chien.*
– *Et qu'est-ce qui te préoccupe dans la vie?*
– *Ce qui me préoccupe, c'est la cruauté envers les animaux. J'ai horreur de ça. Je ne la comprends pas et je ne supporte pas ça. Et puis, les animaux en voie de disparition, que l'homme persécute, cela me préoccupe aussi beaucoup.*

2 – *Qu'est-ce qui est important pour toi dans la vie?*
– *Ce qui est important pour moi, c'est tout d'abord l'argent. Il faut avoir de l'argent pour vivre. Ensuite, mes études. Elles comptent aussi beaucoup pour moi.*
– *Et qu'est-ce qui te préoccupe dans la vie?*
– *Ce qui me préoccupe, c'est l'état de la planète. L'environnement, quoi. Nous abusons de notre planète et il faut arrêter, sinon, ce sera la catastrophe! Nous devons en prendre soin.*

3 – *Qu'est-ce qui est important pour toi dans la vie?*

- *Ce qui est important pour moi, c'est très simple: le foot, puis le foot et … ah oui, le foot!*
- *Et qu'est-ce qui te préoccupe dans la vie?*
- *Ce qui me préoccupe, avant tout, c'est l'injustice, la violence et le racisme. Allez les gars, un peu de respect, c'est quand même important dans la vie. Non?*

4 – *Qu'est-ce qui est important pour toi dans la vie?*
- *Ce qui est important pour moi … Alors, d'abord, c'est ma santé et puis la musique, je crois.*
- *Et qu'est-ce qui te préoccupe dans la vie?*
- *Ce qui me préoccupe avant tout, c'est la faim et la pauvreté dans le monde. Je trouve ça injuste. Chacun a le droit d'être bien nourri.*

Answers

1 Zahra **2** Lucas **3** Karima **4** Manu

Studio Grammaire: direct object pronouns (*me, te, nous, vous*)

Use the *Studio Grammaire* box to review the direct object pronouns *me, te, nous* and *vous*. There is more information and further practice on Pupil Book p. 115.

2 Mets les priorités et les préoccupations des jeunes de l'exercice 1 dans l'ordre d'importance pour toi. (Writing L4)

Writing. Pupils put the priorities and concerns of the teenagers in exercise 1 in order of importance to themselves, putting the most important first.

3 En tandem. Fais trois dialogues. (Speaking L4)

Speaking. In pairs: pupils use the picture prompts to make up three dialogues about what is important to them and what concerns them. They take it in turn to ask and answer. A framework is supplied. *ce qui* is glossed for support.

Starter 2

Aim

To review the language for talking about issues of importance and concern

Give pupils two minutes to write an answer to the following questions, using *Ce qui …*

Qu'est-ce qui est important pour toi dans la vie?
Qu'est-ce qui te préoccupe dans la vie?

Hear answers.

Alternative Starter 2:

Use ActiveTeach p.103 Class activity to practise the language for discussing issues of importance/concern.

4 Lis le texte et choisis le bon mot pour compléter chaque phrase. (Reading L6)

Reading. Pupils read the blog entry and complete the sentences by choosing the correct option from the two given each time. Some vocabulary is glossed for support.

Answers

1. Ce qui est important pour Chloé dans la vie, c'est **le bonheur**.
2. Elle ne peut pas comprendre les gens qui **maltraitent** les animaux
3. Sa famille a adopté un ours polaire, elle pense que c'est **super**.
4. On fait le Pandathlon pour **collecter des fonds**.
5. Il faut avoir seize ans pour **participer au Pandathlon**.
6. Chloé pense que ce serait **stimulant** de travailler pour le WWF.

R Pupils identify in the text in exercise 4 three structures that they will use in their next piece of writing.

5 Écoute Loïc. Prends des notes en anglais sous ces rubriques. (Listening L6)

Listening. Pupils listen to Loïc talking about what is important to him and what concerns him. They make notes in English using the prompts supplied: **Priorities** (3 things), **Concerns** (2) and **Ambition** (1).

Audioscript Track 64

Je m'appelle Loïc et ce qui est important pour moi dans la vie, ce sont mes amis.

Une autre priorité pour moi, c'est le foot, et aussi, ben … il y a mes études, bien sûr. J'adore la biologie et plus tard, je veux être médecin.

Mais ce qui me préoccupe énormément dans la vie, c'est la faim et la pauvreté dans le monde. Je crois que chaque personne a le droit d'être nourrie et logée et malheureusement, il y a beaucoup de personnes dans le monde qui n'ont rien à manger. Puisque ça me préoccupe vraiment, j'ai décidé de devenir membre de l'UNICEF. C'est une organisation qui protège les droits de l'enfant partout dans le monde.

L'année prochaine, quand j'aurai quinze ans, je deviendrai jeune ambassadeur pour l'UNICEF et j'organiserai des projets pour l'organisation au collège.

Answers

Priorities: friends, football, studies
Concerns: hunger, poverty
Ambition: to become a young ambassador for UNICEF

6 Écris un paragraphe sur tes priorités et tes préoccupations dans la vie.
(Writing L5–6)

Writing. Pupils write a paragraph on what is important to them and their own concerns. A framework is supplied. Draw pupils' attention to the tip box on improving writing skills by using more complex language and encourage them to include structures used in texts in the unit.

Plenary

PLTS E

Ask pupils to read out sentences from the texts they wrote in exercise 6. Ask the rest of the class to give constructive feedback on the accuracy of the French. Reward the most imaginative sentences.

Workbook, page 50

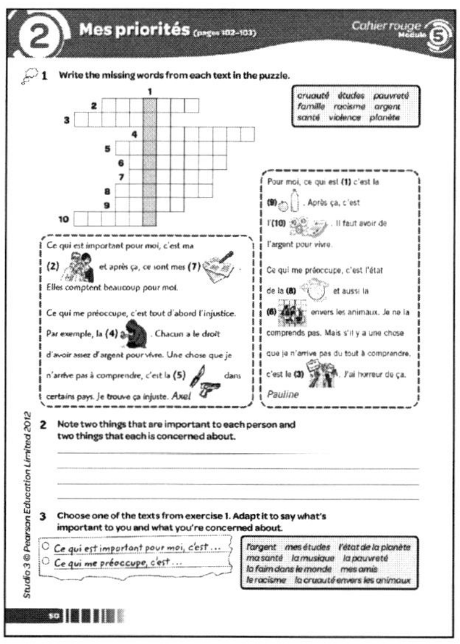
2 Mes priorités (pages 102–103) Cahier rouge Module 5

1 Write the missing words from each text in the puzzle.

cruauté études pauvreté famille racisme argent santé violence planète

Ce qui est important pour moi, c'est ma (2) et après ça, ce sont mes (7). Elles comptent beaucoup pour moi.

Ce qui me préoccupe, c'est tout d'abord l'injustice. Par exemple, la (4). Chacun a le droit d'avoir assez d'argent pour vivre. Une chose que je n'arrive pas à comprendre, c'est la (5) dans certains pays. Je trouve ça injuste. *Axel*

Pour moi, ce qui est (1) c'est la (9). Après ça, c'est l'(10). Il faut avoir de l'argent pour vivre.

Ce qui me préoccupe, c'est l'état de la (8) et aussi la (6) envers les animaux. Je ne la comprends pas. Mais s'il y a une chose que je n'arrive pas du tout à comprendre, c'est le (3). J'ai horreur de ça. *Pauline*

2 Note two things that are important to each person and two things that each is concerned about.

3 Choose one of the texts from exercise 1. Adapt it to say what's important to you and what you're concerned about.

Ce qui est important pour moi, c'est …
Ce qui me préoccupe, c'est …

l'argent mes études l'état de la planète ma santé la musique la pauvreté la faim dans le monde mes amis le racisme la cruauté envers les animaux

Studio 3 © Pearson Education Limited 2012

50

Answers

1 **1** important **2** famille **3** racisme **4** pauvreté **5** violence **6** cruauté **7** études **8** planète **9** santé **10** argent

2 **Axel:** Important: family and studies
Concerned about: injustice, poverty, violence
Pauline: Important: health and money
Concerned about: state of planet, cruelty to animals, racism

3 (Answers will vary.)

Worksheet 5.2 Improving writing

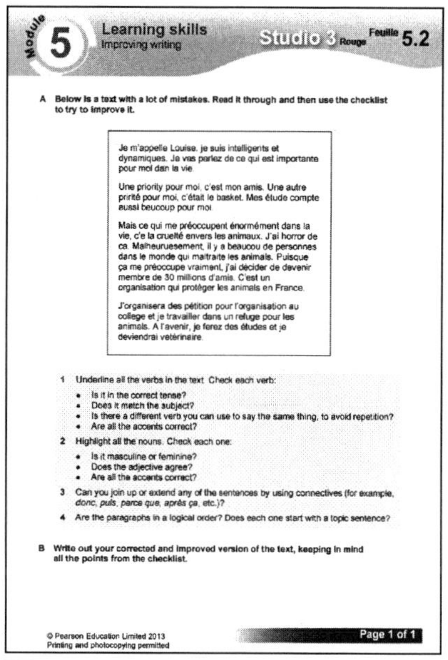
Module 5 Learning skills Improving writing Studio 3 Rouge Feuille 5.2

A Below is a text with a lot of mistakes. Read it through and then use the checklist to try to improve it.

Je m'appelle Louise. je suis intelligents et dynamiques. Je vas parlez de ce qui est importante pour moi dan la vie.

Une priority pour moi, c'est mon amis. Une autre pririté pour moi, c'était le basket. Mes étude compte aussi beucoup pour moi.

Mais ce qui me préoccupent énormément dans la vie, c'e la cruelté envers les animaux. J'ai horror de ca. Malheuruesement, il y a beaucou de personnes dans le monde qui maltraite les animals. Puisque ça me préoccupe vraiment, j'ai décider de devenir membre de 30 millions d'amis. C'est un organisation qui protéger les animals en France.

J'organisera des pétition pour l'organisation au college et je travailler dans un refuge pour les animals. A l'avenir, je ferez des études et je deviendrai vetérinaire.

1 Underline all the verbs in the text. Check each verb:
- Is it in the correct tense?
- Does it match the subject?
- Is there a different verb you can use to say the same thing, to avoid repetition?
- Are all the accents correct?

2 Highlight all the nouns. Check each one:
- Is it masculine or feminine?
- Does the adjective agree?
- Are all the accents correct?

3 Can you join up or extend any of the sentences by using connectives (for example, *donc, puis, parce que, après ça*, etc.)?

4 Are the paragraphs in a logical order? Does each one start with a topic sentence?

B Write out your corrected and improved version of the text, keeping in mind all the points from the checklist.

© Pearson Education Limited 2013
Printing and photocopying permitted

Page 1 of 1

Example answer:

(*Pupils could prepare this as a collaborative writing task and try to address as many of the points on the worksheet as possible.*)

A Je m'appelle Louise et je suis intelligente et dynamique. Je vais parler de ce qui est important pour moi dans la vie.

Une priorité pour moi, c'est mes amis. Une autre priorité pour moi, c'est le basket. Mes études comptent aussi beaucoup pour moi.

Mais ce qui me préoccupe énormément dans la vie, c'est la cruauté envers les animaux. J'ai horreur de ça. Malheureusement, il y a beaucoup de personnes dans le monde qui maltraitent les animaux. Puisque ça me préoccupe vraiment, j'ai décidé de devenir membre de 30 millions d'amis. C'est une organisation qui protège les animaux en France.

J'organiserai des pétitions au collège pour l'organisation et je travaillerai dans un refuge pour les animaux. À l'avenir, je ferai des études et je deviendrai vétérinaire.

B (Answers will vary.)

5 3 Tu vas l'acheter?

Learning objectives
- Talking about things you buy
- Using *si* in complex sentences

Programme of Study references
GV2 Grammatical structures (*si*; direct object pronouns)
LC1 Listening and responding
LC2 Transcription
LC4 Expressing ideas (writing)

FCSE links
Unit 7: Local area and environment (Preferences)

Grammar
- direct object pronouns (*le/la/l', les*)
- *si* … sentences

Key language
bon marché
le commerce équitable
les conditions de travail
écolo
l'éthique sur l'étiquette
l'ouvrier/ouvrière
le produit

PLTS
I Independent enquirers

Cross-curricular
ICT: internet research
PSHE: social and moral dilemmas about the use of money; personal well-being

Resources
Audio files:
65_Module5_Unit3_Ex1.mp3
66_Module5_Unit3_Ex4.mp3
Workbooks:
Cahier d'exercices Rouge, page 51
ActiveTeach:
Starter 1 resource
Starter 2 resource
p.104 Grammar
p.104 Grammar practice
p.105 Grammar skills
p.105 Thinking skills
ActiveLearn:
Listening, Reading
Grammar

Starter 1
Aim

To introduce some language for ethical trade items

Write up the following. Give pupils two minutes working in pairs to identify the items which are sold in the UK as part of an ethical trading scheme, i.e. where the workers are paid a fair amount for their work. Pupils should look up any words they don't know.

tee-shirts	*miel*	*bonbons*
café	*jouet*	*vin*
fleurs	*sacs*	*verres*
chocolat	*raisins sec*	*thé*
ananas	*boucles d'oreilles*	*galettes*

Check answers. (**Answer:** all of them) Ask pupils if they know of any other items sold as part of an ethical trading scheme. Do they buy them?

1 Écoute et remplis les blancs avec la bonne phrase. (1–5) (Listening L4–5)

Listening. Pupils listen to five conversations about shopping choices and complete the gap-fill sentences, using the words supplied. Some vocabulary is glossed for support.

Audioscript Track 65

1 – *Quand tu fais du shopping, comment est-ce que tu fais ton choix, Stella?*
– *Si un produit est écolo, je l'achète, parce que je crois que nous devons protéger l'environnement.*

2 – *Quand tu fais du shopping, comment est-ce que tu fais ton choix, Guillaume?*
– *Si c'est un produit «commerce équitable», je l'achète, parce que je crois qu'il faut respecter les gens.*

3 – *Quand tu fais du shopping, comment est-ce que tu fais ton choix, Christophe?*
– *Si un produit est bon marché, je l'achète, car le prix est la chose la plus importante pour moi.*

4 – *Quand tu fais du shopping, comment est-ce que tu fais ton choix, Laurine?*
– *i un produit me plaît, je l'achète, car les conditions de travail des ouvriers ne m'intéressent pas.*

5 – *Quand tu fais du shopping, comment est-ce que tu fais ton choix, Jade?*
– *Si un produit est bon marché, je ne l'achète pas, parce qu'en général les produits pas chers sont fabriqués dans des conditions de travail inacceptables, souvent par des enfants.*

Answers
1 écolo **2** respecter **3** le prix
4 les conditions de travail **5** bon marché

Studio Grammaire: *si* … sentences
Use the *Studio Grammaire* box to review the direct object pronouns *me, te, nous* and *vous*. There is more information and further practice on Pupil Book p. 115.

2 Fais un sondage dans ta classe. Pose la question suivante et note les réponses. (Speaking L4)

Speaking. Pupils do a class survey on shopping choices. The question to use is supplied. Draw pupils' attention to the tip box on using language from the model text in their responses.

Studio Grammaire: direct object pronouns (*le/la/l', les*)

Use the *Studio Grammaire* box to cover the direct object pronouns *le/la/l'* and *les*. There is more information and further practice on Pupil Book p. 115.

Pupils working in pairs make up four sentences with direct objects and then rewrite them with direct object pronouns.

Starter 2

Aim

To review language for discussing shopping choices

Write up the following. Give pupils three minutes to match the descriptions of the products (1–5) with the reasons for buying them (a–e).

1 *C'est écolo.*
2 *C'est un produit commerce équitable.*
3 *C'est bon marché.*
4 *Je l'aime.*
5 *C'est trop bon marché.*

a *Le prix est la chose la plus importante pour moi.*
b *Si un produit me plaît, je l'achète.*
c *Nous devons protéger l'environnement.*
d *Souvent, les produits pas chers sont fabriqués par des enfants.*
e *Il faut respecter les gens.*

Check answers. (**Answers: 1** c, **2** e, **3** a, **4** b, **5** d)

Alternative Starter 2:

Use ActiveTeach p.104 Grammar practice to practise direct object pronouns.

3 Lis le texte et complète les phrases en anglais. (Reading L5)

Reading. Pupils read the text on ethical trade and complete the sentences summarising it in English.

Answers

1 … made in Asia.
2 … are less expensive.
3 … unacceptable.
4 … very long.
5 … respect workers' rights.
6 … worker.

4 Écoute Quentin. Quelles sont les deux phrases qu'il n'utilise pas? (Listening L6)

Listening. Pupils listen to Quentin talking about ethical trade. They then read the list of sentences and identify the two that Quentin doesn't use. Some vocabulary is glossed for support.

Answers

3, 9

Audioscript Track 66

D'habitude, le shopping ne m'intéresse pas beaucoup. Je préfère surfer sur Internet, mais hier, je suis allé en ville avec mon père et il m'a acheté un beau pyjama qui était très bon marché.

Puis hier soir, j'ai vu le même pyjama sur l'écran de mon ordi. C'était dans un article sur les conditions de travail des ouvriers qui fabriquent des articles pour ce magasin. J'ai été très choqué parce que c'est un enfant qui a fabriqué mon pyjama. À l'avenir, je ferai plus attention. Si un produit est bon marché, je ne l'achèterai pas tout de suite. Je regarderai les étiquettes de plus près, parce que je ne veux pas exploiter les gens.

5 Écris un paragraphe sur le shopping. (Writing L6)

Writing. Pupils write a paragraph on their own shopping choices. Details of the features to include are supplied, along with a list of key language. Draw pupils' attention to the tip box on improving writing skills by using complex sentences using *si* and including opinions.

I

Pupils research on the internet something they have recently bought and something they are thinking of buying, to find out all they can about where and how it is made. They then summarise their findings in French and say whether this information will affect their shopping choices.

Plenary

Ask pupils what affects their shopping choices, and why. Ask about previous purchases and what they will do in future.

Workbook, page 51

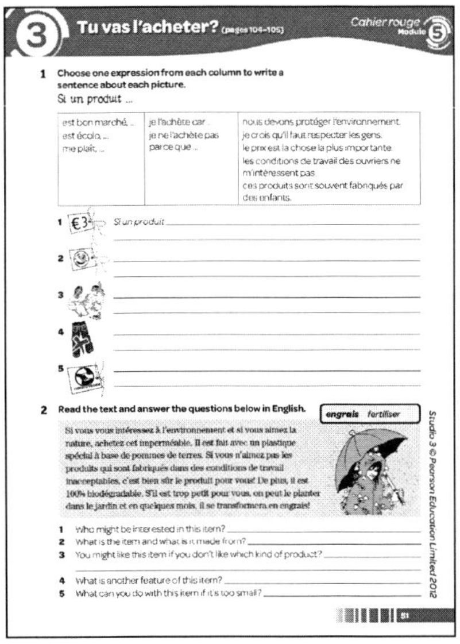

3 Tu vas l'acheter? (pages 104–105) Cahier rouge Module 5

1 Choose one expression from each column to write a sentence about each picture.

Si un produit ...

est bon marché, ... est écolo, ... me plaît, ...	je l'achète car ... je ne l'achète pas parce que ...	nous devons protéger l'environnement. je crois qu'il faut respecter les gens. le prix est la chose la plus importante. les conditions de travail des ouvriers ne m'intéressent pas. ces produits sont souvent fabriqués par des enfants.

1 *Si un produit* ____
2 ____
3 ____
4 ____
5 ____

2 Read the text and answer the questions below in English.

engrais *fertiliser*

Si vous vous intéressez à l'environnement et si vous aimez la nature, achetez cet imperméable. Il est fait avec un plastique spécial à base de pommes de terres. Si vous n'aimez pas les produits qui sont fabriqués dans des conditions de travail inacceptables, c'est bien sûr le produit pour vous! De plus, il est 100% biodégradable. S'il est trop petit pour vous, on peut le planter dans le jardin et en quelques mois, il se transformera en engrais!

1 Who might be interested in this item? ____
2 What is the item and what is it made from? ____
3 You might like this item if you don't like which kind of product? ____
4 What is another feature of this item? ____
5 What can you do with this item if it's too small? ____

Studio 3 © Pearson Education Limited 2012

51

Answers

1 (Example answers:)

1 *Si un produit* est bon marché, je l'achète car le prix est la chose la plus importante.

2 Si un produit est écolo, je l'achète car nous devons protéger l'environnement.

3 Si un produit est bon marché, je ne l'achète pas parce que ces produits sont souvent fabriqués par des enfants.

4 Si un produit est bon marché, je ne l'achète pas parce que je crois qu'il faut respecter les gens.

5 Si un produit est écolo, je l'achète car je crois qu'il faut respecter les gens.

2 1 People who like nature.

2 It's a raincoat and it's made from a special plastic based on potatoes.

3 If you don't like products which are made in unacceptable working conditions.

4 It is 100% biodegradable.

5 You can plant it in the garden and it will be transformed into fertiliser in a few months.

Worksheet 5.3 Direct object pronouns

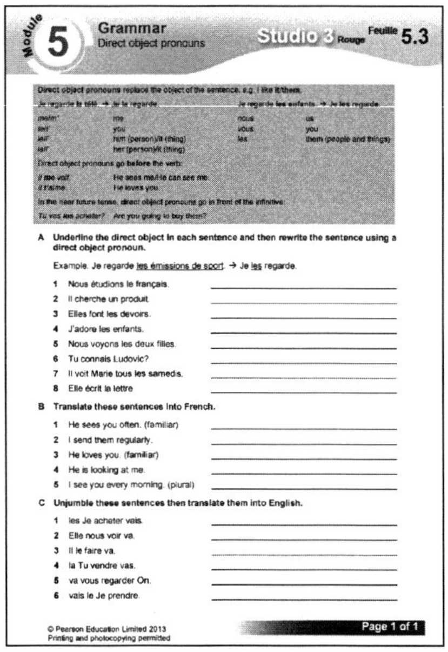

Module 5 Grammar Direct object pronouns Studio 3 Rouge Feuille 5.3

Direct object pronouns replace the object of the sentence, e.g. I like it/them.

Je regarde la télé. → *Je la regarde.* *Je regarde les enfants.* → *Je les regarde.*

me/m'	me	nous	us
te/t'	you	vous	you
le/l'	him (person)/it (thing)	les	them (people and things)
la/l'	her (person)/it (thing)		

Direct object pronouns go **before** the verb:

Il me voit. He sees me/He can see me.
Il t'aime. He loves you.

In the near future tense, direct object pronouns go in front of the infinitive:

Tu vas les acheter? Are you going to buy them?

A Underline the direct object in each sentence and then rewrite the sentence using a direct object pronoun.

Example: Je regarde les émissions de sport. → Je les regarde.

1 Nous étudions le français. ____
2 Il cherche un produit. ____
3 Elles font les devoirs. ____
4 J'adore les enfants. ____
5 Nous voyons les deux filles. ____
6 Tu connais Ludovic? ____
7 Il voit Marie tous les samedis. ____
8 Elle écrit la lettre ____

B Translate these sentences into French.

1 He sees you often. (familiar) ____
2 I send them regularly. ____
3 He loves you. (familiar) ____
4 He is looking at me. ____
5 I see you every morning. (plural) ____

C Unjumble these sentences then translate them into English.

1 les Je acheter vais. ____
2 Elle nous voir va. ____
3 Il le faire va. ____
4 la Tu vendre vas. ____
5 va vous regarder On. ____
6 vais le Je prendre. ____

© Pearson Education Limited 2013 Printing and photocopying permitted

Page 1 of 1

Answers

A 1 Nous l'étudions.

2 Il le cherche.

3 Elles les font.

4 Je les adore.

5 Nous les voyons.

6 Tu le connais?

7 Il la voit tous les samedis.

8 Elle l'écrit.

B 1 Il te voit souvent.

2 Je les envoie régulièrement.

3 Il t'aime.

4 Il me regarde.

5 Je vous vois tous les matins.

C 1 Je vais les acheter.
I am going to buy it.

2 Elle va nous voir.
She is going to see us.

3 Il va le faire.
He is going to do it.

4 Tu vas la vendre.
You are going to sell it.

5 On va vous regarder.
We are going to watch you.

6 Je vais le prendre.
I am going to take it.

Worksheet 5.4 Fact or opinion?

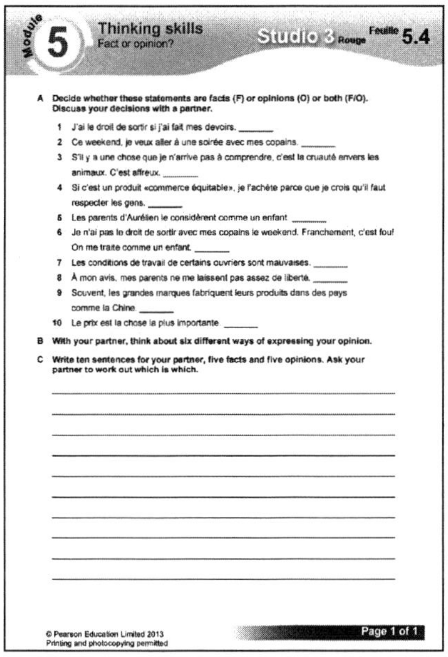

Module 5 Thinking skills
Fact or opinion?
Studio 3 Rouge Feuille 5.4

A Decide whether these statements are facts (F) or opinions (O) or both (F/O). Discuss your decisions with a partner.

1 J'ai le droit de sortir si j'ai fait mes devoirs. ______
2 Ce weekend, je veux aller à une soirée avec mes copains. ______
3 S'il y a une chose que je n'arrive pas à comprendre, c'est la cruauté envers les animaux. C'est affreux. ______
4 Si c'est un produit «commerce équitable», je l'achète parce que je crois qu'il faut respecter les gens. ______
5 Les parents d'Aurélien le considèrent comme un enfant ______
6 Je n'ai pas le droit de sortir avec mes copains le weekend. Franchement, c'est fou! On me traite comme un enfant. ______
7 Les conditions de travail de certains ouvriers sont mauvaises. ______
8 À mon avis, mes parents ne me laissent pas assez de liberté. ______
9 Souvent, les grandes marques fabriquent leurs produits dans des pays comme la Chine. ______
10 Le prix est la chose la plus importante. ______

B With your partner, think about six different ways of expressing your opinion.

C Write ten sentences for your partner, five facts and five opinions. Ask your partner to work out which is which.

© Pearson Education Limited 2013
Printing and photocopying permitted
Page 1 of 1

Example answers

A 1 J'ai le droit de sortir si j'ai fait mes devoirs. **F**

2 Ce weekend, je veux aller à une soirée avec mes copains. **O**

3 S'il y a une chose que je n'arrive pas à comprendre, c'est la cruauté envers les animaux. C'est affreux. **O**

4 Si c'est un produit «commerce équitable», je l'achète, parce que je crois qu'il faut respecter les gens. **F**

5 Les parents d'Aurélien le considèrent comme un enfant. **F**

6 Je n'ai pas le droit de sortir avec mes copains le weekend. Franchement, c'est fou! On me traite comme un enfant. **F/O**

7 Les conditions de travail de certains ouvriers sont mauvaises. **F**

8 À mon avis, mes parents ne me laissent pas assez de liberté. **O**

9 Souvent, les grandes marques fabriquent leurs produits dans des pays comme la Chine. **F**

10 Le prix est la chose la plus importante. **F/O**

5 4 Le bonheur, c'est …

Learning objectives

- Describing what makes you happy
- Using complex structures

Programme of Study references

GV3 Developing vocabulary
GV3 Opinions and discussions
LC1 Listening and responding
LC3 Conversation

Grammar

- *meilleur*
- using different time frames

Key language

Qu'est-ce qui te rend heureux/ heureuse?
Ce qui me rend heureux, c'est de/d' (+ infin)
Ce qui me rend heureux, c'est le/ la/les (+ noun)
Le bonheur, c'est quand …
accro
l'amitié (f)
apprécier
déprimé(e)
décédé(e)
oublier
rester au lit
réussir
se retrouver
se sentir
rigoler

PLTS

R Reflective learners

Cross-curricular

ICT: word-processing
PSHE: personal well-being

Resources

Audio files:
67_Module5_Unit4_Ex1.mp3
68_Module5_Unit4_Ex3.mp3
Workbooks:
Cahier d'exercices Rouge, pages 52 & 53
ActiveTeach:
p.106 Flashcards
p.106 Grammar
p.106 Grammar practice
p.107 Video 11
p.107 Video worksheet 11
p.107 Learning skills
p.107 Grammar skills
ActiveLearn:
Listening, Reading

Starter 1

Aim

To introduce the topic

Ask the class what would make them happier. Note their ideas in English on the board and take a class vote on which is the most popular.

Alternative Starter 1:

Use ActiveTeach p.106 Flashcards to introduce language for saying what makes you happy.

1 Écoute et lis. Trouve la bonne photo pour chaque personne. (Listening L6)

Listening. Pupils listen to five people talking about what makes them happy, and read the texts at the same time. For each person they find the correct photo.

Audioscript Track 67

– *Qu'est-ce que c'est pour toi, le bonheur? Qu'est-ce qui te rend heureux ou heureuse?*
– *Ce qui me rend heureux, c'est d'être avec mon meilleur copain: se retrouver quelque part, sortir ensemble, bien rigoler, quoi! Voilà, pour moi, le bonheur, c'est l'amitié.*
– *Le bonheur, pour moi, c'est de rester au lit au lieu d'aller au collège! Ce que j'adore, c'est quand je me réveille le matin et je n'ai pas de cours parce que c'est dimanche.*
– *Le bonheur, c'est quand mon équipe de foot gagne un match! Quand on a gagné contre le PSG, mes amis et moi étions bien contents. Malheureusement, on a perdu samedi dernier, donc on était tous déprimés.*
– *Ce qui me rend heureuse, c'est d'être en famille. Nous sommes une grande famille et nous sommes très proches. Mon grand-père maternel est décédé l'année dernière et il me manque beaucoup. Alors, j'apprécie surtout de passer du temps avec mes autres grands-parents.*
– *Pour moi, le bonheur, c'est d'avoir de bonnes notes au collège. Une fois, j'ai eu la meilleure note de la classe en sciences et j'étais heureux comme tout! Mes parents m'ont dit que si je réussis mes examens, j'aurai une Xbox 360. Alors, je ferai un gros effort!*

Answers

A Margaux **B** Farid **C** Antonin **D** Éric **E** Cécile

2 Trouve l'équivalent de ces phrases dans les textes de l'exercice 1. (Reading L6)

PLTS R

Reading. Pupils read the texts in exercise 1 again and find the French for the English phrases listed. Draw pupils' attention to the tip box on improving writing and speaking by including more complex structures. Pupils identify structures in the exercise 1 texts that they can use in their own writing and speaking.

Answers

1 Ce qui me rend heureux/heureuse, c'est …
2 Pour moi, le bonheur, c'est …
3 … avoir de bonnes notes au collège.
4 … être avec mon meilleur copain …
5 Nous sommes une grande famille et nous sommes très proches.
6 … rester au lit au lieu d'aller au collège!
7 … si je réussis mes examens, j'aurai …
8 … sortir ensemble, bien rigoler …

Studio Grammaire: *meilleur*

Use the *Studio Grammaire* box to cover *meilleur*.

Pupils write four phrases using the different forms of *meilleur* illustrated in the *Studio Grammaire* box.

3 Écoute. Copie et complète le tableau en anglais. (1–5) (Listening L7)

Listening. Pupils copy out the table. They listen to five conversations about what makes people happy and why. They then complete the table with the details in English.

Audioscript Track 68

1 – *Pardon. Je fais un sondage sur les ados et le bonheur …*
– *Le bonheur?*
– *Oui. Alors … Est-ce que je peux te poser la question suivante: qu'est-ce qui te rend heureux?*
– *Euh, voyons … Alors, ce qui me rend heureux, c'est … mon chien Balthazar!*
– *Ton chien? Pourquoi ton chien?*
– *Parce qu'il est mon meilleur ami! Il est toujours fidèle et aimable. On passe pas mal de temps à jouer ensemble, on fait des promenades … On s'amuse bien ensemble et il me rend heureux. Voilà.*
– *D'accord, merci.*

2 – *Et toi? Qu'est-ce qui te rend heureuse?*
– *Alors … pour moi, c'est le chocolat qui me rend heureuse!*
– *Le chocolat! Ça te rend heureuse, mais tu sais que ce n'est pas bon pour la ligne?*
– *Oui, je sais que c'est mauvais pour la ligne, mais hier, par exemple, j'étais un peu triste, alors j'ai acheté une grosse tablette, j'en ai mangé un peu et voilà, je me sentais mieux, plus heureuse.*
– *Tu es un peu accro au chocolat, alors?*
– *Ah oui, j'imagine que j'y suis accro!*

3 – *Tu as un moment, s'il te plaît? Je fais un sondage sur le bonheur. Qu'est-ce que c'est pour toi, le bonheur?*
– *Ben … pour moi, le bonheur, c'est de jouer sur ma PlayStation.*
– *Pourquoi tu penses que ça te rend heureux?*
– *Je ne sais pas exactement, mais quand tu y joues, tu entres dans un monde fantastique, tu oublies la réalité, tu te perds dans le jeu.*
– *Alors tu préfères le fantastique à la réalité, c'est ça?*
– *Ben … ma famille, mes amis, mon collège, tout ça … c'est important pour moi, mais quand je joue, je m'évade et je suis vraiment heureux, quoi.*
– *D'accord, je comprends. Merci.*

4 – *Et toi? Qu'est-ce que c'est pour toi, le bonheur?*
– *Ça, c'est facile! Pour moi, le bonheur, c'est de partir en vacances!*
– *Les vacances te rendent heureuse? Pourquoi?*
– *Parce que j'adore le soleil! Quand je suis en vacances, je me fais bronzer sur la plage toute la journée. J'ai horreur de l'hiver et du froid. C'est le soleil qui me rend heureuse.*
– *Alors tu voudrais habiter dans un pays chaud?*
– *Ah oui! Ce serait mon rêve d'habiter aux Antilles, par exemple. Je serais tout le temps heureuse!*
– *Bon, merci. J'espère que ton rêve se réalisera!*

5 – *Pardon. Je peux te demander: qu'est-ce qui te rend heureux?*
– *Ce qui me rend heureux, c'est d'aider les autres. Il y a beaucoup de gens dans le monde qui ont besoin d'aide. Par exemple, dans mon collège, on a fait pas mal de choses pour l'organisation Enfants Entraide.*
– *Qu'est-ce que vous avez fait exactement?*
– *Par exemple, on a organisé un marathon à la piscine du collège. On nous a sponsorisés et on a fait des longueurs. Comme ça, on a collecté environ trois cents euros pour Enfants Entraide.*
– *Et pourquoi aider les autres te rend heureux?*
– *Je crois que c'est parce qu'on a l'impression que cela fera une différence pour ces personnes. On sent qu'on peut changer le monde. C'est important pour moi, ça.*
– *D'accord. Merci bien et au revoir.*

Answers

	What makes him/her happy	Why?
1	*his dog*	best friend, faithful and good-natured, play together, go for walks, have fun
2	chocolate	was sad yesterday, ate some, felt better/happier
3	playing on his PlayStation	enters a fantastic world, forgets reality, gets lost in the game
4	going on holiday	loves the sun, gets tanned (on the beach), dreams of living in the Caribbean
5	helping others	feels that it will make a difference, can change the world

Starter 2

Aim

To review language for talking about what makes you happy

Write up the following. Give pupils three minutes to complete the sentence in three different ways, each time giving a reason.

Le bonheur, pour moi, c'est …

Hear answers.

Alternative Starter 2:

Use ActiveTeach p.106 Grammar practice to practise *meilleur*.

4 En tandem. Fais un dialogue au sujet du bonheur. (Speaking L7)

Speaking. In pairs: pupils make up a dialogue on the subject of happiness, taking it in turn to ask and answer. A sample framework is given. Encourage them to use/adapt some of the structures they identified in the texts in exercise 1. Draw their attention to the tip box on improving speaking skills. Play the recording for exercise 3 again, so that they have a clearer memory of the model.

5 Lis le texte. Copie et complète les phrases en français. (Reading L7)

Reading. Pupils read the text. They copy and complete the sentences about Max and Corinne.

Some vocabulary is glossed for support.

Answers

1 Pour Max, le bonheur, c'est **de jouer au hockey sur glace/de participer au sport national canadien.**
2 Il en fait depuis **l'âge de neuf ans.**
3 Il adore ce sport parce qu'il **adore les sensations fortes.**
4 Il faut porter des vêtements protecteurs car **ça peut être dangereux.**
5 Ce qui rend Corinne heureuse, c'est **la danse/de danser le tamouré.**
6 Elle a décidé d'en faire parce que **quand elle était petite, elle regardait sa mère et sa soeur aînée danser le tamouré.**
7 Elle a commencé à en **faire à l'âge de sept ans.**
8 Elle aime beaucoup danser car **quand elle danse, elle oublie tout et elle se sent entièrement heureuse.**

+ Translate the texts round the class, with each pupil translating one sentence.

6 En tandem. Interviewe Max ou Corinne. Utilise les questions suivantes. (Speaking L7)

Speaking. In pairs: pupils take it in turn to play the role of Max or Corinne and to be the interviewer. The questions to ask are supplied.

7 Qu'est-ce que c'est, pour toi, le bonheur? Écris un paragraphe. (Writing L7)

Writing. Pupils write a paragraph on what makes them happy and why. A list of features to include and techniques to use is supplied.

Pupils could do the exercise on computer, to facilitate the production of a second draft.

Plenary

Play a chain game round the class. Ask the class to stand. Start the chain off, e.g. *Pour moi, le bonheur, c'est danser dans la cuisine*. Each pupil repeats the list so far and adds an item, e.g. *Pour moi, le bonheur, c'est danser dans la cuisine et sortir avec mes copains*. Continue the chain. If someone makes a mistake, omits an item or can't add a new item, he/she is 'out' and the chain starts again from the beginning. The last few standing are the winners. Reward them and anyone who came up with a new/amusing idea.

Workbook, pages 52 and 53

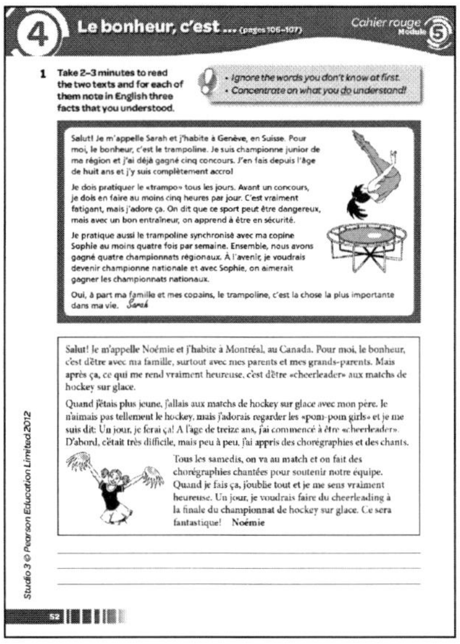

4 Le bonheur, c'est ... (pages 106–107) Cahier rouge Module 5

1 Take 2–3 minutes to read the two texts and for each of them note in English three facts that you understood.

- *Ignore the words you don't know at first.*
- *Concentrate on what you do understand!*

Salut! Je m'appelle Sarah et j'habite à Genève, en Suisse. Pour moi, le bonheur, c'est le trampoline. Je suis championne junior de ma région et j'ai déjà gagné cinq concours. J'en fais depuis l'âge de huit ans et j'y suis complètement accro!

Je dois pratiquer le «trampo» tous les jours. Avant un concours, je dois en faire au moins cinq heures par jour. C'est vraiment fatigant, mais j'adore ça. On dit que ce sport peut être dangereux, mais avec un bon entraîneur, on apprend à être en sécurité.

Je pratique aussi le trampoline synchronisé avec ma copine Sophie au moins quatre fois par semaine. Ensemble, nous avons gagné quatre championnats régionaux. À l'avenir, je voudrais devenir championne nationale et avec Sophie, on aimerait gagner les championnats nationaux.

Oui, à part ma famille et mes copains, le trampoline, c'est la chose la plus importante dans ma vie. *Sarah*

Salut! Je m'appelle Noémie et j'habite à Montréal, au Canada. Pour moi, le bonheur, c'est d'être avec ma famille, surtout avec mes parents et mes grands-parents. Mais après ça, ce qui me rend vraiment heureuse, c'est d'être «cheerleader» aux matchs de hockey sur glace.

Quand j'étais plus jeune, j'allais aux matchs de hockey sur glace avec mon père. Je n'aimais pas tellement le hockey, mais j'adorais regarder les «pom-pom girls» et je me suis dit: Un jour, je ferai ça! A l'âge de treize ans, j'ai commencé à être «cheerleader». D'abord, c'était très difficile, mais peu à peu, j'ai appris des chorégraphies et des chants.

Tous les samedis, on va au match et on fait des chorégraphies chantées pour soutenir notre équipe. Quand je fais ça, j'oublie tout et je me sens vraiment heureuse. Un jour, je voudrais faire du cheerleading à la finale du championnat de hockey sur glace. Ce sera fantastique! **Noémie**

Studio 3 © Pearson Education Limited 2012

52

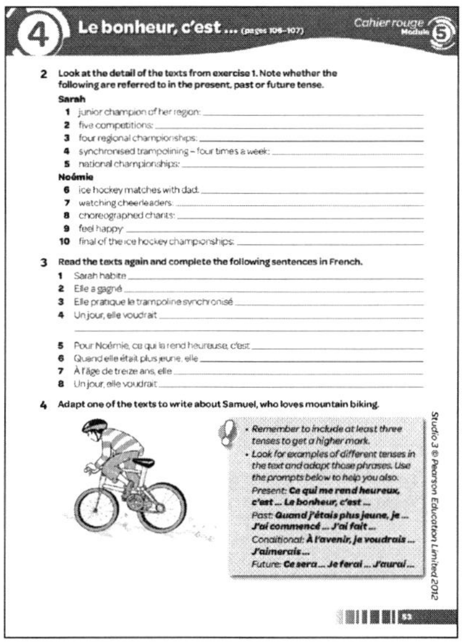

4 Le bonheur, c'est ... (pages 106–107) Cahier rouge Module 5

2 Look at the detail of the texts from exercise 1. Note whether the following are referred to in the present, past or future tense.

Sarah

1 junior champion of her region: ____
2 five competitions: ____
3 four regional championships: ____
4 synchronised trampolining – four times a week: ____
5 national championships: ____

Noémie

6 ice hockey matches with dad: ____
7 watching cheerleaders: ____
8 choreographed chants: ____
9 feel happy: ____
10 final of the ice hockey championships: ____

3 Read the texts again and complete the following sentences in French.

1 Sarah habite ____
2 Elle a gagné ____
3 Elle pratique le trampoline synchronisé ____
4 Un jour, elle voudrait ____
5 Pour Noémie, ce qui la rend heureuse, c'est ____
6 Quand elle était plus jeune, elle ____
7 À l'âge de treize ans, elle ____
8 Un jour, elle voudrait ____

4 Adapt one of the texts to write about Samuel, who loves mountain biking.

- *Remember to include at least three tenses to get a higher mark.*
- *Look for examples of different tenses in the text and adapt those phrases. Use the prompts below to help you also.*

Present: ***Ce qui me rend heureux, c'est ... Le bonheur, c'est ...***
Past: ***Quand j'étais plus jeune, je ... J'ai commencé ... J'ai fait ...***
Conditional: ***À l'avenir, je voudrais ... J'aimerais ...***
Future: ***Ce sera ... Je ferai ... J'aurai ...***

Studio 3 © Pearson Education Limited 2012

53

Answers

1 (Answers will vary.)

2 **1** present **2** past **3** past **4** present **5** future **6** past **7** past **8** past **9** present **10** future

3 **1** Sarah habite **à Genève en Suisse.**

2 Elle a gagné **cinq concours.**

3 Elle pratique le trampoline synchronisé **au moins quatre fois par semaine.**

4 Un jour, elle voudrait **devenir championne nationale et gagner les championnats nationaux.**

5 Pour Noémie, ce qui la rend heureuse, c'est **d'être avec sa famille.**

6 Quand elle était plus jeune, **elle allait aux matchs de hockey sur glace avec son père.**

7 À l'âge de treize ans, elle **a commencé à être «cheerleader».**

8 Un jour, elle voudrait **faire du cheerleading à la finale du championnat de hockey sur glace.**

4 (Answers will vary.)

Worksheet 5.5 Recognising patterns

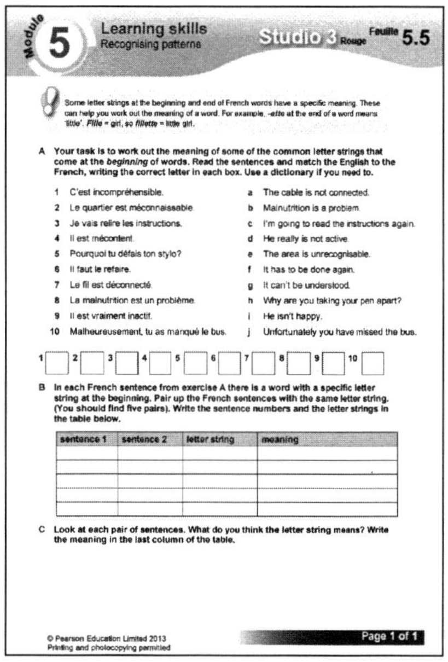

Module 5 **Learning skills** Recognising patterns — Studio 3 Rouge — Feuille 5.5

Some letter strings at the beginning and end of French words have a specific meaning. These can help you work out the meaning of a word. For example, *-ette* at the end of a word means 'little'. *Fille* = girl, so *fillette* = little girl.

A Your task is to work out the meaning of some of the common letter strings that come at the *beginning* of words. Read the sentences and match the English to the French, writing the correct letter in each box. Use a dictionary if you need to.

1 C'est incompréhensible.
2 Le quartier est méconnaissable.
3 Je vais relire les instructions.
4 Il est mécontent.
5 Pourquoi tu défais ton stylo?
6 Il faut le refaire.
7 Le fil est déconnecté.
8 La malnutrition est un problème.
9 Il est vraiment inactif.
10 Malheureusement, tu as manqué le bus.

a The cable is not connected.
b Malnutrition is a problem.
c I'm going to read the instructions again.
d He really is not active.
e The area is unrecognisable.
f It has to be done again.
g It can't be understood.
h Why are you taking your pen apart?
i He isn't happy.
j Unfortunately you have missed the bus.

1 ☐ 2 ☐ 3 ☐ 4 ☐ 5 ☐ 6 ☐ 7 ☐ 8 ☐ 9 ☐ 10 ☐

B In each French sentence from exercise A there is a word with a specific letter string at the beginning. Pair up the French sentences with the same letter string. (You should find five pairs). Write the sentence numbers and the letter strings in the table below.

sentence 1	sentence 2	letter string	meaning

C Look at each pair of sentences. What do you think the letter string means? Write the meaning in the last column of the table.

© Pearson Education Limited 2013
Printing and photocopying permitted

Page 1 of 1

Answers

A 1 g **2** e **3** c **4** i **5** h **6** f **7** a **8** b **9** d **10** j

B and C

sentence 1	sentence 2	letter string	meaning
1	9	in-	not
2	4	mé-	not
3	6	re-	again
5	7	dé-	not (in the sense of reversing/ undoing)
8	10	mal-	not

Worksheet 5.6 Using complex structures

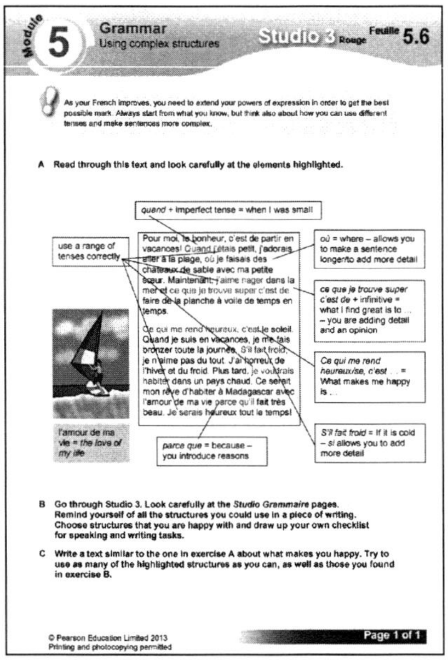

Module 5 Grammar Using complex structures Studio 3 Rouge Feuille 5.6

As your French improves, you need to extend your powers of expression in order to get the best possible mark. Always start from what you know, but think also about how you can use different tenses and make sentences more complex.

A Read through this text and look carefully at the elements highlighted.

Pour moi, le bonheur, c'est de partir en vacances! Quand j'étais petit, j'adorais aller à la plage, où je faisais des châteaux de sable avec ma petite sœur. Maintenant, j'aime nager dans la mer et ce que je trouve super c'est de faire de la planche à voile de temps en temps.

Ce qui me rend heureux, c'est le soleil. Quand je suis en vacances, je me fais bronzer toute la journée. S'il fait froid, je n'aime pas du tout. J'ai horreur de l'hiver et du froid. Plus tard, je voudrais habiter dans un pays chaud. Ce serait mon rêve d'habiter à Madagascar avec l'amour de ma vie parce qu'il fait très beau. Je serais heureux tout le temps!

quand + imperfect tense = when I was small

use a range of tenses correctly

où = where – allows you to make a sentence longer/to add more detail

ce que je trouve super c'est de + infinitive = what I find great is to … – you are adding detail and an opinion

Ce qui me rend heureux/se, c'est … = What makes me happy is …

S'il fait froid = If it is cold – *si* allows you to add more detail

parce que = because – you introduce reasons

l'amour de ma vie = *the love of my life*

B Go through Studio 3. Look carefully at the *Studio Grammaire* pages. Remind yourself of all the structures you could use in a piece of writing. Choose structures that you are happy with and draw up your own checklist for speaking and writing tasks.

C Write a text similar to the one in exercise A about what makes you happy. Try to use as many of the highlighted structures as you can, as well as those you found in exercise B.

© Pearson Education Limited 2013
Printing and photocopying permitted

Page 1 of 1

Answers

(Answers will vary.)

Video

Episode 11: Le bonheur

The team look back at some special moments from the filming of StudioFR, as they talk about the things that make them happy. Video worksheet 11 can be used in conjunction with this episode.

Answers to video worksheet (ActiveTeach)

1 A Suggestions might include: Mehdi – the judo video; Marielle – the one where she met Guillaume; Alex – the fishing video; Samira and Hugo – their date.

B Guesses will vary but may include: Alex – his camera; Mehdi – sport; Marielle – dancing; Samira and Hugo – friendship.

C (Answers will vary.)

2 A Being with friends.

B Fishing.

C *Heureux* is masculine (Alex), *heureuse* is feminine (Marielle).

3 A Hugo

B Marielle enjoyed the fire brigade video, probably because she got picked up by the fireman. Alex liked the fashion sketch – 'in spite of myself' (*malgré moi*) he says – probably because it was his moment in the limelight.

C Food!

D Being chosen to join the team.

E 'Superman'.

F What to do now it's all over.

G Go out with friends (*sortir entre copains*).

H Not using his camera all the time.

I Because it's past tense – it is all over.

5 Bilan et Révisions

Bilan

Pupils use this checklist to review language covered in the module, working on it in pairs in class or on their own at home. Encourage them to follow up any areas of weakness they identify. There are Target Setting Sheets included in the Assessment Pack, and an opportunity for pupils to record their own levels and targets on the *J'avance* page in the Workbook, p. 61. You can also use the *Bilan* checklist as an end-of-module plenary option.

Révisions

These revision exercises can be used for assessment purposes or for pupils to practise before tackling the assessment tasks in the Assessment Pack.

Resources

Audio files:

69_Module5_Rev_Ex1.mp3

Workbooks:

Cahier d'exercices Rouge, pages 54 & 55

1 Écoute. Copie et complète le tableau en anglais. (1–5) (Listening L5)

Listening. Pupils copy out the table. They listen to five conversations and complete the table with the details in English.

Audioscript Track 69

1 – *Tu as le droit de sortir seule?*
– *Non, je n'ai pas le droit de sortir seule, même si mes parents savent où je vais!*
– *Mais, franchement, c'est fou! Tes parents te traitent comme un enfant!*

2 – *Tu as le droit de jouer à des jeux vidéo, le soir?*
– *J'ai le droit de jouer à des jeux vidéo une heure par soir si j'ai fait mes devoirs.*
– *À mon avis, c'est juste. À notre âge, le travail scolaire est plus important que les jeux vidéo.*

3 – *Tu as le droit d'aller sur Facebook?*
– *Non, je n'ai pas le droit d'aller sur Facebook, parce que mes parents n'aiment pas ça. Ils pensent que c'est dangereux, Facebook!*
– *Mais révolte-toi! Il est temps! Tes parents exagèrent!*

4 – *Tu as le droit de sortir avec tes copains, le weekend?*
– *Je n'ai pas le droit de sortir avec mes copains le weekend, même si j'ai aidé à la maison! Je dois rester à la maison. J'en ai marre!*
– *Tu as raison. Ce n'est pas juste!*

5 – *Tu as le droit de regarder la télé dans ta chambre?*
– *J'ai le droit de faire ça jusqu'à dix heures du soir si j'ai cours le lendemain. Sinon, j'ai le droit de la regarder jusqu'à onze heures du soir.*
– *C'est tout à fait normal, à notre âge.*

Pupils include extra details to their answers, as shown in parentheses in the answers opposite.

Answers

	is allowed to ...	is not allowed to ...	other person agrees ✓ or disagrees ✗ with parents?
1		go out alone (even if parents know where she's going)	✗
2	play video games in the evening (for an hour if he's done his homework)		✓
3		go on to Facebook (parents don't like it, think it's dangerous)	✗
4		go out with friends at the weekend (even if she has helped around the house)	✗
5	watch TV in her bedroom (until 10 pm if she has school the next day; if not, until 11 pm)		✓

2 En tandem. Pose les questions suivantes à ton/ta camarade. Utilise les renseignements A ou B ou tes propres idées. (Speaking L5–6)

Speaking. In pairs: pupils take it in turn to ask and answer questions about what is important in their life and what concerns them. They can choose a set of picture prompts to use (two are supplied) or use their own ideas.

3 Lis le texte et termine les phrases en anglais. (Reading L6)

Reading. Pupils read Aïcha's text on what makes her happy and complete the sentences summarising it in English.

Answers

1 … shopping (on Saturday morning, with her friends).
2 … worked in a factory where they made T-shirts.
3 … she worked ten hours a day, six days out of seven.
4 … looks at the label.
5 … buys it (even if it's a bit more expensive).
6 … exploit workers (and we should protect children).
7 … they prefer buying cheap products.

4 Écris ton blog, en utilisant les renseignements suivants. Adapte le texte de l'exercice 3 et ajoute tes propres idées. (Writing L6–7)

Writing. Pupils write a blog entry using the details supplied. They should adapt the exercise 3 text, adding their own ideas. Some vocabulary is glossed for support.

Workbook, pages 54 and 55

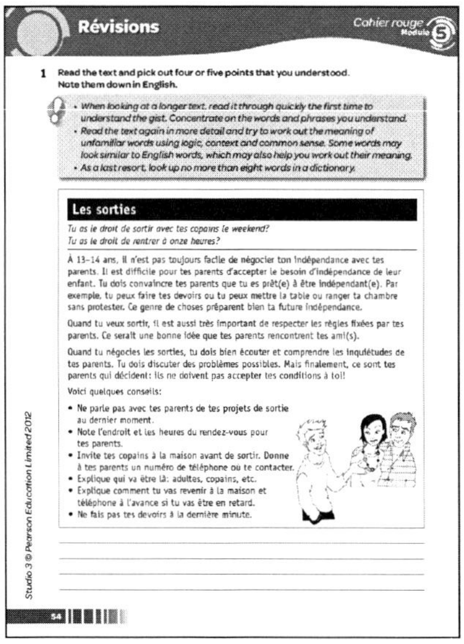

Révisions Cahier rouge Module 5

1 Read the text and pick out four or five points that you understood. Note them down in English.

- *When looking at a longer text, read it through quickly the first time to understand the gist. Concentrate on the words and phrases you understand.*
- *Read the text again in more detail and try to work out the meaning of unfamiliar words using logic, context and common sense. Some words may look similar to English words, which may also help you work out their meaning.*
- *As a last resort, look up no more than eight words in a dictionary.*

Les sorties

Tu as le droit de sortir avec tes copains le weekend?
Tu as le droit de rentrer à onze heures?

À 13–14 ans, il n'est pas toujours facile de négocier ton indépendance avec tes parents. Il est difficile pour tes parents d'accepter le besoin d'indépendance de leur enfant. Tu dois convaincre tes parents que tu es prêt(e) à être indépendant(e). Par exemple, tu peux faire tes devoirs ou tu peux mettre la table ou ranger ta chambre sans protester. Ce genre de choses préparent bien ta future indépendance.

Quand tu veux sortir, il est aussi très important de respecter les règles fixées par tes parents. Ce serait une bonne idée que tes parents rencontrent tes ami(s).

Quand tu négocies les sorties, tu dois bien écouter et comprendre les inquiétudes de tes parents. Tu dois discuter des problèmes possibles. Mais finalement, ce sont tes parents qui décident: ils ne doivent pas accepter tes conditions à toi!

Voici quelques conseils:

- Ne parle pas avec tes parents de tes projets de sortie au dernier moment.
- Note l'endroit et les heures du rendez-vous pour tes parents.
- Invite tes copains à la maison avant de sortir. Donne à tes parents un numéro de téléphone où te contacter.
- Explique qui va être là: adultes, copains, etc.
- Explique comment tu vas revenir à la maison et téléphone à l'avance si tu vas être en retard.
- Ne fais pas tes devoirs à la dernière minute.

Studio 3 © Pearson Education Limited 2012

54

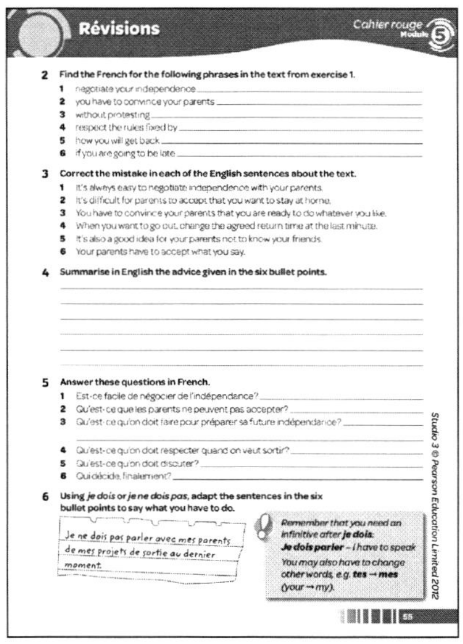

Révisions Cahier rouge Module 5

2 Find the French for the following phrases in the text from exercise 1.

1 negotiate your independence
2 you have to convince your parents
3 without protesting
4 respect the rules fixed by
5 how you will get back
6 if you are going to be late

3 Correct the mistake in each of the English sentences about the text.

1 It's always easy to negotiate independence with your parents.
2 It's difficult for parents to accept that you want to stay at home.
3 You have to convince your parents that you are ready to do whatever you like.
4 When you want to go out, change the agreed return time at the last minute.
5 It's also a good idea for your parents not to know your friends.
6 Your parents have to accept what you say.

4 Summarise in English the advice given in the six bullet points.

5 Answer these questions in French.

1 Est-ce facile de négocier de l'indépendance?
2 Qu'est-ce que les parents ne peuvent pas accepter?
3 Qu'est-ce qu'on doit faire pour préparer sa future indépendance?
4 Qu'est-ce qu'on doit respecter quand on veut sortir?
5 Qu'est-ce qu'on doit discuter?
6 Qui décide, finalement?

6 Using *je dois* or *je ne dois pas*, adapt the sentences in the six bullet points to say what you have to do.

Je ne dois pas parler avec mes parents de mes projets de sortie au dernier moment.

*Remember that you need an infinitive after **je dois**:*
***Je dois parler** – I have to speak*
*You may also have to change other words, e.g. **tes → mes** (your → my).*

Studio 3 © Pearson Education Limited 2012

55

Answers

1 (Answers will vary.)

2
- **1** négocier ton indépendance
- **2** Tu dois convaincre tes parents
- **3** sans protester
- **4** respecter les règles fixées par
- **5** comment tu vas revenir
- **6** si tu vas être en retard

3
- **1** It's **not** always easy to negotiate independence with your parents.
- **2** It's difficult for parents to accept **their child's need for independence.**
- **3** You have to convince your parents that you are ready **to be independent.**
- **4** When you want to go out, **it's important to respect the rules set by your parents.**
- **5** It's also a good idea for your parents to **meet your friends before you go out with them.**
- **6** Your parents **don't have to accept your conditions.**

4 (Example answer:)
Don't leave it until the last minute to talk to your parents about your plans for going out.
Note the place and time of your meeting for your parents.
Invite your friends round before going out – give your parents a telephone number where they can contact you.
Explain who's going to be there: adults, friends, etc.
Explain how you're going to get home and phone in advance if you're going to be late.
Don't leave your homework to the last minute.

5
- **1** Non, ce n'est pas toujours facile.
- **2** Ils ne peuvent pas accepter le besoin d'indépendance de leur enfant.
- **3** On doit faire ses devoirs ou aider à la maison sans protester.
- **4** On doit respecter les règles fixées par ses parents.
- **5** On doit discuter des problèmes possibles.
- **6** Ce sont les parents qui décident.

6 *Je ne dois pas parler avec mes parents de mes projets de sortie au dernier moment.*
Je dois noter l'endroit et les heures du rendez-vous pour mes parents.
Je dois inviter mes copains à la maison avant de sortir. Je dois donner à mes parents un numéro de téléphone où me contacter.
Je dois expliquer qui va être là: adultes, copains, etc.
Je dois expliquer comment je vais revenir à la maison et je dois téléphoner à l'avance si je vais être en retard.
Je ne dois pas faire mes devoirs à la dernière minute.

(Pupil Book pp. 110–111)

5 En plus: Les jeunes contre l'injustice

Learning objective
- Learning about human rights issues

Programme of Study references

GV2 Grammatical structures (*ce qui* and *ce que*)

LC4 Expressing ideas (speaking)

LC4 Expressing ideas (writing)

LC6 Reading comprehension (adapted from authentic)

Grammar
- questions with question words
- *ce qui, ce que*

Key language

Review of language from the module

PLTS

C Creative thinkers

Resources

Audio files:

70_Module5_EnPlus_Ex1.mp3

ActiveTeach:

p.111 Assignment 5

p.111 Assignment 5: prep

Starter

Aim

To introduce the topic

Ask the class what power they think children have to change the world, as an introduction to the story about Craig Kielburger.

1 Écoute et lis le texte. (Listening L7)

Listening. Pupils listen to the feature on the history of Enfants Entraide, an organisation that promotes children's rights throughout the world, founded by Craig Kielburger when he was 12 years old. They read the text at the same time. Some vocabulary is glossed for support.

Audioscript Track 70

L'histoire d'Enfants Entraide

Fondé en 1995 par Craig Kielburger, douze ans, avec l'aide de onze de ses camarades de classe, Enfants Entraide se donne comme mission d'autonomiser les jeunes à surmonter les obstacles qui les empêchent de devenir des citoyens socialement responsables.

Comme tous les matins avant d'aller à l'école, Craig Kielburger feuillette le Toronto Star à la recherche de ses bandes dessinées. Ce matin, son regard s'arrête sur une photo de la page de couverture qui changera sa vie. L'histoire courageuse d'un garçon de son âge: Iqbal Masih, né en Asie du Sud, vendu comme esclave à l'âge de quatre ans. Cet enfant a passé plus de six ans attaché à un métier à tisser. Depuis son évasion, Iqbal parcourait la planète et dénonçait le travail des enfants.

Iqbal a été assassiné pour ses convictions. Il avait le même âge que Craig. Ce que Craig a retenu de cette tragédie, c'est qu'on n'est jamais trop jeune ou trop petit pour s'élever contre l'injustice.

La vision de Craig était claire: libérer les enfants de la pauvreté, libérer les enfants de l'exploitation, libérer les enfants de l'idée qu'ils sont impuissants à changer le monde. Aujourd'hui, plus d'un million de jeunes dans plus de quarante-cinq pays se sont impliqués dans les programmes d'éducation et de développement d'Enfants Entraide.

2 Associe ces mots du texte à leur équivalent en anglais. (Reading L7)

PLTS C

Reading. Pupils match the French phrases from the text with their English equivalents. Draw pupils' attention to the tip box on using reading strategies to tackle the text.

Answers

1 i **2** d **3** a **4** g **5** e **6** j **7** f **8** c **9** b **10** h

3 Relis le texte. Termine les phrases suivantes en anglais. (Reading L7)

Reading. Pupils read the text in exercise 1 again and then complete the sentences summarising it in English.

Answers

1. the help of 11 of his classmates.
2. help young people overcome the obstacles that prevent them from becoming socially responsible citizens.
3. the Toronto Star.
4. sold as a slave.
5. speak out against child labour.
6. age as Craig.
7. stand up against injustice.
8. poverty, exploitation and the idea that they are powerless to change the world.
9. *Enfants Entraide*'s education and development programmes.

4 Imagine que tu es journaliste et que tu vas interviewer Craig Kielburger. Prépare au moins six questions pour Craig. Utilise les mots suivants. (Writing L6)

Writing. Pupils imagine that they are a journalist and are going to interview Craig Kielburger, the founder of Enfants Entraide. They prepare at least six questions to ask. Encourage them to vary the question structures, using question words, *est-ce que* or inversion. A choice of question words is supplied.

Studio Grammaire: *ce qui, ce que*
Use the *Studio Grammaire* box to cover *ce qui* and *ce que*.

5 En tandem. Invente une interview avec Craig Kielburger. Utilise les questions que tu as préparées. (Speaking L7)

Speaking. In pairs: pupils make up an interview with Craig Kielburger, taking it in turn to be Craig and the interviewer. They use the questions they prepared in exercise 4.

6 Lis le texte et choisis la bonne réponse. (Reading L7)

Reading. Pupils read the text and complete the sentences by choosing the correct option from the two given each time. Draw pupils' attention to the tip box on reading skills.

Answers

1. Iqbal Masih était forcé à travailler pour **un fabricant de tapis.**
2. Iqbal était attaché par des chaînes aux **pieds.**
3. Quand Ehsan Khan a découvert Iqbal il était **en mauvaise santé.**
4. Ehsan a libéré Iqbal après **six ans** d'esclavage.
5. Selon Iqbal, les enfants esclaves travaillent **douze** heures par jour.
6. Le gouvernement pakistanais a décidé **d'arrêter l'exploitation des enfants.**
7. Iqbal a été tué par des gens **de la fabrication des tapis.**

7 Quelle est ta réaction personnelle à l'histoire d'Iqbal Masih et pourquoi? Écris deux ou trois phrases. (Writing L3–5)

Writing. Pupils write two or three sentences giving their reaction to Iqbal Masih's story. A sample opening is given.

Plenary

Conclude the topic with a class discussion on what could be done to help children in countries where child labour is used.

Worksheet 5.7 Une poésie

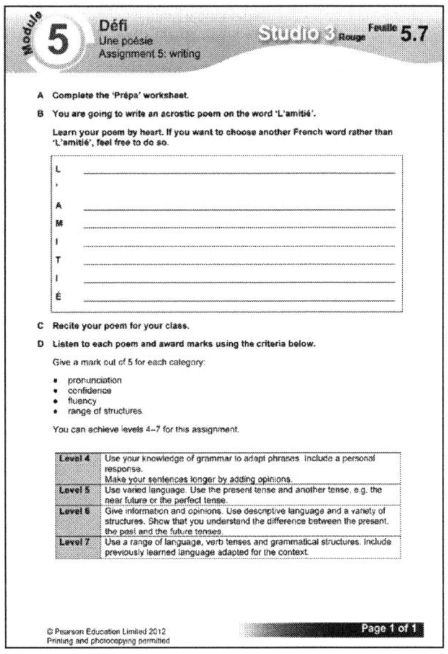

Module 5 Défi
Une poésie
Assignment 5: writing
Studio 3 Rouge Feuille 5.7

A Complete the 'Prépa' worksheet.

B You are going to write an acrostic poem on the word 'L'amitié'.

Learn your poem by heart. If you want to choose another French word rather than 'L'amitié', feel free to do so.

L ______
'
A ______
M ______
I ______
T ______
I ______
É ______

C Recite your poem for your class.

D Listen to each poem and award marks using the criteria below.

Give a mark out of 5 for each category:

- pronunciation
- confidence
- fluency
- range of structures.

You can achieve levels 4–7 for this assignment.

Level 4	Use your knowledge of grammar to adapt phrases. Include a personal response. Make your sentences longer by adding opinions.
Level 5	Use varied language. Use the present tense and another tense, e.g. the near future or the perfect tense.
Level 6	Give information and opinions. Use descriptive language and a variety of structures. Show that you understand the difference between the present, the past and the future tenses.
Level 7	Use a range of language, verb tenses and grammatical structures. Include previously learned language adapted for the context.

© Pearson Education Limited 2012
Printing and photocopying permitted
Page 1 of 1

Worksheet 5.8 Une poésie: Prépa

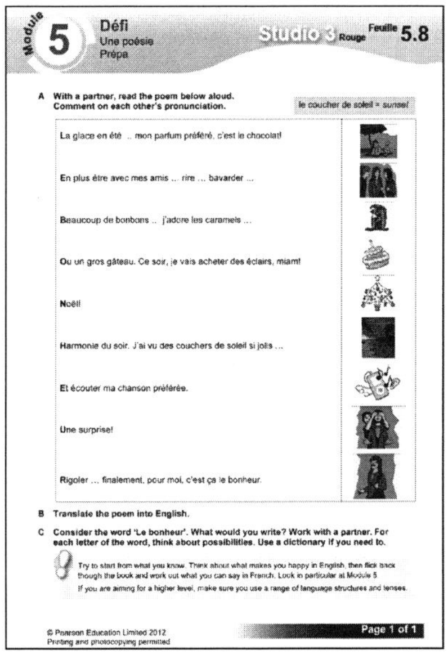

Module 5 Défi
Une poésie
Prépa
Studio 3 Rouge Feuille 5.8

A With a partner, read the poem below aloud. Comment on each other's pronunciation.

le coucher de soleil = *sunset*

La glace en été ... mon parfum préféré, c'est le chocolat!
En plus être avec mes amis ... rire ... bavarder ...
Beaucoup de bonbons ... j'adore les caramels ...
Ou un gros gâteau. Ce soir, je vais acheter des éclairs, miam!
Noël!
Harmonie du soir. J'ai vu des couchers de soleil si jolis ...
Et écouter ma chanson préférée.
Une surprise!
Rigoler ... finalement, pour moi, c'est ça le bonheur.

B Translate the poem into English.

C Consider the word 'Le bonheur'. What would you write? Work with a partner. For each letter of the word, think about possibilities. Use a dictionary if you need to.

Try to start from what you know. Think about what makes you happy in English, then flick back though the book and work out what you can say in French. Look in particular at Module 5.
If you are aiming for a higher level, make sure you use a range of language structures and tenses.

© Pearson Education Limited 2012
Printing and photocopying permitted
Page 1 of 1

Answers

B Happiness is ...
Ice cream in summer ... chocolate's my favourite flavour!
Also being with my friends ... laughing ... chatting ... Lots of sweets ... I love toffee ...
Or a big cake. Tonight I am going to buy eclairs. Yum!
Christmas!
Harmony in the evening. I have seen such pretty sunsets ...
And listening to my favourite song.
A surprise!
Having fun ... in the end that's what happiness is for me.

5 Je parle

The challenge

- Giving a 3-minute video presentation about yourself to convince a French reality TV producer you are right for his show

Overview

Explain how this section works.

- Pupils read the context and what they need to do to complete the challenge.
- They then read the English questions supplied. Explain that they should use these both to help structure their content and as a checklist as part of their final preparations.
- Explain that the exercises which follow in this section are structured to help them prepare for their presentation.
- Before starting, pupils read the POSM feature: this will help them to improve their performance. Encourage them to use this approach routinely in speaking tasks.

Programme of Study references

GV1 Tenses (past, present and future)
GV3 Developing vocabulary
LC4 Expressing ideas (speaking)
LC5 Speaking coherently and confidently

Resources

Audio files:
71_Module5_Jeparle_Ex1.mp3
72_Module5_Jeparle_Ex3.mp3
73_Module5_Jeparle_Ex5.mp3
74_Module5_Jeparle_Ex9.mp3

1 Listen to Emma. Which sentences could she use in her presentation? There are two 'red herrings'. (1–8)

Pupil listen to Emma giving a presentation about herself. They identify the sentences she could use in her presentation. (Two are not appropriate.)

Audioscript Track 71

1 *Coucou! Je m'appelle Emma.*
2 *J'ai quinze ans et j'habite à Hossegor qui se trouve en France sur la côte atlantique.*
3 *J'y habite depuis dix ans.*
4 *Ma passion, c'est le surf.*
5 *Je n'aime pas habiter au bord de la mer.*
6 *J'aime la sensation de liberté. C'est top.*
7 *Je n'aime pas l'histoire.*
8 *Pour moi, le bonheur, c'est le surf.*

Answers
1, 2, 3, 4, 6, 8

2 Write four sentences like Emma's that you could use in your own presentation. Use these prompts.

Using the prompts supplied, pupils write four sentences like Emma's to use in their own presentation.

3 Listen to Emma. Note down what's important to her and what makes her happy.

Pupils listen to Emma and note in English what's important to her and what makes her happy.

Audioscript Track 72

Ce qui est important pour moi dans la vie, ben … mes amis, ma famille et mon chien.

Pour moi, le vrai bonheur, c'est le surf. Quand je suis seule sur ma planche, sous le soleil, je suis heureuse. J'aime la sensation de liberté. C'est top.

Answers

What's important to her: her friends, her family, her dog.

What makes her happy: surfing

4 Think about five things that are important for you and one thing that makes you happy.

Pupils identify five things that are important to them and one thing that makes them happy. A framework is supplied.

5 Listen to Emma talking about something she has done that she was proud of. Choose the correct words to fill in the gaps.

Pupils listen to Emma talking about something she has done that she is proud of. They complete the gap-fill version of what she says, using the words supplied. *fier/fière* is glossed for support.

Audioscript Track 73

J'ai toujours adoré la mer. Quand j'étais petite, je regardais les surfeurs et j'avais moi-même envie de surfer, alors à l'âge de sept ans, j'ai commencé.

Au début, ça a été difficile, mais si on est discipliné et si on s'entraîne régulièrement, on peut faire des progrès très rapidement.

L'année dernière, quand j'ai participé à «l'opération surf», j'étais très fière parce qu'on a collecté de l'argent pour les animaux maltraités et j'adore les animaux. Nous avons surfé pendant dix heures. C'était bien parce qu'on a collecté beaucoup d'argent, mais après, j'étais très fatiguée.

Answers

1 j'étais **2** je regardais **3** j'ai commencé **4** si **5** faire **6** j'ai participé **7** Nous avons surfé **8** C'était

6 Match up the French verbs with their English translations.

Pupils match the French and English verbs.

Answers

j'ai gagné	*I won*
j'ai vu	*I saw*
j'ai participé	*I took part*
j'ai collecté	*I collected*
j'ai écrit	*I wrote*
j'ai commence	*I started*

7 Write a sentence about something you have done that you are proud of!

Pupils write a sentence about something they have done that they are proud of. A framework is supplied.

8 Decode these sentences in the future tense. Then write a similar sentence for your presentation.

Pupils work out the sentences featuring the future tense. They then write a similar sentence to use in their own presentation.

Answers

1. Un jour, j'irai en Guadeloupe où je ferai un «surf camp». Ce sera génial.
2. Un jour, je ferai le tour du monde. Ce sera super.
3. Un jour, j'irai aux États-Unis où je ferai un camp football. Ce sera cool.
4. Un jour, je serai pilote et je voyagerai partout dans le monde. Ce sera intéressant.
5. Un jour, j'irai au Sénégal où je travaillerai comme bénévole. Ce sera top.

9 Listen to Emma's whole presentation. Which of the words and phrases below does she use?

Pupils listen to Emma's whole presentation and identify from the list of words supplied the words she uses. Draw pupils' attention to the tip box on forming extended sentences.

Audioscript Track 74

Coucou! Je m'appelle Emma. J'ai quinze ans et j'habite à Hossegor qui se trouve en France sur la côte atlantique. J'y habite depuis dix ans et ma passion, c'est le surf.

Ce qui est important pour moi dans la vie, ben … mes amis, ma famille et mon chien.

Pour moi, le vrai bonheur, c'est le surf. Quand je suis seule sur ma planche, sous le soleil, je suis heureuse. J'aime la sensation de liberté. C'est top.

J'ai toujours adoré la mer. Quand j'étais petite, je regardais les surfeurs et j'avais moi-même envie de surfer, alors à l'âge de sept ans, j'ai commencé.

Au début, ça a été difficile, mais si on est discipliné et si on s'entraîne régulièrement, on peut faire des progrès très rapidement.

L'année dernière, quand j'ai participé à «l'opération surf», j'étais très fi ère parce qu'on a collecté de l'argent pour les animaux maltraités et j'adore les animaux. Nous avons surfé pendant dix heures. C'était bien parce qu'on a collecté beaucoup d'argent, mais après, j'étais très fatiguée.

Un jour, j'irai en Guadeloupe où je ferai un «surf camp». Ce sera génial.

Answers

quand, où, qui, si, l'année dernière, mais, et, parce que, alors

10 Look back over the module and find some 'wow factor' structures you could use in your presentation.

Pupils identify some structures from Module 5 they can use in their presentation.

11 Now draft your own presentation for the challenge.

Pupils now write their presentation in full, using the language they have developed in the exercises in this section. They check their work to make sure it is logical and accurate.

12 Now memorise your presentation and rehearse it!

Pupils memorise and practise their presentation. Draw their attention to the tip box on improving their presentation. Pupils then give their presentation to a partner, gives suggestions on improving it. Pupils make a note of these suggestions for the next extended speaking task they do.

5 Studio Grammaire

The *Studio Grammaire* section provides a more detailed summary of the key grammar covered in the module, along with further exercises to practise these points. The interactive activities on ActiveTeach pp.114 and 115 are repeated from elsewhere in the module.

Grammar topics

- using different time frames
- direct object pronouns

Resources

Workbooks:

Cahier d'exercices Rouge, pages 56 & 57

Using different time frames

1 Which tense is needed in each gap? Write PR for present, PER for perfect, FUT for future or IMP for imperfect. Use the time expressions and context to help you decide.

Pupils identify the tense required for each missing verb in the gap-fill text, writing PR (present), PER (perfect), FUT (future) or IMP (imperfect) as appropriate. Remind them to use time expressions and context to work out the tense required.

Answers

1 PR **2** PR **3** PR **4** PER **5** PER **6** IMP
7 IMP **8** PER **9** FUT **10** FUT

2 Fill in each gap in exercise 1 using a verb from the list that makes sense.

Pupils complete the gap-fill text in exercise 1 using the verbs supplied.

Answers

1 vais **2** mange **3** joue **4** ai fait **5** suis allée
6 avais **7** étais **8** ai écouté **9** irai **10** sera

3 Put the verbs in brackets into the imperfect tense, then translate the passage into English.

Pupils rewrite the text, replacing the infinitive prompts with the correct form of the imperfect tense. They then translate the completed text into English. *la fouille* is glossed for support.

Answers

1 étais **2** adorais **3** aimais **4** voulais **5** surfais
6 faisais **7** allais **8** participais **9** fascinait
10 était

(Example translation:)
When I was little, I used to love the Indiana Jones series. I also used to like legends and myths a lot. I really wanted to find treasures. I used to surf the internet all the time for information and I used to do some archaeological digs in my garden! Every weekend, I used to go to the archaeological museum in town and take part in digs during the summer holidays. It used to fascinate me, it was my passion! And now, I'm very lucky, because I am an archaeologist!

4 Change the time frame of this text from the future to the past, by putting the underlined verbs into the perfect tense. Start like this:

Pupils rewrite the text to talk about the past, rather than the future. The verbs that need to be changed are underlined. A sample opening is supplied.

Answers

L'année dernière, j'ai fait au moins trente minutes d'exercice par jour. D'abord, je **suis allé** au collège à pied et je **n'ai pas pris** le bus. J'**ai pris** les escaliers au lieu de prendre l'ascenseur et le soir, **j'ai joué** au foot au lieu de jouer à des jeux vidéo. Ensuite, j'**ai mangé** équilibré. Je **n'ai plus mangé** de frites et je **n'ai pas mangé** de sucreries. J'**ai** aussi **bu** beaucoup d'eau.

5 Now imagine Gabriel is writing an article for a magazine, talking about his daily routine. Use the present tense and start like this:

Pupils now adapt the text in exercise 4 to use the present tense to talk about daily routine. A sample opening is supplied.

Answers

Tous les jours, je fais au moins trente minutes d'exercice. D'abord, je **vais** au collège à pied et je **ne prends pas** le bus. Je **prends** les escaliers au lieu de prendre l'ascenseur et le soir, je **joue** au foot au lieu de jouer avec mes jeux vidéo. Maintenant, je **mange** équilibré. Je **ne mange plus** de frites et je **ne mange pas** de sucreries. Je **bois** aussi beaucoup d'eau.

6 Look carefully at the context and put the verbs in brackets into the correct tense.

Pupils complete the gap-fill text by replacing the infinitive prompts with verbs in the correct tense. *un bonnet* is glossed for support. Draw their attention to the tip box on where to find support for this activity.

Answers

1 allons **2** aimons **3** avons fait **4** se baigne **5** prends **6** rentre **7** sort **8** ira **9** ira **10** voyagera **11** prendrai **12** prendrai

Direct object pronouns

7 Copy out these sentences. Underline the direct object pronoun(s), then translate the sentences into English.

Pupils copy out the sentences and underline the direct object pronoun(s) in each. They then translate the sentences into English.

Answers

1. Qu'est-ce qui te rend heureux?
   What makes you happy?
2. Qu'est-ce qui vous préoccupe dans la vie?
   What worries you in life?
3. Ce qui me préoccupe, c'est l'état de la planète.
   What worries me is the state of the planet.
4. Si un produit est écolo, je l'achète.
   If a product is green, I buy it.
5. Si je les aime, je les achète.
   If I like them, I buy them.

8 Translate these sentences into French.

Pupils translate the sentences featuring direct object pronouns into French. Draw their attention to the tip box on the language to use to say 'I think'.

Answers

1. Je les aime (bien).
2. Elle le déteste.
3. Je les regarde.
4. Il nous aime (bien).
5. Tu la regardes./Vous la regardez.
6. Je le trouve sympa/gentil.

Workbook, pages 56 and 57

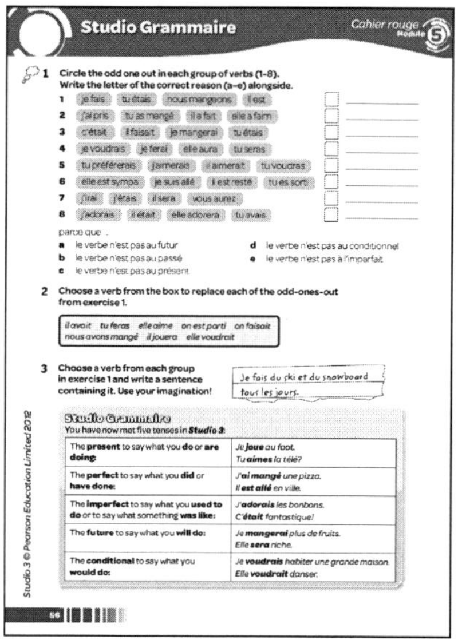

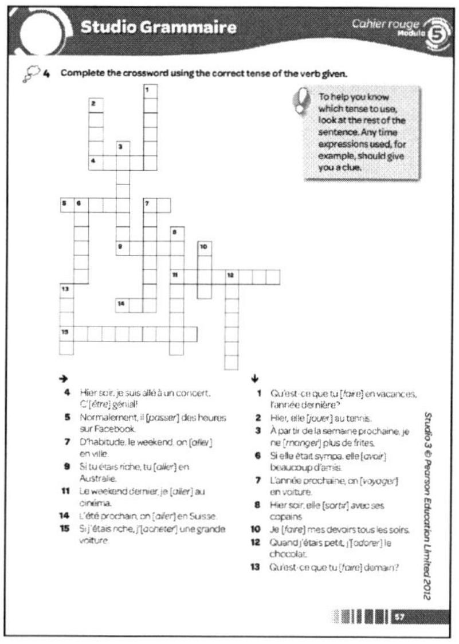

Answers

1 **1** tu étais – **c** **2** elle a faim – **b** **3** je mangerai – **e** **4** je voudrais – **a** **5** tu voudras – **d** **6** elle est sympa – **b** **7** j'étais – **a** **8** elle adorera – **e**

2 **1** elle aime **2** nous avons mangé **3** il avait/on faisait **4** il jouera/tu feras **5** elle voudrait **6** on est parti **7** il jouera/tu feras **8** il avait/on faisait

3 (Answers will vary.)

4 **across: 4** était **5** passe **7** va **9** irais **11** suis allé **14** ira **15** achèterais
down: 1 as fait **2** a joué **3** mangerai 6 aurait **7** voyagera **8** est sortie **10** fais **12** adorais **13** feras

(Pupil Book pp. 126–127)

5 À toi

Self-access reading and writing

A Reinforcement

1 Trouve un copain/une copine britannique pour chaque Français(e). (Reading L5)

Reading. Pupils find a British friend for each French teenager, by matching their interests.

Answers

Mélissa – Lewis

Najim – Jade

Éloïse – Katia

Abel – Amy

Irina – Matthew

2 Écris des e-mails à trouvedesamis.fr pour Ludo et Malika. (Writing L5–6)

Writing. Pupils write emails to the trouvedesamis website for Ludo and Malika, using the details supplied. Draw pupils' attention to the tip box on including different tenses to work towards a higher level.

Example answers

Ludo: Ce qui est important pour moi, c'est la musique et d'aller à des concerts avec mes copains. Ce qui me préoccupe, c'est la pauvreté dans le monde et l'injustice. C'est pourquoi je suis devenu membre d'Amnesty International.

Malika: Ce qui me rend heureuse, c'est de faire les magasins. J'aime aussi partir en vacances, car j'adore le soleil. Cette année, j'irai en Grèce. Ce qui me préoccupe, c'est le racisme et la violence.

3 Tu aimerais être ami(e) avec quelle personne de l'exercice 1? Pourquoi? Tu ne voudrais pas être ami(e) avec qui? (Writing L5–6)

Writing. Pupils choose a friend from exercise 1 and write a paragraph explaining their choice. They then write about a person in exercise 1 they wouldn't like to be friends with, again explaining why. A framework is supplied.

B Extension

1 Copie et complète le texte avec les verbes des cases. (Reading L6)

Reading. Pupils copy and complete the text using the verbs supplied.

Answers

1 viens **2** suis **3** joue **4** veux **5** ai **6** sera **7** avoir **8** fais **9** rend **10** travailler

2 Imagine que tu es Julie. Ta passion, c'est la musique pop. Adapte le texte de l'exercice 1, en utilisant les renseignements suivants. (Writing L7)

Writing. Pupils imagine that they are Julie and write a paragraph about their passion, pop music. They adapt the exercise 1 text, using the details supplied. Draw pupils' attention to the tip box on checking adjective agreement.

Example answer

Je m'appelle Julie et je viens de Belgique. Comme tous les jeunes de mon pays, je suis folle de musique pop! Je chante dans un groupe amateur dans ma ville et un jour, je veux être chanteuse professionnelle. J'ai toujours voulu faire ça, mais je sais que ce ne sera pas facile. Il faut avoir beaucoup d'ambition et, bien sûr, une belle voix! En plus, il faut beaucoup répéter. Quand je ne chante pas, je fais de la natation et je joue au basket. La musique, c'est ce qui me rend la plus heureuse, parce que j'aime être avec mes amis et j'adore quand on joue ensemble.

3 Lis le texte et complète les phrases en anglais. Utilise un dictionnaire, si nécessaire. (Reading L7)

Reading. Pupils read the text and complete the sentences in English. They can use a dictionary. Draw pupils' attention to the tip box on the false friend course.

Example answer

1 ... humanitarian running race.
2 ... school equipment to schools in Senegal, in Africa.
3 ... take part in this extraordinary race.
4 school supplies (rulers, exercise books, pens, pencils – even old-style chalks and slates).
5 ... local schools and businesses.
6 ... run 8–13 kilometres every day to get to different villages.
7 ... the conditions in Senegal are completely different because of the heat.
8 ... that it was an unforgettable experience.